I Am Black
But Comely

The Revelation Of Black People
Throughout Scripture

Psalms 68:31
"Princes shall come out of Egypt;
Ethiopia shall soon stretch out her hands unto God."

I Am Black
But Comely

The Revelation Of Black People
Throughout Scripture

Psalms 68:31
*"Princes shall come out of Egypt;
Ethiopia shall soon stretch out her hands unto God."*

Samuel Greene, *Ph.D.*

Glory Publishing
1301-16 Monument Rd
Jacksonville, FL 32225

Glory Publishing, Inc
1301-16 Monument Road
Jacksonville, FL 32225

Printed in the United States of America
ISBN 978-0-9831696-1-1

Acknowledgements

Thank you to my great friend, disciple, son and scribe, Andrew Jensen, who labored long and hard with me in producing this book. Thanks to the precious saints at Narrow Way Ministries for studying and receiving this book as it was taught.

I express thanks to my lovely wife Katie for once again sharing me with Jesus for many long days and hours. As well, I give thanks to my darling children, for putting up with their Papa being gone so much. I love all of you more than words can say.

Finally, "Thank you Jesus, my lover, my friend, my Savior, and my Lord. You are my Master and I promise to love and walk with you throughout eternity. By the way, thanks for counting me faithful and putting me into the ministry."

Brother Sam Greene
2/14/10

Preface

I only wrote this book because of a Word God spoke to me recently while praying and fasting. The Lord spoke to me and said "I want you to write a book about the great contribution of Black people throughout Scripture." From that Word came some mighty revelations to me. As I searched the Scriptures and took a closer look at history, I came away after writing this with an increased love and appreciation for all that black people have done and gone through throughout history. I marveled to find people who I never thought were black in highly prominent places all through God's Word. I was astounded that I had never in all my forty years as a believer and student of the Word, seen the great truths that the Holy Spirit showed me.

My image of God and His people are forever changed. And my prayer is that as you read and study what this little treatise offers, you will also be astounded and blessed to know just how much and how mightily God used black people in the Scriptures.

I admit that I had to check my opinions at the door every time I studied and wrote. I also had to deal with some personal issues regarding black people in the Bible. But oh, how glad I am for the Holy Spirit being there with me every step of the way.

Jesus said in John 8:32 *"the truth will make you free"* and by the grace of God I was liberated from false teaching, history and just plain old ignorance. I now glorify God on black people's behalf. And I am ever so grateful for all my dear precious black brothers and sisters who allowed God to use them in such mighty, pivotal, and glorious ways.

I've always loved black people and their culture, but now I really do! I suppose the only reason God chose me to write this book was because I'm qualified enough, having lived in the ghettos of Washington, DC for the first third part of my life. I went to all black schools and most of the time I was one of just a few white people there. I freely dated black women and for the most part was a black boy in a white body. I thank God for those years as hard and violent and poor as they might have been, largely because I had the privilege of having many wonderful black friends who were closer to me then my own family. While other families fled to the suburbs, I flourished in the black world I grew up in. Oh, I had to fight almost every day for a long time, but I was eventually accepted fully and embraced as one of them. I will never forget my precious black friends who saved my life on too many occasions. After having to move to an all white community, however, God brought me to Jesus. I had the pleasure then of going back and leading some of my dear friends to Jesus.

This book, however, is about ending racism in the church and seeing the truth about black peoples' contributions throughout the Bible. At times I would get angry at the blatant racism shown by some commentators and white theologians who vainly tried to limit the contributions of black people in the Scriptures. Other times, I would just shake my head in wonder at how ignorant I have been all these years as a teacher and preacher of the Word. It amazed me to see how much was right there all along, yet I never saw it.

I pray this book finally gives black people the honor that is due them. My hope is that many of you will also be enlightened and blessed by what you read here. I'm not foolish enough to think that some will not be furious with me for some of the conclusions I came to as they were so obviously there in Scripture.

But my greatest hope is that this book will serve to honor all that black people have done in Scripture, and awaken the rest of us to their contributions. Furthermore, that racism and prejudice will cease in the body of Christ and that we will learn to receive and love all of God's children, and someday hopefully learn not to judge a man by the color of his skin, but by the content of his character. It is with a humble heart, I present this to you, dear reader, to study and search out what is found here and to see if it's so.

Finally, let me just say out loud and on purpose "I love black people!" And I am so glad God spoke to me to write this book. It is always a pleasure to do the will of God. So please approach this book with an open heart and an unveiled face so that God might speak to you and perhaps give you a look into something you have never considered before. To the end that we as the body of Christ come into greater harmony and unity among all the colors of God's people, this book has been written.

May God the Father speak clearly to you, may Jesus the Son give you great revelation, and may the precious Holy Spirit minister God's grace to you as you read.

Amen!

Table Of Contents

Opening Prayer

Heavenly Father, As we begin to open the Word of God into unknown territories to so many, I would ask you would help every precious reader, that the "eyes of their understanding would be enlightened" and that they would go beyond the letter of the law, but see the "Spirit of the Word" and that more than anything, the content of Your great character shines through everything shared in this book. I pray You would blast away any racism and prejudices and every tendency in us that has anything unclean and dark against any human being in order that we can truly and honestly declare that we have *"a conscience void of offence toward God, and toward men"* (Acts 24:16). We love you dear Jesus and I thank you right now for the Spirit of revelation in Christ Jesus falling upon every reader. "Speak Lord, Thy servants hear Your voice". We promise to give all glory and honor to You. As you settle now upon us, seated upon Your throne, enter into Your rest. Your portion loves you. We sit at your feet and simply say speak Abba Father; and minister Your Word, in the mighty name of Jesus.

Lastly I pray that every devil that would try to bind people's minds from receiving truth, you spirits of religion and traditions of men, spirits of fear and unbelief, I bind you and command you to be gone in Jesus name. "Perfect love casts out all fear" and as we sit at Your feet Jesus, we are sitting at the feet of perfect love. And so Lord, as I minister this Word, let the "precious be taken from the vile" and let wheat come forth, that if there be any chaff, I pray dear reader that with a breath of kindness, you would blow it away so that the kernel of truth may remain and change you into His precious image. Give us a heart like Yours Father, in Jesus' name, Amen!

We Are All God's Offspring
Chapter 1

I would like to say a few things from the outset. It all began the other day. As I was simply waiting on the Lord, He sovereignly spoke to me something that would have never come into my mind on my own. He said to "exhaustively (line upon line) show the contributions of Black people in Scripture." Then He said that He "wants these truths fastened into the hearts of my people." Ecclesiastes 12:11 says, *"The words of the wise are as goads, and as nails fastened by the masters of assemblies, which are given from one shepherd."* The *"one shepherd"* (Jesus – I Peter 2:25, 5:4) gives *"masters of assemblies"* (teachers) *"nails"* or *"goads"* (words of truth) and they are to fasten those truths into the hearts of God's people. This is my intention as you and I will discover the beautiful contributions of Black people threaded throughout Scripture. Actually, the vast majority of people, both in the Old and New Testaments were almost all people of color. There is very little or no presence of Caucasions (white people) until the Romans and their culture enter in. This maybe hard to digest, but if we are going to be true to the scriptures, this is a solid fact."

I can honestly say to you that I have no racist bone in my body. I have been in many nations all over the world and have found precious people in every nation I've visited. As a white person growing up in Washington DC, I grew up in an all-black atmosphere until the age of 15, right before I got saved. For the first 15 years of my life, I lived virtually as a black boy. Then my father moved us to Maryland into an all-white neighborhood. The first year of high school was absolutely horrible for me because even though I was white, I was used to only being around black people. It took a while for me to adjust. Looking back on that I think now how hard it must be for black people to adjust in a white world. How often do white people try to adjust themselves to live in a black world? Beyond this, in these last days, God is asking us to separate ourselves from our cultures, and even our family. This may sound cultish to some, but it is not. Jesus Himself said to his own mother, *"Who is my mother, or my brethren? And he looked round about on them which sat about him, and said, Behold my mother and my brethren! For whosoever shall do the will of God, the same is my brother, and my sister, and mother"* (Mark 3:33-35). In Luke 14:26-27 Jesus said, *"If any man come to me, and hate not his father, and mother, and wife, and children, and brethren, and sisters, yea, and his own life also, he cannot be my disciple."* Until you and I get to the place where we can separate ourselves from the ties of our family, those that keep us from going on with Jesus, we can never fulfill God's call upon our lives, nor ever enter into the true inheritance he desires for us to have. He wants us to be like the "Order of Melchisedec," this highest order in God's kingdom. This precious order no longer claims any lineage; but has found its total life in God, His Word, purpose, people and Kingdom. Hebrews 7:1-3.

But the Lord speaking to me to exhaustively study black people in Scripture delighted me. Honestly, without the Lord sovereignly speaking to me, it wouldn't have entered into my mind. I remember in the early 1980's, I was ministering in Virginia at a church and ministering on "Women in Ministry". During those meetings, the prophetic anointing came upon me, and the Lord spoke and said that in the last great move of God, the two most oppressed people on the face of the earth would be delivered and set free. Those two oppressed people are black people and women. I think all that you and I have to do today is look around now and we see the plethora of black and women ministers. Actually, some of the greatest preachers on the earth today are black men and women. So thinking back to the 1980's when the Lord spoke this, I see that this prophecy has come true.

As I began putting in hours upon hours of research in this subject, one of the things that has really bothered me is many of the commentaries I read seem to be racist. If they weren't racist, they had a subtle form of racism that came through in their teachings. For one thing they try to make sure, whenever somebody black enters the Scriptures, to say that they weren't of the "negroid" (what they called it) section. For example, when talking about the Egyptians, they would talk about two levels of Egyptians, one are light skinned with aquiline noses (i.e. a "white" person's nose) and white people's hair. They go out of their way to say that the Egyptians mentioned in the Bible were from these types of Egyptians. This is simply not true because, Egypt means "black".

There are going to be things in this book that are going to be overwhelmingly revolutional, and for some people, this may cause a problem. For example, you will discover that in the lineage of Jesus, there are black people. Why wouldn't there be?! If He is going to be the Savior of all people, there would have to be. So I ask, if you read something in this book and maybe you don't understand it, don't immediately reject it. Truth sometimes is hard to receive. Just put it on a shelf and wait. It may not be your time to receive it. Or if you search the Scriptures and don't think it is true, then amen. I am not asking anybody to agree with everything I say. However, I can promise you that whatever is written in this book has been thoroughly and exhaustively researched. I know that as this book comes out, there will be a horde of sanctimonious and self-righteous white people lining up to find any error in this book so they can toss it to the wind and say it is error. Even though we have a black president today, racism is still prevalent in our country, and unfortunately also in the church. I found in my life that after I lived up north for so many years and then came to the south that I thought the south would be really racist (and truly some places are), but to be honest, I saw more racism up north than in the south. This is true even in Christianity. One of the chapters of this book addresses the supposed "curse of Ham" which has been used by every white slave owner and every slave owner all over the world. The prophecy given to Canaan (Ham's son) in Genesis 9:25 was, "*Cursed be Canaan; a servant of servants shall he be unto his brethren.*" The racist white plantation owners during the civil war told their slaves that it was the will of God for them to be servants and that if they weren't servants; they would be out of the will of God. Then they would point to the Apostle Paul saying things like "*Exhort servants to be obedient unto their own masters, and to please them well in all things; not answering again*" (Titus 2:9). You see, people can use the Word of God to justify <u>anything</u>. Therefore, you and I not only have to read and search the Scriptures, but we have to listen to the Spirit of God that is in us. As I personally read through dozens of commentators as to what they had to say, every one of them (except maybe one or two), the witness inside of me discerned they were departing from the truth and moving into another area when addressing black people in Scripture if they addressed them at all.

Now I believe that some white people (and black people) are racist because of the way they grew up. They were taught to be racist just as they were taught to eat with a fork and a knife. It was ingrained in them to hate people of another skin. The only source of deliverance for this is in Jesus. I have personally known just as many racist blacks as I've known racist whites. So I am not pointing the finger at anyone people, I am pointing the finger at all people, myself included.

Maybe the Lord might speak to you and bring correction. Don't be afraid of this. If Jesus opens up a door in your heart (a chamber) and shows where you really have been racist and treated other people in a way that they shouldn't have been treated just by virtue of their social status or the color of their skin, don't be alarmed. We do all this stuff many times subconsciously. For example, when we get on an elevator and there are three gangsters rap black guys and you are the only white person in there; you may pull your purse tighter or move your briefcase away from them. Why? Because the stereotype is that if a black person looks a certain way, you think he wants to rob or do something violent to you. Well, I'd rather somebody walk up to me dressed up as a gangster rapper than some of these criminal investors from wall street that steal hundreds of millions of dollars from people in silence and quietness. Which is worse? There is evil in all the hearts of men, and no one race has a monopoly on evil in them.

Now in this chapter, I want to simply show you that racism is not of God because we are all the "offspring of God". The first thing I want to look at is in Ephesians 1:10. Let us read this verse in context by beginning in verse 8,

"*[8]Wherein he hath abounded toward us in all wisdom and prudence; [9]Having made known unto us the mystery of his will, according to his good pleasure which he hath purposed in himself: [10]That in the dispensation of the fullness of times he might gather together in one all things in Christ, both which are in heaven, and which are on earth; even in him.*" This means that there is a time coming when God is going to gather together in one, all things in Christ, in heaven and on earth and <u>even in Him</u> (this means the body of Christ). So when it is speaking of earth here, it is not speaking of Christians, but of unsaved people. At some point, God is going to be all in all and we have to get this in our head, that He is the Supreme Ruler, Pontiff, and Sovereign Lord over the whole universe. God is gathering together <u>in one</u> <u>all things</u> in Christ. You can see it in the earth that Muslims are gathering, atheists are gathering, homosexuals are gathering, abortionists are gathering, etc. Everything is coming to fullness. Darkness is coming to fullness but at the same time there is a light that shines on the earth, there is a candle that blazes, and it is called the body of Christ! God does not want His people separating because of the color of everybody's skin, but He is gathering <u>all</u> of us together black, white, red, brown, yellow etc...

Secondly, the Scriptures are very clear that we are all (all nations) the offspring of God. This is very clear in a passage in Revelation 5. What we know and how we learned what we know must always bow to truth. When faced with truth, even though we may not like it, we need to bow to it. David said in Psalms 51:6, "*Behold, thou desirest truth in the <u>inward parts</u>: and in the hidden part thou shalt make me to know wisdom*" and the Bible plainly declares we are all the offspring of God. In Revelation 5, this is the chapter when the lamb opened the book and worship pursues. John had been weeping and Jesus had prevailed and in verse 9 it reads, "*And they sung a new song, saying, Thou art worthy to take the book, and to open the seals thereof: for thou wast slain, and hast redeemed us to God by thy blood out of <u>every kindred, and tongue, and people, and nation</u>.*" Now this is either true or it isn't. This is speaking of all the nations, races, tribes, ethnic groups, etc. and God has redeemed everyone of them! Does John 3:16 only say, "*For God so loved the <u>Caucasians</u>...*"? I don't think so. But there is a vast number of people that believe that white people are now the Jews because during the dispersion of the Jews, they claimed that Jeremiah went to Europe, that Paul actually preached in England or Scotland, and it is such a bizarre and ridiculous story, but you would be surprised at how many people believe this doctrine called "British Isralism". They believe that the Jews that were dispersed (Judah – the real Jews), they moved and became Europeans, and then moved to America and so on, and so now Jews are all the white people. Sounds pretty crazy and far out, but a lot of smart people believe this. To me, all you have to do is read Revelation 5:9 and that puts an end to this.

15

Secondly, the Bible clearly states that God is no respecter of persons (Acts 10:34, 15:9). John 3:16 says, "*For God so loved the world...*" When we think back to slavery, slave owners would kill, torture, and sell slaves and think it was right. What black people were forced to do was unspeakable. But then to have ministers put their stamp of approval on it is unimaginable. Even up until the late 1960's famous white ministers taught segregation and the theory they used was this: that Black people are not human beings and that they are called the "beasts of the earth" or rather the "living creatures" (i.e. Genesis 1:24-27 distinguishing between God creating living creatures and then creating man). Now obviously the Scriptures do not mean this. This was racist men putting their pre-supposed opinions to explain the Word of God. This is why even we, when looking into the Word of God, have to be careful not to do the same thing. When approaching the Word of God, we cannot have a pre-conceived idea about what the Bible says because we can find a passage to support any claim we might have. Cults are famous for doing this. We have to search the Scriptures with an open heart and allow the Scriptures to speak for itself. But these racist preachers also say that the reason for the curse on Cain after he killed his brother Abel came about from the fact that since there was no other woman on the earth at the time, Cain married one of these black living creatures creating the ungodly line of Cain. This is a shocking tale, but this is what they believe. They also go on to teach about the so-called curse of Ham to support the claim that the black people are a servant race (Genesis 9:25, "...*Cursed be Canaan* (one of the sons of Ham); *a servant of servants shall he be unto his brethren*"). They teach that their whole existence (why they were created) is to serve and be slaves to other people and try to use to Word of God to support this. And up until the 1960's, when all of the civil right's activity was happening, many white preachers (especially in the south) taught this very doctrine, that black people are beasts and not human beings. My heart in writing this book is to shatter this lie with a mighty sword, God's word of truth! I am not afraid of any racist person because I know Jesus! The little song we used to sing as little children is so true, "*Red and yellow, black and white, they are precious in His sight.*" Especially today, we need to teach our children and raise them up in the "good and right way". We have to teach our children when they are young because I remember my racist father everyday speaking his racist rants. He hated the Jews, Blacks, Chinese, Mexicans, etc. and had a racist name for all of them. I remember looking at my racist dad, knowing he only had an eighth grade education, and he is pontificating to me how white people are this and that, and thinking what a joke. What really made it a joke was my family was on welfare and many of my black friends weren't on welfare. He would curse at them being on welfare, speak how lazy and terrible other races were, and how they would use the government to support their evil ways. But he was the one doing that very same thing. I went to a school for the first 15 years of my life with all black people and sure there was violence

16

and a lot of uncomely stuff, I had to endure, but when my family moved to Maryland and went to an all white school, I saw the same things, but just in a different way. Racism is a devil and it is a spirit from hell and it originated in Babylon (Genesis 11:1-9 – Nimrod founded the Tower of Babel which led to all of the races being separated).

God loves the whole world (John 3:16). In Matthew 28:19 Jesus says, "*Go ye therefore, and teach all nations, baptizing them in the name of the Father, and of the Son, and of the Holy Ghost.*" God wants us to make disciples of all nations. This is every nation and every kind of ethnic group. Mark 13:10 says "*the gospel must first be published among all nations*" before Jesus returns.

Look next at Acts 17. Let us start in verse 22 so we can read it in context. This is Paul while he was in Athens speaking on Mars' hill where all the Greek scholars came from, "*22Then Paul stood in the midst of Mars' hill, and said, Ye men of Athens, I perceive that in all things ye are too superstitious. 23For as I passed by, and beheld your devotions, I found an altar with this inscription, TO THE UNKNOWN GOD. Whom therefore ye ignorantly worship, him declare I unto you...*" I love the way Paul preached. How would you feel sitting in a congregation and somebody calls you ignorant? It is very similar to Jesus saying to the woman at the well in John 4:22, "*Ye worship ye know not what...*" So many people get offended and leave when something is said that challenges them. We need to understand that God does this on purpose to get our attention because many times His people are not listening. He needs to say things many times to jar us and wake us up. Paul then continues, "*24God that made the world and all things therein, seeing that he is Lord of heaven and earth, dwelleth not in temples made with hands; 25Neither is worshipped with men's hands, as though he needed any thing, seeing he giveth to all life, and breath, and all things; 26And hath made of one blood all nations of men for to dwell on all the face of the earth, and hath determined the times before appointed, and the bounds of their habitation; 27That they should seek the Lord, if haply they might feel after him, and find him, though he be not far from every one of us: 28For in him we live, and move, and have our being; as certain also of your own poets have said, For we are also his offspring...*" In verse 27 when Paul is saying that God is not far from every one of us, he is addressing the world here. All of the unsaved people that we see everyday do not know this, but God is not very far from them, if they would just reach out. He created all peoples, all of us came from the original Adam. So in truth we are all connected in some ways as brothers and sisters. Everything God does is about family. He the Father created sons and daughters in His own image. Believe it or not we are all one family no matter what color or ethnic background or nation we were born in. We are Gods great created family.

All of us come from Adam, but more importantly, the second Adam (Jesus). Never forget this, when you got saved, you became a new creation (II Corinthians 5:17, Galatians 6:15). In the Greek it means a "new species". When you become a Christian, you are no longer white, black, or any color. You are now a son of God which is a species that is not of this earth. Hallelujah! We all come from one blood, and that is the "precious blood of Christ"!

Romans 12:2-3 says, "*And be not conformed to this world: but be ye transformed by the renewing of your mind, that ye may prove what is that good, and acceptable, and perfect, will of God. For I say, through the grace given unto me, to every man that is among you, not to think of himself more highly than he ought to think; but to think soberly, according as God hath dealt to every man the measure of faith.*" We are not to think of ourselves more highly than we ought to think. This is also true when considering the races.

Romans 10:10-13 says, "*[10]For with the heart man believeth unto righteousness; and with the mouth confession is made unto salvation. [11]For the scripture saith, Whosoever believeth on him shall not be ashamed. [12]For there is no difference between the Jew and the Greek: for the same Lord over all is rich unto all that call upon him. [13]For whosoever shall call upon the name of the Lord shall be saved.*" There is no difference between the Jew and the Greek. God is no respecter of persons (Acts 10:34-35). This is true of black and white, brown or yellow.

Let us go back now to the beginning to the book of Genesis. Here in Genesis 1:26-27 it says, "*And God said, Let us make man in our image, after our likeness...*" In other words, all human beings have been created in the image and likeness of God. I believe that just as Jesus was able to hide Himself from His disciples (like in Luke 24 when they couldn't recognize Him, or Mary at the garden didn't know who He was, etc), the Lord many times changes the way He looks purposely for whatever reason. I have no problem with a black person seeing a black Jesus. I believe God speaks to people where they are at. So if you are a rapper that just got saved, God, when He speaks to you, may just say "Yo, what up dog! I have a word for you today." And if He is speaking to some redneck white boy in the back woods of Tennessee, He may just say, "Howdy!" He will be whatever He has to be to reach us and I believe that when you see the face of God, you see the face of every color and every culture. God is so big and so deep, we can't even begin to comprehend these things. For a minute, He may have a black face, and then a Hispanic face, or a Jewish face, or a white face. Man was made in the image of God and He made man to have dominion, "*...and let them have dominion over the fish of the sea, and over the fowl of the air, and over the cattle, and over all the earth, and over every creeping thing that creepeth upon the earth. [27]So God created man in his*

18

own image, in the image of God created he him; male and female created he them."

We are all the offspring of God. Here in Ephesians 2:18-19, *"[18]For through him we both have access by one Spirit unto the Father. [19]Now therefore ye are no more strangers and foreigners, but fellow citizens with the saints, and of the household of God..."* You and I are no longer strangers and foreigners. Once we come to Jesus, we realize that we are a new creation in a new Kingdom and the same God that created people in the beginning in His image and even though man fell, that now that we are born again, we are now restored to that initial creation in our spirits. A Christian's spirit is made perfect created in the image of God (Hebrew 12:23) which is called being "born again" (justification). This allows God then for the rest of our lives to conform our soulish man into His image through His workings (sanctification). Eventually, at the coming of the Lord, our bodies will be glorified (glorification). This is also known as our three-fold salvation.

Acts 2 is the account of the day of Pentecost. *"[1]And when the day of Pentecost was fully come, they were all with one accord in one place. [2]And suddenly there came a sound from heaven as of a rushing mighty wind, and it filled all the house where they were sitting. [3]And there appeared unto them cloven tongues like as of fire, and it sat upon each of them. [4]And they were all filled with the Holy Ghost, and began to speak with other tongues, as the Spirit gave them utterance. [5]And there were dwelling at Jerusalem Jews, devout men, out of every nation under heaven..."* Just in case you thought or were taught salvation is only for Jewish people, when the day of Pentecost came, there was an explosion of the Holy Ghost into the entire world! *"...[6]Now when this was noised abroad, the multitude came together, and were confounded, because that every man heard them speak in his own language. [7]And they were all amazed and marvelled, saying one to another, Behold, are not all these which speak Galilaeans? [8]And how hear we every man in our own tongue, wherein we were born? [9]Parthians, and Medes, and Elamites, and the dwellers in Mesopotamia, and in Judaea, and Cappadocia, in Pontus, and Asia, [10]Phrygia, and Pamphylia, in Egypt, and in the parts of Libya about Cyrene, and strangers of Rome, Jews and proselytes, [11]Cretes and Arabians, we do hear them speak in our tongues the wonderful works of God."* This includes all nations. When God does anything, He doesn't want to limit it to a particular race or nation, but He wants the world to receive it! So when the day of Pentecost came, He made sure there were representatives from all of the nations of the earth present. So today millions of Christians of all colors and nations are truly saved and filled with the Holy Ghost. I've found them in every nation I've traveled. All colors, all backgrounds, all walking in the things of God. All of them are our brothers.

In Ephesians 3:14-21 it reads, *"[15]For this cause I bow my knees unto the Father of our Lord Jesus Christ, [15]Of whom the whole family in heaven and earth is named."* Paul is bowing his knees and praying that every one in heaven and every one on earth, *"[16]That he would grant you, according to the riches of his glory, to be strengthened with might by his Spirit in the inner man; [17]That Christ may dwell in your hearts by faith; that ye, being rooted and grounded in love, [18]May be able to comprehend with all saints what is the breadth, and length, and depth, and height; [19]And to know the love of Christ, which passeth knowledge, that ye might be filled with all the fullness of God..."* God desires all people to be filled will all of the fullness of God! Titus 3:3-4 says *"[3]For we ourselves also were sometimes foolish, disobedient, deceived, serving divers lusts and pleasures, living in malice and envy, hateful, and hating one another. [4]But after that the kindness and love of God our Saviour toward man appeared."* These little statements and wordings such as *"toward man"* can be passed up but you have to realize, the kindness and love of God our Saviour was towards all men. If God created you, whoever you are, He has not forsaken you! Isaiah 52:10 says, *"The LORD hath made bare his holy arm in the eyes of all the nations; and all the ends of the earth shall see the salvation of our God."* God wants every one in the world to come to Jesus. Zechariah 2:8 say, *"For thus saith the LORD of hosts; After the glory hath he sent me unto the nations..."* Every person God created, God feels a responsibility to. When Adam was created, we were there inside of Adam (in a sense). We were the same one who was created in the image and likeness of God. There were no languages then, only one. There were no colors then, only whatever Adam looked like. All of us come from the same place. When we look at our black brother or we look at our Hispanic brother or any people different from ourselves, we need to realize, Jesus died for them too. Jesus even died for that person from another race that you maybe can't stand, but because many don't know the love of God, many don't walk in the love of God, leading many to resort to holding onto petty prejudices and racist thoughts. Most are smart enough now to keep this all held in and not show to others their racist thoughts, but think privately within themselves. Inside of these people, they're judging, criticizing, and thinking all manner of things, not realizing that whoever they are judging, they are the offspring of God. Oh how surprised we are going to be in heaven! We will see every color, nation and ethnic group there. We will have to adjust our thinking for sure.

There is no difference between peoples anymore. Galatians 3:26-28 says, *"[26]For ye are all the children of God by faith in Christ Jesus. [27]For as many of you as have been baptized into Christ have put on Christ. [28]There is neither Jew nor Greek, there is neither bond nor free, there is neither male nor female: for ye are all one in Christ Jesus."* You and I have to get to the place where this revelation is a reality to us. For example, when we look at a sister, we don't see her anymore as a woman or when we look at a Jewish person, we don't see them as a Jew. This was the revelation of Paul and he was hated for it because Jews in the early church wanted to still feel superior to the Gentiles. Many of the early church fathers didn't want the Gentile believers to come in or if they did, they had to follow strict Jewish Laws. Thank God for the Apostle Paul who fought against this when others didn't. Paul had a revelation and the Lord taught him as he spent years by himself. He said in Galatians 1:12, *"For I neither received it of man, neither was I taught it, but by the revelation of Jesus Christ."* And 14 years after God had given it to him; he went up to Jerusalem and confronted the church fathers there. As a matter of fact, he even rebuked Peter while he was there because Peter showed some serious racism. Peter was eating with Gentiles and when James (who was one of the heads of the church there) came in, Peter quickly disengaged himself from the Gentiles and from that moment on only ate with Jews. Paul happens to come by later and sees Barnabas (who was one of his sons in the faith) doing the same thing and he gets infuriated (Galatians 2:11-14). In Galatians 2:11 it says Paul withstood Peter to the face. This was a big deal because this was Paul bringing blame on the Apostle Peter, not just anybody. And this was the same Paul who killed Christians earlier in his life (Peter could've brought this up and not listen to Paul, but he didn't). But Paul says of himself in Acts 23:1 that he has *"lived in all good conscience before God until this day"* as well as in Acts 24:16 he says, *"And herein do I exercise myself, to have always a conscience void of offence toward God, and toward men."* What a man of God Paul was! When he said he had a conscience void of offence toward God and men, he really meant it. Only a man with a pure heart and a true ministry of God could point to one of the greatest men of God in history and say to him basically, how can you do such a thing?! Paul had to do it because Peter feared the elders. Fear and racism go hand in hand. But I am here to tell you that there is neither Jew nor Greek, male nor female, bond or free, but we are <u>all one</u> in Christ Jesus. All this talk of women not being able to be in the ministry is not true either. What women? We are all sons of God now. All of us have started over because we are all a new species in Christ Jesus.

Next, Ephesians 2:10-15 reads *"[10]For we are his workmanship, created in Christ Jesus unto good works, which God hath before ordained that we should walk in them. [11]Wherefore remember, that ye being in time past Gentiles in the flesh, who are called Uncircumcision by that which is called the Circumcision in the flesh made by hands; [12]That at that time ye were without Christ, being aliens from the commonwealth of Israel, and strangers from the covenants of promise, having no hope, and without God in the world: [13]But now in Christ Jesus ye who sometimes were far off are made nigh by the blood of Christ. [14]For he is our peace, who hath made both one, and hath broken down the middle wall of partition between us; [15]Having abolished in his flesh the enmity, even the law of commandments contained in ordinances; for to make in himself of twain one new man, so making peace."* When we come to Jesus, all of the divisions cease. There is no difference anymore! If you are in Christ Jesus, worldly opinions are finished. They are done with.

In Acts 15, Peter is trying to defend himself in going to Cornelius' house and he stands up in verse 7, "*7And when there had been much disputing, Peter rose up, and said unto them, Men and brethren, ye know how that a good while ago God made choice among us, that the Gentiles by my mouth should hear the word of the gospel, and believe. 8And God, which knoweth the hearts, bare them witness, giving them the Holy Ghost, even as he did unto us; 9And put no difference between us and them, purifying their hearts by faith. 10Now therefore why tempt ye God, to put a yoke upon the neck of the disciples, which neither our fathers nor we were able to bear?*" God "*bare them witness, giving them the Holy Ghost*" which were the Gentiles. The Gentiles consist of anybody that doesn't know Jesus. Gentiles represent every nation. And God "*put no difference*" between the Jews and the Gentiles. In verse 11 it continues, "*But we believe that through the grace of the Lord Jesus Christ we shall be saved, even as they.*" There is no difference now once we have been born again.

Song of Solomon 4:7 says, "Thou art all fair, my love; there is no spot in thee." When God is talking to the bride of Christ in Song of Solomon, He is talking about everybody in that bride. When it speaks of Jesus in Song of Solomon 5:16 it says, "*He is altogether lovely.*" The many-membered Jesus (His bride) will be altogether lovely!

Colossians 3:10-11 reads "*10And have put on the new man, which is renewed in knowledge after the image of him that created him: 11Where there is neither Greek nor Jew, circumcision nor uncircumcision, Barbarian, Scythian, bond nor free: but Christ is all, and in all.*" So when we are born again all of this ceases and we simply are all children of God, by faith in Christ Jesus.

Acts 10:34-35 reads "*34Then Peter opened his mouth, and said, Of a truth I perceive that God is no respecter of persons: 35But in every nation he that feareth him, and worketh righteousness, is accepted with him.*" Amen!

There is no difference between Jews, Gentiles, and whoever tells you otherwise are teaching in error. Let us never forget that we are all the offspring of God and that there is no difference any more between any of us. We are all the children of God by faith in Christ Jesus! God is not willing that "none should perish". He loves everybody! Help us to see with Your eyes Father for Your "*eyes behold the nations*" (Psalms 66:7). You made bare Your arm of salvation, not for just the Jews, but to all nations! Lord, give us a bigger heart than we have now and bigger eyes to see. Give us a greater vision. As we walk this earth, let us be living flames of fire that You have called us to be, lights in the midst of a perverse generation. You said the world would know we are your disciples because of the love we would have for one another. This was your command to us in John 13:34-35, "*[34]A new commandment I give unto you, That ye love one another; as I have loved you, that ye also love one another. [35]By this shall all men know that ye are my disciples, if ye have love one to another.*" This means black, white, yellow, red, etc. Right now Jesus, we lift up our hearts in our hands and we ask you to expose anything you need to. We really want to be free. We want to have freedom and deliverance from any racist and ungodly thinking. We want it wiped out of us, so we can be true ministers of the gospel, the good news. "*How beautiful are the feet of them that preach the gospel of peace, and bring glad tidings of good things!*" (Romans 10:15). This is the good news that the whole world should be saved.

God Does Not Tolerate Racism
Chapter 2

In this chapter I would like to share that God does not tolerate racism by first looking at a story in Numbers 12. First of all, God just doesn't like racism, and He will not tolerate it. As we'll find in this story, there is nothing like interracial marriage to make people's true racism come out. This subject will be covered in its own complete way later in a chapter all it's own. But here we see in God's Holy Word his attitude towards racism.

If you or I find ourselves walking in a mall today and we see a black man with a white woman together, we may feel something. Why is this? You can't consciously explain why you do, but something in you moves. If you are a black woman and you see a black man walking down the street with a white woman, you feel something move inside of you. Of course nobody will admit this, but it is true. These things many times are subconscious and they live inside of us and until God opens up that chamber in our heart, we may be carrying around racism that we don't even know is there. It is all subtle because the devil is subtle, and he's the Father of racism. When God said to the children of Israel to not marry another tribe, He was not saying you can't marry somebody of another race. He was saying to not marry outside the Kingdom of God or outside of His people (the Nation of Israel). We will see this when we talk about the curse of Ham. Israelites were especially not to marry Canaanites.

As we begin in Numbers 12, we see that Miriam and Aaron definitely had a problem the woman Moses married. They had a problem with this woman not only because she was black, but also an Egyptian. Remember the Egyptians had held Isreal in bondage for many years. So there was obviously some resentment for being simply all an Egyptian woman, and then also because she was black." So Let us read starting in verse 1, *"[1]And Miriam and Aaron spake against Moses because of the Ethiopian woman whom he had married: for he had married an Ethiopian woman..."* An Ethiopian woman is a black woman. No matter how commentators or whoever try to act like she is not, she was black. Many commentators go to great lengths to twist this fact to say she wasn't black. Moses married a black woman, and Miriam who was a worship leader and was commended in the book of Micah for being one of the leaders in the Exodus, and Aaron, who really acted cowardly and did what others say (e.g. gave into the people to build them a golden calf), had a problem with this. When we consider Aaron as a leader, if we look back to Exodus 3, God really never intended Aaron to be there. God called Moses alone to deliver His people. It reminds me of Kathryn Kuhlman who was a sister who had a tremendous healing ministry for many years. It always bothered me when she would say, "I know that a man is supposed to be doing my ministry". Secretly in her heart she knew this wasn't true. She was saying that to appease all of the chauvinist males as if God couldn't use a woman in ministry to work miracles. But this kind of thinking is ingrained in us. You see, 20-30 years ago it was ingrained in women that they were to stay at home and do anything and everything their husband said. I was there in the 1970's when this was happening. The submission teachings came out. Shepherds came out and told women that they had to submit to anything and everything their husband said. Out of this came multitudes of divorces 10 or 20 years later when everybody realized it was bad teaching and error. We are to submit to one another in love. A wife is to submit to her husband in the Lord. When a husband tells his wife to do something that defiles her conscious, she doesn't have to do it because our first and greatest husband is Jesus.

So Moses had married this black woman. In verse 2, Miriam and Aaron continue, "*²And they said, hath the LORD indeed spoken only by Moses? Hath he not spoken also by us?*" There is tremendous revelation here. Miriam and Aaron didn't come out and say they are troubled because of the black woman. They use another angle. People will not confess that they are realy a racist, but they find another excuse to express their dissatisfaction. God does not like this, which is why He makes it clear in verse 1 that their speaking against Moses was due to the black woman. If we look towards the end of the story, we will see that Miriam gets leprosy and Aaron doesn't, which shows Miriam was the real racist here. This reveals that Miriam was like the woman described in Ecclesiastes 7:26, "*And I find more bitter than death the woman, whose heart is snares and nets, and her hands as bands: whoso pleaseth God shall escape from her; but the sinner shall be taken by her.*" She had a controlling spirit. Aaron, like so many husbands we see, just went along with whatever Miriam said. When you consider also what they said, "*Hath the LORD indeed spoken only by Moses? Hath he not spoken also by us?*" it sounds like an Absalom spirit as well. They were maybe waiting to take some of the credit for leading God's people out of bondage.

"*...And the LORD heard it.*" You better circle this in your Bible because we need to always remember the Lord hears everything. He hears it when we think it too. Every idle word we speak will be accounted for in our life. We better watch what we say. We all should understand a day of judgment is coming (Luke 8:17 & Luke 12:2). Certainly we must know we cannot hide anything from the Holy Ghost. Just consider Ananias and Sapphria in Acts 5; and that should be sufficient evidence.

"*³(Now the man Moses was very meek, above all the men which were upon the face of the earth.)*" Moses grew up in Pharaoh's house and was a prince of Egypt. He had everything, but the 40 years in the wilderness broke him so completely, that he became the meekest man on the face of the earth.

Meekness does not mean weakness because how many of us have stood before Pharaoh with just a staff or held up our rod before the Red Sea and it parts. Meekness means Moses was pliable, teachable, humble, and didn't think he had it all. Let's just consider a few scriptures about man and his worthiness. Romans 7:18 says *"For I know that in me (that is, in my flesh,) dwelleth no good thing: for to will is present with me; but how to perform that which is good I find not."* Psalms 39:5 adds, *"...verily every man at his best state is altogether vanity. Selah."* Jeremiah 17:9 plainly says, *"The heart is deceitful above all things, and desperately wicked: who can know it?"* Isaiah 40:17 reads *"All nations before him are as nothing; and they are counted to him less than nothing and vanity."*

What else does the Bible say about man? Job 15:14 says, *"What is man, that he should be clean? and he which is born of a woman, that he should be righteous?"* Psalms 143:3-4 says, *"³For the enemy hath persecuted my soul; he hath smitten my life down to the ground; he hath made me to dwell in darkness, as those that have been long dead. ⁴Therefore is my spirit overwhelmed within me; my heart within me is desolate."* Isaiah 53:6 says, *"All we like sheep have gone astray; we have turned every one to his own way; and the LORD hath laid on him the iniquity of us all."* We see in Psalms 14:2-3 that *"²The LORD looked down from heaven upon the children of men, to see if there were any that did understand, and seek God. ³They are all gone aside, they are all together become filthy: there is none that doeth good, no, not one."* Micah 7:2 says *"The good man is perished out of the earth: and there is none upright among men..."* Romans 3:10-13 clearly defines man and says, *"¹⁰As it is written, There is none righteous, no, not one: ¹¹There is none that understandeth, there is none that seeketh after God. ¹²They are all gone out of the way, they are together become unprofitable; there is none that doeth good, no, not one. ¹³Their throat is an open sepulchre; with their tongues they have used deceit; the poison of asps is under their lips:"* And finally, Jeremiah 17:5 says, *"Thus saith the LORD; Cursed be the man that trusteth in man, and maketh flesh his arm, and whose heart departeth from the LORD."* All of us must eventually come to this conclusion that without Him we are nothing.

"⁴And <u>the LORD spake suddenly</u> unto Moses, and unto Aaron, and unto Miriam, Come out ye three unto the tabernacle of the congregation. And they three came out." God was so upset about this, He moved immediately. *"⁵And the LORD came down in the pillar of the cloud, and stood in the door of the tabernacle, and called Aaron and Miriam: and they both came forth."* Let me say this first: if you have been the subject of racism or if you've been the person whom racism has been used against and you are a child of God, the Lord will hear it and the Lord will call them out and He will come down! The audible voice of God spoke. If I was Miriam or Aaron, I would be afraid by now. This reminds me when I used to get my reports cards in school. I would have stomach aches all the way home. If I couldn't convince my sisters to

change my grades, then I knew I was going to get a serious whipping at home, so I had a terrible feeling all the way home that judgement was coming. So God comes down in His glory and singles out Miriam and Aaron to come here. If I was them, I would've been on my face screaming at the top of my lungs saying "I'm sorry, have mercy, Moses is a great man of God!" God comes down suddenly. He didn't even give them a chance to think about what they did.

"*6And he said, Hear now my words: If there be a prophet among you, I the LORD will make myself known unto him in a vision, and will speak unto him in a dream. 7My servant Moses is not so, who is faithful in all mine house 8With him will I speak mouth to mouth, even apparently, and not in dark speeches; and the similitude of the LORD shall he behold: wherefore then were ye not afraid to speak against my servant Moses? 9And the anger of the LORD was kindled against them; and he departed.*" When somebody talks about a man or woman of God in an unrighteous way, they better be careful. That goes for all of us. You see, there is something greater than a prophet and the five-fold ministry. The similitude of the Lord is the face of God. This tells me maybe many ministers do not behold the face of God, which is the manifest presence of God. The word "presence" in Hebrew means "face, or the turning of the face towards". You can be a prophet and yet never even have the manifest presence of God as Moses. There is something greater than the five-fold ministry and it is called Brideship. It is called intimacy with God. God was basically saying to Miriam and Aaron, "you know I have a special relationship with Moses and you've seen Me come down to meet with Moses causing him to have to cover his face because of the glory, why then were you not afraid to speak against Moses?" Do you not think Miriam and Aaron should have thought twice before speaking unrighteously about Moses? I encourage all of us to wait a moment before we open our mouths. Never answer anything quickly or hastily. You and I learn this most of the time by making mistakes. You can even say the right thing at the wrong time. Consider all that Moses had done: how God dealt with him for 40 years; how God used him against the entire nation of Egypt and brought 3 million Israelites out with mighty signs and wonders and beyond that how God had given him the 10 commandments burned into stone (twice); Moses had fasted 80 days; they saw Moses go up into the mountain to be with God and when he would come back the glow of God's glory upon him was too much that they made Moses put a veil on his face, etc. Miriam and Aaron did not consider this.

The truth is, for many people, everything you or I do is never enough. They will criticize one petty thing and overlook the thousand selfless things we do. For example, I hear criticism all of the time about our worship services at the church I pastor. Some say it is too loud or it is too long, etc. They are speaking about creature comforts and the flesh. Now should we go on forever and ever and ever? Certainly not, every worship session should be different in time limits. If God is done in 20 minutes, I will put my guitar down. Sometimes it is an hour and a half, sometimes it is 45 minutes. You can't say, we are going to only worship for 30 minutes. If you do this then you are touching the ark of God and somebody may just die. I will never try to touch and control the Holy Spirit. The ark of God should always be free to move until it is in its right place and we've lead everybody in the room to the Most Holy Place. Once we are in there, than we can stop. God is never satisfied until He meets with His people face to face in there. You see, when you or I receive the Word of God in the outer court, we really don't get it like we could. When you receive the Word in the Holy Place, there is a little more chance, but when you receive the Word of God in the Most Holy Place, it is a living Word and when God speaks in the Most Holy Place, He writes it upon the table of our hearts. It is engraved into your nature! This is why we just don't have meetings to have meetings. We have visitations with God and while we are there, He engraves on our hearts what He wants to say. It is an impartation of His character. We don't realize how Babylonish we really are many times in our church gatherings. Our purpose for meeting should always be about Jesus and meeting with Him. We don't come to church to receive and just do things. We come to give, to *"bring the sacrifice of praise into the house of the Lord"* (Jeremiah 33:11), to *"bring ye all the tithes into the storehouse"* (Malachi 3:10), etc. We are supposed to bring an offering with us as in Exodus 25:1-2, *"[1]And the LORD spake unto Moses, saying, [2]Speak unto the children of Israel, that they bring me an offering: of every man that giveth it willingly with his heart ye shall take my offering."* The Lord spoke to His people to bring an offering in order to build the house of the Lord, *"[8]And let them make me a sanctuary; that I may dwell among them"* (Exodus 25:8). We don't come to church to get, but we come to church to give. Many times I feel like a voice crying in the wilderness and there is a great hurricane and winds blowing all around me. And I am screaming at the top of my lungs, but my voice is overshadowed by the winds and storm and people just don't get it. So much of what we still do is founded in religion, not the Spirit of God. Oh it is going to require a great shaking to bring forth that remnant, but it is happening even now. A remnant will not have "Mystery Babylon" written on their foreheads, but the image of Christ will be on their forehead. Glory to God!

But in this story, God is challenging Aaron and Miriam as to why they were not afraid to speak against Moses. Now God doesn't want us afraid of men or women of God, but He does want us to give honor where honor is due. I Timothy 5:17 says, *"Let the elders that rule well be counted worthy of double honour, especially they who labour in the word and doctrine."* So the anger of the Lord was kindled against Miriam and Aaron. *"[10]And the cloud departed from off the tabernacle..."* God got so mad the cloud departed. Haven't you seen someone so mad that they just left the room? This is the picture I get

28

about what happened. You can be sure that when God sees racism, even when it is done subtly, he will leave. He will remove his manifest presence. He will not tolerate it. Men are so caught up in themselves and their own ministry, they don't even recognize the Lord has departed. Ministers especially should be concerned about racism, for they will receive the greater judgment. But how many hide behind the scriptures and pervert the Word of God, by their subtle racism.

And then, "...*behold, Miriam became leprous, white as snow: and Aaron looked upon Miriam, and, behold, she was leprous.*"

"*[11] And Aaron said unto Moses, Alas, my lord, I beseech thee, lay not the sin upon us, wherein we have done foolishly, and wherein we have sinned.*" Just in the last few months, somebody called me and for an hour they just lit into me. They cursed at me, said stuff to me, screamed and yelled, and told me I was everything but a man of God, for an hour. I kept my peace, didn't lose control, and tried to end the conversation peaceably. And then an hour or two later they called back and said they acted foolishly and said they were sorry for what they said. Now, I was glad to say I forgive you, but you know, you wound people when you talk like this. Every one of us needs to be careful. Yes, I forgave them instantly, but the damage people do when your mouth becomes an agent of Satan accusing others and speaking abusively, full of pettiness and disputing, and then you realize you made a mistake, you know, sometimes it is not enough just to say you are sorry. You might want to grab the person and say, "look at me, I'm really sorry, because I know I might have hurt your heart when I did that." If you are going to be a man or a woman of God, a true minister, than you are going to have to be able to forgive and love people in spite of what they do. If you can't do that, than go back to college and get a degree in something you can make money in because you are not going to make it in the ministry. Everybody will always have something to say about everything you do in ministry. It is a way of life. Also, we have to be able to be people who are able to listen because God can speak through anybody.

At the same time, God gets angry when others speak unrighteously about others, especially those in leadership. It is amazing to me that people will lie right to your face and then turn around and smile at you when they see you and act like they didn't just cut you to shreds. Solomon says in Ecclesiastes 10:20 "*Curse not the king, no not in thy thought; and curse not the rich in thy bedchamber: for a bird of the air shall carry the voice, and that which hath wings shall tell the matter.*" I remember I was in a restaurant one time sitting in a booth and as I was eating I heard on the other side of the partition between booths two people talking about a man called Sam Greene. So I listened as I was eating my food these two people ripping me to shreds with their judgements. I left the restaurant before they were able to see me and when I saw them on Sunday morning they were just sitting there smiling and saying they loved me. God is watching and when you hurt a man or woman of God, God gets upset. In I Samuel 8, Samuel was so upset at what the people were saying God had to speak to Samuel and say, *"Samuel, Hearken unto the voice of the people in all that they say unto thee: for they have not rejected thee, but they have rejected me, that I should not reign over them."* (I Samuel 8:7). Ultimately people will get mad about what God has done in you that has pointed out their indiscretion and they use you as the whipping post. But every word that is spoken is written down and God hears it, especially if it is about somebody who is in the glory because we really have to be careful then.

Aaron continues crying out to Moses in verse 12, *"[12]Let her not be as one dead, of whom the flesh is half consumed when he cometh out of his mother's womb..."* Look at Moses reaction, *"[13]And Moses cried unto the LORD, saying, Heal her now, O God, I beseech thee. [14]And the LORD said unto Moses, If her father had but spit in her face, should she not be ashamed seven days?..."* As precious as Moses was, he was trying to get Miriam to have no punishment, but God was not going to let that happen. The Lord continues, *"...let her be shut out from the camp seven days, and after that let her be received in again."* What does this mean, seven days? Miriam is not allowed back in the congregation until the seventh day, that is, until that thing has been perfected in her life and she's not going to do it again.

"[15]And Miriam was shut out from the camp seven days: and the people journeyed not till Miriam was brought in again." This is very interesting. Do you realize when we do things like what Miriam did, we not only harm ourselves, but the rest of the body can't go on either. And this was all because Moses married a black woman and they were such cowards they couldn't even say the real reason why they were mad. Let us not be like Miriam. This was racism at its purist and God despised it!

The next Scripture I would to mention regarding God does not tolerate racism is in Luke 6:30-37, particularly in verse 32 where Jesus says, *"For if ye love them which love you, what thank have ye? For sinners also love those that love them."* The Lord expects us to love everybody. Amen!

Matthew 25:31-45 is the story of the people of God standing in the last days, and God divides the sheep and the goats. The sheep were those that visited the prisons, took care of the hungry and thirsty, clothed the naked, etc, and did it in a merciful way. So much of our own religious works in the respect of this time and age is done in a way that looks down upon the needy and the strangers. There is nothing worse than treating a person like they are beneath you. Years ago, when I was a young man and moved to Jacksonville, FL from

Washington D.C., I had no money, worked a job to make just enough money to get by so I could go to all of the meetings night and day, so I rarely had money for frivolous things like restaurants and movies. Occasionally when I would want to go out to eat, sometimes people would say they would take care of me, but in doing so they would make it very clear when we were sitting at the table that they were taking care of the food for me and would embarrass me completely. I remember one time when it was a cruel embarrassment (I was thankful for the food), but as I went home that night I was in the presence of the Lord and the Lord said He allowed this to happen to me because it is a learning experience for you to learn what not to do. And I remember asking the Lord when the day comes that I get to the place where I have a flow of money and am not in constant need that I will always look to pay for others and I will never make them feel obligated, expecting nothing in return and never embarrass them. We are not to give loans, expecting a return. We don't remind people how much we've given or treat them like they are beneath us. Jesus expects us when we go to the prisons, to treat prisoners with respect. Or if we see strangers or clothe the naked, we don't act like we are big-shots giving them clothes to wear like we are something great. We don't do things to be seen of men. Matthew 6:3 says, *"But when thou doest alms, let not thy left hand know what thy right hand doeth."* Everything we do is unto the Lord. God is watching and especially the way we treat people who are different from us or of another race and at the judgment seat there will be many people saying to the Lord, *"when saw we thee an hungred, and fed thee? Or thirsty, and gave thee drink? When saw we thee a stranger, and took thee in? or naked, and clothed thee?"* (Matthew 25:36). Jesus responded and said, *"Inasmuch as ye have done it unto one of the least of these my brethren, ye have done it unto me."* God does not tolerate racism in any shape or form.

I Peter 2:17 says, *"Honour all men. Love the brotherhood. Fear God. Honour the king."* He tells us four major things to do here. We are to honor the king (e.g. our president), fear God, love our brothers in Jesus, and honor all men. Even worldly people, we are to treat them with respect.

We must all be careful not to judge people according to their appearance. We have all done it but God is not pleased with it. John 7:24 says, *"Judge not according to the appearance, but judge righteous judgment."* I can honestly say to you I have done this also. Upon meeting somebody for the first time, we immediately just size them up. We compartmentalize people in our brain. Even with somebody's name, we judge them unrighteously. For example, if I knew a girl named April years ago and I meet somebody else named April, somehow my brain thinks the new April is like the April I knew years ago. We have to be careful because we can put people in a box and expect them to be a certain way when they are not like that at all. God made it clear in I Samuel 16:7 when Samuel saw Jesse's first son and said basically, "wow, this guy is beautiful, surely the Lord's anointed is before me." And God set Samuel straight when He said *"Samuel, Look not on his countenance, or on the height of his stature; because I have refused him: for the LORD seeth not as man seeth; for man looketh on the outward appearance, but the LORD looketh on the heart."* Here is some help in doing this. When you meet somebody, let them talk. Give thhyuiem 5 minutes or so because that is all it will take. Our mouths will always betray us because our hearts and our mouths are connected. In 5 minutes, they will say something to let you know what kind of spirit they have. You will have a witness about what kind of person they are by what they say. We can't just immediately make judgments, especially on the outward appearance. This is really a racist act, whether we know it or not. God doesn't like this. We are to honor all men and not to judge them unrighteously. Let us give people a chance. Let's not judge them, immediately. Let's wait and discern a righteous judgement. Don't judge a man by his appearance, the clothes he wears, the color of his skin, etc... Let's wait and let God show us the true heart of an individual, lets judge them by their fruit, and the content of their character.

In Isaiah 65:5 the Lord is speaking here, *"Which say, Stand by thyself, come not near to me; for I am holier than thou. These are a smoke in my nose, a fire that burneth all the day."* This reminds me of a person that came to the church I was pastoring and came with great need. We helped this person tremendously, but then one day I was counseling this person in my office and this person actually said to me, "You know, I thought the people here at Narrow Way were spiritual, but you all don't even come anywhere close to the kind of glory I tap into when I am alone." Now knowing this person, knowing the extreme problems in their life, that I had just dealt with. I couldn't h.... having entered into any great level of glory, because her life was so messed up and confused. Yet she still felt superior to the rest of us. And knowing the witness of the Holy Ghost, I couldn't tell if they even entered into any level of glory. The audacity for this person to say they are in a greater place spiritually than all of us is amazing. First of all, if you were, you would never say it. Actually, this person went on to criticize another member of the church and the way they prayed and that it didn't meet up to her standards. I responded and said, "First of all, this is Jesus' church, and I am the pastor and those are my sheep you are talking about." Then I said, "You are spooky, not spiritual". I see this person from time to time and they just go from church to church, and subtly I see there is a spirit of rebellion. This holier than thou attitude, God says, is a smoke in His nostrils and it infuriates Him.

I remember when I moved to Jacksonville, FL as a teenager, I only had a brown paper bag containing 2 sets of underwear, 2 pairs of jeans, a couple pair of socks, a pair of Chuck Taylor tennis shoes, a couple of shirts, and a pair of overalls, and that was all I owned. It all fit in one paper bag. I slept on a floor for a couple of months initially until I moved into a house with a couple of brothers. Remember now, I came from the ghetto and could remember the times walking with my mama to pick up our government cheese and powder milk. I came out of poverty and know all about it. As I began to grow in the Lord, I eventually got sent out to pastor in Chicago for a couple of years, then I came back to Jacksonville and was put on staff of a pretty large church, I was making a pretty good salary, had a couple of suits, and all that goes with a little success. Well, one day after I led the worship during a service and the glory was in the room, I had my nice new brown suit on and I smelled real good and I went to sit down in the front row. After I sat down, I remember smelling this awful smell. Immediately I knew the smell because homeless people have a certain stench to them when they don't take showers for a long period of time. Well, sitting there was this man, obviously in dire need of a shower, several shaves, and probably needed to be bathed in cologne for 2 weeks. And immediately this thing rose up in me and I began to be very critical of him thinking how can he come to church smelling and looking like that. As I was thinking this, the pastor got up to the microphone and said, "I would like everyone to turn to the person next to you and give them a Holy Ghost hug!" Well, there was only one person next to me and I immediately cringed thinking I had to touch this filthy and dirty man. As I was thinking of someway to get out of this because I didn't want my suit spoiled and stained (some people can be so nasty the smell on then can remain on your clothes), the voice of the Lord came to me saying, "I remember a young man..." He didn't have to say anything else. I immediately received the rebuke, walked over to the man, and embraced him. I never saw him again. It is amazing how you can be poor and poverty stricken, get a little money, and become so self-righteous and "holier than thou". This can happen to any of us.

In Acts 10:28 when Peter is rehearsing before the council there, he says, *"And he said unto them, Ye know how that it is an unlawful thing for a man that is a Jew to keep company, or come unto one of another nation; but God hath shewed me that I should not call any man common or unclean."* He was rehearsing the fact when God had visited him at Cornelius' house. God doesn't want us calling any man, nation or ethnic group, common or unclean. God created all men, and he expects us to treat people as he does. Let's remember we are all God's children, we are all his creation, so we need to give respect to every man.

Lastly, let us look at the parable in Luke 18:9-14, *"[9]And he spake this parable unto certain which trusted in themselves that they were righteous, and despised others..."* We are talking about the attitude of racism or self-righteousness, God hates it. Jesus speaks this parable to everybody but He knows there are certain people in the midst who are like this. You see, when a word comes forth, it may not be for you. If you are not self-righteous, don't get upset. You just need to realize that certain among us have that problem. Just listen and let God hammer this truth deeper into your heart. Sometimes God just has a word for certain people in the midst. If the shoes fits wear it, and if not don't come under bondage or condemnation. Many times, the Lord will say things publicly so He doesn't have to embarrass or single people out. I always loved what William Branham used to do when the Lord would give him words of prophecy that exposed the sin in their lives. He would put his hand over the microphone and whisper in their ear. It is not the will of God to embarrass people or prophesy horrible things to them in front of other sheep. We see this happen all of the time in the body of Christ and it is not of God and we need to not be a part in it.

Continuing in the story, "*¹⁰Two men went up into the temple to pray; the one a Pharisee, and the other a publican. ¹¹The Pharisee stood and prayed thus with himself...*" What does this mean that he "*prayed thus with himself*"? It means God didn't hear his prayer. He was just praying to himself. God doesn't hear selfish, arrogant, and racist prayers. He was just talking to himself and said, "*...God, I thank thee, that I am not as other men are, extortioners, unjust, adulterers, or even as this publican. ¹²I fast twice in the week, I give tithes of all that I possess...*" I am going to tell you a little secret. Every person, whether they consciously thought about it or not, has done the exact same thing. Maybe we didn't say these same words, but something in us was like that at some point. God wants to help us and remove this thinking from us. Jesus always stands with the accused. You and I have to be able to talk to the poorest of the poor and the richest of the rich and still be the same person. I know so many brothers who could not make it into the ministry because they couldn't speak to millionaires because they were so insecure and intimidated. They couldn't talk to people of greater social rank or greater intelligence than them and they never wanted to excel or progress where they could do that. Jesus was able to sit in a rich man's house and converse freely and He was able to talk to harlots. We are to be all things to all people. We have to learn to be transparent and have "*always a conscience void of offence toward God, and toward men*" (Acts 24:16).

"*I fast twice in the week...*" I remember when fasting really became popular in the early 1970's. Everybody fasted. It was one of the things that poured through the charismatic movement. People fasted every other week back then because it was the thing to do. I have fasted much in my Christian life so far and I have found many times that I was fasting because it was the thing to do (everybody else was doing it). I remember the Lord speaking to me once during one of these times and said I wasn't really fasting, I was just making myself hungry, and He never called me to fast. Everything that God institutes is beautiful, but we can make it religious and become self-righteous with it. First of all, if we fast, we don't need to tell anybody about it. Now sometimes, we can't help and tell others because we have to, but I always got amused when I would ask a brother to get a bite to eat and they would immediately say, "No, I'm fasting". Why couldn't they just say, "No, I'm busy" or something like that. It's always, "No, I'm fasting", and immediately you feel inferior to the "great faster"

Here's another one, "*I give tithes of all that I possess...*" Just tithe and keep quiet. It is like when people give testimonies. Sometimes I would hate testimony time at the church I grew up in because sure enough ten people would always get up and give a testimony and it was always, "I went to the hospital, and I prayed for people, and God used me, and God anointed me" and it never seemed to end up being a testimony of the goodness and grace of God, but a testimony of their greatness. It felt like instead of singing the song to God "How Great Thou Art" we needed to sing to the person "How Great You Are!"

"*[13]And the publican, standing afar off...*" How many are standing a far off? How many times do we not include people of color in our lives? We don't really accept or honor them, we simply tolerate them. This tells us something right here. He wouldn't even come close, but "*a broken and a contrite heart, O God, thou wilt not despise*" (Psalms 51:17). "*And the publican, standing afar off, would not lift up so much as his eyes unto heaven, but smote upon his breast, saying, God be merciful to me a sinner. [14]I tell you, this man went down to his house justified rather than the other: for every one that exalteth himself shall be abased; and he that humbleth himself shall be exalted.*" Amen! We need to humble ourselves. Jesus said it perfectly in Matthew 11:29, "*Take my yoke upon you, and learn of me; for I am meek and lowly in heart: and ye shall find rest unto your souls.*" We don't have to impress anybody. Impress Jesus with the way you live and treat others. Let's do everything we do to the Lord, and not to men. Keep your heart, examine yourself, and try not just other people's spirits, but try your own spirit to see whether it is of God. Judge a righteous judgment! Don't judge according to the outward appearance. There is a lot of stuff the Lord has to work out of us. This is why sanctification, the second aspect of our salvation, takes a lifetime. Don't be discouraged if you have these issues still in you and the Lord is working on them. Ultimately, God will deliver you which is why you are going through it.

But God hates racism. God hates that class mentality that somebody is better than somebody else. The craziest thing is I have seen poor ignorant rednecks who didn't even have an education (they quit school during elementary school) act like they are the greatest thing in the human race. I've seen rich wealthy people act like complete fools. Everybody is tempted with these issues, but we are not of this world anymore. We are in a new Kingdom! Let the glory of the Lord descend now upon every reader and seal this word in their hearts. We want to be like Jesus! Amen! Let us resolve to never, judge a man after the outward appearance, or just an initrul meeting. But rather judge them by their fruits, heart, and content of their character. Let us never judge a man simply because his skin color is different from ours. Or his culture is different from ours. Let's learn to rejoice in God's great diversity of people, and try to learn something from them, rather than rejecting them. I believe most Christians, desire to do good, to act and respond as Jesus did with people; but many times we are a product of our environment. If our parents were racist or we've had bad experiences with people of whatever color, if the people that we're around or grown up with had racist tendencies, it tends to form an opinion in our minds or subconscious, and we then act on those impulses that have been ingrained in us from our youth. Remember every man and women are different, they have their own unique personality we just have to stop lumping people of a different color, and generalizing them by thinking all people of that skin color are alike. They just aren't, if we truly yearn to be like Jesus then we're going to have to act like him. "With God there is no respecter of persons..." Let this be our motto, and way of life from now on. We can bring an end to racism. Actually, the body of Christ should lead the way. How else can the world see the love of God, if we don't walk, talk, live and act like Him? I pray that from this day on together we will not be self righteous, proud, arrogant or judgmental, or racist. But we will learn of him where the scriptures say "I am meek and lowly of heart", or "For God so loved the world" or "they will know that you are my disciple because of the love you have one to another." Why don't we as Philippians 2:15 declares, *"That ye may be blameless and harmless, the sons of God, without rebuke, in the midst of a crooked and perverse nation, among whom ye shine as lights in the world;"* Finally then this scripture will be fulfilled; Matthew 5:13-16, *"Ye are the salt of the earth: but if the salt have lost his savour, wherewith shall it be salted? it is thenceforth good for nothing, but to be cast out, and to be trodden under foot of men.* [14] *"Ye are the light of the world. A city that is set on an hill cannot be hid."* [15] *"Neither do men light a candle, and put it under a bushel, but on a candlestick; and it giveth light unto all that are in the house."* [16] *"Let your light so shine before men, that they may see your good works, and glorify your Father which is in heaven."*

The Truth About The Curse Of Ham
Chapter 3

I need to preface before I begin with the story of Noah and Ham a few things to you because some of you may have not heard of the curse of Ham or even be aware of the circumstances surrounding it. I want to give you a brief historical record. The story here is about after God judged the earth because man was doing much wickedness after the imagination of his heart. Man was unrestrained in his evil. It had reached a point where every person did whatever they thought immediately and it got to a place of such wickedness that in Genesis 6:1-4, the "*sons of God*" (speaking of demonic angels or spirits) "*came in unto the daughters of men, and they bare children to them.*" The offspring that was created by this union was a race of giants called Nephilim. These giants went on to become the Anakims, Goliath, Og, etc. But God wanted to destroy this and wipe it off the face of the earth, so He sent a flood and kept only 1 righteous man, Noah. Noah prepared diligently beforehand for a hundred years and preached for a hundred years that God was going to judge the earth. Can you imagine this? I wonder how Noah felt after the 67th year and nothing had come yet. But he did what God told him to do. As impossible as it was, he built an ark of gopher wood and God spoke to him and said take yourself, your wife, your three sons and their wives, two of each animal on the face of the earth, get it into the ark because He was going to judge the earth with water. So the heavens were opened and floods of water came and everything on earth was utterly destroyed. The water came up until it went completely above every mountain and highest peak on the earth and for 150 days, Noah had to wait for the waters to assuage. This is 5 months they had to wait for just the water to recede. God had to so judge the earth to clean it from the filth and the sin.

And so here you have now the only people again, like Adam was, on the face of the earth. Noah, a man who found favor with God, and his three sons, Ham, Shem, and Japheth were blessed by God to "*be fruitful, and multiply, and replenish the earth.*" We find in many countries and cultures that speak of a great flood. They may have not called it Noah's flood or Noah's ark, but they record some kind of cataclysmic flood in their history. This is just confirming the Word of God is true!

All of the earth had to be repopulated by Noah's sons, Ham, Shem, and Japheth. Noah had no more children. Therefore, all of the races of the earth can be traced to Ham, Shem, or Japheth. After God had brought them out of the ark, we see as time progresses that as one of the descendents of Ham (Nimrod) started Babylon, God had to destroy the Tower of Babel and scatter the people throughout the earth and change the languages of everybody. No longer did the people of the earth speak one language. Babel in Hebrew means "confusion". They all began to speak in other languages (it was a supernatural thing). God restores this in the day of Pentecost in Acts when He brought all of the nations of the earth together and turned them back into one pure language, speaking in tongues. Zephaniah 3:9 says, *"For then will I turn to the people a pure language that they may all call upon the name of the LORD, to serve him with one consent."* We are going to be one again! Babylon is what started all of the confusion and all of the racial problems. No wonder then that spiritual Babylon in the church today is full of racism.

Most of the commentaries that we normally would look to, to find great help in searching the Scriptures basically aren't completely truthful because if they were to say certain things and admit that certain people were black in the Scriptures, it would totally throw them off-kilter. So they go out of their way to try to manufacture and make up things using the Word of God deceitfully to give a foundation for what they've done. These three sons became the three sons that re-populated the earth. Out of Shem (the godly line – Noah says in Genesis 9:26 *"Bless be the Lord God of Shem"*) came forth the Hebrews. Shem's descendents were all the Hebrew and Arabic peoples of the earth. Out of Japheth and all of the Caucasian and the entire myriad of Caucasian (French, German, Scandinavian, etc.) peoples. Japheth's people were white. Shem's people were olive skinned. Jesus was not white. He was olive skinned. And I have to tell you that just as there are as many subtle white racists, there are many black racists who will tell you Jesus was black and I am sorry, this just isn't true. Many say this because in Revelation 2 it says Jesus' feet were like burned brass and His hair white as wool, meaning He was black. This is not describing what race Jesus was, but describing what Jesus looked like after being in the glory for 70 plus years. Eventually, everybody's coming color in eternity will be bronze/amber/gold. We will shine with the glory of God! So Jesus was neither white nor black. You can go off on either side. What we need is sound doctrine and the truth. This is the problem many times. People don't search the Scriptures for the truth. They search the Scriptures to find what they want. Adam was not a black man because his name literally means "to blush". Now I was born and grew up in the ghetto and I never saw a black person blush. Now I know they get embarrassed like everyone else, but they have the ability to hide it. When I do something stupid, it shows up on my face. But Adam wasn't white either. Adam was the created being of God. Actually he was more red than anything. So you and I do not want to go off on the deep end either way. Lastly, Ham was the father of all Black races. When I say Black races, I am talking about all of the different shades of black. But this is where I saw that white commentators try to deceive us and it gets so awful it left me disgusted where I don't know if I will ever search from certain commentators again.

38

So out of these three sons, we will read in the story in Genesis 9, that something bad happens to Noah and Noah speaks and gives a curse. Now the Bible clearly states Noah cursed Canaan, but many preachers in history say he cursed Ham because everybody believes Ham did the evil deed, whatever it was. And so, people took this curse and used it to prove that Black people are cursed and to be servants to Shem and Japheth. They are not only to be a servant, but a servant of servants (Genesis 9:25). So all down through history we see slavery existing. Slavery has happened to almost every race of people. Jews have been slaves and even today young white girls are forced into slavery. Slavery is happening even today. You would think we've grown enough and would have stopped this by now throughout the human race, but it is a demonic and hateful spirit that is subtle. This is why Jesus tells us to be *"wise as serpents, and harmless as doves"* (Matthew 10:16). We have to be just as wise as the devil to stop what he does and the only way we can do that is to know the Word of God. Jesus always responded to the devil with the Word of God. Many times in Matthew 4 Jesus told the devil, *"it is written"*. We are always to talk to the devil out of the Scriptures and he will flee. So many have used this supposed "curse of Ham" to justify their buying and selling of human beings. I would encourage you to watch the 2006 movie called "Amazing Grace" which was the story based on the life of antislavery pioneer William Wilberforce. He was this English man who was this Christian and when he found out what was happening on the slave ships, he spent the rest of his life trying to get England to stop doing it. The difficulty was so much money was being made that people didn't want slavery to stop.

Let's bring it closer to home, in America. White ministers preached that white people came from the line of Shem and this is a lie. Whites are not olive skinned. They would preach out of the Scriptures to justify slavery that the curse of Ham proves Black people are cursed and that they have to be servants. They would even convince the Black preachers in Black churches. I studied many of the early Black clergymen who admitted Ham was cursed and that Black people were supposed to be slaves. This tells me that if you tell a lie long enough, it will actually be true to you. If you tell a lie long enough to people, then they will believe it is true. We were told a lie, even as children. I was told by my father everyday, "Watch out for those," expletive for black people." My father cursed every race in front of me as a child as we were living in the ghetto. I was the only white boy in an all black school. I would listen to my racist father, but at school I would have some of the most precious friends on earth and I knew what my father was saying to me was a lie, even before I got saved. Every one of us, if we tell the truth, carries within them some sort of racist feeling because we were taught it from our youth.

This "curse of Ham" doctrine has been taught throughout history and even has been taught by many famous white preachers even up to the mid 1960's.

39

They would teach blacks are under a curse. In the deep south all over, this is believed still and the only way to expose a lie is to bring the truth, the sword of the Spirit, which is the Word of God (Ephesians 6:17).

I lived in the Ghetto in the early and mid 1960's. I was there when the riots broke out when Martin Luther King was killed. I fought most of my young life as many as 5-10 people at a time. I fought because I didn't want to be considered soft or a coward and I finally ended up in a black gang. For all intents and purposes, I was a black person in a white body. Then my father moved us to an all white school and it was hard for me even though I was white. I have seen racism on both sides. I don't want to be racist or have any racist thoughts in my being at all. I can tell you as I am writing this that I don't, because of the grace of God who allowed me to live among only black people for the first 15 years of my life. I saw through the lies and generalization that was spoken about black people. I thank God for allowing this in my life, so that from an early age, I experienced the true black reality.

Well let us read now in Genesis 9 to see who God really cursed and what this curse means so we can understand the truth about black people. In verse 13 we see God setting the rainbow in the clouds as a token of a covenant between them and the earth and in verse 18 we continue, *"And the sons of Noah, that went forth of the ark, were Shem, and Ham, and Japheth..."* And I want you to note what it says next because it is very important as we will see, *"...and Ham is the father of Canaan."* Now the Bible doesn't mention at this point who one of Shem's sons were or who one of Japheth's sons were. It makes a point of saying right away that *"Ham is the father of Canaan."* You can find the descendents of Shem in Genesis 10:21-31. He was father of the olive skinned people or the Semitic peoples of the earth. It is called a branch of the Afro-Asiatic language family. It includes both Hebrew and Arabic peoples. Shem's name means in Hebrew "a name celebrated, distinguished, and renowned". He was the ancestor of the Hebrews because Eber was one of his descendents (Genesis 10:21) which became the Hebrews. Japheth was father of all of the fair descendents or the Caucasians (Genesis 10:2-5) and in Genesis 10:5 it mentions the Gentiles as the descendents of Japheth. Japheth's name in Hebrew means "enlargement, extension, let him enlarge, he that persuades beauty". The European civilization is what descended from him (Greek, Roman, Norse, English, French, Spanish, etc.). Ham is the father of all the Black races in the earth. Through him Egypt was founded. Egypt was called the "land of Ham". It is noteworthy to mention Psalms 78:51, *"And smote all the firstborn in Egypt; the chief of their strength in the tabernacles of Ham:"* Psalms 105:22-23, *"To bind his princes at his pleasure; and teach his senators wisdom. [23]Israel also came into Egypt; and Jacob sojourned in the land of Ham."* Psalms 105:27, *"They shewed his signs among them, and wonders in the land of Ham."* Psalms 106:22, *"Wondrous works in the land of Ham, and terrible things by the Red sea.*" The land of Ham is always associated with Egypt. This is important because many white commentators try to deceive us. If you look up Egypt in your Bible, you are going to see that Egypt was a black nation. Ham's descendents settled in Africa, Egypt, Babylon, Assyria, and Philistia and they are named in Genesis 10:6-20. The Bible spends more time mentioning the genealogy of Ham compared to Noah's other two sons. It says twice "Ham was the father of Canaan". Ham was the father of Cush which became Ethiopia, Mizraim which became Egypt, Phut which became Libya and the Moores, and then Canaan which became all of the tribes the children had to destroy in the promise land. These tribes were the enemies of God. Now not all of the Canaanites were black, but they were certainly people of color. Cush, Phut, and Mizraim were black, but not all of the Canaanites were black.

Continuing now in the story in Genesis 9, "*[19]These are the three sons of Noah: and of them was the whole earth overspread. [20]And Noah began to be an husbandman, and he planted a vineyard [21]And he drank of the wine, and was drunken; and he was uncovered within his tent...*" Now I will stop here and say a few things before we continue with the story. The word uncovered in Hebrew means "to unclothe in a disgraceful sense, to reveal something". Most Hebrew scholars think this is speaking of something immoral or shameful. Some other translations of this phrase "*uncovered within his tent*" include: "*he was uncovered and lay naked*", "*he was shamefully exposed*", "*unclothed*". So here is Noah uncovered within his tent and verse 22 continues by saying "*And Ham, the father of Canaan...*" Here we see this phrase for the second time, "*Ham, the father of Canaan*", pointed out to us. Two is the number in Scripture for witness and separation. Matthew 18:16 says, "*in the mouth of two or three witnesses every word may be established.*" Why didn't it say "Ham, the father of Cush" or one of his other sons? Everywhere else in the Bible is says the land of Ham is Egypt. But in this particular chapter twice it says "*Ham, the father of Canaan*". This is so very important. God is trying to get us ready for something. "*[22]Ham, the father of Canaan, saw the nakedness of his father, and told his two brethren without...*" It does not say Ham uncovered Noah but simply saw the nakedness of his father and told his two brethren without, "*[23]And Shem and Japheth took a garment, and laid it upon both their shoulders, and went backward, and covered the nakedness of their father; and their faces were backward, and they saw not their father's nakedness.*"

Now there are some Scriptures in the Old Testament that if you looked up the word uncovered and nakedness, you will find that most of it is dealt with when it comes to incest or having sex with your father's wife (Leviticus, Numbers, Deuteronomy, and even in Exodus you will find this). The term uncovered is a term speaking of some kind of sexual sin within the family.

"[24]And Noah awoke from his wine, and <u>knew what his younger son had done unto him</u>. [25]And he said, <u>Cursed be Canaan</u>; a servant of servants shall he be unto his brethren. [26]And he said, Blessed be the LORD God of Shem; and Canaan shall be his servant..." Now this is the only time in the Bible where Noah speaks. There is not another place in the Old Testament where we hear Noah saying anything and the only time we hear him is when he is prophesying here. Noah is prophesying here. He is not just running his mouth. He is doing exactly what Jacob did in Genesis 49 with his sons. When Jacob was getting ready to die, he called all of his children in and prophesied over them. In the old days, this is what an old man would do before his death. He would lay on a bed and call all of his children in and bless them and as he blessed them prophetic words would come forth over their lives. So this is exactly what Noah is doing. Now Noah is not ready to die. He doesn't die for another 350 years. But he is prophesying here.

So Ham saw his father's nakedness, told his 2 brothers who covered him up without looking at him. The word uncover, we saw, has sexual connotations to it. In speaking with a close friend who is a Scholar who asked Rabbi's about this story, this is what they believe happened. They thought that Ham castrated Noah. Now he didn't have any more children, but I don't think this happened. Jewish Rabbi's many times sit around a table and take a verse of Scripture and look at it from every possible angle using their intellect. The problem with this is you and I cannot intellectually receive revelation. Matthew 16:17 says, *"flesh and blood hath not revealed it unto thee, but my Father which is in heaven."* Another idea that Rabbi's have is they think Ham slept with his mother and Canaan was the offspring. There is really nothing in the Scriptures to support this idea. Another idea is Ham performed a sexual act on his father. Now God is very gracious in the Scriptures many times and doesn't reveal exactly what happens because what really happened in Noah's case was terrible. This is similar to Job 1 when is says that Job prayed for his sons and daughters fervently because he knew they were having a party. Why would Job fervently be praying for them? God tries to hide it and He doesn't expose it. What was going on with Job's brothers and sisters was incest. Proverbs 26:2 says *"the curse causeless shall not come"*. In the book of Job, God allowed Satan to do what he did because what the sons and daughters were doing was terrible. Ecclesiastes 10:8 says *"He that diggeth a pit shall fall into it; and whoso breaketh an hedge, a serpent shall bite him."* God is not going to tell Satan to come and destroy you. We have a hedge around us to protect. It is only when we break the hedge through un-repented sin in our life that Satan can come in and do stuff to us. If something happens to us and we haven't sinned, it is only because God has allowed it. The devil is on a leash. Jesus is Lord of all and has the keys of hell and death. He is in control of everything and many times He will allow in His wisdom what He can prevent in His power for a higher purpose.

42

So Noah awakes and knows *"what his younger son had done unto him"*. He is prophesying now as he begins to curse. Now let us read this curse again, *"[25]And he said, Cursed be Canaan; a servant of servants shall he be unto his brethren."* I would like to address Canaan for a moment here. Canaan's name in Hebrew means "merchants, traders, a servant, low, humble" and comes from a root word that means "to humble, to be subdued, to be brought low". Canaanites were known for their licentious, immoral, and repulsive behavior. God told His people to never compromise with Canaanites and have nothing to do with them. He especially said don't marry their daughters or sons because they are an evil perverted, immoral, and wicked people. You will find this in Leviticus 18:1-2, 18:27-28, and Deuteronomy 12:28-32. Some of Canaan's descendents in Genesis 19 were Sodom and Gomorrah. Are you getting a picture here? Canaan became the tribes that Israel had to conquer (Amorites, Girgashites, Hivites, etc). Basically they were the enemies of God's people. So who is Noah cursing? I don't find Ham's name here. Therefore first of all, I don't know why others in the past have called this the curse of Ham. There is nothing in this story that says Ham was cursed. But in every commentary and in every Bible dictionary, it will say the curse of Ham. Why? Because they want you to believe that black people are under a curse. Let me say clearly: Black people are not cursed! It is a lie and I am telling you when those white preachers stand before the judgment seat of Christ, I wouldn't want to be them. I know even as I am writing this, I will make enemies, but it doesn't matter to me. We need to tell the truth. We are living in the last of the last days. We need to speak the truth in our hearts. We have to be able to have a conscious void of offence toward God and toward our fellow brothers and sisters (Acts 24:16). We need to be able to do like the old Hebrews used to do. When they saw their brother or sister, they would say "Shalom" and their brother or sister would say back to them "Shalom" which means they are telling each other they have nothing against each other, their hearts are right and free towards one another, and that they love one another. But in the Pentecostal Charismatic communities today, you have people sitting in the same church that hate each other and don't do the Word of God anymore. If they are offended from another brother or sister, they don't go to them to make it right. Of all of the sins the Lord hates in Proverbs 6, you would think it would be some really serious ones. There is only one physical sin mentioned in this list (*"hands that shed innocent blood"*). The rest are heart issues that the Lord hates because we can hide our heart issues. But you and I can't hide them from the Holy Ghost or a true man or woman of God.

✓The rest of Noah's prophecy to his sons was, *"Blessed be the LORD God of Shem; and Canaan shall be his servant. God shall enlarge Japheth, and he shall dwell in the tents of Shem; and Canaan shall be his servant."* The only one who got blessed in this prophesy was Shem. Shem is blessed because out of him would come the Messiah (the lineage of Jesus). Japheth is symbolic of the Gentiles who were grafted in (Romans 11:17) to the vine of the Hebrews through Jesus. So Japheth dwelling in the tents of Shem represents the Gentiles receiving the Lord Jesus as their Saviour. Canaan will be Japheth's servant too.

In verse 24 it says when Noah awoke he knew "*what his younger son had done unto him*". He does not curse Ham in the next verse, but Noah curses Canaan. Below are the reasons why I believe Ham did not molest his father but Canaan did. Ham had simply discovered it, told his two brothers so they could try to fix the situation. The first reason I believe Ham did not molest his father is every time it mentions Ham's name it points out he was the father of Canaan. Canaan is not a good name. Canaanites were filthy, immoral, and terrible people. And whatever Canaan did, it was sexual, it was awful, immoral, and it was shameful. He may have laid with Noah's wife because the Scriptures say in Leviticus and Deuteronomy that someone to be uncovered means that incest has happened somehow.

Secondly, there is no word for "grandson" in Hebrew. In Genesis 31 when Jacob was fleeing with his sons and daughters and Laban (Jacob's father-in-law) came chasing after them, he said "*Wherefore didst thou flee away secretly...and hast not suffered me to kiss my sons...*" (Genesis 31:27-28). But they weren't his sons he was talking about. They were his grandsons! I could give you a multitude more of Scriptures to back this up where you can see the many times this language is used to describe grandsons. People are spoken to as sons when they are grandsons in the Old Testament because there is no Hebrew word that denotes a grandson. Many of the Jewish scholars take the word "*younger son*" here to mean "smaller son" which denotes a "grandson".

Thirdly, God is not going to curse somebody for what somebody else did. This would be unrighteous and unscriptural. The Scriptures do not directly tell us what happened, but God saw what happened. Proverbs 26:2 says, "*the curse causeless shall not come*". Canaan was cursed by God for something he did. God called out the perpetrator.

Fourthly, none of Ham's other sons were cursed. Egypt became one of the greatest and most intellectual places on the face of the earth. Some of the most beautiful pictures come from Africa and the civilization that was built there by the descendents of Ham and Cush. Now Nimrod was bad and some of the black theologians will try to tell you he was some great man, but Genesis 10:9, which says Nimrod "*was a mighty hunter before the Lord*", in the original Hebrew it should read Nimrod "*was a mighty hunger against the Lord*". Some black theologians try to promote Nimrod as this great black man. I don't care if Nimrod was black or white, I would not want to associate myself with someone who was against the Lord and built Babylon.

Fifthly, God had already blessed Noah and his sons in Genesis 9:1 and God never takes a blessing back! Genesis 9:1 says, "*And God blessed Noah and his sons, and said unto them, Be fruitful, and multiply, and replenish the earth.*" This reminds me of Numbers 22-23 when Balaam kept trying to curse Israel, God sad to him, "*thou shalt not curse the people: for they are blessed*". Even though Balaam tries later to curse them, he finally gives up and says "*How shall I curse, whom God hath not cursed?*" (Numbers 23:8), and says later on in verse 20 (speaking of God), "*he hath blessed; and I cannot reverse it*". Balaam could not curse whom God has blessed! Hallelujah! People can lie about it like they have in history, but Ham is blessed! The curse of Canaan had nothing to do with cursing a skin color, but everything with what he had done. God looks upon the heart (I Samuel 16:7) and not on the outward appearance. God does not see color, nor would He ever curse someone because of the color of their skin. Curses come because of the condition of people's hearts and their evil deeds.

And by the way, doesn't Jesus break the power of all curses anyway. Don't we read in Galatians 3:13, "*Christ hath redeemed us from the curse of the law, being made a curse for us: for it is written, Cursed is every one that hangeth on a tree.*" So even if Ham was cursed, the curse is gone in Jesus anyway.

Here is another thought. In Exodus 20:5-6 it says a Biblical curse lasts only to the 3rd or 4th generation. I am treating this accusation that black people are cursed like we are in a court trial and so even if Ham was cursed, the curse has been dead for thousands of years and we couldn't use it anymore if it existed. It has run out. The statute of limitations is gone.

Proverbs 26:2 says again, "*the curse causeless shall not come.*" Canaan was cursed because of something he had done. God never cursed Ham. He cursed Canaan. The curse on Canaan was finally fulfilled when the Canaanites were utterly defeated and destroyed by Joshua; this is found in Joshua 9:23 and I Kings 9:20-21. The Canaanites were completely demolished eventually. But of all the people that Israel fought, all of them were Canaanites.

Here's another question many people have: Was Ham even a black man? Ham's name means "hot, warm, and dark". If Noah wasn't black, how could Ham have been black? What happened is these people moved to these areas of the country and eventually became Black, Oriental, White, etc. When God dispersed every one, everybody moved. Those living in hot climates became darker skinned because of the sun and those in colder climates ended up becoming white.

This lie of God cursing Ham has been perpetrated for thousands of years because of racial hatred. The reason for this racial hatred is Africa had some of the most brilliant people in history. Consider the pyramids. Scientists today still can't even catch up with the intelligence that was founded in those pyramids. Those black people were some of the most intelligent and brilliant people on the face of the earth and white people didn't want people to know this. They wanted us to think that black people are the opposite. They want us to believe that they are on welfare, all looking for a hand-out, and not wanting to go to school. They have made many black people have no self-esteem and have ruined generations of young black men and women making them think they were nobody when their ancestors were some of the greatest and most intelligent people on the face of the earth.

Let me finish by looking at come passages of Scripture about what God says about His beautiful Black people. Now remember Cush, whose name means "black". Let these sayings sink down into your heart. In Amos 9, God is speaking to Israel and in verse 7 He says, *"Are ye not as children of the Ethiopians unto me, O children of Israel? Saith the LORD..."* In other words, God is saying the children of Ethiopia are to be just like the children of Israel. Psalms 68:31 says, *"Princes shall come out of Egypt; Ethiopia shall soon stretch out her hands unto God."* How can Black people be cursed when God is blessing them over and over again?! Here in Psalms 87 God is talking about Zion and who makes up Zion. Let us read the first six verses, *"[1]His foundation is in the holy mountains. [2]The LORD loveth the gates of Zion more than all the dwellings of Jacob. [3]Glorious things are spoken of thee, O city of God. Selah. [4]I will make mention of Rahab and Babylon to them that know me: behold Philistia, and Tyre, with Ethiopia; this man was born there. [5]And of Zion it shall be said, This and that man was born in her: and the highest himself shall establish her. [6]The LORD shall count, when he writeth up the people, that this man was born there. Selah."* There are at least four peoples mentions here that will be in Zion and one of them is Ethiopia! Next in Zephaniah 3, let us read beginning in verse 9, *"[9]For then will I turn to the people a pure language, that they may all call upon the name of the LORD, to serve him with one consent. [10]From beyond the rivers of Ethiopia my suppliants, even the daughter of my dispersed, shall bring mine offering..."* This referring to Black people!

Matthew 27:32 mentions Simon, a man of Cyrene. Cyrene people are Black people. Simon was the man chosen to carry the cross of Jesus. God could've chosen a white person, or even a Hebrew, but He purposely didn't because He wanted us to understand that Black people are in His heart, that they have a great part when it comes to the salvation that is being worked out in the earth today. Moreover this very Simon later on has two sons name Rufus and Alexander who actually become members of the local church and God uses them so much that Paul makes mention of them. In Acts 13:1 it mentions those who were certain prophets and teachers in the church that were at Antioch and one of them was black, being from Cyrene.

In Acts 2, we see that not only were black people involved in our salvation, but in the baptism of the Holy Ghost as well. When the Holy Ghost fell on the day of Pentecost there, among all of the nations that were gathered who came to worship at the feast, were Black nations! Acts 2 8-10, *"And how hear we every man in our own tongue, wherein we were born?"* [9.] *"Parthians, and Medes, and Elamites, and the dwellers in Mesopotamia, and in Judaea, and Cappadocia, in Pontus, and Asia,"* [10.] *"Phrygia, and Pamphylia, in Egypt, and in the parts of Libya about Cyrene, and strangers of Rome, Jews and proselytes,"*

Lastly, we see the Ethiopian eunuch in Acts 8 who was riding in a chariot. Philip was taken by the Spirit of God (translated) to this eunuch and he finds him reading out of Isaiah in the chariot, *"[30]And Philip ran thither to him, and heard him read the prophet Esaias, and said, Understandest thou what thou readest? [31]And he said, How can I, except some man should guide me?..."* This word guide means to teach. Hear me, we need men of God teaching the Scriptures. We don't need men handling the Word of God deceitfully, using the Word of God for gain, and telling lies to protect images. How many black slaves, after working all day in the field and going to their little shanty church, were told that God created them to be slaves?! The zeal of the Lord of hosts eats me up inside thinking about this. How many thousands of black men and women heard this lie and believed it? But they stayed with Jesus anyway. Even in their life, if all they knew and believed was slavery, they had hope of a promise of freedom. Today, we can't even get people to walk with Jesus or come to the meetings and they are blessed beyond belief. So this story of the eunuch ends with Philip explaining to him Jesus and the eunuch ends up getting saved and baptized in water and went back to Candace, the queen of Ethiopia at that time. A memorial plaque to the place and to the church where this Ethiopian eunuch went to and preached the gospel to the Ethiopians is still there to this day. Revival came through this black man!

In 1983, I was in Virginia at a conference that I was invited to do on "Women in Ministry". There were hundreds of people there and during one of those meetings, I began to prophesy that in the last days, the two most oppressed people were going to be set free by God and God was going to overrule men and their hatred and chauvinistic ways and these two oppressed peoples were going to be the leading figures in the last great move of God, namely black people and women. I prophesied this over 25 years ago, now I ask you who are some of the greatest preachers on the earth today? Black people and women!

47

I finish in Revelation 5:9 which says Jesus redeemed us by His blood *"out of every kindred, and tongue, and people, and nation"*. People may not like this, but we are all in the same family. I may be the red-headed, one-eyed and toothless stepchild to you, but I am in your family. Hatred can only live if we give into the baser inclinations in our heart. How can a man can call himself a man of God and hate at the same time? It does not make sense to me, but it is a new day!

Galatians 3:28 says *"There is neither Jew nor Greek, there is neither bond nor free, there is neither male nor female: for ye are all one in Christ Jesus." "Therefore if any man be in Christ, he is a new creature: old things are passed away; behold all things are become new"* (II Corinthians 5:17). There is no difference between us anymore. God is no respecter of persons and He tells the Jews, 'don't you know I love the Ethiopians just as much as I love you. They are my children too and a day is coming when Ethiopia shall raise her hands to me.' Finally God's curse was not upon Ham, but upon Canaan. Canaan was the evil doer; and he and his descendants were judged for it. Just remember the scripture says "cursed be Canaan not Ham or his black descendants."

The Presence Of Black People
Beginning In Genesis
Chapter 4

As I was studying for this book, the Lord really began to open to me the presence of Black people in the Scriptures. There are several things we need to keep in remembrance as we approach this subject. I said these things in another chapter but it is worth repeating them again. First of all, the people who translated the Bible, translated it according to their own opinions many times. Now we know God oversaw all of this and we believe the Bible is perfect and we believe God ordered the Canon of Scriptures. This is why God left us the original Hebrew and Greek languages so we can look up ourselves and determine what a translated word really means. You have to know that racism has been around since the beginning. Most commentators and most of the older writers literally were constantly trying to move people away from the presence of Black people in the Scriptures and trying to falsely prove that the people under whom I will mention in this chapter were really white Caucasian people. But this is simply not true and I would like to prove this by the Scriptures. Secondly, commentaries are simply men's opinions about the Scriptures. They are commentating on the Scriptures. But the truth is found within the Word of God and men can't do anything to the truth. This is why you and I need to search the Scriptures, look at the original Hebrew and Greek, and allow the Word of God to reveal the truth. Psalms 119:130 says *"The entrance of thy words giveth light; it giveth understanding unto the simple."* God's Word is the only thing that can put an end to things we cannot see. It divides the soul and the spirit and is a living thing (Hebrews 4:12) that separates the precious from the vile. If we don't know the Bible and if we don't know the keys on how we research it, than we are left to whatever somebody has told us and will be living in another man's revelation and not in the truth. I don't claim to have all truth, far from it. In writing this book, I've called every man and woman of God that I am submitted to and asked them, talked to them, and the funny thing I found out was there was a great measure of ignorance or a not wanting to touch the subject. But believe me, in writing this book I have studied hours upon hours, spent much time in discussion with others, to make sure everything I write here is not only true, but scholarly written, so that nobody can gainsay against it.

I would like you to read a copy from a great painter, poet, and theorist from 1837 who was instructing his students about how to draw and how to recreate art. This was absolutely astounding to me when I first read it. He wrote these words as a manual for artists. For us they starkly demonstrate how deeply and in how many varied ways black and white symbolism is a part of Western culture. He said:

"White is the symbol for divinity or God. Black is the symbol of the evil spirit or demon. White is the symbol of light. Black is the symbol of darkness and expresses all evils. White is the emblem of harmony. Black is the symbol for chaos. White signifies supreme beauty. Black signifies ugliness. White signifies perfection. Black signifies vice. White is symbol of innocence and black is that of sin, guilt, and moral degradation. White, a positive color, indicates happiness. Black, a negative color, indicates misfortune. The battle between good and evil is symbolically expresses by the opposition of white being good and black being evil."

This is just one statement from one man who I'm sure from his birth, just as you and I have, had been thoroughly engrained into our hearts and into our minds things that other people have said and thought, mostly by people we've trusted (our own mothers and fathers, grandfathers, and so on). When you and I were a little child whatever our momma or papa said is pretty much what we believed about life. If it comes from so-called authorities (people with doctorates, scholars, theologians, teachers, preachers, etc..), we think subconsciously that they would never say anything that isn't true, but racism is a subtle and sly spirit that works its way into our subconscious and we don't even realize how the devil uses racism in our life until somebody points it out for us. Everything that was said above is pretty much what we've all been taught in some form or fashion. Now, nobody may have directly sat us down and said white means this and black means that. Certainly in the Scriptures the color white represents purity, holiness, or righteousness and the color black represents judgment, darkness, famine, or sin. But God never meant it to be anything other than representative of a color and not people. Many have perverted the Scriptures by trying to make them say things that are absolutely not true.

Let us begin by looking at the story of the Garden of Eden in Genesis 2. We want to look at where Black people first enter the Scriptures. Now first of all let me say there are black teachers who teach black liberation theology and a portion of what they say is right. Certainly sometimes it comes from a hateful and divisive standpoint rather than trying to bring people into unity. But I don't blame them because of the oppression that black people have suffered. If you haven't seen the recent movie called "Amazing Grace", you need to watch it. It was very good, and historically true. The things that were done to black people are unspeakable. They weren't the only oppressed people of the earth, but Americans (our fathers) did these things to them. Now I personally have never persecuted a black person in my life and this is what many people will say too, that they don't owe the black person anything because they never personally did anything to them. I think one of the greatest things America could do is if we had a day of repentance all across the country and an acknowledgement of what we did when we took this nation from the American Indians as well when we subjected black people into slavery for all those years. We need to repent as a nation. II Chronicles 7:14 says, "*If my people, which are called by my name, shall humble themselves, and pray, and seek my face, and turn from their wicked ways; then will I hear from heaven, and will forgive their sin, and will heal their land.*" Many white people will get mad at this. It will all be private and hidden like Miriam and Aaron in Numbers 12. The Bible says they really got mad at Moses for marrying a black woman, but they said they were mad because they were questioning whether the Lord only spoke to Moses. They really never said what they really meant because what they really felt is ignorance personified. Far too many people accuse or say things to us, but don't really tell us why they're really upset with us. They hide behind a lie because if what they were really feeling was exposed, they know they would been seen as racists or petty fools.

Let me state conclusively, some Black liberation theologians says that Adam was black and then go out of their way to prove that Jesus was black and they use foolishly the Scripture in Revelation 1:14-15 that says of Jesus, "*...his hairs were white like wool...and his feet like unto fine brass, as if they burned in a furnace...*" This is speaking of the now glorified Jesus. The burnished brass is the glory on His feet. This has nothing to do with race. There is no race in glory. The word Adam itself means "red", "So whoever Adam was, he wasn't white or black." Adam is the father of all peoples. God then judged the earth with a flood and destroyed everybody but Noah and his family. Noah's three sons (Shem, Ham, and Japheth) then repopulated the earth. From these three sons come all of the races of the world. Understanding who their sons were and what happened to them, we can then see history unfold in a godly way. But we have to be willing to see things that we don't want to see. Here is the thing I learned years ago. You and I can never go to the Scriptures to prove what we want to see. We must allow the Bible to speak for itself. Don't even believe everything I say. Search the Scriptures to see if these things are so. When I teach, I take it to heart what James said, "*My brethren, be not many masters (Greek – "teachers"), knowing that we shall receive the greater condemnation*" (James 3:1). In Revelation 22:18-19, Jesus warns us if we add anything or take away anything from this book there will be a punishment. So I try my best that whatever comes out of my mouth is something that has been totally searched out. There are times like Paul in I Corinthians 7 when he first says in verse 10, "*I command, yet not I, but the Lord...*" and then later in verse 12 says "*to the rest speak I, not the Lord...*" We need to differentiate when it is God and just somebody's opinion. But when we try to teach our opinions and say it is God, this is error in its highest form.

We must understand that when we speak of the people, we should really say African. Not all Africans are black, but they are certainly people of color, (Semitic Bedouin) looking folks as well as black darker skinned people.

Whether these were of the darker type, only God really knows, but one thing for sure they weren't white. We should also note that some of the people I will refer to as black, were simply Africans, some darker or light skinned. But they were people of color. They were however African and in most cases this would speak of being black or dark skinned people. I am not a scientist or an archeologist, or an anthropologist, I am just a humble teacher of the scriptures, and I might quickly add, I certainly don't know everything. In fact I acknowledge my weakness here, I am simply trying to obey God and search the scriptures for biblical conclusions to these mothers. So when I say black, I will be speaking of Africans: I pray that no one takes offense at this. Throughout this study I will refer to Africans from many countries, but I will use the term black; simply because I think it's important to give honor where honor is due, and to set the record straight that there were no white people present at that time.

So we want to look back at the original Garden of Eden and see the first entrance of the black race here. In Genesis 2, God has just created man, put him in the midst of the garden, and in verse 10 we begin, *"¹⁰And a river went out of Eden to water the garden; and from thence it was parted, and became into four heads..."* White commentators have told us that the original Garden of Eden is in Iraq because Iraq is lighter skinned people (this is where they probably would like it). But when you take the maps and you follow these rivers listed in verses 11-14, you find that it was in Africa.

Let us consider the first river mentioned in verses 11-12, *"The name of the first is Pison: that is it which compasseth the whole land of Havilah, where there is gold; And the gold of that land is good: there is bdellium and the onyx stone."* Note this is before the fall of Adam. The garden of Eden had a river just like the throne of God has in Revelation 22:1, *"And he shewed me a pure river of water of life, clear as crystal, proceeding out of the throne of God and of the Lamb."* This is the glory of God or the essence of God Himself pouring out. And so God's intent was not to just keep it in the garden, but to fill the entire earth (*"four heads"* – four is the number in Scripture for creation). Psalms 72:19 says, *"And blessed be his glorious name for ever: and let the whole earth be filled with his glory; Amen, and Amen."* The name of this first river, Pison, means "great diffusion of waters, a flowing stream" and it comes from a root word that means "to push, to disperse, to multiply, speed, and increase" all representing again God's glory flowing this way. The name Havilah in Hebrew means "something that suffers pain, bringing forth, trembling with pain" and it comes from a root word that means "pang, pain especially of a pregnant woman". This Pison River, when I searched it out, literally was found in the land of Cush who was one of the sons of Ham (Genesis 10:6). The name Cush means "a black countenance, region of burnt faces, blackness". This river flowed to a black land, where, verse 11 tells us, is

52

Gold! The gold of this land "*is good*". You see, everything in Genesis and Revelation are not only speaking about what is happening then, but it is a prophetic and spiritual picture. For example, when we consider Adam when God created him, He created all of us in him. So Adam is a type or picture of all of us or mankind. Therefore these rivers flowing out were not only a natural occurrence, but the lands they flow into are very important. The sense of the definition of Havilah is like being in anguish as a pregnant woman and in Havilah there is gold and it is the good kind of gold which speaks of the Divine character of our great God.

The next river is found in verse 13, "*And the name of the second river is Gihon: the same is it that compasseth the whole land of Ethiopia.*" Gihon means "a great breaking forth of waters, a river, a valley of grace". Some scholars think this was the Nile river, but I don't want to worry about that. Scripturally, Ethiopia is the same thing as Cush. If you look up Ethiopia, it will say it is the same as Cush. Cush's name means "a black countenance, region of burnt faces, blackness". So the second river that flows out of the Garden of Eden encompassed the entire land of Ethiopia or a land of black people.

These were the first countries named in Scripture and they were lands that would be ultimately inhabited by black people. The other two rivers go elsewhere, but the significant thing here is the first two rivers surrounded and flowed through black people's lands. Ultimately what that is saying is both in Havilah and in Ethiopia that God is going to visit them with His glory! We find the fulfillment of this in Acts 8:26-39 when the Ethiopian eunuch is going home and Philip is caught up to his chariot and the eunuch is reading the book of Isaiah and Philip says, "*Understandest thou what thou readest?*" (verse 30). The eunuch responds and says, "*How can I, except some man should guide me?*" (verse 31). The irony of this is I wonder how many black slaves held the Bible up to a white preacher and said I need to understand this book and the answers they got were not the living Word of God, but an answer that subjugated them and kept them in bondage. A famous fundamental preacher in today's time even admitted that up until the 1960's he preached segregation and went along with everyone else that taught about the curse of Ham meaning that all black people are cursed. I will address this in another chapter. Many types of Bibles had this same type of teaching written in their margins until people got angry and they had to remove it. Mormons taught this as a major tenant of their faith and wouldn't allow black people into the Mormon Church until people started finding out what they believed and now all of the sudden Black people can come in.

The facts of these first two rivers in Genesis 2 is tremendously important and a big deal. It reveals to us that from the moment of creation God is prophesying that in the future Ethiopia, the land of Havilah will have a visitation of God to them and like pregnant women, pregnant with the bride of Christ, they are going to be a very integral part of the last great move of God. Glory to Jesus!

So the first countries named in Scripture were not America, England, Britain, Russia, France, etc, but they were African nations. The Bible has its roots in Africa. The world, the creation, has its roots in Africa. Some white people will hear this and they will get upset. But I say to them or you dear reader, if you are upset, don't attack me or hate yourself, maybe God is simply opening a chamber inside of your heart that you didn't even know you had is trying to change you. It is said everywhere that 10:00 on Sunday morning is the most racial time in America. I've made it my purpose in life to destroy this and make it a myth. There is no difference anymore. As Christians, we are a new species. I am not white. You are not white, black, red, or whatever, for "*if any man be in Christ, he is a <u>new creature</u>* (Greek – "new species")*: old things are passed away; behold, all things are become new*" (II Corinthians 5:17). This is why in Joel chapter 2's army is says the earth has never seen the like of these people that are the remnant of God (Joel 2:1-11). We are a species that are above the pettiness, racism, and violence. But what has happened and is so disgusting, the Catholic Church being the worst perpetrator in history, enslaved, murdered, and killed all in the name of Jesus. Is it any wonder the Jews hate the name Jesus? Is it any wonder then that many black people do not want to worship the God that their mothers and fathers worshipped? Because they feel like it is an Uncle Tom religion and nobody has ever introduced them to the real Jesus and told them when they become a Christian they were no longer black nor white, but are now a new species called the sons of the living God with a new Father in heaven. God becomes your new Father and the church becomes your new mother. Out of the joining of the mother and Father is going to come the Bride of Christ. (Revelation 12).

The second instance of Black people in Scripture is found in Genesis 9. God has now judged the earth because man at that time did every wicked thing that he imagined and God was greatly upset and I think also He was trying to rid the world of the Nephilim (the giants). Remember in Genesis 6 that the sons of God (angelic beings) had gone into the daughters of men and had produced a race of giants called Nephilim. Probably in Genesis or in that time period, as Goliath was (by the way, Goliath was a black man because he was part of a tribe that was black), so were these Nephilim. All of these pictures of David slaying Goliath need to be fixed. We don't know exactly what shade he was, but he was part of a black tribe. He could have been lighter skinned or very dark and to some this may be a big deal. There is racism even among blacks too. Light skinned blacks are hated by dark skinned blacks because they think they have too much white in them. All of us have some sort of mixture of many, many races. If you are white, there may be black blood in your line somewhere. We are really just a big mixture, some darker and some lighter. But truthfully, what difference does it make? We can say for sure however, that most or many of the people found in the Old Testament were people of color.

By Genesis 9, God has judged the earth, wiped it out with water, and makes a covenant with Noah and his sons that He will never destroy the earth with water again. People living on the earth when the ark rested were Noah, his three sons, and their wives. That was it. So out of Noah's three sons, Shem, Ham, and Japheth, come all of the nations and peoples of the earth. Up until Genesis 10, everybody spoke the same language. Nimrod (a black man), a descendent of Cush, built Babylon (Tower of Babel – Genesis 11) and God had to deal with this foolishness by confounding the languages and scatter people all over the earth (Genesis 11:7-8). It is amazing that in the history of different countries, they all record a flood and after the flood people were sent throughout the entire earth. God's original intention was that we all spoke the same language. But he ultimately had to confuse the languages. The beauty of this is found in Zephaniah 3:9 when the Lord says *"For then will I turn to the people a pure language, that they may all call upon the name of the LORD, to serve him with one consent."* What is this pure language? It is speaking in tongues. Glory to God!

In the story in Genesis 9, let us start in verse 18 *"And the sons of Noah, that went forth of the ark, were Shem, and Ham, and Japheth: and Ham is the father of Canaan..."* Notice it says right away *"Ham is the father of Canaan"* without saying anything about Shem and Japheth and their sons. This tells me there is something going on with Ham and Canaan. God makes a point here of mentioning Ham is the father of Canaan. *"[19]These are the three sons of Noah: and of them was the whole earth overspread..."* I have already addressed this story in verses 20-26 about the supposed "curse of Ham" in another chapter. Right here, I want to simply talk about Ham. Ham's name in Hebrew means "heat, hot, warm, black, or dark". Ham is considered by most scholars to be the first black man. My question is, do we believe that Ham was black, and Shem was white, and Japheth was another color and Noah was a rainbow color? I don't think so. I believe this is a picture again. In other words, I believe Ham is representative of all his descendents. Whatever Noah's color was, Ham was probably the same color. As far as we know whatever color Adam was the Bible describes him as red or blushing. So whatever color this was, Ham probably had it too. But here is the thing, Ham represents the Black nations just as Japheth represents Caucasians, and Shem (the godly line) represents the Semitic peoples (ultimately the Hebrews). Ham's descendents ultimately ended up in Egypt, Ethiopia, Babylon, Philistia, and Assyria.

Ham's four son's are found in Genesis 10:6, *"And the sons of Ham; Cush, and Mizraim, and Phut, and Canaan."* Let us look at what their names mean and ultimately where each ended up and what part of the earth they populated. Most scholars will agree that Cush's name means "blackness, black". Cush and his people ended up in Ethiopia which is a black nation. He was the father of Nimrod who ended up being the father of Babylon. Mizraim's name means "tribulations, two distresses, two-fold Egypt, or oppressors". His ancestors ended up in Egypt. This is where the white commentators try to use a little subtlety. They speak of a lower Egypt and a higher Egypt. In other words they try to say there were white people living in the higher part of Egypt and black people living in the lower part of Egypt. Even as they write this in their commentaries, you can almost feel the deception. They don't want us to even consider the fact they were simply a black nation because the connotations mean anybody from Egypt early in the Scriptures was black. So they had to come up with something to cover this up. In the Scriptures, the term Mizraim is always referred to as Egypt. The third son was Phut. His name means a bow, extension, or brown. They populated Africa, the Moore's, and Libya. The last son of Ham was Cannan. Canaan's name means "merchants, traders, servants, to be brought low, subdued, and humbled". They use this definition again to pressure black people to think they were just to be servants on the earth. Canaan's descendents went on to be the Amorites, the Girgasites, the Hivites, Sodom & Gomorrah, all the tribes of Palestine, and all of the nations that Israel had to fight in their 40 years journey.

In the Scriptures, the land of Ham is pretty much spoken of as Egypt. If it is true that Ham's name means black, dark, hot, or heat and he represents the black races (all Scholars agree on this), it contradicts their opinion on this lower and higher Egypt. There are four places in Scripture where God Himself associates the land of Ham with Egypt. In Psalms 105:23 it reads *"Israel also came into Egypt; and Jacob sojourned in the land of Ham"* and in verse 27 of the same chapter it reads *"They shewed his signs among them, and wonders in the land of Ham."* Where were the children of Israel when they were in bondage? They were in Egypt. So the land of Ham is Egypt. In Psalms 78:51 it reads *"And smote all the firstborn in Egypt; the chief of their strength in the tabernacles of Ham."* Egypt and Ham are one in the same. Ham then represents the black race after the fall.

In Genesis 15:13 God says *"Know of a surety that thy seed* (which are the children of Israel) *shall be a stranger in a land that is not theirs, and shall serve them; and they shall afflict them four hundred years."* This is the definition of Egypt. One of the definitions of the word Egypt in Hebrew literally means "oppressors". God is telling Abraham here that His people (Israel) will go into Egypt and be subjected to slavery. The ancient Egyptians were an African race established first in Ethiopia. They always painted their gods black. The Sphinx is the image of the Pharaohs and their faces portray a black man.

The next black person in Scripture is found in Genesis 16. The name of Abraham's second wife was Hagar. Starting in Genesis 16:1, *"Now Sarai Abram's wife bare him no children: and she had an handmaid, an Egyptian, whose name was Hagar."* Hagar was black. Hagar's name means "flight, fugitive, immigrant, the sojourner, ensnaring, and wanderer" and comes from a root word that means "to flee, a stranger". She was made a stranger. Abraham is the father of our faith. Sarah is the mother. They are spoken well of in Hebrews 11 and we thank God for them. What Sarah did in this story in Genesis 16 was wrong. She asked Hagar to do what ultimately happened and then ended up despising her. As we look at this story, you will see the great man of God Abraham cuts off his black wife and his mixed race son (Ishmael) because of his wife not being able to deal with it. He totally ignores him. What you have to understand is Ishmael is both Jew and Black and Hagar is the mother of all Muslims. The fight that goes on today started right here because Ishmael was the eldest son. Ishmael was due the firstborn's inheritance but he was robbed of it and sent into the wilderness. He was ignored and that is why there is animosity, even until this day between the Jews and the Muslims over whose right it is to own that land. Now the Bible tells us we need to pray and support Israel, but I say (and I know I will have arrows shot at me for saying this) God assured Hagar He was her God and that Ishmael was His son as well. God was clear in pointing out the problems Ishmael would have, but God didn't forsake Hagar or forsake Ishmael. God didn't despise them or disown them. So even today in the midst of the great struggle in Palestine, let's not be so zealous just for Israel that we forget that Ishmael is a person. Ishmael is a people and God loves them just as much. Not only this, but this story is just the beginning and a picture of how the church gets rid of that which it is threatened by. How would you feel if you were disowned? The problem was Abraham really loved Ishmael. It broke his heart to send him away. Abraham's name means "father of a multitude". His name was Abram, which means "exalted father", but he became Abraham ("father of a multitude" or "father of many nations") because he had a father's heart. Sarai (or Sarah) was a princess. She got her way. Ultimately God blessed her and Abraham and praise God for that. But how would you like to be disowned at the age of 14 or 15 like Ishmael was, told by your father you must leave, sent off to the wilderness to live, and was only given a bottle of water and some bread? Wouldn't you feel a little resentment when you know it is a big thing in the custom of the day for the eldest son to receive the double portion and you realize you are getting nothing? This is just a thought.

In this story, it is not just about black people and hating black people. It is also about hating Muslims, Palestinians, or Jews. Racism is a devil, period, and we don't need to hate anybody! If someone asks you, "whose side are you on in the fight between Israel and Palestine?" You should say, "I am on God's side." Remember when Joshua met the Lord near Jericho (Joshua 5:13-15) and Joshua asked Him if He was for them or for their enemies. The Lord answered and said, neither! God is the God of everybody. He loves everybody He created. We make demons out of people we don't like. God help us to grasp this. Perfect love casts out fear (I John 4:18). Some people fear to embrace black people, have them as friends, and enter into a relationship with them because of fears that were planted in them that weren't even their fault (fears put in them from their mothers and fathers, and other family members, etc). Everyday as a child I heard racial slurs from my father against every race, especially black people. Now I never believed him because I went to a school of all black people as a white boy and knew it wasn't true. My father would feed me this foolish nonsense every night but living among black people everyday, I found what he said wasn't true at all. On the contrary, my family was the family on welfare and seemed to have the issues. I don't blame people for having racist tendencies because I don't think they came to those conclusions by themselves. They were put in them by others. Now that we are new creations in Christ Jesus, we have to be washed. Those chambers in our souls have to be opened, exorcized and replaced with truth. Jesus said in John 8:32, *"And ye shall know the truth, and the truth shall make you free."*

Let us read the story in Genesis 16 continuing in verse 2, *"²And Sarai said unto Abram, Behold now, the LORD hath restrained me from bearing: I pray thee, go in unto my maid; it may be that I may obtain children by her. And Abram hearkened to the voice of Sarai. ³And Sarai Abram's wife took Hagar her maid the Egyptian, after Abram had dwelt ten years in the land of Canaan, and gave her to her husband Abram to be his wife. ⁴And he went in unto Hagar, and she conceived: and when she saw that she had conceived,* her mistress was despised in her eyes. *⁵And Sarai said unto Abram, My wrong be upon thee: I have given my maid into thy bosom; and when she saw that she had conceived, I was despised in her eyes: the LORD judge between me and thee. ⁶But Abram said unto Sarai, Behold, thy maid is in thy hand; do to her as it pleaseth thee..."* I have a problem here with Abram. If he was the head of the house, he shouldn't let his wife tell him what to do. He just let her do whatever she wanted. We know Abraham was weak at times. Twice he told other kings his wife was his sister because he was afraid. The Bible doesn't hide any of these traits in people. We all have issues. Obviously, Abraham was a weak man when it came to strong women.

"...And when Sarai dealt hardly with her, she fled from her face. ⁷And the angel of the LORD found her by a fountain of water in the wilderness, by the fountain in the way to Shur..." Shur in Hebrew means "a point of observation, a fortified city, a watcher". This would make Hagar an intercessor as far as I

am concerned. She didn't know what to do so she went to a fountain of water in the wilderness to watch and intercede to find out what was the next move. This angel of the Lord was Jesus. It is called a Theophane, in theological terms, a divine appearance.

"*8And he said, Hagar, Sarai's maid, whence camest thou? and whither wilt thou go? And she said, I flee from the face of my mistress Sarai. 9And the angel of the LORD said unto her, Return to thy mistress, and submit thyself under her hands. 10And the angel of the LORD said unto her, <u>I will multiply thy seed exceedingly</u>, that it shall not be numbered for multitude...*" Notice the Lord didn't say to her and Abraham's seed, but "*thy seed*". Hagar was an African. She was black and the son that she and Abraham produced would never fit it, would always be despised, discarded, and rejected. He obviously didn't get his portion. "*11And the angel of the LORD said unto her, Behold, thou art with child, and shalt bear a son, and shalt call his name Ishmael...*" Once again, maybe Abraham bowed to a strong woman because he obviously went along with this because his name ended up being Ishmael.

"*...because the LORD hath heard thy affliction; 12And he will be a wild man; his hand will be against every man, and every man's hand against him; and he shall dwell in the presence of all his brethren.*" Ishmael had a reason to be angry. Ishmael had reasons to be resentful. This doesn't make what he did right, but you and I have to be people who can look through and discern where somebody is coming from. When you or I hear somebody speak, we need to understand that whatever they are saying, it is their <u>perception</u> of what happened and we need to discern the precious from the vile. When you see somebody hurt or wounded and out of that hurt and wound it caused them to react in a certain way, you have to be big enough (especially if it concerns you) to overlook it in order to minister to them to bring them out of their bondage. Ishmael was a wild man. Consider all of the suicide bombers that are everywhere now. Muslims really are soldiers. To be a Muslim leader you have to memorize the entire Quran. Christian leaders certainly don't memorize the entire Bible. The task seems incredibly daunting for us, but Muslims really do this. This is how dedicated and committed they are and that is why Islam is the fastest growing religion on the earth. We can't even get most Christians to ever read their Bibles. God help us I pray he brings a new fresh desire to read and study the scriptures to the body of Christ. We need to be more dedicated to the true and only God. "Study to shew thy self approved unto God a workmen..." Lord Jesus please bring this zeal for the Word to your people.

Ishmael's name means "he will hear God, he will be heard of God, or whom God hears". "*13And she called the name of the LORD that spake unto her, Thou God seest me: for she said, Have I also here looked after him that seeth me?*" I believe this is where Allah comes in for the Muslims. The word

59

she spoke was "El Roi" and this is the only time it is used in the Scriptures. "El Roi" means "God is seen or the well of Him that sees". Notice where she was too. *"¹⁴Wherefore the well was called Beer-lahai-roi; behold, it is between Kadesh and Bered."* Beer-lahai-roi means "the well of the life of vision, the well of her that lives and/or him that sees, preserves me in life, the well of the living who sees me". In other words, Hagar being despised and rejected, God did not reject her. God met her in a fountain of water in the desert! God will meet black people by a fountain of water in the desert and rather than making you bitter, let it make you better and give you vision. Glory to God!

Let us now look at the end of Ishmael. It is found in Genesis 21. Previously, Hagar ends up going back to Abraham and Sarah, births Ishmael and in Genesis 21, Isaac is born and in verse 8 a great feast is made the day Isaac was weaned. In verse 9 it then says, *"And Sarah saw the son of Hagar the Egyptian, which she had born unto Abraham, mocking."* I wonder why Ishmael was mocking Isaac. He probably felt the resentment and bigotry coming from the household and Sarah who hated him because he was black. He was the eldest son and deserved the first born birthright blessing. In verse 10 it continues, *"Wherefore she said unto Abraham, Cast out this bondwoman and her son: for the son of this bondwoman shall not be heir with my son, even with Isaac."* We know Paul in the New Testament uses this as an allegory in Galatians while talking about the difference between the Law and grace in Christ Jesus. *"¹¹And the thing was <u>very grievous</u> in Abraham's sight because of his son."* Even though Sarah hated Ishmael, Abraham knew he was his son and he obviously loved him dearly. It was grievous to him to do what Sarah was asking. *"¹²And God said unto Abraham, Let it not be grievous in thy sight because of the lad, and because of thy bondwoman; in all that Sarah hath said unto thee, hearken unto her voice; for in Isaac shall thy seed be called."* God has to speak here to encourage Abraham and watch how he does it, *"¹³And also of the son of the bondwoman will I make a nation, because <u>he is thy seed</u>."* God here still calls Ishmael <u>Abraham's seed</u> (Galatians 3:16). Out of the seed of Abraham came the Lord Jesus, so Black people, Muslims, and whoever, they are under the covenant of Abraham's seed and all can come to Jesus. Glory to God!

Continuing in Genesis 21, *"¹⁴And Abraham rose up early in the morning, and took bread, and a bottle of water, and gave it unto Hagar, putting it on her shoulder, and the child, and sent her away: and she departed, and wandered in the wilderness of Beer-sheba. ¹⁵And the water was spent in the bottle, and she cast the child under one of the shrubs. ¹⁶And she went, and sat her down over against him a good way off, as it were a bowshot: for she said, Let me not see the death of the child. And she sat over against him, and lift up her voice, and wept. ¹⁷And God <u>heard the voice of the lad</u>; and the angel of God called Hagar out of heaven..."* Hagar and Ishmael are in the middle of the wilderness by themselves and they hear the <u>audible voice of God</u> saying, "...*What aileth thee, Hagar? fear not; for God hath heard the voice of the lad where he is.* [18]*Arise, lift up the lad, and hold him in thine hand; for I will make him a great nation.* [19]*And God opened her eyes, and she saw a well of water; and she went, and filled the bottle with water, and gave the lad drink.* [20]*And God was with the lad; and he grew, and dwelt in the wilderness, and became an archer.* [21]*And he dwelt in the wilderness of Paran: and his mother took him a wife out of the land of Egypt.*" Hagar went back to her own people. Ishmael also married a black woman. It's encouraging to know, even though men and women reject us because of the color of our skin our precious heavenly Father never does. He is truly a great Father, and loves all of his children he is "the friend that sticketh closer than a brother. Oh how great is our God, faithful, compassionate, caring, loving, kind, and will never leave us or forsake us". He has not, nor will he ever forsake his precious black children. Glory to His name!

Black People Throughout Scripture
Chapter 5

There is really quite a lot to share about the Black race in the Bible. One of the things I really want to be let known is nobody knows for sure really who the Canaanites ended up being as far as what color they were. When people try to draw conclusions about this, to me this is wrong because we can't really tell. Now the descendents of Ham, Cush, Mizraim, and places like Cyrene, Libya, and Egypt were black skinned people we know. There are some who take the Scriptures way too far and they get into supposition and we can't do that as well. I don't believe Ham was a black man. I believe he was the father of the black races. Whatever color Noah was, his sons had the same color. Ham represented black races. Shem represented the Asiatic/Israel/Arab races, and Japheth represented Caucasians and the Europeans definitely. Whether they became black instantly, white instantly, etc, I don't know. The Scripture is a spiritual book and we don't want to be foolish with this. When God sent these three sons to re-populate the earth, they and their descendents all traveled to different places in the earth and I think ultimately their descendents became the races and skin colors that they represent.

The first thing we must note is this. Any vision of a white Jesus, white Apostles, even the early church being white is totally erroneous. We don't see the influx of white people until Cornelius comes on the scene. This is when the Gentiles began to open their hearts to receive the Word of God. Most of the early Christians were not the white skin color that we've come to see in great paintings, movies, and so on. No scholar can argue against this. There is no place in history, in the Bible, or in actuality where you or I can prove differently. Jesus was a man of color, most likely olive-skinned. Those who say Jesus was a black man because of the passage in Revelation 1:14-15 says He had bronze feet and white hair is foolish. This passage is describing Jesus in the glory, just as Moses when he came in and out of the glory and was changed in his appearance. Revelation 1:14-15 is describing Jesus after being in the glory for 70 years or so after He was resurrected. This will happen to us as well. Our bodies will radiate the glory of God and all of us will have the color of burnish bronze or an amber/glory color. So we need to be free to tell people this. There was no white Jesus. The disciples were not white. The Gentiles don't even come promptly into the picture in scripture until Cornelius and his band: Acts 10.

Now I want to try to go quickly through this. The history of races, especially in the Scripture is a very deep study and would take somebody years to detail where each of Noah's sons and their descendents traveled too, where their tribes ended up, etc. It is not something you can do in a week or two. It would probably take a lifetime of study to follow the history of races however they went. Because of this, to me, I am only going to speak of those that I know were absolutely black for sure. The rest is up to conjecture and maybe we will find out later. For our own knowledge, there are certain names in the Scripture where they are identified as black and there is no question about it. For example Cush, one of the sons of Ham, means blackness. Then there is Kedar which means in Hebrew "to be powerful, dark skinned, black skinned", Egypt which means "black", Niger which means "black", and Mizraim who really is an ancestor of the Egyptians. One of the tribes of the Canaanites we know can be black is the Philistines. The Philistines came out of Mizraim. This is very important. Another place is Cyrene which is an ancient city in North Africa (ancient name of Tripoli) and later becomes Libya.

Cush, the son of Ham, fathered Egypt, Libya, etc. Canaan was a son of Ham too, but I do not believe that Canaan was a black race (certain tribes maybe, but you would have to study this much further to attempt to figure this out). In this chapter, I would like to continue to talk about the presence of Black people in Scripture. We already looked at some in the book of Genesis and I would like to continue.

Did you know Moses received the Ten Commandments in Africa? We already saw that creation began in Africa. Mount Sinai is located on the Sinai Peninsula which is in the northeast portion of Egypt and Egypt is in Africa. Moses was raised as an African Prince. Now we all know the story in Exodus 2 on how this happened (Moses taken by Pharaoh's daughter), but I would like to look at what the Bible says in Acts 7:22 about him. Acts 7:22-23 says *"And Moses was learned in all the wisdom of the Egyptians, and was mighty in words and in deeds. And when he was full forty years old, it came into his heart to visit his brethren the children of Israel."* Moses was born a Hebrew, but it is interesting to note that Moses skin color had to be somewhat dark or he would have never have passed as a son of an Egyptian. He obviously was a man of color. He was a Hebrew. One of the thing histories tells us is that a lot of the things we do as civilized nations came from the Egyptian people. They had circumcision. They set up the family structure. And many of the things we do today came from the wisdom found in Egypt. Many have done great studies on the pyramids and whoever constructed them were geniuses. Egyptians knew how to embalm people, they believed in an afterlife, etc. They were a wise and civilized people who had a great civilization in much science and wisdom. The next thing we need to note is many Egyptians, once God brought Israel into Egypt (Exodus 12:37-38, Deuteronomy 23:7-8), went with Israel and traveled with Israel during the forty years. They were called the mixed multitude.

Let us look next in I Chronicles 2:34-41. The remainder of this chapter will not be in chronological order. As I said before, I am only going to list those who I know for certain were black. Every time you see the word Canaan or Canaanite, it doesn't mean somebody was black. I have a problem when people do this because I do not believe this can be proven. If we look in I Chronicles 2:1, we see this chapter is listing the *"sons of Israel"*. Here in I Chronicles 2:34 we read; *"Now Sheshan had no sons, but daughters. And Sheshan had a servant, <u>an Egyptian</u>, whose name was Jarha. And Sheshan gave his daughter to Jarha his servant to wife; and she bare him Attai..."* He came out of the tribe of Judah, so in the line of the tribe of Judah, we know absolutely for certain there was a black representative. Judah is the Messianic line that Jesus descended from in his earthly state.

I don't know why it is that white people are afraid to give black people their due. I think it really comes down to this. It is a basic insecurity and inferiority in white people that cannot stand to even imagine that God would grant to the black race more then them. This is why I had to deal with the supposed "Curse of Ham" because it is a lie and needed to be exposed because all of our civilization is predicated on the fact that black people are cursed and white people are blessed. This is not true at all! The Hebrew nation and Black people were very close together and in some cases cousins. There was a lot of intermarriage going on between them. God only knows what the result was as far as how they looked, but one thing is for sure, in the genealogy of the Lord Jesus, there are black representatives and why not so? If Jesus is going to represent the whole world (*God so loved the world* John 3:16), why would He not be part of everybody in the world? I pray God illuminates the foolishness of wondering about the skin color of a person. I also pray that we the "Body of Christ" can set the example of living in true harmony with all believers, no matter what their color, nationality, culture. Only you and I hold the key to this happening, it begins with us. Lord lift us above pettiness, racism, hatred, etc...And make us true Christians.

In I Samuel 30, Ziklag had been taken and burned, and all of David and his men's wives and possessions had been taken. David's men wanted David stoned and so David goes out to capture the people who had stolen from him. Look here starting in verse 10, *"But David pursued, he and four hundred men: for two hundred abode behind, which were so faint that they could not go over the brook Besor. [11]And they found an Egyptian in the field, and brought him to David, and gave him bread, and he did eat; and they made him drink water..."* Now I could preach on this verse. The revelation that is here about the black race and about this Egyptian man being in the field is tremendous. Scripturally, what does the field represent? It represents the world, Jesus said, and the place of ministry. But anyway, continuing in verse 12, *"And they gave him a piece of a cake of figs, and two clusters of raisins..."* Now there didn't seem to be any racism in David. It was probably because he was brought up around black people. *"...and when he had eaten, his spirit came again to him: for he had eaten no bread, nor drunk any water, three days and three nights."* This is the principle of the third day. In other words God is going to visit Egypt, a part of the world. *"¹³And David said unto him, to whom belongest thou? And whence art thou? And he said, I am a young man of Egypt, servant to an Amalekite; and my master left me, because three days ago I fell sick. ¹⁴We made an invasion upon the south of the Cherethites, and upon the coast which belongeth to Judah, and upon the south of Caleb; and we burned Ziklag with fire. ¹⁵And David said to him, Canst thou bring me down to this company? And he said, Swear unto me by God, that thou wilt neither kill me, nor deliver me into the hands of my master, and I will bring thee down to this company. ¹⁶And when he had brought him down, behold, they were spread abroad upon all the earth, eating and drinking, and dancing, because of all the great spoil that they had taken out of the land of the Philistines, and out of the land of Judah. ¹⁷And David smote them from the twilight even unto the evening of the next day: and there escaped not a man of them, save four hundred young men, which rode upon camels, and fled. ¹⁸And David recovered all that the Amalekites had carried away: and David rescued his two wives. ¹⁹And there was nothing lacking to them, neither small nor great, neither sons nor daughters, neither spoil, nor any thing that they had taken to them: David recovered all."* Who gave David the eyes to find the enemy, the Egyptian, a black man? Many people have long said that black men and women are the eyes of God. To see into the realm of the sup

Ernatural, all he wanted was a promise from David that he was not going to be turned over to his former master (who would be a type of Satan). And without hesitation, he helped David recover everything that they had lost!

Let us look at the story of Joseph (one of Jacob's sons) in the book of Genesis. Joseph was sold by his brothers (Genesis 37:28) to the Ishmaelites (a black people) for 20 pieces of silver and the Ishmaelites *"brought Joseph into Egypt"*. Continuing his story in Genesis 39:1, *"And Joseph was brought down to Egypt; and Potiphar, an officer of Pharaoh, captain of the guard, an Egyptian, bought him of the hands of the Ishmeelites, which had brought him down thither. ²And the LORD was with Joseph, and he was a prosperous man; and he was in the house of his master the Egyptian. ³And his master saw that the LORD was with him, and that the LORD made all that he did to prosper in his hand. ⁴And Joseph found grace in his sight, and he served him: and he made him overseer over his house, and all that he had he put into his hand. ⁵And it came to pass from the time that he had made him overseer in his house, and over all that he had, that the LORD blessed the Egyptian's house for Joseph's sake; and the blessing of the LORD was upon all that he had in the house, and in the field. ⁶And he left all that he had in Joseph's hand; and he knew not ought he had, save the bread which he did eat. And Joseph was a goodly person, and well favoured..."* I want to talk about Potiphar for a moment. Potiphar was Egypt's military commander. In verse 1, it says he was *"an officer of Pharaoh, captain of the guard"*. Potiphar saw that the Lord was with

Joseph. Once again we see this ability in black people to recognize the hand of God or to have discernment about what God is doing. This black man was very trusting and trusted Joseph with all he had. How different from white people. He was so trusting he didn't know what he had or owned except for the food that was put before him everyday. This speaks of a man who has great trust, a gentle heart (even though he was a military commander), and one who recognizes authority and God's favor. Joseph should have been killed for what he did, but Potiphar spared him and put him in prison. Potiphar was an honorable, caring, black man. Who could discern or recognize what God was doing. It makes me wonder how many precious black intercessors have helped God's people by their remarkable ability to understand the times, to see what God wants and have aided the kingdom of God throughout history. These almost unknown, wonderful people had to have God's true heart.

From Potiphar's house, Joseph went to prison for many years, until finally Pharaoh had a dream he couldn't interpret. Joseph stood before Pharaoh and interpreted the dream, and Pharaoh made Joseph overseer over all he had, just like Potiphar did. Once again we see this trust factor. He put everything in Joseph's hand. Joseph even had the ring that signified Pharaoh's authority. Joseph could have put his hand to any piece of paper and it would say that Pharaoh had signed this. This is how important Joseph was in the house of Pharaoh. Why is it that black people seem to have been willing to trust other races and even give them positions of power and trust? But white people, up to this point have tried to stymie and hold back, and not trust their black brothers. This has to be a tremendous insecurity in them, along with great jealously. Now to help Joseph become more acclimated to being with Egyptian people (Joseph was Hebrew), Pharaoh encouraged him to marry a black woman. We see this story in Genesis 41, *"³⁹And Pharaoh said unto Joseph, Forasmuch as God hath shewed thee all this, there is none so discreet and wise as thou art: ⁴⁰Thou shalt be over my house, and according unto thy word shall all my people be ruled: only in the throne will I be greater than thou. ⁴¹And Pharaoh said unto Joseph, See, I have set thee over all the land of Egypt. ⁴²And Pharaoh took off his ring from his hand, and put it upon Joseph's hand, and arrayed him in vestures of fine linen, and put a gold chain about his neck; ⁴³And he made him to ride in the second chariot which he had; and they cried before him, Bow the knee: and he made him ruler over all the land of Egypt. ⁴⁴And Pharaoh said unto Joseph, I am Pharaoh, and without thee shall no man lift up his hand or foot in all the land of Egypt. ⁴⁵And Pharaoh called Joseph's name Zaphnath-paaneah; and he gave him to wife Asenath the daughter of Poti-pherah priest of On. And Joseph went out over all the land of Egypt. ⁴⁶And Joseph was thirty years old when he stood before Pharaoh king of Egypt..."* Joseph's new name that he was given was Zaphnath-paaneah. If there is any type of the Lord Jesus in the Old Testament, it is Joseph. His new name means "Savior of the age, savior of the world, giver of the nourishment of life, revealer of secrets, and treasury of the glorious rest". And this is an Egyptian name. Joseph had a character change in Egypt. The woman that God had him marry was an Egyptians whose name was Asenath. Her name means "who belongs to Neith (which was an Egyptian Goddess)". She was the mother of Manasseh and Ephraim (verses 50-52). She was also a daughter of a priest of On. This is a black woman Joseph married. This made Manasseh and Ephraim a mixed race and went on to become part of the tribes of Israel. Even within the nation of Israel, there is a portion of black people. It is simply astounding how trusting this black leader was. He obviously was not prejudiced or racist. He didn't distrust or feel insecure about promoting Joseph. Why can't we as white leaders do the same I believe that if we can receive this revelation and act accordingly, black people everywhere would flock to Jesus. There could be an unprecedented move of God among black people if we could learn from Pharaoh and trust, promote, and bless our black brothers and sisters.

Next, look at what Jacob did in Genesis 48. This reminds me of what God did to the Gentiles when He said they are adopted in. Genesis 48, "*[1]And it came to pass after these things, that one told Joseph, Behold, thy father is sick: and he took with him his two sons, Manasseh and Ephraim. [2]And one told Jacob, and said, Behold, thy son Joseph cometh unto thee: and Israel strengthened himself, and sat upon the bed. [3]And Jacob said unto Joseph, God Almighty appeared unto me at Luz in the land of Canaan, and blessed me, [4]And said unto me, Behold, I will make thee fruitful, and multiply thee, and I will make of thee a multitude of people; and will give this land to thy seed after thee for an everlasting possession. [5]And now thy two sons, Ephraim and Manasseh, which were born unto thee in the land of Egypt before I came unto thee into Egypt, are mine; as Reuben and Simeon, they shall be mine. [6]And thy issue, which thou begettest after them, shall be thine, and shall be called after the name of their brethren in their inheritance...*" Glory to God! Manasseh and Ephraim were both people of color and their seed were completely adopted within the household of faith. Why can't we do the same thing? I pray we begin to see each other as God sees us. Thank God for our beautiful black brothers. It can only help us grow stronger. We need white people to embrace our black brothers. Promote them, encourage them and release them in to greater roles of leadership within the Kingdom of God!

When Israel finally entered into the promise land, the two sons of Joseph, Manasseh and Ephraim took the place of Joseph and Levi and became part of the twelve tribes of Israel. In Deuteronomy 33 we see the blessing Moses placed on them. Moses is prophesying over all of the sons of Israel. Now Joseph's sons were Manasseh and Ephraim. So in Deuteronomy 33:13-16, "*And of Joseph he said, Blessed of the LORD be his land, for the precious things of heaven, for the dew, and for the deep that coucheth beneath, [14] And for the precious fruits brought forth by the sun, and for the precious things put forth by the moon...*" Look at how all of sons of Joseph were blessed. "*The dew*" represents the anointing. "*The deep*" represents the deep things of God. "*The precious fruits*" represent the fruits of the Spirit. The moon in Scriptures is a type of the bride of Christ (it has no glory on its own, but only reflects the glory of the sun). Moses continues with the blessing upon Joseph, "*[15]And for the chief things of the ancient mountains, and for the precious things of the lasting hills, [16]And for the precious things of the earth and fulness thereof, and for the good will of him that dwelt in the bush: let the blessing come upon the head of Joseph, and upon the top of the head of him that was separated from his brethren. [17]His glory is like the firstling of his bullock, and his horns are like the horns of unicorns: with them he shall push the people together to the ends of the earth: and they are the ten thousands of Ephraim, and they are the thousands of Manasseh.*" So this prophesy and proclamation was given to Manasseh and Ephraim, who were two multi-colored men (from a mixed marriage, their mother again being a black woman). Why don't we help to see this prophecy be fulfilled, and with open arms and hearts, embrace and love are dear black brothers. Whether we like it or not, God has already spoken of his intentions. So it is now up to us. Let's pray that a mighty move of reconciliation and repentance zealously sweep over the body of Christ; and we live up to God's word, and receive, embraces and show the world we will obey God's command to "Love one another with a pure heart."

In I Samuel 17 we find the story of David defeating Goliath. Goliath was Ham's descendent and we can conclude he was black because he came from Mizraim whose lineage we saw was from Egypt. Look again at Genesis 10 where we see the generations of the sons of Noah, Shem, Ham, and Japheth. Starting in verse 6 we read the sons of Ham, "*And the sons of Ham; Cush, and Mizraim* (his name again means blackness and became Egypt), *and Phut, and Canaan. [7]And the sons of Cush; Seba, and Havilah, and Sabtah, and Raamah, and Sabtecha: and the sons of Raamah; Sheba, and Dedan. [8]And Cush begat Nimrod: he began to be a mighty one in the earth...[11]Out of that land went forth Asshur, and builded Nineveh, and the city Rehoboth, and Calah, [12]And Resen between Nineveh and Calah: the same is a great city. [13]And <u>Mizraim begat Ludim, and Anamim, and Lehabim, and Naphtuhim, [14]And Pathrusim, and Casluhim, (out of whom came Philistim,)</u> and Caphtorim...*" If you look up Philistim, they always refer you to the Philistines. So the Philistines came from Mizraim or Egypt. Therefore the Philistines were descendents of the black Mizraim, Cush's son. This is without question. This is the lineage of Goliath. Goliath was a black man. There are some people who believe that when Israel went to spy out the promise land and they saw the giants of Anakim (out of whom Goliath came out of), the people who they saw who were so powerful that made them so afraid were black people. They went back and told Moses that they were grasshoppers in their sight. They were overwhelmed by them. In addition, David called Goliath an uncircumcised Philistine. Therefore there is no question about Goliath being black because Philistim, which is Philistine, came from Mizraim (Egypt).

Next, let us look at II Samuel 6 and look at Obededom, the man who had the ark. Obededom was a Gittite (verse 10). In Joshua 13:1-3, we read, *"¹Now Joshua was old and stricken in years; and the LORD said unto him, Thou art old and stricken in years, and there remaineth yet very much land to be possessed. ²This is the land that yet remaineth: all the borders of the Philistines, and all Geshuri, ³From Sihor, which is before Egypt, even unto the borders of Ekron northward, which is counted to the Canaanite: <u>five lords of the Philistines</u>; the Gazathites, and the Ashdothites, the Eshkalonites, the <u>Gittites</u>, and the Ekronites; also the Avites..."* The Philistines had 5 major lords over their peoples and one of those peoples was the Gittites. Philistim out of which came the Philistines is black because of Mizraim (we saw this in Genesis 10:13 – one of Ham's sons). Obededom was a Gittite and was a decendent of Ham. So in II Samuel 6 we find the story of David trying to bring the ark back home to him and because David didn't do it after the due order, God smote Uzzah. *"⁹And David was afraid of the LORD that day, and said, How shall the ark of the LORD come to me? ¹⁰So David would not remove the ark of the LORD unto him into the city of David: but David carried it aside into the house of Obed-edom the Gittite..."* (II Samuel 6:9-10). David left the ark in the hands of a black man. Maybe David was seeing what was going to happen to Obededom because the ark just killed Uzzah. Maybe David was thinking because he was black, he was going to be destroyed. Let us continue in verse 11, *"And the ark of the LORD continued in the house of Obed-edom the Gittite three months: and the LORD blessed Obed-edom, and all his household. ¹²And it was told king David, saying, The LORD hath blessed the house of Obed-edom, and all that pertaineth unto him, because of the ark of God. So David went and brought up the ark of God from the house of Obed-edom into the city of David with gladness."* Obededom was a black man, he had the ark, which is a type of the manifest presence of God, in his house, and the Lord blessed him mightily because of it. Now Obededom's story is not finished here. In I Chronicles 15 David is building the Tabernacle of David. He builds a tent for the ark which becomes the Tabernacle of David and this is where 24 hour worship began. David then begins to name and appoint singers of songs, the instruments of music, the chief musician, etc. We pick up the story in verse 22, *"And Chenaniah, chief of the Levites, was for song: he instructed about the song, because he was skilful. ²³And Berechiah and Elkanah were doorkeepers for the ark. ²⁴And Shebaniah, and Jehoshaphat, and Nethaneel, and Amasai, and Zechariah, and Benaiah, and Eliezer, the priests, did blow with the trumpets before the ark of God: and <u>Obed-edom</u> and Jehiah were <u>doorkeepers for the ark</u>..."* In other words, Obededom was called to be a guardian of the ark of God or a doorkeeper to bring the people into the presence of God!

Next, let us shift to a not so pleasant story, Solomon and his many women. I Kings 11:1-4, *"But king Solomon loved many strange women, together with the daughter of Pharaoh, women of the Moabites, Ammonites, Edomites, Zidonians, and Hittites; ²Of the nations concerning which the LORD said unto the children of Israel, Ye shall not go in to them, neither shall they come in unto you: for surely they will turn away your heart after their gods: Solomon clave unto these in love. ³And he had seven hundred wives, princesses, and three hundred concubines: and his wives turned away his heart. ⁴For it came to pass, when Solomon was old, that his wives turned away his heart after other gods: and his heart was not perfect with the LORD his God, as was the heart of David his father."* Many of these tribes and women that Solomon married were black women. There were just as many black women in Solomon's harem as there were anybody else. I don't think there were any white women there though. In I Kings 3 we read *"And Solomon made affinity with Pharaoh king of Egypt, and took Pharaoh's daughter, and brought her into the city of David, until he had made an end of building his own house, and the house of the LORD, and the wall of Jerusalem round about."* Solomon made a treaty with Pharaoh, king of Egypt, and he took Pharaoh's daughter to be his wife. Following this through, we find in I Kings 9:15-16 *"And this is the reason of the levy which king Solomon raised; for to build the house of the LORD, and his own house, and Millo, and the wall of Jerusalem, and Hazor, and Megiddo, and Gezer. For Pharaoh king of Egypt had gone up, and taken Gezer, and burnt it with fire, and slain the Canaanites that dwelt in the city, and given it for a present unto his daughter, Solomon's wife."* Solomon therefore was married to at least one black woman and also had many black concubines.

Now let us talk about the Queen of Sheba in I Kings 10. Sheba was in the lineage of Cush. Cush's name again means "black". She was the queen of Ethiopia and was a very wise black woman. Even though it cannot be proven, some people believe she carried Solomon's seed back with her to Ethiopia and with that there came forth a root of people in Ethiopia that knew the God of Israel. They believe this is why we see later in Acts 8 the reason for the Ethiopian eunuch being sent by the Queen of Ethiopia (Candace). Candace sent this eunuch to worship at the feast in Jerusalem. Solomon gave the Queen of Sheba everything, more than anybody else. He really opened his heart to her and she took the stuff back with her. Isn't it interesting we find in Sheba the same interest and hunger for God as this eunuch sent by Candace? In Kings 10 we read, *"¹And when the queen of Sheba heard of the fame of Solomon concerning the name of the LORD, she came to prove him with hard questions. ²And she came to Jerusalem with a very great train, with camels that bare spices, and very much gold, and precious stones: and when she was come to Solomon, she communed with him of all that was in her heart. ³And Solomon told her all her questions: there was not any thing hid from the king, which he told her not. ⁴And when the queen of Sheba had seen all Solomon's wisdom,* *and the house that he had built, ⁵And the meat of his table, and the sitting of his servants, and the attendance of his ministers, and their apparel, and his cupbearers, and his ascent by which he went up unto the house of the LORD; there was no more spirit in her..."* When was the last time you communed with somebody everything that was in your heart? There must have been something going on between Sheba and Solomon. I believe there was no more spirit in Sheba after she saw and heard all that Solomon spoke and showed her was because of two reasons: 1) what she saw was beyond anything that she could have hoped for, and 2) because it rivaled her own nation. Her own civilization was just as rich, just as educated, and just as wise as Solomon's and it blew her mind that this Hebrew king had the same revelation and more. *"⁶And she said to the king, It was a true report that I heard in mine own land of thy acts and of thy wisdom. ⁷Howbeit I believed not the words, until I came, and mine eyes had seen it: and, behold, the half was not told me: thy wisdom and prosperity exceedeth the fame which I heard. ⁸Happy are thy men, happy are these thy servants, which stand continually before thee, and that hear thy wisdom. ⁹Blessed be the LORD thy God, which delighted in thee, to set thee on the throne of Israel: because the LORD loved Israel for ever, therefore made he thee king, to do judgment and justice. ¹⁰And she gave the king an hundred and twenty talents of gold, and of spices very great store, and precious stones: there came no more such abundance of spices as these which the queen of Sheba gave to king Solomon...¹³And king Solomon gave unto the queen of Sheba all her desire, whatsoever she asked, beside that which Solomon gave her of his royal bounty. So she turned and went to her own country, she and her servants."* Now, what did she take back? Some people say she and Solomon fell in love and they had a relationship but ultimately she had to go back because she was the queen of another nation. Some people quote this from Jewish Rabbis, but we do know this: she saw in the heart of Solomon the truths of the God of Israel and carried this back to her black nation and a remnant of people held onto this truth. How many people know of the story of the Ethiopian Jews? For the last 20 years, they have been making their pilgrimage back to Israel. Where do we think these Ethiopian Jews came from? Some Jews maybe traveled and settled in Ethiopia, but for the most part, I believe, it came as God brought this revelation through this precious black woman.

In Jeremiah 38, there is a man name Ebedmelech. In this story, a bunch of men had come to Zedekiah the king and said that Jeremiah's prophecy that all of the Israelites should go to Babylon (the Chaldeans) and not fight meant that Jeremiah was not a man of God. So they ended up throwing Jeremiah in prison. God's will actually was for the people of God to go to Babylon. Let us read in Jeremiah 38, starting in verse 5, *"Then Zedekiah the king said, Behold, he is in your hand: for the king is not he that can do any thing against you. ⁶Then took they Jeremiah, and cast him into the dungeon of Malchiah the son of Hammelech, that was in the court of the prison: and they let down Jeremiah* *with cords. And in the dungeon there was no water, but mire: so Jeremiah sunk in the mire..."* Jeremiah sunk in the mire. This reminds me of the passage in Ezekiel 47 where the only place where the glory would not heal was in the miry places (Ezekiel 47:11). Jeremiah was put into a place where the glory could not reach (the dungeon). Jeremiah needed somebody to help him. Now watch as we continue the story, *"⁷Now when Ebed-melech the Ethiopian, one of the eunuchs which was in the king's house, heard that they had put Jeremiah in the dungeon; the king then sitting in the gate of Benjamin; ⁸Ebed-melech went forth out of the king's house, and spake to the king, saying, ⁹My lord the king, these men have done evil in all that they have done to Jeremiah the prophet, whom they have cast into the dungeon; and he is like to die for hunger in the place where he is: for there is no more bread in the city. ¹⁰Then the king commanded Ebed-melech the Ethiopian, saying, Take from hence thirty men with thee, and take up Jeremiah the prophet out of the dungeon, before he die. ¹¹So Ebed-melech took the men with him, and went into the house of the king under the treasury, and took thence old cast clouts and old rotten rags, and let them down by cords into the dungeon to Jeremiah. ¹²And Ebed-melech the Ethiopian said unto Jeremiah, Put now these old cast clouts and rotten rags under thine armholes under the cords. And Jeremiah did so. ¹³So they drew up Jeremiah with cords, and took him up out of the dungeon: and Jeremiah remained in the court of the prison..."* Look how God blesses this precious Ethiopian for helping Jeremiah. We find this in Jeremiah 39 starting in verse 15, *"Now the word of the LORD came unto Jeremiah, while he was shut up in the court of the prison, saying, ¹⁶Go and speak to Ebed-melech the Ethiopian, saying, Thus saith the LORD of hosts, the God of Israel; Behold, I will bring my words upon this city for evil, and not for good; and they shall be accomplished in that day before thee. ¹⁷But I will deliver thee in that day, saith the LORD: and thou shalt not be given into the hand of the men of whom thou art afraid. ¹⁸For I will surely deliver thee, and thou shalt not fall by the sword, but thy life shall be for a prey unto thee: because thou hast put <u>thy trust in me, saith the LORD</u>."* So Ebedmelech had become a convert to the God of Israel and because of what he did to free Jeremiah, God honored him in the process.

Next, in Matthew 27:32 and in Luke 23:26, there was a man name Simon the Cyrenian whose was asked to carry the cross of Jesus. He was a descendent of Ham through Phut (one of Ham's sons). We don't see any Romans (the white people in the picture) carrying the cross, nor any Hebrews, not even Peter, James, or John. This was a black man going out of the town into his own country and they compel him to carry the cross. Well, Simon's story doesn't end here. Look in Mark 15:21, *"And they compel one Simon a Cyrenian, who passed by, coming out of the country, the father of Alexander and Rufus, to bear his cross. ²²And they bring him unto the place Golgotha, which is, being interpreted, The place of a skull."* So Simon was the father of Alexander and Rufus. Rufus is mentioned in Romans 16:13 which says *"Salute Rufus chosen* *in the Lord, and his mother <u>and mine</u>."* Scholars all agree that this is the son of Simon. Paul called Rufus's mother his own mother. Wow! There was obviously no racism in the heart of the apostle Paul. On the contrary he knew and acted like they were his family as well. Lord help us to follow Paul's example.

Also in Acts 13 we see there are black prophets and teachers in the early church. Acts 13:1 reads *"Now there were in the church that was at Antioch certain prophets and teachers; as Barnabas, and Simeon that was called Niger, and Lucius of Cyrene, and Manaen, which had been brought up with Herod the tetrarch, and Saul."* In others words, two of these people mentioned were black men. *"[2]As they ministered to the Lord, and fasted, the Holy Ghost said, Separate me Barnabas and Saul for the work whereunto I have called them..."* We see this again in Acts 11:19-21. *"[19]Now they which were scattered abroad upon the persecution that arose about Stephen traveled as far as Phenice, and Cyprus, and Antioch, preaching the word to none but unto the Jews only. [20]And some of them were men of Cyprus and Cyrene, which, when they were come to Antioch, spake unto the Grecians, preaching the Lord Jesus. [21]And the hand of the Lord was with them: and a great number believed, and turned unto the Lord."* You have to understand something. This is revolutionary. In nothing we have ever written or seen before has there been any presence of a black person in the early New Testament church. But on the contrary, we find some of the most affluent and most important prophets and teachers named by the Word of God were those black men in Acts 13. Others whose names are not even mentioned in Acts 11 were black men preaching the gospel and the hand of the Lord was upon them and great things were done by them! What an injustice has been done, not only to the Word of God, to black people, as well as to us as students of the Bible. We've been lied to. It is way past time to honor all that black people have done for the kingdom of God. This story must be told, we absolutely need to see the great ministry that so many black people brought to the Body of Christ.

We can't approach the Word of God with our intellect. II Corinthians 3:18 says, *"But we all, with open face beholding as in a glass the glory of the Lord..."* We have to approach the Word of God with an *"open face"* or an "unveiled face". We cannot read the Bible with prejudice eyes. We can't even come to this Word with doctrines we were taught as children that our mothers and fathers believed. We have to open this book and let it speak for itself. We have to search the Scriptures to see if these things are so (Acts 17:11). I don't even like using terms "black" and "white" when talking about my brothers and sisters in the Lord because when we do this we're not living as true sons of God. But because of such a lack of education and a lack of revelation we find people talking like this in today's world. Here is the thing. It just didn't end with the early church covering all of this over and acting like it was something different. All of the early portraits of the Hebrew people and all of the portraits of people born in the beginning of time showed their skin being dark. It wasn't until about the 15th century that people began to change the features in the people and make them white, all the while totally distorting the Scripture. The King James Version has serious holes in its translation, but thank God for this version as well for translating things correctly when it comes to black people in Scripture. If you read some of these newer translations, they won't say Simon of Cyrene or somebody from Egypt or Ethiopia. They will say a "Cushite" instead of "Egypt" where you would know that that man was black. To me it is a subtle way of trying to hide it and it amazes me that this went down all through history and even to the early 1900's when God at Azusa Street began to pour out His Spirit and who did He use? He used a little partially blind black man name William Seymour who had a box for a podium. Every night he would hide behind that box and just pray until the glory fell and he let anybody minister (inter-racial meetings). In the Old Testament, we see Potiphar and Pharaoh (black rulers) giving Joseph free reign over their stuff and never having a problem with the issue that Joseph was another race. White people don't seem to do the same thing. At the Azusa Street revival, there were so many white people getting filled with the Holy Ghost and speaking in tongues that a group of white ministers met (some of whom are some very famous names that I will not mention) and decided that something needed to happen. So these white ministers started having their own meetings (kind of "whites only" or "whites in charge") and the different denominations began out of this. Black people were left then without a place and weren't wanted so they began the "Church of God in Christ" which is a Spirit-filled Black denomination. I wonder how many great preachers and teachers have lived and have never had the opportunity because of some racist white person who had no anointing stood and hindered them. I'm telling you there is going to be such judgment at the coming of the Lord, I fear for people who still are walking in this racism today. When you think of the early prophets and teachers in Jerusalem, we've been trained to think of them as white people but they were all people of color, many of whom were black. There were no white people there until Cornelius. Many of the prophets that sent out Barnabas and Paul (that laid hands on them and had the authority to do so) were black. The early church didn't have racism because they were all people of color! It is only when white people come into the scene that problems occur. It is amazing and we don't like to admit it, but it is the truth. White people are always famous for wanting to say races have certain characteristics. Well, what are the characteristics of the white race? – conquering, stealing what somebody else has done, taking what doesn't belong to them, stealing other peoples civilizations and claiming it as their own. If you are looking for a white Jesus in heaven, you won't find Him. He just may be black. It doesn't matter to me because the same Jesus I have been talking to all this time is going to be the same Jesus no matter what color He is, so what difference should it make to us?

74

At the day of Pentecost, who was there? Acts 2:5-11, *"⁵And there were dwelling at Jerusalem Jews, devout men, out of every nation under heaven. ⁶Now when this was noised abroad, the multitude came together, and were confounded, because that every man heard them speak in his own language. ⁷And they were all amazed and marveled, saying one to another, Behold, are not all these which speak Galilaeans? ⁸And how hear we every man in our own tongue, wherein we were born? ⁹Parthians, and Medes, and Elamites, and the dwellers in Mesopotamia, and in Judaea, and Cappadocia, in Pontus, and Asia, ¹⁰Phrygia, and Pamphylia, in Egypt, and in the parts of Libya about Cyrene, and strangers of Rome, Jews and proselytes, ¹¹Cretes and Arabians, we do hear them speak in our tongues the wonderful works of God."* Of these nations included the black nations of Egypt, Libya, and Cyrene when the Holy Ghost fell.

Let us look next at the Ethiopian eunuch in Acts 8:26-39. The story begins by an angel appearing to Philip to go to a certain place. Philip didn't put on his shoes and go. He was translated to this place and this is the only occurrence in the Scripture where a man goes from one place to another place immediately, or is translated to meet up with a black man because that black man was very important. So Philip appears next to the chariot of this Ethiopian eunuch as he is going home after being sent by the queen (Candace) to go worship at Jerusalem. Philip meets up with this eunuch as he is reading out of the book of Isaiah and Philip asks the eunuch if he knew what he was reading. The eunuch says he doesn't understand and wants to know if Isaiah is speaking about himself or some other man. The eunuch also says to Philip in verse 31, *"How can I, except some man should guide me?"* He is saying to Philip how can I know what Isaiah is saying unless somebody teach me? We see great humility and meekness in this eunuch. In other words it is like John having to go to the messenger in Revelation 10:9 and say *"give me the little book"*. But in history we see what terrible things were taught to black people over the years and what judgment awaits those who taught them. This Ethiopian was a eunuch. Jesus said in Matthew 19:12, *"For there are some eunuchs, which were so born from their mother's womb: and there are some eunuchs, which were made eunuchs of men: and there be eunuchs, which have made themselves eunuchs for the kingdom of heaven's sake. He that is able to receive it, let him receive it."* Eunuchs for the Lord are one of the highest ranks in the body of Christ. They are totally devoted and given up their lives to serving and worshipping Jesus. They deny their own sexual urges and Jesus has become their all in all. This Ethiopian was a eunuch. He gets saved in the story and they pass by water and he gets water baptized. In verse 39 it says about this *"And when they were come up out of the water, the Spirit of the Lord caught away Philip, that the eunuch saw him no more: and he went on his way rejoicing."* My take on this is: when the eunuch came up out of the water of baptism, the Spirit of the Lord fell on the eunuch and he started speaking in tongues as Philip was being taken away and he went on his way rejoicing (speaking in tongues). How many precious, hungry black saints have looked to white preachers or teachers to open the Word of God to them, but were ignored. What a terrible injustice this is. I know at the judgement seat of Christ there is going to be some punishment given to every man or women of God who has lied, deceived or did violence to the Scriptures by not telling the truth to black saints. God help everyone in the five fold ministry to see this, and to begin to share the whole truth in scripture, thereby releasing a mighty force of black men and women of God into their ministry.

Deuteronomy 23:7 says "...*thou shalt not abhor an Egyptian...*" This is God speaking. We are not to abhor a black person. Psalms 68:31 says "*Princes shall come out of Egypt; Ethiopia shall soon stretch out her hands unto God.*" Psalms 87:4-5 says that Zion is made up of Ethiopian people. In Amos 9:7 God is speaking to Israel, "*Are ye not as children of the Ethiopians unto me, O children of Israel?*" In Isaiah 11:10-12 when the day of the Lord comes the remnant shall return from Egypt, Cush, etc. In other words, the remnant is in all of these dark skinned places. Zephaniah 3:10 says "*From beyond the rivers of Ethiopia my suppliants* (or my worshippers), *even the daughter of my dispersed, shall bring mine offering.*" Glory to God!

Lastly, let us turn to Revelation 5. We find in this chapter that Jesus is the lamb that had the authority to open the book that nobody else could open and in verse 7 it says, "*And he came and took the book out of the right hand of him that sat upon the throne. [8]And when he had taken the book, the four beasts and four and twenty elders fell down before the Lamb, having every one of them harps, and golden vials full of odours, which are the prayers of saints. [9]And they sung a new song, saying, Thou art worthy to take the book, and to open the seals thereof: for thou wast slain, and hast redeemed us to God by thy blood out of every kindred, and tongue, and people, and nation; [10]And hast made us unto our God kings and priests: and we* (every kindred, and tongue, and people, and nation) *shall reign on the earth.*" Amen! It is way past time to give these great black soldiers in the kingdom of God, the honor and respect they are due. I pray the Lord opens the "eyes of our understanding" also I pray that the racist scales upon eyes fall; and that we clearly see and acknowledge the tremendous contribution our dear black saints have made to the kingdom of God. Oh Lord, let us come together as one people, let us rejoice in God's diversity rather than hide pretending not to see. Open the eyes of our heart Lord, and let us rise and leave behind the petty prejudices of yesteryear, and welcome with arms wide open to all the body of Christ. Let there be true unity and communion between all of God's great family of believers and thereby giving the unbelieving world a picture of the true love of God. Let's make a point to reach out and prove that our God is truly the only wise God our savior; and that we show his love to everyone we meet. Once that happens we prove his love.

Racism & Loving One Another
Chapter 6

Dear reader, I know that you would want to have and be all that God has for you. Of all of the things that the world has puts us through and what our family has passed down to us, through genetics you and I want and need to be free from any chain or bondage. We don't want the racisms of our mothers and fathers to pass to us. It dies with our generation! So as we approach the Word of God regarding the subject of racism, we want to see the heart of God. If you have an ear to hear what God is saying, then lay your head upon the breast of Jesus and as you see His heart, let it become bone of your bone and flesh of your flesh. Dear Father in heaven, let your Spirit of revelation be upon these words and let your overshadowing glory rest upon every reader as they hear your Word and heart regarding this subject.

Thus far, we have taught on how God despises racism, how we are all of God's offspring, the different black people in Scripture, and the "curse of Ham". We learned there was no "curse of Ham". The curse was on Canaan. Canaan was the one who did the evil deed to Noah. Ham did not do it. Canaan molested his grandfather and the curse was brought upon the Canaanites. Now Ham is the father of the black races, but not all Canaanites were black. Cush, Mizraim, and Phut (the other three sons of Ham) relate to Egypt, Ethiopia, and all of the other black nations in Africa. Their civilizations were some of the greatest civilizations the world has ever known. Most of the inventions of the world came out of the early black civilizations. All you have to do is look at the pyramids. Some people believe that those pyramids pointed to the Messiah coming. The civilization that came out of Egypt was awesome. Creation began in that area. Adam was not white or black. Adam was created in the image of God and his name means "red or ruddy."

We learned Ham is the father of all Black nations. Shem is the father of the Semitic races (Israel, Arabs, etc), and Japheth is the father of all White races that spread. Was Ham himself black? I don't think so. Since Noah wasn't black, it is logical that Ham, Shem, or Japheth wasn't black. But these three sons are pictures or types of what would ultimately come. Ultimately as the descendents of Ham, Shem, and Japheth traveled throughout the earth to different places, their skin color changed over hundreds and thousands of years. But the sad thing is, the thing that is so treacherous and horrid, is that white people and even Jewish people have taken the so-called "curse of Ham" and have used it to enslave black people for centuries. So much so, they indoctrinated black clergy men to even believe this and they taught the slaves on plantations that they were called by God to be a *"servant of servants"* so just rejoice and pick cotton. Hundreds of years of slavery was built upon a lie. If you read almost every commentator, you have to be careful, because there is subtle racism hidden in much of what they say when it comes to the subjects where black people are concerned. They try to tell you that Egypt had one white people section at the upper part of Egypt and a black section at the lower part of Egypt. This is not so. Egypt was a black nation period. Something in us does not want us to rejoice in the inventions that black people have brought to the earth. We love to glory in German scientists and other Caucasian races, but if you want to get right down to it, science began in the black community. This is the truth. In researching for this book, I read every Black theologians book too on purpose and I saw the same kind of racism that the whites use. Jesus is not black because it says in Revelation 1:14-15 that His hair is white as wool and His feet burned like bronze. This is describing Jesus in the glory of God. What people fail to understand is that when we got saved we became a new creation or a new species. Get this in your head. There is neither Jew nor Greek, bond nor free, black nor white, male or female, because as Christians, we are not of this world. Our Kingdom is the Kingdom of God and God is no respecter of persons. He is putting an end to these lies. It has to happen!

Even in today's generation, one very prominent evangelical minister has clearly stated he taught this curse of Ham and segregated theology up until the 1960's. We even find this in other religions such as with the Mormons. Fifteen years ago, a black person could not join the Mormon Church because of the curse of Ham. Ham was never cursed, though, Canaan was. The Canaanites were the enemies of Israel and they have been the enemies of God since the beginning. So the curse was upon the Canaanites. As history unfolds, we see that all of the tribes of Canaan ended up being very immoral and grossly sexually perverted. So God said He didn't want Israel having anything to do with these tribes. He told Israel they couldn't marry people from these tribes. It had nothing to do race, but it had everything to do with the condition of their hearts.

In this chapter, I want to go to a couple of places in Scripture, many of them you may know. In all of our hearts there is still, I believe, some semblance of racism that lives there (be it black, white, or whoever). I believe that as the Word of God comes forth, we can be delivered! I believe that as the Word of God is revealed and enters your heart, you can be free.

As I quote certain passages of Scripture, let the Word wash over you. John 7:24 says *"Judge not according to the appearance, but judge righteous judgment."* This means we are not to judge based on the way things look with our natural eyes. If we are going to be like Jesus we need to do what I Samuel 16:7 says *"But the LORD said unto Samuel, Look not on his countenance, or on the height of his stature; because I have refused him: for the LORD seeth not as man seeth; for man looketh on the outward appearance, but the LORD looketh* on the heart." I love what Martin Luther King said once, "*I have a dream that my four little children will one day live in a nation where they will not be judged by the color of their skin, but by the content of their character.*" It is not a matter of what you are, but who you are. Even though this Scripture plainly tells us not to judge by the outward appearance, how many of us still judge according to the appearance everyday? For example, if we meet somebody, we make a judgment immediately. I'll never forget about a situation in my church many years ago. There was a brother that I allowed once to share a Word during a service while I was absent, who had a black beard. After that there was a sister around the same time I noticed started missing a couple of meetings in a row. So I went to this sister to see if there was anything wrong and she told me she was never coming back to our church ever again. After asking her why, she asked me how I could have asked the brother with the beard to minister. I was puzzled because everyone else who was at the meeting said he shared a great word and the meeting was glorious. Well she said she couldn't take it because he was full of demons. I said with a puzzling look, "Demons? I've known this brother for 30 years. How is he full of demons?" She said, "Brother, he had a very dark and black beard". Now I know this is foolish, but it really happened. She judged this man unrighteously because he had a beard. People that are racist are very ignorant and they need to be told so. I wish black people would tell other black people and white people would tell other white people to stop doing the same thing and tell them they are acting like a fool. Especially if we are Christians, we ought not to be even listening to foolish racist remarks, beliefs, or nonsense. Our people are not those with the same skin color anymore, but are those, as Jesus said, Luke 8:21, "*And he answered and said unto them, My mother and my brethren are these which hear the word of God, and do it.*"

I John 4:11 says, "*Beloved, if God so loved us, we ought also to love one another.*" Didn't Jesus say in John 3:16, "*For God so loved the world that he gave his only begotten Son, that whosoever believeth in him should not perish, but have everlasting life.*" He didn't say, "For God so loved the white people...", nor did He say, "For God so loved the black people..." God loves everybody, all nations. He loves Russians, Haitians, Jamaicans, Asians, Blacks, Whites, Spaniards, etc. He loves the entire world! If you are going to be like Jesus, then you are going to have to love the world (not meaning the things of the world, but the peoples of the world).

Galatians 6:10 says "*As we have therefore opportunity, let us do good unto all men, especially unto them who are of the household of faith.*" We are to do good unto all men. Jesus said in John 15:12 "*This is my commandment, that ye love one another, as I have loved you.*" I John 3:16 says, "*Hereby perceive we the love of God, because he laid down his life for us: and we ought to lay down our lives for the brethren.*" Are you willing to lay down your life for others, even those of every race or color? Luke 6:32 says *"For if ye love them which love you, what thank have ye? "For sinners also love those that love them."* Just because somebody is different, it doesn't mean that anything is wrong with them. Maybe you don't understand where they are coming from. How many of us judge people just by the way they dress? This too is a subtle form of racism. The first time we meet somebody, we have to train our mind not to judge after the outward appearance. This is unrighteous.

I John 4:21 says *"And this commandment have we from him, That he who loveth God love his brother also."* I Peter 2:17 says *"Honour all men. Love the brotherhood. Fear God. Honour the king."* When it is talking about loving the brotherhood, he is speaking of the body of Christ, but he also says to honor all men, that means every one in the world. Moreover we are told to not just love all men, but honor all men as well. You or I need to learn to honor even the lowliest person on the face of the earth. I've heard of churches say they are only starting a church just for a certain segment of society. Let me ask you, would Jesus do this? I don't think so. How can others say things like this and call themselves Christians? If you start a church, everybody should be welcome. I knew a friend who was on the praisers at this church who was heavy set and the leadership walked up to her and said, "We're making some changes to the praisers and limiting the number on the praisers and you are going to have to go". So she pressed it further and she found out the truth was that when the camera was on the stage, that they didn't want the "fat" woman to be seen, so the "fat" woman had to be removed, because appearance wise it didn't look good. Where do we find this in scripture? It is all about style now and not about substance. I'd rather listen to a toothless person sing with the glory than somebody singing who has shiny bright teeth with no anointing. God rarely chooses the rich and beautiful, only occasionally. Most of the time, He chooses the despised ones, the weak ones, the base ones, etc. Why does He do this? Because they know what it is like to experience being judged according to your appearance. They know what it is like to have racism attached to their life. They are not wanted because they don't measure up to somebody else's standard of what is beautiful. Beauty is in the eye of the beholder. Who are we to say who is beautiful or not. Have we forgotten the little children's song we used to sing? *"Jesus loves the little children. All the children of the world black and yellow, red and white are all precious in His sight. Jesus loves the little children of the world."* We sang it as a little kid, but as adults we don't live it.

When we got saved Romans 5:5 says *"the love of God is shed abroad in our hearts by the Holy Ghost which is given unto us."* You may say or think you don't know how to love black people or love white people because they do this differently than you, or their culture is different. We must rise above this kind of thinking.

I Thessalonians 3:12 says *"And the Lord make you to increase and abound in love one toward another, and <u>toward all men</u>, even as we do toward you"*. We are not to abound in love towards just some men, but all men.

Look with me at the early church now. Looking in Acts 6:1, *"And in those days, when the number of the disciples was multiplied, there arose a murmuring of the Grecians against the Hebrews, because their widows were neglected in the daily ministration..."* If you follow this through God goes on and chooses deacons, but what jumped out at me in this story was that the Jews were purposely not taking care of the Greeks. I wonder why. Maybe they thought Grecians weren't as good as the Hebrews. Sadly racism is in the church. What amazes me is how a man can hold onto his own personal prejudices, after he has come to Jesus. We're supposed to be changed. Where is the love of God? Racism is in the church and God wants it out. We also must be zealous for these uncomely attitudes to go, as leaders we must live the things we preach. We must set an example of how we as children of God should treat each other.

Luke 10 is the story of the Good Samaritan which starts in verse 25, *"And, behold, a certain lawyer stood up, and tempted him, saying, Master, what shall I do to inherit eternal life? [26]He said unto him, What is written in the law? how readest thou? [27]And he answering said, Thou shalt love the Lord thy God with all thy heart, and with all thy soul, and with all thy strength, and with all thy mind; and <u>thy neighbour as thyself</u>. [28]And he said unto him, Thou hast answered right: this do, and thou shalt live..."* In other words, Jesus was telling this many he didn't love his neighbor as thyself. *"[29]But he, willing to justify himself, said unto Jesus, asnd who is my neighbour?"* What a phony question this was. If Jesus told you to love your neighbor, couldn't you figure it out what that meant? The body of Christ is good at lying and is excellent at wearing masks. The body of Christ is excellent at thinking one thing and acting another. *"[30]And Jesus answering said, A certain man went down from Jerusalem to Jericho, and fell among thieves, which stripped him of his raiment, and wounded him, and departed, leaving him half dead..."* Now those of you that have never lived up north don't know what it is like in big cities. I have walked on the streets of Chicago where people were laying in the streets robbed, beaten, or obviously having much trouble, and people walk right past them. Just recently there was a story of a man beating up a woman on a bridge because she was driving too slow and he threw her over the bridge. This all happened in traffic with many witnesses and nobody did anything to help her. Nobody seems to want to get involved. Is this the heart of God? Years ago I was at the beach just worshipping and praying by myself and all of a sudden a couple passed by me screaming down on the other side of the beach, obviously having an argument. Then I saw the man begin to hit the woman. When this happens and I am present, I always ask myself, "why me?" However, I screamed at him to take his hands off that woman. And he turned around and started running towards me. I could've kept my mouth shut or made an excuse like I didn't see them, but I couldn't. Now I was thinking what I was going to do when he gets to me. I'm a Christian and I'm not allowed to hit him or fight. Luckily for me the woman ran after him and jumped on him to hold him back and they left. But he didn't hit her anymore.

We live in a society where we don't want to get involved if it might damage us. If our reputation might get affected by us being around someone who other people don't think highly of, we don't want them to know that they are our friends. There is such a lack of loyalty in the body of Christ and so little real love going on (I Corinthians 13 – the "agape" God kind of love). Love is patient, kind, and seeks not its own. The God kind of love loves in spite of, not expecting anything in return. Do you walk in love? What about those at your work you have trouble with? Proverbs 15:1 says "*A soft answer turneth away wrath: but grievous words stir up anger.*" Do you walk past an argument when somebody is being abused and not at least try to step in and bring peace? Evil will always prosper when good men and women do nothing. The easiest thing for most of us to do is to stay quiet, get a situation out of our thoughts (so we don't carry around the judgment of us failing our brother), and leave. In Luke 10, here is a man lying half-dead in the street and low and behold, look at what happens.

"*[31] And by chance there came down a certain priest that way: and when he saw him, he passed by on the other side...*" How could it be that men of God would cross the street to get away from such a needy person? It is the duty of a man of God to help and to reach out to the needy. Sadly it seems now that the charismatic church has turned into more of a business now. In many places pastors no longer pastor people, they administrate an organization. Jesus in Matthew 25:31-46 told many believers that they are to not stand with the sheep but to get over on the left side where the goats are because "*I was an hungred, and ye gave me no meat: I was thirsty, and ye gave me no drink: I was a stranger, and ye took me not in: naked, and ye clothed me not: sick, and in prison, and ye visited me not.*" (Matthew 25:41-42). Every time I am in the grocery store, if somebody doesn't have enough money, I will give it to them right on the spot. I will never forget one of the times I was away at a hotel room and one of the maids came knocking on the door to see if I needed anything. I told her I didn't need anything and she left. Immediately after she left, I had a witness to give this woman the hundred dollar bill that was in my pocket. So I went out of my room to find her. She was at the end of the hallway. I told this maid I don't know who you are, but Jesus Christ, the Son of the Living God, told me to give you this and I placed in her hand the hundred dollar bill. I didn't wait around for her to tell me how great I was and how thankful she was. I just walked immediately back and closed the door to my room. Six months later I am at a gas station that was right across the street from this hotel and as I was pumping gas, I hear this joyous shriek and turned and saw a woman wanting to speak with me. At first, I didn't recognize her and just said hello to her. She reminded me that she was the woman who was the maid at the hotel that I gave the hundred dollars to and, she added I just want you to know that I am in church and I am worshipping Jesus now. She began walking with Jesus because of a hundred dollars. How can a man of God walk by someone in need? God is watching the pastors in every city and seeing what they are doing. No pastor will be sent out under my ministry that doesn't try to know everybody in their congregation. I will not tolerate anything less. We are not building kingdoms to men. We are building people and the Kingdom of God. The Bible exhorts us in I Thessalonians 5:12 *"to know them which labour among you..."* Jesus said in John 10:14 *"I am the good shepherd, and know my sheep, and am known of mine"* and in John 10:27 *"My sheep hear my voice, and I know them, and they follow me."* As pastors, we can't stay hidden with our phone turned off. We have to meet with the people. I know it is hard and yes they will take advantage of you. But you shouldn't be in the ministry if you don't care for people or you don't want to minister to people in their time of need.

This reminds me of a story years ago. Now I love the sport of boxing and this story was during the time years ago when Sugar Ray Leonard had just started fighting. Now I lived in a house at the time by myself at the end of a street and I had a gravel driveway. Now during this particular day Sugar Ray Leonard had an important fight that was airing on TV that I really wanted to watch. So I was at home fixing myself a bowl of popcorn and pouring myself a large glass of coke getting ready to watch this fight in the comfort of my house. When I got situated with my snack and was sitting right in front of the TV ready for the fight to start I hear the sound of gravel move in my driveway. So I peek out of one of the blinds and it was this sister that went to my church. I'll call her Susie in this story. Now Susie was one of those people who always took up all of my time. She never did a thing I said, but she constantly wanted attention and to be ministered to. So as I see her pulling up to the house I became upset, but immediately had a great idea. I grabbed my popcorn and drink and hid it, turned out the lights and the TV and decided to hide. My front door had a diamond shaped window in it and I decided a great place to hide was under this window so when she looked in, she would see that nobody was in there. My rationale was Susie wasn't going to do anything I said anyway and all she was going to do was steal my time and rob me of watching this fight and I wasn't going to let her do that. So I am literally crouched under the window by my front door waiting for her to recognize nobody was there and then leaving. The doorbell rings and I am as quite as possible. She then starts banging on the door (these types of people sure are persistent) and I'm thinking just another minute now and she will leave. I'm thinking when I hear the gravel sound again, I'll get up. Maybe I will only miss the first round at the most. But as I was bent over hiding, the voice of the Lord came to me and actually said in a whisper, "Sam, what are you doing?" I said to the Lord "I'm hiding". He then said "What are you hiding from?" I said "Susie". He said "Why?" I said "You know Susie like I know Susie". And He said "Son, if you are going to be a man of God, you have to be one all the time". So I popped up my face in the glass with a big smile on my face and let her in and don't you know she stayed for exactly an hour and a half. As soon as she left I quickly flipped on the TV only to find the credits from the fight were rolling. True men of God cannot ignore the people of God. It is another form of subtle racism.

Continuing in Luke 10, "*32And likewise a Levite, when he was at the place, came and looked on him, and passed by on the other side...*" Nobody ever wants to go to the "other side" except Jesus. In Mark 5:1-15 Jesus "*came over unto the other side*" to minister to the demon possessed man in the country of the Gadarenes. Most people don't want to be around the people who really need help. But if you are a minister these are the people you want and need to be around. God wants to send you to help them, not ignore them. When real revival comes to America, the first thing He will do is shake His church. He is doing it right now actually. I have never seen such warfare in my entire life as a believer. I have been in the ministry since 1975, pastoring since 1977, and I have never seen the attack on families like what is happening right now. So as believers, we need to be coming together so much the more as we see the day of the Lord approaching in order to stay encouraged, to provoke one another to love and good works, and to comfort one another. We are not to be passing to the other side because we know there is a "Gadarene" person there. Many times did I see the elders above me in the first church I was a part of ministering only in the affluent parts of town and when there was an opportunity to minister at a black woman's house in the ghetto (as an example), they would send me instead. I gladly went and those elders in the church (who really shouldn't have been elders in my opinion) never went. This was nothing other than subtle racism on their part. Jesus said in Matthew 25:40 "*Inasmuch as ye have done it unto one of the least of these my brethren, ye have done it unto me.*" Do you have a problem with the "*least of these*"?

But look who goes to help the wounded man in Luke 10, a Samaritan. "*33But a certain Samaritan, as he journeyed, came where he was: and when he saw him, he had compassion on him, 34And went to him, and bound up his wounds, pouring in oil and wine, and set him on his own beast, and brought him to an inn, and took care of him...*" Samaritans were half-breeds and were looked down upon in Israel at the time. It seems like the only people God can get to go and help His people are those who themselves have suffered under the hands of racism, or suffered under the hands of bad leadership.

85

Have you ever thought when you met people how their life made them what they are? For example, so many people when you meet them can be very offensive and rude and instead of being mean back to them try to understand that what they are really doing is a mechanism to protect their insecurities. They try to keep people out because they don't want anybody getting close. Fellowship exposes sin. People that don't like to fellowship are hiding something. This is a fact. Secondly, people that have a spirit of rejection carry that thing with them and when they get around people, the people feel it and start feeling and acting funny because of it and it only confirms the rejection that the person is carrying around. You and I have got to be bigger than pettiness. We should desire to be men and women of substance that sees beyond where a person is at and instead of "seeing them clearly" as the blind man said, but we see them as "men as trees walking" (Mark 8:22-25). We see them as God wants them to be. When I sit and listen to people tell me their stories, I take note at what they are saying because I realize that people are who they are because of their environment, their parents, the authority figures in their life, the things that happened to them along their journey, and lastly the things they've inherited through no fault of their own from their parents. I have seen the hand of God take people who were unruly, unkind, and rebellious, and after they allowed Jesus to give them some inner healing, they became precious, sweet, and wonderful people. If you would have known me before I got saved, I promise you, you would have thought of me as a criminal, a person, full of rebellion with no hope. I used to sit on the floor in my high school in the hallways with my ankles crossed, smoking a cigarette in front of everybody daring somebody to say something to me. One time a teacher tried to come by and tell me to stop, but all that happened is I said a lot of terrible things to her and then flicked my cigarette at her when she walked away. That was pretty bad. But look at how sweet I am now! You see hidden behind all of my rebellion was a young boy who never saw anybody in authority being kind and caring. Nobody ever put their hand on my shoulder and said I love you to me. My father never said one kind word to me in all of my life. My mother was weak and couldn't leave my abusive father. So I hated all authority and let them know it. But the day I got saved, I was instantly changed. The truth was all that time I wanted to be under somebody with true godly authority and I believe most people are like that but if you would have met me you would have looked at me and said there was no hope for me. But I declare to you there is hope for all of those around you. There is hope for your children when they are acting weird and rebellious. I'm telling you, if you could've seen me you would have said there was no way anything good would have come out of my life. One instance comes to my mind. I called my high school years after I graduated to get my transcripts to attend college and the secretary of my high school answered and when she recognized my voice she said "Mad Dog! How are you doing?" That's the name I was called in high school. Then I got to witness to her and told her I was Mad Dog no more and that I was a Jesus freak now. Wow! Was she surprised? People are just waiting for some kindness, some tenderness, someone to show them unconditional love. I know that in my heart, even though I pretended to be cool and rebellious, inside I was screaming for guidance and love.

Next, let us look at Luke 7, starting in verse 36, "*And one of the Pharisees desired him that he would eat with him. And he went into the Pharisee's house, and sat down to meat. [37]And, behold, a woman in the city, which was a sinner, when she knew that Jesus sat at meat in the Pharisee's house, brought an alabaster box of ointment, [38]And stood at his feet behind him weeping, and began to wash his feet with tears, and did wipe them with the hairs of her head, and kissed his feet, and anointed them with the ointment. [39]Now when the Pharisee which had bidden him saw it, he spake within himself...*" Before I continue, let me say that racists always secretly think things but they never say it. It was like when we saw Moses married an Ethiopian woman and Miriam and Aaron were furious about it and rather than say they were furious about Moses marrying a black woman they said to Moses "*Hath the Lord indeed spoken only by Moses? Hath he not spoken also by us?*" Racists will never tell you what the real problem is. They will use an excuse to hide their racism. God so hated what Miriam and Aaron did, He turned Miriam's skin leprous. If you have ever judged inter-racial marriages, you need to read this story in Numbers 12. Be very careful because the Lord does not like it and you might turn out like Miriam.

So this Pharisee "*spake within himself saying, This man, if he were a prophet, would have known who and what manner of woman this is that toucheth him: for she is a sinner.*" This Pharisee was upset this harlot was in the house because she wasn't invited. This was a Pharisee's house and she was a known sinner by everybody. But she had the guts to push her way through because she heard that Jesus was there!

Years ago I worked as a cook at a restaurant at the beach and I worked the graveyard shift when all the bars would close and all of the bad people would come in to eat. I wore a shirt that people could read on my back as I was cooking that said "Smile, Jesus love you". Well, one of the guys that was a waiter there was gay and very flamboyant. It was during the Elton John days where people wore platform shoes and the big glasses and he dressed and acted like this. Well he heard me witnessing to some people and he said to me "tell me about your church". And I said, "Oh, it's a place you would never want to go. We worship Jesus freely and dance, shout, and speak in tongues". I said this to him thinking it was going to get him away from me. To my surprise he says, "Hey, I would like to see that and go...when is your next meeting?" I said, "Friday night". He said, "Can I come?" I said, "I can give you directions". He said, "No, you can take me there. I would like to go with you".

I said begrudgingly, "I guess". So on Friday night, he walks into church right next to me with his platform shoes, his shirt unbuttoned half way revealing his chest hairs, a couple of medallions hanging, and his big and gaudy Elton John glasses. I'm telling you, I didn't want to be seen with him. I would have never invited him to church. So the meeting starts and we start clapping during the first praise song. Even the way he was clapping was bothering me and all the while I was thinking I have lost my reputation and people are going to think weird things about me. Well during the meeting the pastor gets up and says "I think there are people here tonight those needs to get saved. Who here wants to give their life to Jesus?" The first hand that went up was my gay co-worker. The pastor immediately said, "Sam, did you bring him here tonight?" I said softly, "Yes". He said, "Alright, bring him on up here". I would have never thought it, but he radically got saved and filled with the Holy Ghost on his knees that night. The very ones you think there is no chance or hope for are the very one crying out. This Pharisee was thinking within himself in Luke 7 who is this sinner!? The answer is every one of them, including him. We are all saved by the grace of God.

But Jesus always stands with the accused. Jesus always stands with the people who nobody else wants. If the whole world hates you, Jesus will love you. If Christians won't even stand with you because they are afraid their reputation is going to be damaged, Jesus will. As a Pastor, I am not afraid to minister to people who have blown it and who have made mistakes. I'll receive them because I believe that is exactly what Jesus would do. Also, I have made far too many mistakes myself to judge any other man.

What is in your heart today? Do you ever think badly sometimes when you get on an elevator with somebody who is different than you? Do you feel awkward to sit down in a restaurant when you are surrounded by people of a different race? If there is only one seat left in a movie theater and it is between two people with another skin color, do you try to find another seat or do you boldly go where no man has gone before? Revelation 5:9 says *"And they sung a new song, saying, Thou art worthy to take the book, and to open the seals thereof: for thou wast slain, and hast redeemed us to God by thy blood out of every kindred, and tongue, and people, and nation."* We all come from the same Father. Acts 17:26 says the same thing, *"And hath made of one blood all nations of men for to dwell on all the face of the earth, and hath determined the times before appointed, and the bounds of their habitation"*

We may act or feel fearful in situations with another race but the Bible says in I John 4:18, *"There is no fear in love; but perfect love casteth out fear..."* Some people have never been around people of another race much in their life. Many black people have never known a white person intimately and vice versa. As a white boy, I grew up in an all black environment. I know now that God purposely did this in my life so I could understand black people. I can boldly declare that I do not have one racist bone in my body. I truly believe my culture is the Kingdom of God. Psalms 45:10-11 boldly challenges us *"Hearken, O daughter, and consider, and incline thine ear; <u>forget also thine own people</u>, and thy father's house. So shall the king greatly desire thy beauty: for he is thy Lord; and worship thou him."* Jesus said, *"My Kingdom is not of this world"* (John 18:36). As Christians, we are like Jesus and are in God's Kingdom now which is not of this world. We are a new creation or a new species, created in Christ Jesus. Ephesians 2:19 says *"Now therefore ye are no more strangers and foreigners, but fellowcitizens with the saints, and of the household of God."* Black, white, yellow, brown, and red people are all one now. The world will never be won until they see this.

I'm begging every reader to see other people with the eyes of God. Never unrighteously judge according to the outward appearance again. The people who are different deserve a chance. Don't believe anymore that all black people are violent or lazy. My father said this to me every night but I had to go with my mom once a month to pick up our government cheese and powdered milk, we were the ones on welfare. Racism is ignorant, irrational, and foolishness, and is based upon fear and hatred. But today, the God that created us all out of one blood will touch your heart if you let Him. Lift you heart unto the Lord as I pray.

"Father, root out all hatred and racial prejudices in our lives. I know it is a process, but begin the work today as we make this confession to you. If you have faith to do it, repeat this words: Dear Jesus, I ask you to forgive me right now for being unkind to a person of another color, to anyone that didn't fit my so called standards. I ask you for forgiveness and I ask you to wipe that stuff out of the chambers of my heart. And if I have inherited something from my ancestors, I ask you to break the power of that curse today. If I have learned information in my head that I learned from my parents as a child that is not of you, please remove it from me. I want to love like you Jesus. I want to love like the Good Samaritan. No longer will I judge people by their appearance. No longer will I judge people by their reputation. I yield my heart to you and I ask you to once again let the love of God be shed abroad in my heart by the Holy Ghost"

Begin to pray in the spirit now and let out of your belly flow rivers of living and healing water. Father, drive out all uncleanness, all racism, all thinking of superiority. Drive out everything in us of pride and arrogance, and fill us Lord with Your Spirit. Give us that meek and lowly spirit and attitude in Jesus' name.

Jesus gives us a new commandment in John 13:34-35, "*A new commandment I give unto you, That ye love one another; as I have loved you, that ye also love one another. <u>By this</u> shall all men know that ye are my disciples, <u>if ye have love one to another</u>.*"

Where Do We Come From?
Chapter 7

In this chapter I would like to talk about where mankind came from and the original color of man. So let us begin at the beginning in Genesis 1:1, "*In the beginning God created the heaven and the earth.*" We see a similar passage to this in John 1:1, "*In the beginning was the Word, and the Word was with God, and the Word was God.*" Jesus in Revelation 1:8 says, "*I am Alpha and Omega, the beginning and the ending...*" We want to keep in mind that before there was anything, there was God, God the Father, Son, & Holy Ghost living in their great triune nature. The word "beginning" does not refer to the beginning of God, but to the origin of the recorded history of universe. The reference is to the time when there was nothing created, no universe, nothing except God Himself. Before there was anything created or conceived, there was God all alone existing in the tri-unity

In Revelation 13:8, it reads that Jesus was the "*Lamb slain from the foundation of the world.*" In Psalms 102:25 it says, "*Of old hast thou laid the foundation of the earth: and the heavens are the work of thy hands.*" In Jesus' great prayer He spoke about being given again the glory that He had with the Father before the world began (John 17:24). Zechariah 12:1 reads, "*The burden of the word of the LORD for Israel, saith the LORD, which stretcheth forth the heavens, and layeth the foundation of the earth, and formeth the spirit of man within him.*" God is the original cause. He is the first cause period. Isaiah 48:12-13 says, "*Hearken unto me, O Jacob and Israel, my called; I am he; I am the first, I also am the last. [13]Mine hand also hath laid the foundation of the earth, and my right hand hath spanned the heavens: when I call unto them, they stand up together.*" There He is again, the Creator, our great God. Ephesians 1:4 says, "*According as he hath chosen us in him before the foundation of the world, that we should be holy and without blame before him in love.*" So we see several things from the above passages of Scriptures. First, Jesus was the Lamb slain before the foundation of the earth. Second, we were chosen in Him before the foundation of the earth. Then before God did anything, He and the triune God (God Head) decided that they were going to create the world and the heavens as we look back at Genesis 1:1-2.

"*[1]In the beginning God created the heaven and the earth. [2]And the earth was without form, and void; and darkness was upon the face of the deep. And the Spirit of God moved upon the face of the waters.*" Now just very quickly I want to say that between Genesis 1:1 and Genesis 1:2, I believe firmly that there was a catastrophe that took place because everyone of the words after Genesis 1:1 and is used for create really means "re-create". Man was told to in Genesis 1:28 to "*replenish the earth*". So between Genesis 1:1 and Genesis

91

1:2, we find a great catastrophic event had occurred which was the overthrow of Lucifer and him being cast out of heaven (found in Isaiah 14 and Ezekiel 28). In Ezekiel 28:13 is says of Lucifer, *"Thou hast been in Eden the garden of God..."* There are three gardens in Scriptures. The first is the garden of God that is in the third heaven (paradise). Next, there is the garden of God in the original earth. And then there is the garden of God in our hearts.

In Isaiah 14:12-14 we see why Lucifer fell: *"[12]How art thou fallen from heaven, O Lucifer, son of the morning! how art thou cut down to the ground, which didst weaken the nations! [13]For thou hast said in thine heart, I will ascend into heaven, I will exalt my throne above the stars of God: I will sit also upon the mount of the congregation, in the sides of the north: [14]I will ascend above the heights of the clouds; I will be like the most High..."* Lucifer thought he was beautiful and the revolt happened and we know that at least a third of the angelic host went with him. This says to us that we can be in the glory and still be deceived, even one such as Lucifer who was the *"anointed cherub that covereth"* (Ezekiel 28:14). So when Lucifer's overthrow happened, God destroyed the then-known earth which at that time was a holding place. Satan had control over the earth.

Lucifer, as the son of the morning, was the next closest thing to God and when he revolted and God judged him and threw him out of the third heaven (that is why he dwells now in the second heaven with those angels that went with him which is the kingdom of darkness – *"principalities...powers...rulers of the darkness of this world...spiritual wickedness in high places"* (Ephesians 6:12)). But at that time there was an earth and Ezekiel 28:16-19 talks about the *"multitude of thy merchandise"* and the *"iniquity of thy traffick"* all talking about Lucifer. In other words trade was going on. Who lived before Genesis 1:2, we really don't know. But this can answer clearly for us where dinosaurs came from. I have no problem agreeing with scientists who say the earth is millions of years old because we don't know the time period between verses 1 and 2 of Genesis 1. To try to say the earth is only 7,000 years old is perhaps not correct. So God cast out Lucifer and destroyed the earth and everything on it (dinosaurs, unicorns even, and all of the things found hidden deep within the earth found by scientists). The earth perished not only in Noah's flood, but in this catastrophic event.

We have further Scriptural evidence of this event between verses 1 and 2 because God doesn't create anything void and without form. Jeremiah 4:23-27 clearly shows this, *"[23]I beheld the earth, and, lo, it was without form, and void; and the heavens, and they had no light. [24]I beheld the mountains, and, lo, they trembled, and all the hills moved lightly. [25]I beheld, and, lo, there was no man, and all the birds of the heavens were fled. [26]I beheld, and, lo, the fruitful place was a wilderness, and all the cities thereof were broken down at the presence of* the LORD, and by his fierce anger. [27] For thus hath the LORD said, The whole land shall be desolate; yet will I not make a full end." Isaiah 45:18 says "For thus saith the LORD that created the heavens; God himself that formed the earth and made it; he hath established it, he created it not in vain, he formed it to be inhabited: I am the LORD; and there is none else." The literal translation of this verse reads, "For thus saith the Lord that created the heavens, God Himself that formed the earth and made it, he hath established it, He created it not a chaos or waste, he formed it to be inhabited." So the first creation is Genesis 1:1 and the re-creation begins from Genesis 1:2 on. So between these two verses could be millions of years. We just don't know.

But in the beginning, before the foundation of the world, God had already planned and ordained the Lamb of God slain and that we were chosen in Him that we should be holy and without blame before Him in love. God is sovereign and in complete control of the universe. Everything has already been planned and will proceed as He sees fit. Nothing is going to happen without His knowledge. Satan is a tool in the hand of God. God uses him. There is no greater king than the Lord Himself. Matthew 25:34 says, "Then shall the King say unto them on his right hand, Come, ye blessed of my Father, inherit the kingdom prepared for you from the foundation of the world." Every one of us was already in God. He knows the end from the beginning (He is the Alpha and the Omega, the beginning and the end). So God in His great all-knowing (omniscient) wisdom decided to create beings that He could fellowship with. He first started with, as Job 38:6-7 calls them, the morning stars. Most scholars believe this is talking about the angelic host. In the Job chapter 1, God asks Satan "Whence comest thou?" (Job 1:6-7). And Satan answers and says, "From going to and fro in the earth, and from walking up and down in it". The first earth was destroyed after Lucifer was cast out of the third heaven. He now lives in the second heaven. We also see him as the serpent in the second garden in Genesis 3. The first garden was made of stones and was full of jewels and beauty. This was the garden of God, the Eden in the third heaven. This second garden of God, the Eden in Genesis 3, was a mineral garden with plants, trees, etc. There is a difference between these two, but when we are talking about races and genealogies and cultures, we need to understand that all of us were already in the mind of God millions of years ago. So God decided to do this thing called creation knowing full well everything that would happen, for Jesus was the lamb slain before the foundation of the world. Also, God had in His heart a people. This entire exercise of creation and world history is for the sole purpose for God to get what He originally wanted, somebody to fellowship with. It is this simple. Think about it. God has everything, knows everything, has all power, etc, and it might get lonely. I don't think God is lonely as we get, but His nature and heart is so precious that He wanted to share all that He has and is. God knows everything and He created everything. And all of this was already in His heart before the foundation of the earth.

But Lucifer saw that he was beautiful and rebelled leading to the rebellion of a third of the angelic host. Then even when God created the earth, Adam and Eve both reject Him. Then you find the children of Israel, His chosen people, rejecting Him. You also find even after the resurrection of Jesus after He appeared to over 500 people and tells them to meet Him in Jerusalem on the day of Pentecost, we see only 120 showed up. It is an amazing thing that God is the most rejected being ever in history of the universe.

Let us now look at the creation of man and the first man. There are many theories about Adam and I believe this, that Adam was a figure himself, but also represented all of mankind. In other words, Adam's name is the same Hebrew word for "man". So mankind is found in Adam. Beginning in Genesis 1:26-27, "*²⁶And God said, Let us* (here is the triune God – "Elohim", I John 5:7) *make man in our image, after our likeness: and let them have dominion over the fish of the sea, and over the fowl of the air, and over the cattle, and over all the earth, and over every creeping thing that creepeth upon the earth. ²⁷So God created man in his own image, in the image of God created he him; male and female created he them.*" There are a lot of things I want to share related to this creation of man. First of all, Eve was in Adam. God later caused a deep sleep to come upon Adam and the Bible says in Genesis 2:21 that He "*took one of his ribs*" to form Eve, but this actually means "alter ego". God took the female characteristics out of the man and made a woman. This says to us that God Himself has both male and female characteristics. We know this is true because one of God's covenant names is "El Shaddai" which means "the breasty one, all sufficient, all powerful one". This is the motherly aspect of the divine nature. So in God are both male and female dimensions. We are created in the image of God; therefore, we would have the same thing. This is what the beauty of marriage is (naturally and spiritually). Eve came out of Adam just like the bride of Christ is going to come out of body of Christ. Paul calls this a mystery (Ephesians 5:31-32). When a man and a woman come together, they form a unity that was found in the original man (if they can walk in this unity).

Some other translations of Genesis 1:26-27 read, "*Then God said, Let us make human beings in our image, to be like ourselves.*" This brings out the Adam represents all human beings. Other translations read, "*God spoke, Let us make human beings in our image, make them reflecting our nature*", "*God created them human beings, He created them god-like*". Many have a problem with this saying, "*god-like*", but it is true. Adam was given dominion. He was the god of the earth. Our whole redemption is a returning to this, returning to paradise. We lost paradise because every one of us was in Adam (we would have done the same thing). It says of the remnant in Joel 2:3 that it is like the garden of Eden before them. This means that the remnant will have entered into paradise and wherever they go, they bring that with them. One last translation reads, "...*and now we will make human beings; they will be like us and resemble us.*"

Next, we need to understand a couple of important words. God created man in His image. The word "image" in Hebrew means "to shade, resemblance, a figure, something cut out, representation". The word image in Greek (this is important because of passages like Romans 8:29, "*For whom he did foreknow, he also did predestinate to be conformed to the image of his Son...*") means "a likeness, a profile". In other words, we were created in the image of God and means we were created to represent and resemble and be a figure of God in the earth.

The word "likeness" in Hebrew means "resemblance, model, shape, like as, a form or a pattern, to be like or act like". God created man in His own image and likeness. This means that we are the model of God, and that we are to be like and act like God. This is how the original man was created. David says in Psalms 17:15, "*As for me, I will behold thy face in righteousness: I shall be satisfied, when I awake, with thy likeness.*" You see "the likeness of God", when Adam fell, was taken from man. Man became a fallen being and he lost that likeness and image because he chose the tree of the knowledge of good and evil over the tree of life. The tree of life is Jesus and is all that is God. Adam knew what to do. Eve didn't and Adam did not stop her. Wouldn't you think it unusual for a serpent to talk? Adam didn't and he allowed the serpent to keep talking to Eve. This tells me Adam was part of it and must have been conversing with the serpent already. Adam was already beginning to move in a bad direction and allowed Eve to fall because secretly he wanted to taste of the tree of the knowledge of good and evil himself. And so when they chose this, God comes and says "Where are you Adam?" God wanted to know where Adam was because Adam was created to resemble, be like, act like, and be the image of God on the earth. And now God finds Adam hiding himself from the presence of God, where once Adam lived in the presence of God. At this point, Adam becomes a fallen being, but in the beginning we were created just like God. Now God is a spirit (John 4:24) and how do you resemble a spirit? Now these things may be beyond our understanding now, but let me say God is a triune being (Father, Son, and Holy Ghost) and we are a triune being as well (spirit, soul, and body – Hebrews 4:12, I Thessalonians 5:23). Our spirit, soul, and body correspond to the Father, Son, and Holy Ghost.

Next, let us look at the word for man. The word for "man" in Hebrew is the same word for "Adam". The Hebrew word is pronounced *Aw-dawm*' and it means "to be ruddy, a human being, an individual, species, mankind". This word ruddy means having a fresh health, red color, or reddish. This Hebrew word for "man" or "Adam" comes from a root word pronounced *Aw-dam*' and it means "to show blood in the face, to flush or blush, or turn rosy, be red". So who is this man? Well if people are going to fight and argue about what color Adam was, we can clearly say whoever he was, he was ruddy, red, or reddish. We know that the ability to see him blush had to be present. His countenance was one who had an ability to blush and be red. He certainly wasn't white, nor was he black.

Something else to note is man was created on the sixth day (Genesis 1:31). Man was created on the sixth day and interestingly enough so was the serpent. Six is the number of man and Satan. 666 is the number of the anti-Christ. Many say this will be one man. But it may be something else as well. Six is man, six is Satan, and the third six is like taking it to its zenith, so 666 simply means the fullness of Satan in the fullness of man. This is anti-Christ and is a spirit. John said in I John 2:18 that *"even now are there many antichrists"*. So once man fell, where at once he lived in paradise and walked with God in the cool of the day, now he had a fallen nature, had listened to Satan, and in the chamber of his soul (which was no longer pure) he begins to live by the knowledge of good and evil. From this point on, man has digressed to where now (thousands of years later in the recreated earth), we find it almost like Genesis 11 where is says, *"Behold, the people is one...and now nothing is restrained from them, which they have imagined to do"*. There is nothing sacred anymore. I was turning the channel on my television the other day and two men were kissing and I couldn't believe it. I grew up watching "Leave It To Beaver", "The Donna Reed Show" and "Father Knows Best" and none of that stuff happened on those shows. But things aren't a shock to me as much anymore because I have been a pastor since 1977 and have ministered to every kind of fowl thing you can imagine (unspeakable things – things that are very dark and things that nobody see go on, but they do in many people's lives). It is unspeakable what goes on in the world now. Whatever is in the imagination of men's hearts is being done right now because we are reaching the time of fullness. Satan has been loosed and there are more demons in this earth than ever before. But wait until the manchild is caught up and kicks Satan out of the second heaven (Revelation 12) Satan comes down to the earth. Woe to the earth then! But just as evil is coming to fullness, God is bringing a people into the fullness of righteousness who will have paradise again and walk free from sin. So you, where does racism begin? It begins when you look at someone and categorize them according to the color of their skin. This is knowledge. When you are living from the tree of life, all you see is the heart of the person. Racism comes out of the fallen nature of man. We see in another chapter that racism is actually an evil spirit that causes people to be racist.

Let us next read Genesis 2:7, *"And the LORD God formed man of the dust of the ground, and breathed into his nostrils the breath of life; and man became a living soul."* Let me try to explain this. Man is three-fold (just like God). The word "formed" means "molded". God molded man out of dust and then breathed into this clay form. God breathed into man, his spirit. And when the spirit entered this clay figure, man became a living soul. This is important. When someone dies, their soul and body dies and their spirit does not. Their spirit is eternal. While a person is alive, their spirit and body are constantly fighting with the soul to have precedence. The body without the spirit is dead. The soul is the connecting thing between the spirit and the body. This is why we experience a wrestling match between our spirit and our flesh. Galatians 5:16-17 says *"Walk in the Spirit, and ye shall not fulfil the lust of the flesh. For the flesh lusteth against the Spirit, and the Spirit against the flesh: and these are contrary the one to the other..."* Matthew 26:41 reads *"the spirit indeed is willing, but the flesh is weak."* So the whole battle in the fallen man is taking place in the soul. Once God breathed the breath of life, the living essence, into mankind, and once it flowed into that clay figure, a soul came forth. This soul is the only thing man owns. Our body and our spirit belong to God. I Corinthians 6:19-20 says, *"What? know ye not that your body is the temple of the Holy Ghost which is in you, which ye have of God, and ye are not your own? [20]For ye are bought with a price: therefore glorify God in your body, and in your spirit, which are God's."* The only thing we really own is our soul which is made up of our mind, emotions, affections, thoughts, imaginations, desires, intellect, etc. This is why so many people are depressed and tormented because their soul is the place of warfare. Our spirit, once we are born again is made perfect just like Jesus when He walked the earth. He was the Son of God, but He was also the son of man, meaning He had a human soul and body, but his spirit was all God.

As Christians, we now have the Spirit of God living in us. God's Spirit and our spirit become one. I Corinthians 6:17 says *"But he that is joined unto the Lord is one spirit."* And out of our spirit man now comes forth the river of God. John 7:38 says *"He that believeth on me, as the scripture hath said, out of his belly shall flow rivers of living water."* Belly here represents our spirit. Psalms 46:4-5 says *"There is a river, the streams whereof shall make glad the city of God, the holy place of the tabernacles of the most High. [5]God is in the midst of her..."* Revelation 22:1 says *"And he shewed me a pure river of water of life, clear as crystal, proceeding out of the throne of God and of the Lamb."* Inside of everyone of us is a pure river that is flowing if we activate it. Well, how do we activate God's river? Job 32:18-20 says *"[18]For I am full of matter* (Hebrew – words), *the spirit within me constraineth me. [19]Behold, my belly* (again, this is our spirit) *is as wine which hath no vent; it is ready to burst like new bottles. [20]I will speak, that I may be refreshed: I will open my lips and answer."* This is why the baptism of the Holy Ghost and speaking in tongues is so important. The only way to release the spirit of God or the river of God within you is by praying in tongues. You cannot worship God in the Spirit if you don't pray or sing in the Holy Ghost. As you and I begin to speak in our heavenly language, the river of God begins to churn and begins to rise up and flow out of us and as it does, it flows over our soulish man with all those chambers in it (that have been messed up by life, familial genetics, experiences, etc). The key for us then is to learn to be led by our spirit. Romans 8:14 says *"For as many as are led by the Spirit of God, they are the sons of God."* The Spirit of God lives in our human spirit. Jesus doesn't come down to you, He wants to come out of you. Out of us flows the river of God! And I say this to my precious Baptist and denominational brothers and sisters who refuse the baptism in the Holy Ghost: The baptism of the Holy Ghost is not an option God gives us. Jesus died not only for us to be saved, but in order that we might receive the promise of the Spirit through faith. Jesus died for us to make us ready to be filled with the Holy Ghost! Galatians 3:13-14 clearly reveals this to us, *"[13]Christ hath redeemed us from the curse of the law, being made a curse for us: for it is written, Cursed is every one that hangeth on a tree: [14]That the blessing of Abraham might come on the Gentiles through Jesus Christ; that we might receive the promise of the Spirit through faith."* The blessing of Abraham is righteousness by faith. Galatians 3:6 says *"Abraham believed God, and it was accounted to him for righteousness."* So the blessing of Abraham is our born again salvation experience. So Jesus died in order that we might receive the blessing of Abraham, and (as we keep reading verse 14) *"that* (or *in order that*) *we might receive the promise of the Spirit through faith"*. Well, Acts 2 clearly defines that the promise of the Spirit as the baptism of the Holy Ghost. Peter said in Acts 2:39, *"For the promise is unto you, and to your children, and to all that are afar off, even as many as the Lord our God shall call."* So the day of Pentecost, when the Holy Ghost fell, is unto us, our children and to as many as the Lord our God shall call! Jesus died not only to deliver us from the curse of the law and save us from an eternal damnation, but He did it in order to prepare us to receive the baptism of the Holy Spirit which fills you with the river of God.

But looking back at the creation of man in Genesis 2:7, let us look at some other translations which will help us understand something about Adam's color better. *"And God formed man of the soil of the ground..."* Now what does soil look like? It definitely isn't white. Another translation reads, *"God formed man out of dirt from the ground and blew into his nostrils the breath of life. The man became alive, a living soul."* Another one reads, *"Lord God formed man of the slime of the earth and breathed into his face the breath of life and man became a living being."* So whoever Adam/man was (ruddy, to blush, reddish in color), he was made and formed by the dust, dirt, soil, and slime or the ground. Now reader, people can say anything they want, but the original man was not a white man. I don't even believe he was a black man. He was somewhere in between.

The word "formed" in Hebrew means "to press or squeeze into shape, to mold into form like a potter, to fashion, form, frame, or make purpose". In

Genesis 2:6, it says there was a mist that watered the whole face of the ground. This wasn't rain. It was just a mist that made the ground a clay-like substance out of which God molded or formed man. When God formed man in the beginning and man fell, what do you think God is doing right now to us? We are being conformed to the image of Christ Jesus who is the second Adam! Paul says in Galatians 4:19 *"My little children, of whom I travail in birth again until Christ be formed in you"*. Romans 8:29 says *"For whom he did foreknow, he also did predestinate to be conformed to the image of his Son..."* II Corinthians 3:18 says, *"But we all, with open face beholding as in a glass the glory of the Lord, are <u>changed into the same image</u> from glory to glory, even as by the Spirit of the Lord."* So God is now re-forming (not man's body), but his soul! Our soul is the place that needs to bear the image of God again. This is where man fell in the first place by eating of the tree of the knowledge of good and evil.

The word "dust" in the Hebrew is *"ophar"* which means "dust as powdered or gray, clay, earth, mud, ashes". It comes from a root word, *"aphar"*, which means "to be gray, to pulverize into powder". Now I am trying to form a picture in all of us of this man. Let us look at I Corinthians 15:47-49 which is important to this subject, *"[47]The first man is of the earth, earthy: the second man is the Lord from heaven. [48]As is the earthy, such are they also that are earthy: and as is the heavenly, such are they also that are heavenly. [49]And as we have borne the image of the earthy, we shall also bear the image of the heavenly."* This means simply that mankind originally was made in the image of God. I believe he was a glorious being. Adam was in glory.

The next word I want to look at is "ground". In Hebrew it is the word *"adamah"* which means "soil, earthy, land" and comes from a root word *"adam"* which means "to show blood in the face, flush, blush, or turn rosy, red, ruddy". This was the same root word translated "man" or "Adam".

So what do all of these definitions mean for us? I get out of all of the definitions above that the original man must have been a reddish gray color. If this is accurate, he couldn't have been a black man because we wouldn't see him blush. Also, he couldn't have been white because he couldn't have been likened unto soil or dirt. Somehow or another, the original man was a reddish clay like color or formation. So whatever anybody says, this is the truth as found in the Scriptures. Somehow you could've seen the original man blush and have a rosy countenance and at the same time resemble the clay, dirt, and soil out of which he was formed. So the conclusion we must come to is the formed Adam was the color of grayish red.

Continuing in Genesis 2:8, *"And the LORD God planted a garden eastward in Eden; and there he put the man whom he had formed."* Some other translations read *"And the Lord God planted a garden toward the east, in Eden (delight) and there He put the man whom He had formed, framed, constituted"*, *"The Lord God planted an orchard in the East, in Eden, and there He placed the man He had formed"*, and *"The Lord God planted a paradise of pleasure from the beginning where in He place man"*. This is where we are headed! The Hebrew word for garden means "a garden as fenced, to hedge about, to protect, to defend, enclosure, surround, cover, a plot of ground protected by a wall or hedge". So this garden in the earth was a protected place. This is why many believe this garden is just a spiritual thing and was not a natural place. I can flow with this. I don't know, but yet because I live in this natural world, I'd like to think it was a natural place. But whatever it was, it was enclosed away from the rest of the world. It was a special place hedged about.

As we search the Scriptures, what is the garden now? There are actually three gardens. Two of them you and I have to go through to get to the third. The first is the garden of Gethsemane (Matthew 26:36, Mark 14:32). Gethsemane means "olive press". It is the place where God presses out of us or crushes us so the oil can flow. This takes place in our soul. Keep this in mind. Next, in John 19:41 it says *"Now in the place where he was crucified there was a garden."* The second aspect of the garden we must go through is to bear the cross and die to ourselves in order to get to the third garden, which is paradise. For right now though, the garden of the Lord is our soul. Song of Solomon 4:12-16 (the Bridegroom speaking to the Bride) says *"[12]A garden inclosed is my sister, my spouse; a spring shut up, a fountain sealed. [13]Thy plants are an orchard of pomegranates, with pleasant fruits; camphire, with spikenard, [14]Spikenard and saffron; calamus and cinnamon, with all trees of frankincense; myrrh and aloes, with all the chief spices: [15]A fountain of gardens, a well of living waters, and streams from Lebanon. [16]Awake, O north wind; and come, thou south; blow upon my garden, that the spices thereof may flow out. Let my beloved come into his garden, and eat his pleasant fruits."* All of these spices, fruits, and terms are all of the things in the garden of God in our soulish realm (for example, myrrh is suffering or bitter experiences, etc). Song of Solomon 5:1 continues, *"I am come into my garden, my sister, my spouse: I have gathered my myrrh with my spice; I have eaten my honeycomb with my honey; I have drunk my wine with my milk: eat, O friends; drink, yea, drink abundantly, O beloved."* The honeycomb is the Word of God. Wine is the Holy Ghost. Milk once again is a type of the Word of God. Jesus, when He comes into His garden, this garden is within you and I. This garden is the soul of man and God brings into our soul a Word, the glory, the anointing, the spices (all of the characteristics of the Lord), and He also comes with myrrh which means again suffering or bitterness. Jesus went through this Himself as a man in the garden of Gethsemane. When Jesus visits our garden, He brings these things to us. Our garden must be crushed, so the oil and spices can flow out. Our garden must be crucified so we can go back and enter into paradise, the final garden.

Once our soul has been changed into the image of God, out of our spirit will flow the river of God, and it will no longer be hindered at all because our soul will have become like the Garden of Eden again and it will flow right into your body, causing your body to be glorified. Philippians 3:21 says, *"Who shall change our vile body that it may be fashioned like unto his glorious body..."* So the garden is the soul of man. Other passages related to this include Isaiah 51:3, Isaiah 58:11, Jeremiah 31:12.

The word Eden itself is masculine and feminine and it means "pleasure, delight, delicate" and comes from a root word that means "to be soft, pleasant, to live voluptuously, to delight". This is paradise. There are only three places found in Scripture where the term paradise is found. The first is in Luke 23:42-43 during the interaction of Jesus and the thief on the cross, *"⁴²And he said unto Jesus, Lord, remember me when thou comest into thy kingdom. ⁴³And Jesus said unto him, Verily I say unto thee, To day shalt thou be with me in paradise."* The second time is Paul saying *"How that he was caught up into paradise, and heard unspeakable words..."* (II Corinthians 12:4). The third time is in Revelation 2:7 where Jesus is saying, *"...To him that overcometh will I give to eat of the tree of life, which is in the midst of the paradise of God."* The word paradise literally means in the Greek "an Eden, a park, a grand enclosure". So this garden that was planted in the earth has been planted inside of us now in our soul. When you live in the presence of God, you are living in paradise. Can you imagine living voluptuously in your soul and experiencing paradise and delight?! Many of us are tormented, depressed, and melancholy and do not live in the liberty we claim we should. There are very few truly free people. But there is an Eden inside of you if you let it come forth. That is why praying in tongues is so important. Jude 20 says *"But ye, beloved, building up yourselves on your most holy faith, praying in the Holy Ghost."* The Holy Ghost always prays for things according to the will of God. I Corinthians 14:2 says *"For he that speaketh in an unknown tongue speaketh not unto men, but unto God: for no man understandeth him; howbeit <u>in the spirit he speaketh mysteries</u>."* As you and I pray in tongues, we bring forth the deepest part of God and the deepest part of yourself and it looses the heavenly paradise into your soul. For those of you who struggle with your mind, God has a glorious provision for us! There's a garden within you containing everything you need. You just have to go and eat, live, and drink from the tree of life. This is what man was originally supposed to do.

Continuing in Genesis 2:10, *"And a river went out of Eden to water the garden; and from thence it was parted, and became into four heads."* The river was one initially. One is the number in Scriptures for God and unity and only after leaving paradise does this river part into four heads. Four is the number for creation. So the river is flowing from God out to creation. We already talked about this river and how inside of every Spirit-filled believer there is a river that flows from the throne of God. If you follow the source of the river, it will always lead you to God. He is the initial, first, and only cause that there is. The river then divides into four heads and I only bring this up because I want you to know that one of the first countries named in the Bible was an African country. The first river mentioned is Pison (verse 11), *"The name of the first is Pison: that is it which compasseth the whole land of Havilah, where there is gold; ¹²And the gold of that land is good: there is bdellium and the onyx stone."* Note this is before the fall of Adam. God's intent was not to keep the river just in the garden, but to fill the entire earth. This is why the Lord says in Numbers 14:21, *"But as truly as I live, all the earth shall be filled with the glory of the LORD."* How is this going to happen? This will happen out of the sons of God in the last days. This is called the manifestation of the sons of God (Romans 8:19). The manifestation of the sons of God is simply the sons of God being totally perfected in their soulish man. They have the image of Christ Jesus and the river will flow out of their garden to the rest of the world and this will bring the last great move of God. The last great move of God is not going to come down; it is going to come out of a people. Isaiah 60:1-2 says *"Arise, shine; for thy light is come, and the glory of the LORD is risen upon thee. ²For, behold, the darkness shall cover the earth, and gross darkness the people: but the LORD shall arise upon thee, and his glory shall be seen upon thee."* Paul says in II Thessalonians 1:10 *"When he shall come to be glorified in his saints..."* The first coming of the Lord is in a people and then Jesus will come where every eye will see Him. So once the sons of God are filled with the image of God in their soulish man, they've gotten back to paradise, are walking in dominion and the river of God is flowing out of them, instead of there being just one Jesus on the shores of Galilee, there will be millions of Jesus' all over this earth. The sons of God won't be Jesus, but they will be like Him in every way, walking the earth like Jesus did 2000 years ago. Jesus Himself said in John 10:34, *"Is it not written in your law, I said, Ye are gods?"* Jesus here was quoting out of the book of Psalms which says, *"I have said, Ye are gods; and all of you are children of the most High."* Our calling is to be god-men on the earth, but we will always only be the children of the Most High God, the Chief Shepherd and Bishop of our souls. This is doing no despite to the glory of God. Jesus *"thought it not robbery to be equal with God"* (Philippians 2:6). Neither should we when it comes to our calling. To say we can never be like Jesus is just phony and false humility. The truth is we should want to have dominion, be walking in paradise, and have the image of our God like we were originally created. Literally, God wants us to be god-like.

Please let this revelation be imparted to your heart. You see, when the glory fills a meeting or comes into a room, how does it really come? It comes because a person or a people bring it. This means that you and I become the carrier of the glory of God in the earth. I remember years ago I was having a great struggle as an assistant pastor in the certain church, before I started pastoring myself. It was a very large church and I pretty much did everything. I led the worship, did all of the counseling, had two home meetings, was head of the intercessors, etc. And as a young minister, I struggled in watching the elders above me say one thing to the congregation and do the opposite in their daily life. Their faith wasn't following the end of their conversation. Now I had my own issues, but I tried to do and live the Bible and remain transparent before the people and I found that the men above me weren't doing that and I was in a great struggle about it. So I went to see my father in the Lord who was pastoring in another state at the time. I drove three hours to talk to him and his wife. I was really in a depressed state and wanted to quit and give up the ministry. So I arrived and walked into their sanctuary to meet them. We worshipped for a bit and I'll never forget what they said to me. His wife walked up to me and begins to prophecy over me and this is what she said to me, "Son, thou art a beast of burden". Now I'll be honest with you. I got furious. Now mind you, I drove three hours to get ministered to and would have to drive three hours back and this is what was said to me. Why did I drive three hours to be called a beast? As they were prophesying over me I was only thinking they are saying I'm a beast because of my weight which made me more upset. So my mind was just sailing and being foolish, but that is all that they had to say to me, "Thou art a beast of burden". And as I sat there, thoroughly upset, mad, disappointed, and still depressed, God spoke to me in such a gentle voice. I'll never forget it. He said, "You don't know anything, do you?" I replied and said, "I guess I don't". He said, "You are a beast". I said, "Thank you. You could've told me these three hours ago and saved me the drive because I have to drive another three hours home". He then said to me. "Son, you are a beast, and a beast carries burdens. You will carry the burden of the glory of God". Now this happened to me in the early 1980's. There were no "glory meetings" back then. There were no "river meetings". So for the Lord to tell me that I am called with the burden to carry the glory of God wherever I went was a new revelation. From that point on when I began pastoring myself after moving on from that large church, God told me to turn my attention to His people. My ministry from that point on and still remains today is to minister to the bride of Christ. I have evangelists and people who will bring the people in, but my God given job was to disciple God's people and make them ready for the coming of the Lord.

At the time in the early 1980's, I never knew all the struggles I had up to that point (and continue to have), God was trying to make me into a proper vessel (or beast) that would be worthy of handling and bearing the most precious commodity in the universe, the glory of God. Now I've said all this to humbly say this, the older I've become in the Lord, the closer I've gotten to God and the more I live in Him. The more I live in Him, the more He lives in me, and the more the glory abides in my life. This means, you and I can literally change the atmosphere in the room when we walk in it because we bring with us paradise. We bring with us all of those fragrant spices, all the beauty of paradise, as well as the river and glory of God. A man can bring this while on the earth. Many have mocked me for teaching this over the years, but I say to you, *"He that hath an ear, let him hear what the Spirit saith unto the churches; To him that overcometh will I give to eat of the tree of life, which is in the midst of the paradise of God."* (Revelation 2:7). Anybody who can hear what the Spirit of God is saying will know it comes from a place of great humility and brokenness. I have laid my life down so I can be a true beast of burden and I beg you to do the same. You have to give up everything of self to receive Him. Paul says in Galatians 2:20, *"I am crucified with Christ: nevertheless I live; yet not I, but Christ liveth in me..."* As you and I die to ourselves, we can literally take the real Jesus wherever we go. We even saw in Peter's life in Acts 5:15-16 that people tried just to get in his shadow to be healed. Why? Peter was walking in the glory. When talking about Jesus to Mary in Luke 1:35, *"the angel answered and said unto her, The Holy Ghost shall come upon thee, and the power of the Highest shall overshadow thee: therefore also that holy thing which shall be born of thee shall be called the Son of God."* The overshadowing anointing causes the seed in the womb to grow. So if you and I have that overshadowing anointing and walk into a room, the seed of the Spirit of God that is in every believer can come forth and become the son of God they are called to be. This is God's highest tribute and way of blessing His people. If God sends you somewhere to minister, He is not just sending you. In you is a garden and when you open your mouth and sing or speak, out of you will flow the *"pure river of water of life, clear as crystal"* (Revelation 22:1). And as that pure river flows to people, it cleanses, sanctifies, strengthens, heals, encourages, delivers, and also promotes the growth of the incorruptible seed in every person to grow up into His image!

Well, back to Genesis 2 and this first river called Pison. Pison means "a great diffusion of waters, a flowing stream" and comes from a root word that means "to push, to disperse, to multiply, to twist or whirl" all representing God's glory flowing this way. The river Pison *"compasseth the whole land of Havilah"*. The name Havilah means "something that suffers pain, bringing forth, trembling with pain" and it comes from a root word that means "pang, pain especially of a pregnant woman". This means that the river comes to take the seed in the womb and make it grow. Now when I searched out to where this river Pison was, it is found in the land of Cush who was one of the sons of Ham (Genesis 10:6). The name Cush means "a black countenance, region of burnt faces, blackness". This river first flowed to a black land. Glory to God! So if God reached out to anyone first, it was to the black race. And God also mentions that in this land was this special kind of gold. Gold in the Scriptures always speaks of the character and nature of God.

"And the name of the second river is Gihon: the same is it that compasseth the whole land of Ethiopia." Many scholars think this is the Nile River, but I don't think that is important. All I know is, Ethiopia is the same thing again as Cush. If you look up Ethiopia, you will see it is the name Cush which means again "a black countenance, region of burnt faces, blackness". So this second river that flows out of the Garden of Eden covered the either land of Ethiopia or the land of black people. Also consider these were the first countries named in Scripture and they were lands that would be ultimately inhabited by black people.

So what have we seen so far in creation? The first man created was not white. He was a reddish gray color (earthy). The first countries mentioned in the Bible are in Africa. The first places where the rivers flowed to were to Africa, Iraq, and the regions around there. Psalms 68:31 reads, *"...Ethiopia shall soon stretch out her hands unto God."* Once man fell, Africa became a place where many false gods and false idols were worshipped. And in God's plan of redemption, He returns Ethiopia back to Himself. It is a seen in a figure in Acts 8 where Philip is immediately translated in the Spirit right next to a chariot with a man who was the eunuch of great authority under Candace, queen of the Ethiopians. He was a black man and he was reading the book of Isaiah and didn't know what it meant. And listen to this, the chariot is traveling and Philip is traveling with it. Philip had no horse. This was supernatural! And Philip asked the eunuch if he understood what he was reading and the eunuch responded, *"How can I, except some man should guide (or teach) me?"* You see, this is the judgment that is coming upon the white race (and already has come). For years, the white race has refused to teach the truths of Scripture to black people. For generations, they told the black people they were only servants and slaves (segregational doctrine). Some people taught that black people weren't even human but they were beasts of the earth. Black people weren't allowed to learn how to read or write. They were told what the Bible said about them because they couldn't read themselves. These were terrible and unrighteous things done to black people. But look what black people did with the little they received? Some of the greatest songs ever written came out of the slavery experience by black people.

But I also mention that the greatest persecution of black people were blacks themselves who sold their own black brothers and sisters. Where do you think the black people came from? They were bought. Black people enslaved black people and sold them to white men who traded them. And there is still slavery in Africa today. But it still does not negate the horrors that white people have put upon black people.

This is why I believe I was born in the ghetto and was there for the first 15 years of my life. I was a black person in every possible way (except for my skin being white). I was even allowed to say the epithet that is used for black people. To be allowed to call other black people that (especially as a white person) was a sign of being received. When I was growing up, this epithet was said more in a brotherly way. When I joined and was accepted in a black gang, I was allowed to say this very thing to my brothers in the gang. I reached a point of being completely received, so I understand the black experience completely. Then, after 15 years, I was dropped completely in a white community. Did I see racism in the ghetto? Absolutely! I've seen things done to white people that are unspeakable, but when I moved into an all white community I saw things done to black people that were just as unspeakable. As white people, our history also shows us enslaving Indians as well as the blacks. It seems like all the white people want to do is take over everybody else's stuff. I'm not tremendously proud of my heritage, but I am a white man (at least to this world). But in the Spirit, I am the color of amber and I have a feeling that it is going to be a kind of reddish gold! Glory to God!

But God doesn't always move quickly, but eventually He moves. Israel were slaves in Egypt for over 400 years, but the day came. The day always comes when the Lord says, "Let my people go!" So Philip in Acts 8 teaches to that black eunuch the gospel. This says to us that the black race in the last days will be loosed. I remember prophesying this in 1984 that the two greatest and oppressed groups of people that will be loosed in the last days will be women and black people. There were no famous black preachers in 1984. There certainly weren't many women teachers back then either. But now, some of the greatest preachers today are black men and women. Some of the greatest teachers are women.

So Acts 8 is a type of the black race being taught about Jesus in the last days and they will immediately receive Him and stretch out their hands to God (Psalms 68:31). God will redeem those initial people and restore them. So our heritage is not really Judeo-Christian, but really is Afro-Judeo-Christian. Israel lived in Egypt for 400 years. Who did they marry? They married black men and women. There were only 70 of them when they went down to Egypt. But when they came out there were 3 million of them. Do the math. The olive skinned Israelites married black men and women. This is what happened and when they came out of Egypt, they were not white people, but they were a people of color. Why would this offend anyone? It surely doesn't offend me. If God was actually black, I'm all for it. Black is beautiful. Black, but comely! I want to be part of the restoration, how about you?

Forgetting Your Own People
Chapter 8

I would like to talk about our family in two ways. One, God wants us to forget our earthly family and realize as Christians we are part of a heavenly family, and two define for us what this heavenly family is. In this chapter, I would like to look at that God calls us to forget our earthly family. First of all, when someone gets saved, they are a new creation in Christ Jesus. The Greek word for creation means "species". We become a new kind of species when we get saved. From the moment we get saved, we are no longer white, black, Jew, Gentile, or even male or female. We become sons of God.

One of the things in the Bible that will surprise many is what God says to do with our natural family in relation to walking with the Lord Jesus. Remember when Elijah took his mantle and walked past Elisha and threw his mantle on him (I Kings 19:19-21). What did Elisha do in response? What Elisha did is what every one of us should do when the call of God and the anointing of God fall on us. Elisha burned every thing that was important to him (everything from his former life), kissed his father and mother goodbye, and followed the man of God. I believe this is what God wants from all of us, but this is not an easy thing. This is hard because culture is so driven into us. We are told we're being an "uncle Tom" or a "house negro" and told we are betraying our race and family. I've been told many times by family and others previously close to me that they don't understand how I can leave my people. But my answer is simple. My people are the people of God now.

When the Lord fell on me as a teenager, I knew it meant leaving all that I knew and running after Him. This is what Jesus told His disciples, *"Follow me, and I will make you fishers of men"* (Matthew 4:19). Jesus wanted an immediate response. In Matthew 8:19-22 when a certain disciple told Jesus he would follow him but first asked, *"suffer me first to go and bury my father"*, Jesus' response was *"Follow me; and let the dead bury their dead."* In other words, Jesus was saying to this person your family needs to be dead to you. Jesus says in Matthew 23:9, *"And call no man your father upon the earth: for one is your Father, which is in heaven"*, getting us to see that we have a new family with God as our Father.

We will see the multitude of Scriptures that declare that upon coming into the Kingdom of God, we then begin to move away from our family and the culture we grew up in. This is not going to be an easy voice for many to hear but those who want to prepare themselves to be the bride of Christ and prepare themselves for the ages to come, need to hear this.

Let us begin in Psalms 45. This is a great passage about the bride of Christ. Beginning in verse 9 it reads, *"Kings' daughters were among thy honourable women: upon thy right hand did stand the queen in gold of Ophir."* This queen in gold of Ophir is the bride of Christ. *"¹⁰Hearken, O daughter, and consider, and incline thine ear; forget also thine own people, and thy father's house; ¹¹So shall the king greatly desire thy beauty: for he is thy Lord; and worship thou him."* I don't think this can be expressed more plainly. We are to forget our own people. This sounds radical, but we will see later that Jesus actually says this Himself. Yes, we will forever be connected with our family by blood and have relationships with them and honor and love our natural mother and father, brothers and sisters, etc. But you and I as well as our natural family have to understand things change and become different upon our salvation and we are no longer bound to them like we were because we enter a new Kingdom. As Christians we live in this world, but we are no longer of this world.

At the age of 17 when I got on a Trailways Bus to go on with Jesus, leaving Washington D.C. and moving to Jacksonville, FL after graduation, I knew it was forever. For 25 years my family held this against me and refused my entrance into any of their lives apart from cursory talking until my mother passed away. My mother begged me to do her funeral which I didn't want to do, but of course I did. This was the first time in all of my life and ministry (25 years later) that my family ever heard me preach, sing, or have ever seen me in my element as a minister. But when the funeral was over, each one of my siblings came up to me and told me they now understand why I had left and had to separate myself so many years previously. All of the animosity faded away and now I have a great relationship with all of them even though I don't speak to them that often. Over the years, I led all of them to Jesus and got them filled with the Holy Ghost. I even moved two of them to Florida with me after I moved down there, but they turned around two weeks later and went back home. You can't make people walk with Jesus. But for me to have stayed in Washington D.C. at the age of 17 would have meant me getting caught up in my family life ultimately drowning me in a sea of issues. That is why I knew I had to go at 17 without ever even knowing the Scriptures at the time.

"Forget also thine own people and thy father's house". Let the Lord speaks this to you today. *"¹¹So shall the king greatly desire thy beauty: for he is thy Lord; and worship thou him."* Verse 11 cannot happen without doing the previous verse. The King (type of Jesus) will only desire your beauty if you've left your father's house. I understand this is hard. It is hard when you have a wife, children, brothers, sisters, mothers, fathers, cousins, nieces, nephews, grandfathers, grandmothers, etc, but nonetheless, we have to understand this. We need to teach people this when they get saved so we can train and teach them up in the good and right way, separating the precious from the vile and

letting them know what they need to do. We are not talking about radically saying you can't talk to your family ever again. We are talking about putting our natural families in their proper place, *"for he is thy Lord; and worship thou him."*

Now this is going to be especially hard on my precious black brothers and sisters because in the black culture, everybody is a brother. Because of the persecution that black people had to endure, they bound together as a group of people and have a family like mentality when it comes to their culture and their race. They had to because they had nobody else. To leave your family and culture is very hard because you will bear a reproach from others (especially from your family or those formerly close to you) as you press on in Jesus. But I tell you, as Christians, we are not to look for the approval of men, we look for the approval of God on everything we do. I pray every morning for the love of God to be shed abroad in my heart by the Holy Ghost towards every person.

Let us look next at Matthew 10 to see what Jesus had to say about this principle, starting in verse 34, *"Think not that I am come to send peace on earth: I came not to send peace, but a sword."* This sword is the Word of God. The Word of God is what does the separating. *"[35]For I am come to set a man at variance against his father, and the daughter against her mother, and the daughter in law against her mother in law. [36]And a man's foes shall be they of his own household."* After pastoring now since 1977, I've seen that one of the greatest hindrances and one of the greatest problems in many disciples' lives come from their own household or family. David said *"I will walk within my house with a perfect heart"* (Psalms 101:2). I wonder how many of us actually try to do this?

Jesus continuing in verse 37, *"[37]He that loveth father or mother more than me is not worthy of me: and he that loveth son or daughter more than me is not worthy of me. [38]And he that taketh not his cross, and followeth after me, is not worthy of me. [39]He that findeth his life shall lose it: and he that loseth his life for my sake shall find it."* The Greek word for life here is *"psuche"* meaning our soulish life. Once we were born again, our spirits were made perfect with God. Our bodies belong to the Lord (they are the temple of the Holy Ghost – I Corinthians 6:19). The only thing you and I have control over in our own existence is our soul. David said in Psalms 119:109, *"My soul is continually in my hand"*. Psalms 25:1 says *"Unto thee, O LORD, do I lift up my soul."* Our soul is all we own. The rest of us were bought by Jesus, *"For ye are bought with a price: therefore glorify God in your body, and in your spirit, which are God's."* (I Corinthians 6:20). We have the choice to decide whether to let the Spirit of God within us to lead and direct us or do we let the soulish, physical rule and reign in our life. So the principle Jesus is talking about in Matthew 10 is not us hating our mother and father, sons or daughters. God doesn't want us to hate anybody. Jesus is simply saying like Paul said in II Timothy 2:4, *"No man that warreth entangleth himself with the affairs of this life; that he may please him who hath chosen him to be a soldier."* Entanglements are going to come from our own household. In these last days, we are going to have to make declarations and steps that will cost us. To go on with Jesus cost me personally 25 years of brothers and sisters who I loved who didn't understand what I was doing. God doesn't want us to hate our mother and father. He wants us to love them, but you have to put your relationship with them in perspective. It must be Jesus first. Jesus has to be the first cause in all of our lives period. Every relationship we have has to come second to our relationship with Jesus. You cannot serve two. You will either hate the one or love the other. I even remember telling my wife Katie before we got married that marrying me was not going to be easy because she won't be first. The Master comes first.

Taking this a step further, I remember my children being upset because of all of the time I spend going to meetings, teaching and ministering to people. They started saying it seems I love the people more than them. Now hearing this from your children is like a dagger, but I sat down with my children (they were still pretty young) and I said, "Listen, your papa loves you very much but you have to understand something. I'm a papa to other people as well. God's people are my children as well." Believe it or not, my young children received it and released me. Praise God! None of my children say things like that to me anymore. They know what I'm doing, why I am doing it, and they are at peace with it and so is my wife. Our relationships have to be in perspective. So Jesus says these radical words like He does in Matthew 10 to get our attention. Are you consumed with your family? Are you so consumed with your spouse that it rules your life? We cannot allow this to happen, especially in these last days.

Next, let us look at Matthew 19:27-29. Starting in verse 27, *"Then answered Peter and said unto him, Behold, we have forsaken all, and followed thee; what shall we have therefore?"* Peter left all to follow Jesus and was asking Him what he was going to get out of following Him. *"[28]And Jesus said unto them, Verily I say unto you, That ye which have followed me, in the regeneration when the Son of man shall sit in the throne of his glory, ye also shall sit upon twelve thrones, judging the twelve tribes of Israel."* What a tremendous reward! Jesus answered Peter for what he get for following Him. But the reward is not now. It's a coming Kingdom. We need to get the body of Christ to wake up to this fact. The 80 years or so that we have on the earth will determine how we live in the rest of the ages to come.

Jesus then goes on to say, *"[29]And every one that hath forsaken houses, or brethren, or sisters, or father, or mother, or wife, or children, or lands, for my name's sake, shall receive an hundredfold, and shall inherit everlasting life."*

110

Many people say there is only one reason for divorce in the Scriptures and that is fornication or adultery. I don't believe this. Having pastored since 1977, I would have to say only 35-40% of marriages are marriages that God put together. Jesus said in Mark 10:9 *"What therefore God hath joined together, let not man put asunder."* People spend years trying to make something work that God never joined and when children come things get worse and then when they are 50-60 years old they hardly know their spouse. I don't believe anybody should go after divorce or use divorce as a way to get out of something. But I do believe there is a provision when you are going on with God that sometimes it may cost us in a relationship, and this is what Jesus is talking about. Jesus said this, not me: *"And every one that hath forsaken houses, or brethren, or sisters, or father, or mother, or <u>wife</u>, or children, or lands, <u>for my name's sake</u>..."* This means for God's character and reputation, you forsake something so you can go on with God.

How many women have submitted to ungodly husbands and have been made to do things that God never required of them to do. I remember the 1960's and early 1970's and the teaching on submission. Women were told to submit to anything and everything her husband wanted. This is insanity. God never said to do this. In Matthew 19:29, *"And every one that hath forsaken houses, or brethren, or sisters, or father, or mother, or wife, or children, or lands, for my name's sake, shall receive an hundredfold, and shall inherit everlasting life"*. He's busy saying the opposite. And as we approach the end of the last days, that which is not of God is going to burst apart. Everything is going to be shaken. Those whom God has joined will stand as a partnership through the storms of life. This is the good part of a family and the way it should be. It should be heaven on earth. But when you have a husband or wife constantly going in another direction, the turmoil and contention is overwhelming and trust me, I understand this. I went through this, years ago horribly. I am absolutely not advocating divorce, but what I am saying is at some point you have to look at your husband or wife and say, "listen, I love you with everything that is within me, but you have to understand something. I am not going to be influenced by you to stop me from walking with Jesus. I will be there to help and carry you the whole way, but if you begin to try to cut me off, persuade me, and use situations to try to make me not go on with Jesus; you have to understand I have only one Master. I can't serve two."

A perfect example of this was years ago I led a young lady to the Lord. She was gloriously saved and was filled with the Holy Ghost. She started to sit under the teachings and everything was going great with her. And I'll never forget when asking her about her husband she said, "he will never get saved and come to this church because he hates everything that has to do with church." I told her she had to stop confessing this. But after about a year, during a teaching one night a man who I'd never seen before (which was this woman's husband) walked in and sat in the meeting. At the end of the meeting he said he never heard anything like this before and said he wanted to get saved. So I led him to Jesus and he got filled with the Holy Ghost and began to sit under the Word night and day. He was at every meeting. Well, I thought the sister, the wife, would be ecstatic about the change in her husband. Within a few months she made an appointment with me and told me she was having a problem with my husband going to too many teachings. I told the sister she was the one who wanted this and God has given her a miracle. What ended up happening over the next three years is he ran hard after the Lord with a tremendous passion and she, once being confronted with true discipleship (because affliction arises for the Word sake), she committed adultery and ran off with another man. But he is still going on with Jesus even today.

Luke 2:42-51 is the story when Jesus was a little boy. This story always amazes me because there is no way Joseph and Mary would forget Jesus. God allowed this to happen on purpose because He was trying to make a statement to us. How can Joseph and Mary not know where their son was for 3 days? But after not knowing where Jesus was, they find Him at the temple talking and contending with the Scribes and Pharisees about the Law. Already at the age of 12, Jesus is feeling the call of God. And when Joseph and Mary finally found Jesus at the temple, "...[48]*they were amazed: and his mother said unto him, Son, why hast thou thus dealt with us? Behold, thy father and I have sought thee sorrowing.* [49]*And he said unto them how is it that ye sought me? wist ye not that I must be about my Father's business?* [50]*And they understood not the saying which he spake unto them...*" Mary and Joseph didn't understand what it meant when Jesus said He must be about His Father's business. Many spouses or family members do not understand us when somebody gets saved and begins to give themselves to the things of God, especially when they forsake all to follow the call of God.

Later we find Jesus in John 2:1-4 at the age of thirty, "[1]*And the third day there was a marriage in Cana of Galilee; and the mother of Jesus was there:* [2]*And both Jesus was called, and his disciples, to the marriage.* [3]*And when they wanted wine, the mother of Jesus saith unto him, They have no wine.*" So Jesus' mother wants Jesus to do something because there is no wine. "[4]*Jesus saith unto her, Woman, what have I to do with thee? mine hour is not yet come...*" Jesus was waiting Himself for the moment in time when God the Father would say His ministry begins now. This is similar to Joseph's testimony in Psalms 105:19, "*Until the time that his word came: the word of the LORD tried him.*" "Mine hour" in this story can also speak of the hour of Jesus' death. Everyone of us are called to an hour of death. Dying to self is an appointment we have. But Jesus, calling His mother "*Woman*" and then saying "*what have I to do with thee?*", was trying to communicate that even though

112

Mary was His mother, to Jesus she was just a woman to Him now. For us, it comes down to a simple principle. Is Jesus first in our lives?

Next, let us look in Luke 14:16-24. *"¹⁶Then said he unto him, A certain man made a great supper, and bade many:"* This supper is the marriage supper of the Lamb and this certain man is God the Father. *"¹⁷And sent his servant* (this is the Holy Ghost) *at supper time to say to them that were bidden, Come; for all things are now ready. ¹⁸And they all with one consent began to make excuse."* What does this mean that they all began with one consent to make excuse? It means there was some consenting taking place. In other words, this is communication between people as to what they are supposed to do and coming to an agreement. Are we influenced by what other people think? Does their opinion weight more in our life than it should? As far as I am concerned, the only opinions that mean anything to me are the opinion of God the Father, the witness of the Holy Ghost, the men and women whom I have submitted my life to, my wife, and lastly to the leadership at my church. But in this story they were consenting to come up with a reason to make an excuse. You see, people who go on with God exposes those who do not especially if they are living together. One is constantly about the things of God, studying the Bible, worshipping, going to meetings and the other is consumed with the cares of this life like Martha in Luke 10:38-42. Martha was upset with Mary who sat at Jesus' feet while she was *"cumbered about much serving"* (or as the Greek reads, *"distracted with care"*). But Jesus' response was, *"Martha, Martha, thou art careful and troubled about many things: ⁴²But one thing is needful: and Mary hath chosen that good part, which shall not be taken away from her."* I guess this means that Martha hath chosen the bad part, namely, allowing other things and cares to distract and fill her life instead of sitting at Jesus' feet. Jesus was not first in Martha's life. What is first in your life? Martha was demanding that her sister (another family member) help her. But Mary had a revelation of Jesus and she sat at His feet and was despised by her sister for doing it. Don't consent with others who will take you away from a deeper walk with God.

"¹⁸And they all with one consent began to make excuse. The first said unto him, I have bought a piece of ground, and I must needs go and see it: I pray thee have me excused." This speaks of our possessions being more important that our relationship with Jesus. *"¹⁹And another said, I have bought five yoke of oxen, and I go to prove them: I pray thee have me excused."* This speaks of our job being more important. *"²⁰And another said, I have married a wife, and therefore I cannot come."* Here is the excuse of our family keeping us from going on with God. These are the excuses Jesus brings out that people consent to. *"²¹So that servant came, and shewed his lord these things. Then the master of the house being angry..."* Jesus is trying to show us that God gets angry about the fact that people were making excuses. Have you ever tried to throw a

party and one by one people start calling you up and say they can't come. You went through all of the trouble preparing for the party and people start telling you they can't make it. Well if one does this, it is okay. If the second person calls canceling it may begin to ruffle you. But usually by the third cancellation, you may get angry and upset. By the fourth, you cancel the party. And the excuses people usually make are phony anyway. Well, what if these same people that cancelled you find out later that they just went to somebody else's party. It would hurt you deeply. How do you think God the Father feels when we make excuse about spending time with Him? He's given us everything He has. *"For God so loved the world, that he gave his only begotten Son..."* (John 3:16). How much more can He give? He's promised us rewards that are absolutely phenomenal. He's promised us we can have His image and to be like him. What more do we want? No, many would rather stay home and watch T.V. instead of wanting the heavenly treasures He's prepared for us. How would we feel if we were God? We would think those people don't love us or they don't care about us.

Look at the same chapter in verse 25-27, *"And there went great multitudes with him: and he turned, and said unto them..."* I love this. When the power of God is present and people are getting healed and delivered, the multitudes will follow. Knowing this, Jesus turned and addresses the multitude. This means something to me. I get a picture of Jesus walking with this crowd of people behind him and it caused Jesus to respond. So Jesus purposely turns and says to them, *"[26]If any man come to me, and hate not his father, and mother, and wife, and children, and brethren, and sisters, yea, and his own life also, he cannot be my disciple. [27]And whosoever doth not bear his cross, and come after me, cannot be my disciple."* You see, Jesus just gave the parable about people making excuses and it is like He knows they didn't understand what He was trying to say to them. So He says plainly to them, you have to hate your father, mother, wife, etc. and hate your own life also. He is trying to get their attention and convey that He is to come first in their life, not their family or their own desires. He doesn't actually want us to hate our family, but he is saying, our families have to find their proper place. Jesus is not advocating hate, rather he is imploring us to put our walk with him first.

In the book of Ruth 1 we see this same situation. This is the story where Naomi and her husband backslide, leave Bethlehem-Judah with their sons, and go into the country of Moab to live. Over time Naomi's husband dies and the two sons die as well and Naomi is left in Moab with her two sons' wives. Naomi wants to head back to Bethlehem-Judah and says to her two daughters in law *"[8]Go, return each to her mother's house: the LORD deal kindly with you, as ye have dealt with the dead, and with me. [9]The LORD grant you that ye may find rest, each of you in the house of her husband. Then she kissed them; and they lifted up their voice, and wept."* (Ruth 1:8-9).

Before we go on in the story, I want to look at verses 19-21 (describing her return) to show you what Naomi's spirit was like, *"¹⁹So they two went until they came to Bethlehem. And it came to pass, when they were come to Bethlehem, that all the city was moved about them, and they said, Is this Naomi? ²⁰And she said unto them, Call me not Naomi, call me Mara: for the Almighty hath dealt very bitterly with me. ²¹I went out full, and the LORD hath brought me home again empty: why then call ye me Naomi, seeing the LORD hath testified against me, and the Almighty hath afflicted me?"* Naomi is bitter against God, but the truth was her and her husband backslid and went to a country God didn't want them to have anything to do with. But we learn in this story that this was still all in the sovereign plan of God. Naomi is bitter. She lost her husband and her sons. So when she is telling her daughter-in-laws (Ruth and Orpah) to go back it is because she doesn't want them coming with her. She really doesn't seem to want to go back herself, but she has to do it because she is forced to.

So Naomi continues speaking to the daughter-in-laws in verse 11, *"And Naomi said, Turn again, my daughters: why will ye go with me?"* She had no conception to what God was doing, bringing in a Gentile, a Moabite. She didn't realize God was working. In our lives we don't realize the circumstances that we are in have much more to do with hundreds of lives by the decisions we make. We cannot be bitter against God. Acts 24:16 says *"And herein do I exercise myself, to have always a conscience void of offence toward God, and toward men."* We cannot live with anything in our heart against the Lord or we will miss being part of His Divine purposes. Ruth is part of the Messianic line and Naomi didn't know it.

So she continues her nonsense, *"¹²Turn again, my daughters, go your way; for I am too old to have an husband. If I should say, I have hope, if I should have an husband also to night, and should also bear sons; ¹³Would ye tarry for them till they were grown? would ye stay for them from having husbands? nay, my daughters; for it grieveth me much for your sakes that the hand of the LORD is gone out against me."* God's hand had not gone out against her. Naomi had gone against God. *"¹⁴And they lifted up their voice, and wept again: and Orpah kissed her mother in law; <u>but Ruth clave unto her</u>. ¹⁵And she said, Behold, <u>thy sister in law is gone back unto her people</u>, and unto her gods: return thou after thy sister in law. ¹⁶And Ruth said, Intreat me not to leave thee, or to return from following after thee: for whither thou goest, I will go; and where thou lodgest, I will lodge: <u>thy people shall be my people</u>, and <u>thy God my God</u>: ¹⁷Where thou diest, will I die, and there will I be buried: the LORD do so to me, and more also, if ought but death part thee and me. ¹⁸When she saw that* *she was stedfastly minded to go with her, then she left speaking unto her."* You have Orpah and Ruth doing two different things which are two types of the church. Ruth's name means "someone worth seeing, friendship". Orpah's name means "the neck of an animal, hardened, double-minded". Naomi was trying to dissuade both of these Gentiles from coming into the things of God. After hearing Naomi, Orpah was given enough reason to stay with her family in Moab. But Ruth, somehow in her time with Naomi and her husband, had seen something about God and she decides to give up everything she knows to follow God. She decided to leave her country and her people and confessed that the people of God will be her people now. The principle is this, we have to be separated from our family if you are going to go on with God and be in the bride of Christ.

Jeremiah 3:14 says, *"Turn, O backsliding children, saith the LORD; for I am married unto you: and I will take you one of a city, and two of a family, and I will bring you to Zion."* Not everybody in a family responds to the call of God. In this case two. Two is the number in Scripture for witness and separation. You may be the two in your house. You are the witness and the separation. It was true in my family. When I was a teenager I was the only witness for Jesus in my family and I had to separate myself from my family and all of their insecurities and bondages. It was hard at the time and I didn't want to do it, but staying with my family would have robbed me of my calling in God. In II Kings 7:3 when the people of God were being besieged by the enemy four leprous men who were sitting at the entrance of the gate said, *"Why sit we here until we die?"* If they stayed they figured they would die and if they went out of the city the enemy would be there. So they said, we should just go for it and God answered these lepers and made the enemy flee before them. These four lepers end up walking into an empty enemy camp with all of their possession left for them.

"Two of a family" – The Bible says in Genesis 5:24, *"Enoch walked with God: and he was not; for God took him."* Have you ever wondered that Enoch had children and a wife? The Bible doesn't say they walked with God. You see where ever you are in life and God's mantle falls upon you and God's call touches your heart, there is no going back. You just follow it and go for it because it is Him calling you and deep is calling unto deep (Psalms 42:7). I know it is hard to separate ourselves from soulish ties. Believe me, I know. But in the end you will be better for it and it may be by your separating yourself; you become a witness to those who are left behind.

Lastly, we finish in Hebrews 7:1-3 which talks about Melchisedec. Hebrew 7:11 talks about the *"order of Melchisedec"*. "Order" means rank. There isn't just one person in an order. It is a company or rank of people. I Corinthians 15:23 talks about every person will be resurrected *"in his own* order". This is the same word meaning rank. There are ranks within the body of Christ and there are ranks in the priesthood. To understand this better, all you have to do is read Ezekiel 44 and you will find the Levites who have turned away from the Lord. They were allowed to minister to the house only. The sons of Zadok (Melchi-zedek) were allowed to minister to the Lord. So the highest priesthood we can ever enter into is the order of Melchisedec (Melchizedek – Hebrew). I believe there are priests and then there are priests of God. There are Eli's and then there are Samuel's (I Samuel 3). There are priests like Eli's wicked sons and then there are the David's. Just being a priest in the Levitical order means nothing, but being a part of the order of Melchisedec (which means "son of righteousness") is earned. I believe Melchisedec was the Lord Jesus (First seen in Genesis 14:18-20). This was God in the flesh. Many disagree with this, but I can't help but compare the two. Melchisedec was the "*King of peace*" (Hebrews 7:2) and Jesus is the "*Prince of peace*" (Isaiah 9:6). Melchisedec was the "*priest of the most high God*" (Hebrews 7:1) and Jesus is the "*high priest*" (Hebrews 6:20). Let us read in Hebrews 7, "*¹For this Melchisedec, king of Salem, priest of the most high God, who met Abraham returning from the slaughter of the kings, and blessed him; ²To whom also Abraham gave a tenth part of all; first being by interpretation King of righteousness, and after that also King of Salem, which is, King of peace;*"

So this Melchisedec is Jesus. When Jesus' mother sought after Jesus in Mark 3:32-25, Jesus answer His mother by saying, "*Who is my mother, or my brethren? ³⁴And he looked round about on them which sat about him, and said, Behold my mother and my brethren! ³⁵For whosoever shall do the will of God, the same is my brother, and my sister, and mother.*" Now for us, to be in the "order" of Melchisedec, let us continue in Hebrews 7:3 to look at the defining things about it, "*³Without father, without mother, without descent, having neither beginning of days, nor end of life; but made like unto the Son of God; abideth a priest continually.*" If you and I are going to be a true priest of God, like Jesus, we have to be disengaged from what we were, disengaged from our natural family, culture, and previous life and now live to God!

These truths are not easy for any of us, but Jesus said in Matthew 19:11, "*All men cannot receive this saying…*" So I pray that each reader has ears to hear what the Spirit is saying to the church and that we would see that Your heart is to show us the good and right way and that You are our true Father. We want to be the bride of Christ. So today, we forget also our own people because You are our Lord and we worship You. May Your grace and anointing fall upon every reader as this is walked out in all of their lives, in Jesus' name. Amen!

Racism And The Scriptures
Chapter 9

It is sad to say but racism exists in many parts of the world in some form or fashion and it has found its way into the fabric of humanity's everyday life. Even though this is horrible, we can somewhat understand "heathens" or non-believers walking this way. Christianity should however counter the exclusion and alienation of racism. Christianity is supposed to promote love, joy, peace, and good will towards <u>all men</u> (Luke 2:14). I understand that even in our born again experience we still wrestle with our Adamic nature. However, I cannot understand how anyone who; is saved, filled with the Holy Ghost, and is a true disciple, that is, one who studies the Scripture, has intimate times of worship and intercession with our precious, loving, and merciful God, can still hate or despise someone for the color of their skin or culture.

We will see in this chapter what the Scriptures say about racism. We will also see the instances in the Bible of racism. The Bible is our plumb line. It is our guide for all that we do, so let us allow the Holy Scriptures to teach us what God has to say and then let us do it. No matter what anyone else is doing, we will do the Word of God and hopefully leave an example and an impression of the loving character of our God in this world. We should be, and act like, the city set on a hill.

Let us turn to Philippians 2. This is how Christians should really be living as far as the Lord is concerned. Looking in verse 14-15, "*Do all things without murmurings and disputings: [15]That ye may be blameless and harmless, the sons of God, without rebuke, in the midst of a crooked and perverse nation, among whom ye shine as lights in the world. [16]Holding forth the word of life...*" As Christians, we are in this world, but we are not of this world. My prayer is that Jesus will shine through you and me, and by doing the Word, show the world the true nature of Christ. As these Scriptures point out, we may be the only Jesus people will ever see. Matthew 5:14-16 reads, "*[14]Ye are the light of the world. A city that is set on an hill cannot be hid. [15]Neither do men light a candle, and put it under a bushel, but on a candlestick; and it giveth light unto all that are in the house. [16]Let your light so shine before men, that they may see your good works, and glorify your Father which is in heaven.*" In other words, when you or I encounter racism or prejudice of any kind, it is our opportunity to be the light of the world in that darkness. I don't care if you or I are in an elevator, in a break room at work, or we are driving in the car with some friends and somebody manifests some racism or prejudice. When this happens, this is our time to shine. We are not trying to be some strict religious law oriented people. But you can tell when somebody says something and it isn't right. If it is something that you cannot tell in front of the particular people you are talking about, than maybe you ought not to say it. But when we see racism or hear a derogatory comment about another race, then that is our time to shine as light before men. You know, Jesus said in John 13:35, *"By this shall all men know that ye are my disciples, if ye have love one to another."* If the world cannot see the love of God operating amongst the different cultures and peoples in the body of Christ, where are they going to see it?

Next, I want to talk about some important facts about racism. I am even going to go into things that are a little different and even look at some scientific facts. In writing about this subject, I really wanted to research this so I am confident in what I am saying and that whoever reads this will not be able to gainsay or resist it. The theory of races pretty much really did not become a big deal until Charles Darwin wrote his book called *"On the Origin of Species by Means of Natural Selection, or the Preservation of Favored Races in the Struggle for Life"*. What most evolutionists don't understand is when they say they believe in evolution, they are saying they are an absolute racist. Now there have always been prejudices among races throughout history and certain races enslaving other races because of the evil of men's hearts. But as far as theories go, it wasn't until Charles Darwin's book that things were written about races like this. In truth, his *"On the Origin of Species"* is a racist philosophy because it teaches that different groups or races of people evolved at different times and rates. So some groups are more like their ape-like ancestors than others. For example the Australian Aborigines (dark-skinned people who were the earliest inhabitants of Australia) were considered to be the missing link between the ape-like ancestor and the rest of mankind which resulted in terrible injustice and prejudice toward those Aborigines. They were treated as non-humans. Once this evolution theory became popular, biological arguments for racism increased. Even scientists weighed in with their racist propaganda. Fueled by this theory, a noted African explorer captured an African pygmy and later had him displayed with an orangutan in a cage at the Bronx Zoo, with the obvious inference that black people are deficient. Consider the horror of this. But great prejudices began with this type of teaching that some races are more elevated intellectually than others.

As a result of Darwin's theory, therefore, people began thinking about different people groups around the world as representing different races, thereby encouraging great prejudice. Out of this sprang numerous terrible theories. One of these theories was when Cain was cast out of the garden, the "mark" (Genesis 4:14) that was put upon him was that he became black. In response to this hideous theory, if you really search the Scriptures, if there is any mark God gives people when He is angry, it is white. When people were cursed they did not turn black, they turned white with leprosy. We even see in the book of Leviticus (Leviticus 13) that when discussing about the plague of leprosy, if a black hair appears, the person is pronounced clean. Nobody has ever seen this before. But these things are ingrained in us from childhood, and we grow up thinking and feeling these things. You see, Satan has had all those years early in our lives to train us in racism and we don't even realize it.

A second theory discussed when Cain had left the family of God, who did he marry? They say there were no other peoples on the earth so he must have married one of these things they called the "beasts of the earth/living creatures", that being black people. This theory was commonly held and preached in this country for hundreds of years and not until around 1960 did that theory begin to fade and be exposed. They tried to say blacks were some of the beasts (different from animals and humans) that were on Noah's ark. They say blacks were half way between animals and humans and that they did not have a soul at all.

Obviously these theories can sound ridiculous to us, but people can pervert the scriptures and cause us to believe anything they want. And if people have tendencies in them to be racist or hateful, such theories and teachings will feed and encourage those tendencies. But it all started with Darwin's theory, and I think now of all the left leaning liberal people who constantly hold onto evolution do not realize how racist they are being. Black people as a group should rise up and see through this nonsense. That is why we believe God created mankind. We did not evolve. The whole evolutionary principle, asserting that some evolved faster than others, opens wide the door for racial prejudice.

Scientists however classify all human beings as Homo sapiens sapiens (modern human beings are the species Homo sapiens of which the only subspecies is known as Homo sapiens sapiens). They conclude there is only one race of humans and that the theory of race has no basic biological reality. They say that the differences that separate us are cultural, not racial. Some suggest that the word race should be abandoned because it is meaningless. We only accept the idea of race because it is a convenient way of putting people in broad categories to suppress them. Hitler's Germany provides the most hideous example. Hitler did not hate only Jews, but black people too. He used the scientific racist theories to assert that white people were a superior race, and the Jews inferior human beings because they did not evolve like white men did. Due to the suppression of blacks in the USA at the time, Hitler actually believed that America at some point would join him in his destruction of the Jews.

Classifying people according to their race is so ingrained in our natural thinking. Immediately if we see a white person or a black person, our response changes based on the color of their skin. This is because we have been trained to judge by the outward appearance. We have to guard ourselves. I Samuel

120

16:7 says, *"the LORD seeth not as man seeth; for man looketh on the outward appearance, but the LORD looketh on the heart."* It has been ingrained in us to look at each other's skin color and their outward appearance. For example, we judge somebody by whether they are "beautiful" or "ugly", or by their weight, and all kinds of things, instead of discerning who they are on the inside, in the hidden man of the heart, where true beauty lies.

The Bible does not even use the word race in references to people, except for certain versions. These versions include the New International Version (NIV), the English Standard Version, and "God's Word". The NIV Bible in two places (Ezra 9:2 and Romans 9:3) uses the word race. Ezra 9:2 is where they inter-married with tribes outside of the family of God. The subject of inter-marriage has been perverted by people as well, but we will look at that in another chapter. The word translated "race" in the NIV literally means in the Hebrew language, "seed". It does not mean race. The other passage (Romans 9:3) where the word "race" is used in the NIV reads (in the KJV), *"For I could wish that myself were accursed from Christ for my brethren, my kinsmen according to the flesh."* They translate this "race" but the actual Greek reads, "my relatives according to the flesh". Classifying people according to their skin color is racism, no matter who is applying it to whom. We have to understand something. If we believe the Bible then we believe God made <u>one man</u>, and we are all of <u>one blood</u> and have <u>one father</u>.

I want to solidify this into our hearts. Ephesians 1:10 states, *"That in the dispensation of the fulness of times he might gather together in one all things in Christ, both which are in heaven, and which are on earth; even in him."* You see, in the last days Ephesians 4:13 tells us we all are going to *"come in the unity of the faith, and of the knowledge of the Son of God, unto a perfect man, unto the measure of the stature of the fulness of Christ."* This perfect man is going to be made up of every skin color in the world, every ethnicity, every tribe, every nation, and every people. They will have one knowledge, one faith, and will be one people. They form the literal and spiritual body of Christ on the earth.

In Acts 17 Paul is dealing with some people in Greece. He is really rebuking them because they have an altar for the "unknown God" and he says in verse 25, *"²⁵Neither is worshipped with men's hands, as though he needed any thing, seeing he giveth to all life, and breath, and all things; ²⁶And <u>hath made of one blood</u> <u>all nations of men</u> for to dwell on all the face of the earth, and hath determined the times before appointed, and the bounds of their habitation."* I'm sorry Mr. Darwin, you were wrong. God has made of one blood all nations of men!

The next passage I want to look at is found in Revelation 5:9. This was after John is weeping because nobody was found worthy to open the book and now the Lamb has prevailed and has overcome. It reads, *"And they sung a new song, saying, Thou art worthy to take the book, and to open the seals thereof: for thou wast slain, and hast redeemed us to God by thy blood out of every kindred, and tongue, and people, and nation."* One translation reads, *"every ethnicity"*. Verse 10 continues, *"And hast made us unto our God kings and priests: and we shall reign on the earth."* Especially as believers, we have to realize God has redeemed everyone that is born again and He has done it out of every nation, not just one.

These passages are so important. As Christians, we have to get it together. If the body of Christ does not come into unity and stop racism, I don't know how it could ever stop in the world. In Ephesians 3, Paul is praying. Beginning in verse 14 is says, *"[14]For this cause I bow my knees unto the Father of our Lord Jesus Christ, [15]Of whom the whole family in heaven and earth is named."* We are all from the same family! Galatians 3:26-29 says, *"[26]For ye are all the children of God by faith in Christ Jesus..."* Do you know that the heretical doctrine the black people couldn't be saved because they had no soul existed? Many people believed this. Another theory purported was that because blacks were the "beasts of the earth" it was their reason for existence to be burden bearers or slaves to the greater races to the earth. They used the supposed "curse of Ham" to support this theory as well. Now we might think this comical, but it is very serious because it was taught for hundreds of years by white ministers. This was especially taught in the south by slave owners. They hammered it into the black man's thinking that he was only to be a burden bearer.

We have to understand from the creation of Adam, a reddish clay, there were no white people until the scattering of Japheth to the Caucus mountains. And they only became white because of the climate that they were in. Even today, most of the world is brown. So it seems awfully silly to think that the smallest population of people in the world (white people) controls most of the world. Look at what the white race has done. Let us just confine ourselves to America and know that I love my country. I cry when I hear Whitney Houston singing the Star Spangled Banner every time. I believe that God brought it together, but even the men that started our country had slaves, were racist, and held to these viewpoints I've been sharing with you. What is the first thing the father's of our country did? They were escaping England to get away from religious tyranny. This is good. But we come in and drive out the inhabitants of this nation, the Indians. Now we don't just ask them if we can share their land. No, we take the land by domination and by force until eventually the Indians were almost wiped out. Then, we had the nerve to put them on reservations almost like prison camps. This is the truth. It is disturbing, horrible, and vile, but it is the truth nonetheless. We massacred perhaps millions of Indians to take their land. Well, we need to repent of that. Secondly, we begin to do what all the other countries were doing – bring in slaves. And for hundreds of years, slavery existed in this country. Men were not taught how to read or write. They were told they were inferior beings. The women were used maliciously. I guess there were many "good" slave owners (the irony is comical). Well maybe one white man didn't beat his slaves, but he still had slaves. And as I was mentioning earlier about the civil war, the north really didn't care to free slaves. They were mad because the south was seceding. The south had all the cotton and stuff the north wanted for trade. It wasn't about freeing black people. But after blacks were so called "freed", from the north came these carpet baggers who brutalized many black people. Out of this came groups like the K.K.K. Laws were passed and even though blacks were supposedly emancipated by a proclamation, not much change really happened. The Law still did not allow them to vote or have any say. And so, when black people were freed the racist would point the finger and say "look at them, they can't read, write, or do anything". Well, if the people we were a part of weren't taught how to read or write from generation to generation, we wouldn't fair well either. This went all the way up to the Jim Crowe laws in the 1950's and 1960's until, thank God, people like Martin Luther King came along. Suppose Martin Luther King was a violent person like H. Rap Brown and Stokely Carmichael were. I lived where these men came and preached their racial hatred. H. Rap Brown and Stokely Carmichael were always in Washington D.C. stirring things up. But Martin Luther King, a Christian, left a tremendous legacy. In a nonviolent Christian's way, he fought for the liberty of his people. And he set in motion the groundwork for Black people to gain the right to even vote and gain all their rights as citizens of our country. Before the mid 1960's black people couldn't even vote in our country. I don't know if the younger black population actually realizes the change that has taken place over the last 40-50 years. Now even though the laws were passed that brought change, the same racism still existed in our leaders. There are still men in the Senate today who voted for desegregation in the 1960's. One of them died a few years ago, but one of them is still alive right now and in the Senate. But if we examine ourselves as a nation, we find that laws cannot remove racism. Racism still exists in America today.

Thinking back to the atrocities in our modern history that racism brought, it is unbelievable. I could never think of owning a slave. It staggers my mind when I see how the Jews were slaughtered not that long ago because of racism. That was in the 1930's and 1940's (less than 100 years ago!). This is not that long ago. And now in Germany there is more anti-Semitism than there has even been since the war. It seems to be starting up all over again.

Back to Galatians 3, "*27For as many of you as have been baptized into Christ have put on Christ. 28There is neither Jew nor Greek, there is neither bond nor free, there is neither male nor female: for ye are all one in Christ Jesus. 29And if ye be Christ's, then are ye Abraham's seed, and heirs according to the promise.*" First of all, the Bible clearly is stating here that there is no difference between Jews and Greeks. Please note this because we have many Messianic churches today and by them calling themselves Messianic Christians, there is a slight inference that they are better Christians than Gentile Christians and I don't believe it is of God. There is neither Jew nor Greek! But Paul also says here we are <u>all one</u> in Christ Jesus. This means black, white, red, yellow, and brown people are all heirs and all one in Christ Jesus. Romans 10:11-13 echoes this and says, "*11For the scripture saith, Whosoever believeth on him shall not be ashamed. 12For there is no difference between the Jew and the Greek: for the same Lord over all is rich unto all that call upon him. 13For whosoever shall call upon the name of the Lord shall be saved.*"

Now in Acts 10:24 we find Peter walking through the door in Cornelius' house. God had just given Peter a vision of a great sheet knit at the four corners with all manner of beast, creeping things, and fowls, falling to the earth. All these creatures were unlawful for Jews to eat, but the Lord tell Peter to kill and eat because "*What God hath cleansed, that call not thou common*" (verse 15). At the same time Cornelius had a vision (he was a centurion of the band called the Italian band) to send for a man by the name of Peter. Then we pick up the story in verse 24 as Peter is walking through the door in Cornelius' house, "*24And the morrow after they entered into Caesarea. And Cornelius waited for them, and had called together his kinsmen and near friends. 25And as Peter was coming in, Cornelius met him, and fell down at his feet, and worshipped him. 26But Peter took him up, saying, Stand up; I myself also am a man. 27And as he talked with him, he went in, and found many that were come together. 28And he said unto them, Ye know how that it is an unlawful thing for a man that is a Jew to keep company, or come unto one of another nation; but God hath shewed me that I should not call any man common or unclean.*" This is the Bible!

John 3:16 says, "*For God so loved <u>the world</u>, that he gave his only begotten Son, that whosoever believeth in him should not perish, but have everlasting life.*" Jesus did not come for one nation, but for the whole world. Jesus died and rose again for all people making us His body. Romans 12:3-5 says, "*3For I say, through the grace given unto me, to every man that is among you, not to think of himself more highly than he ought to think; but to think soberly, according as God hath dealt to every man the measure of faith. 4For as we have many members in one body, and all members have not the same office: 5So we, <u>being many</u>, are <u>one body in Christ</u>, and every <u>one members one of another</u>.*" I Peter 2:17 says to "*<u>Honour all men</u>. Love the brotherhood. Fear God. Honour the king.*" John 15:12-13 says, "*12This is my commandment, That* *ye love one another, as I have loved you. [13]Greater love hath no man than this, that a man lay down his life for his friends."* Jesus loved everybody and expects the same from us. Ephesians 2:18-19 says, *"[18]For through him we both have access by one Spirit unto the Father. [19]Now therefore ye are no more strangers and foreigners, but <u>fellowcitizens</u> with the saints, and of the household of God."*

The next thing I want to look at in this chapter is some scientific proof about how there is no difference between the races. The truth is that there are only minor variations among people groups. Scientists have found that if you take two people from anywhere in the world, the basic genetic differences between them would be typically around 0.2 percent, even if they came from the same people group. Next, even when we speak of the different so-called racial characteristics that many think are major differences (such as skin color, eye shape, nose size, lips, etc), they only account for 6 percent of this 0.2 percent variation which amounts to a mere 0.0012 percent difference genetically. Basically, there is no difference genetically making racial differences trivial. For instance, this is also true when looking for a tissue match for an organ transplant. You may hate black people, but if you need a liver and there is a black man's liver that just came available, what are you going to do? Don't worry, it will work fine! It is all in your racial head. Racism and prejudices are in the soul of a man, not in the spirit or body of a man. Another point to make is we know that all peoples can freely interbreed and produce fertile offspring. If we were so different, we couldn't do this.

The next fact is we all have the same coloring pigment in our skin and this is called melanin. This is a dark brownish pigment that is found in special cells in our skin. If we have no melanin, we are albinos. Albinos simply do not have any ability to produce melanin or color in their skin. If we produce a little melanin, it means we will be European white. If we produce a great deal of melanin, we will be black and in between there are all shades of brown. The first man Adam from whom all other human beings are descended, within him were all the factors of skin color (black, white, red, and brown). They were all in him. We saw that Scriptures seem to point out that Adam was a reddish clayish color. So white had to be in Adam. Black had to be in Adam, etc. Pretty much everybody in the beginning up until the flood were the same color. When the flood destroyed the earth, things changed environmentally. And then we know that from that flood, Shem, Ham, and Japheth were told to replenish the earth. This is found in Genesis 10, *"[1]Now these are the generations of the sons of Noah, Shem, Ham, and Japheth: and unto them were sons born after the flood...[32]These are the families of the sons of Noah, after their generations, in their nations: and by these were the nations divided in the earth after the flood."* There was no separation of color until then nor language as we read Genesis 11:1, *"And the whole earth was of one language, and of one speech."*

Everybody was the same, a reddish clay color. But when God saw in Genesis 11 that all the people were one and were trying to build a tower to heaven God separated them, *"⁵And the LORD came down to see the city and the tower, which the children of men builded. ⁶And the LORD said, Behold, the people is one, and they have all one language; and this they begin to do: and now nothing will be restrained from them, which they have imagined to do..."* Before we see how God handled this, I want to bring up an important point we see here. We can even have unity in the flesh. And when we have unity in the flesh, we can accomplish tremendous things. Why is it we find Christians have such a hard time coming together, which is probably why Jesus said if just two of us agree together we can see God move. Jesus had to simplify it for us I guess. Can you imagine when we as Christians come into the unity of the faith, what will be possible? Ephesians 4:13 says we can reach fullness is Christ, *"Till we all come in the unity of the faith, and of the knowledge of the Son of God, unto a perfect man, unto the measure of the stature of the fulness of Christ."* Forget about the Tower of Babel, we are going to be God-like again, men and women as they were in paradise.

Continuing in Genesis 11, *"⁷Go to, let us go down, and there confound their language, that they may not understand one another's speech. ⁸So the LORD scattered them abroad from thence upon the face of all the earth: and they left off to build the city. ⁹Therefore is the name of it called Babel; because the LORD did there confound the language of all the earth: and from thence did the LORD scatter them abroad upon the face of all the earth. ¹⁰These are the generations of Shem..."* So after God scatters the people across the face of the earth, He begins sharing on the descendents of Noah's three sons, Shem, Ham, and Japheth. As these three groups migrated away from Babel they encountered new and different climate zones. And accordingly their skin color changed to protect them. Our skin will react to the climate and make us the color it needs to be for the environment we live in. If you are living in the cold mountains like the white people, they didn't need dark skin. But if you are living around the equator where the sun is closest to the earth, you need to have more melanin produced and darker skin to protect your body. This is the whole thing about color. It was simply designed by God to protect the human that lives within.

Lastly, I want to look at two Scriptural terms. Did you know that the words "nations" and "Gentiles" are the same Hebrew and Greek words for the most part? In the Hebrew and Greek "nations" and "Gentiles" are synonymous. If you look up the Hebrew and Greek words for "nations" and "Gentiles", you will find the same words. The Hebrew word for both "nations" and "Gentiles" means "a foreign nation, heathen, people" and comes from a root word that means "person or baby". The Greek word means "a race (as of the same habit), a tribe, foreign, non-Jewish, by implication a pagan" and comes from a root word that means "to be used by habit or conventionality, be custom". The importance of this definition is it is not really about a race of people. This is why they put in parenthesis "as of the same habit" because what we are really talking about are just people groups with different culture. You see, we confuse races with cultures. We tend to find things in other people's culture and we make it racist in select groups. We applaud one culture and use another culture to foster racism. Why is this? Is there a reason for this? Yes. Is there a reason why black people think white people are cruel and mean many times? Yes. Why would a black man have to steal? Because he wasn't provided the same rights as other people, so as a culture growing up with no laws on their side, and growing up being persecuted and told you were inferior your whole life (generation after generation), as a culture maybe perhaps violence and stealing is a product of it.

What I am trying to say is a person, when they come into the earth, only know what they see around them. We are shaped by what our parents said and the environment in which we live and grow up in. We have no control over this. I'll be honest with you, for the first 14 years of my life I stole something pretty much everyday. I stole my lunch money everyday or I would shake people down and take it from them. Why did I do this? My parents were on welfare. We had no money. I never had a bicycle, baseball glove, etc. I never learned how to swim. You name it, I never had anything as a child unless I stole it. There is a reason why people are the way they are. Many things have been ingrained into some black people's thinking. We can't generalize a whole group of people, but this is still true. Now during this last generation where blacks have the same rights as whites, we see blacks running companies now. We have a black man who is president. Black people fill all aspects of society once given the chance to learn. You see, ignorance is bliss. This is why rappers and people like that to me act foolishly. They foster ignorance and stereotypes and simply encourage racism as far as I am concerned.

How do you think a black person feels when a white person walks into a room? If they feel the white person is smarter, superior, it is because they were told for generations that is the way it is. We think and do what our fathers did and what the culture that is within us does. What I am trying to tell you now, is when a man or woman is born again; they become a new creation in Christ Jesus. Old things pass away and all things become new! But there are not only bad things but precious things in every culture. For instance, every black guy calls every other black guy a brother. Every black woman will call another black woman a sister. Why is this? Because all they had were each other for hundreds of years. So a sense of family developed in their culture. Blacks have a sense of family far greater than white people. White people don't call each other brothers and sisters. In fact, there is a great amount of pride within the white race that separates them socially. I bet you President Obama could walk into the ghetto, walk up to a basketball court and say he wants to play and they will say, "Sure brother, let's play". Now if a white man driving a Rolls Royce comes into a country restaurant with rednecks that aren't very educated, is he going to call the waitress, "sister"? I don't think so. You see, there are good and bad things in every culture. We ought to rejoice in the diversities among us rather than pick out the things that are bad, especially now that we are born again. You and I are the only ones that can eliminate racism. World leaders can have every summit they want and racism will never stop. We can all get together around the white house and all hold hands and sing "Kum By Ya" and promise to never hate again, and I tell you it is not going to work because in the soul of mankind there is inbred hatred for other peoples simply because of the color of their skin. When in actuality, that person that is standing next to you of another color is somewhere at sometime in history been a part of your own family. We are of one blood of all nations of the earth.

Let me pray dear reader. As I pray, believe with me, that somehow, someway, you and I can break free from racism. I thank God everyday for the privilege He gave me (and I didn't even know it when it was happening) of the ability to live in the black culture. I was basically a black boy with white skin. I have seen things on both sides and I pray that what I shared will cause you to turn your heart to the Lord and do as Paul tried to live his life, "*And herein do I exercise myself, to have always a conscience void of offence toward God, and toward men*" (Acts 24:16). And as God told Peter not to call any man common or unclean, let us do the same. We are the lights of the world. I pray right now that you loose the hold of racism in our souls. Lord, the things we learned that weren't our fault, the things ingrained in our minds from our parents and grandparents and by generations of people that lived before us, deliver us. We want the image of Christ Jesus in our soul. You loved the whole world and were willing to die for it. Let us have your heart Jesus. And I bind every racist devil in our souls, minds, and bodies. I bind those devils, in you that are reading this; I bind those devils in you right now and cast them out. Be gone in Jesus name!

Lord, you said in Romans 5:5 that "*the love of God is shed abroad in our hearts by the Holy Ghost which is given unto us.*" May the Holy Ghost shed abroad in every heart the love of God right now. We give you honor and praise today Jesus! We thank you for our brothers and sisters and thank you for being a loving and merciful God to us. In Jesus' name, Amen!

The Spirit Of Racism And Hate
Chapter 10

This chapter in this book will be for me very, very personal. We have seen so clearly in the Word that Black people have played a great and pivotal role throughout the Bible and we have seen that we all come from the same human family. To God, we are all equal and precious in His sight. *"God is no respecter of persons"* (Acts 10:34) nor has He chosen any race, color, ethnic group, tribe, or peoples above others. He sees all of us through the blood of Jesus. We that have been born again are a *"new creation"* (II Corinthians 5:17, Galatians 6:15) and in the Greek this means a *"new species"*. We now (that is, all of God's people) belong to His great family. We are all the *"offspring of God"* (Acts 17:29) and His precious blood has cleansed all of us and brought us into our new family, the Kingdom of God: *"Therefore if any man be in Christ, he is a new creature: old things are passed away: behold, all things are become new"* (II Corinthians 5:17). We are now brothers and sisters, or as the scriptures declare, we are all now *"the sons of God"* (I John 3:1). We all now have the same color in the Spirit, that is the color of the glory of God, and that color is amber or gold or burnished brass. So for me it is impossible for someone who has been touched by the grace, mercy, and love of God, to hate someone because of the color of their skin, origin, culture, etc. This is even without looking into the principle of how we are *"to love one another as Christ has loved us"* (John 13:34, 15:12). The Bible is very clear that he who hates his brother is a murderer (I John 3:15, Matthew 5:21-22). These are extremely strong words that come roaring out of the Word of God. So first of all, if someone is going to call themselves a Christian, Biblically they are without excuse. How anyone could stand in God's divine, manifest glory and presence and hate is unfathomable to me. We are no better than Cain who *"slew his brother...because his own works were evil, and his brother's righteous"* (I John 3:12). Any honest believer who will have *"truth in the inward parts"* (Psalms 51:6) can never, ever, be a racist or hold racist ideas and love God at the same time. The verdict is in, the Scriptures are absolutely clear; we cannot be a racist or have tendencies like it and have a true walk with God.

Now I want to speak personally from my own experience and show you that racism stems from extreme pride, ignorance, and fear. I have lived my life in both the black and white world and feel I am more than equipped to speak on this subject. I have suffered racism at the hands of both black and white people. Having been raised in the black culture, God has allowed me to see both sides of this problem. I have seen racism in both black and white cultures. God sovereignly allowed me to be born in an all black community and live there for the first 15 years of my life. He then moved me to an all white neighborhood and allowed me to experience that culture as well. My

129

hope is, as you listen to my story, it will not only help you to see that racism is a spirit, but also that we don't have to be a product of our environment, but through the *"shedding of the blood of Jesus Christ"* we actually do become a *"new creation"* (Greek – *"new species")*, and are therefore part of a new family, the family of God. We have in Jesus been restored to the original unity found in the Garden of Eden and have been delivered from Babylon where the people of God were scattered and became what we have now, all the different races and cultures and colors (Genesis 11:1-9). In Jesus this is broken and destroyed and we are now people of the Kingdom of God. So here is my life story told in a concise way. I ask the Holy Spirit to give me the right words so that like an *"arrow of truth"* perhaps we can begin to go beyond our racist attitudes.

I want to begin by talking about two things. Racism and the hatred of someone for their culture or color of their skin stem from an evil spirit and secondly, I want to bring out how genetically speaking how that as we have come into this world, the environment we live in, we are part and parcel of our mothers and fathers all the way back through the generations.

First of all, racism is an evil spirit. It doesn't care what race or color. It just wants you to hate. From the beginning of my life, all of my parents, grandparents, aunts, uncles, etc. always used a derogatory word for black people when describing them. I believe this is true in most cultures. They speak privately of other races in a demeaning and incendiary way. They tell disgusting jokes, stories that aren't true to emphasize their hatred. Only, and I repeat only a demon that entered into our ancestors, years ago, and has been passed down from generation to generation can be this vile. When you consider all the scriptures in the Bible that tell of God's love and how He commands us to love one another and even to love our enemies, you have to realize at that point it is Satan that is behind all the hate. There are thousands of scriptures that speak of God's love, His grace, and His mercy. Racism is not just something people do, but it is a vile spirit that is operating in them. Satan was a *"murderer from the beginning"* (John 8:44) and until we are born again we are *"of your father the devil"* (John 8:44). The Bible declares that every one who is not saved has one or more devils in them, *"the spirit that now worketh in the children of disobedience"* (Ephesians 2:2). Satan causes men to hate. Sometimes even after we are born again these enemies of God will hide in the deeper chambers of our soul. We must renounce Satan and his devils, then receive some deliverance, and delve into the Word of God. Then we will start to understand God's character as well as start to allow the Holy Ghost to sanctify and cleanse us, we begin to walk in the love of God and we then can completely be made free from racism.

So let's clearly show how the spirit of racism and hate is from the Devil. In John 8:42-44, Jesus of course is wrestling with the Pharisees, the scribes, and the law-givers. *"Jesus said unto them, If God were your Father, ye would love me: for I proceeded forth and came from God; neither came I of myself, but he sent me. Why do ye not understand my speech? Even because ye cannot hear my word. Ye are of your father the devil, and the lusts of your father ye will do. He was a murderer from the beginning, and abode not in the truth, because there is no truth in him. When he speaketh a lie, he speaketh of his own: for he is a liar, and the father of it."* You have to understand when he says *"if God were your Father"*, he is talking to the priests, the ones who spend all day searching the scriptures. These are men who know God and Jesus says if God were your Father. I want to emphasize here, *"ye are of your father the devil and the lust of your father you will do"*

Racism at its very core stems from an evil spirit. We go all the way back to Cain slaying his brother Abel because his deeds were righteous. Remember the Lord speaking to Cain after he didn't receive his sacrifice. He told him that sin was crouching at the door and warned him to be careful about his attitude, but it didn't help. Why? Because Satan was allowed into the earth by Adam and Eve and man had become a fallen being. Now, in our fallen nature Satan exploits it. Once in the garden, where our spirit, soul, and body were living in complete paradise, in complete oneness with God man walked with God in the cool of the day. In the Hebrew means he rested comfortably with God. Everything was wonderful until they ate from the tree of knowledge of good and evil. This is when Adam, (man, mankind) fell and chose to go with the knowledge. The devil wanted back in and Adam and Eve allowed him to come back in.

We see in Job that when all the angels were reporting into God that Satan also came to report. God is still in charge and Satan and all that follow him have to report to Him. It says that Satan was walking back and forth. What was he looking for? He was and is looking for just a small crack in someone's soul that will allow him to come in and try to take control. We have to be so very careful with all the gates into our life. We have to protect ourselves. David said *"I will set no wicked thing before mine eyes."* In my own life it has taken years to finally get a hold of that principle. Protect yourself and realize that Satan is not omniscient, but he has certain demons that follow each of us to see what we do. He doesn't know our minds and he can't read our thoughts. All he knows is what we say and what we do. So we need to be like David when he said *"put a watch over my lips."* Let your words always be seasoned with salt and with grace.

So Satan is walking around, to and fro, basically looking for someone he can violate. Consider the temptation of Jesus that is in Matthew 4 and Luke 4 when Jesus was led of the Spirit into the wilderness and fasted 40 days. Afterwards he was tempted of the devil. You see the devil came after the 40 day fast before Jesus had eaten. He waited for what he thought was the right time, the time when Jesus would be at his weakest point. Then he begins to tempt him on so many different levels. Jesus passed the test by using the Word of God which is significant to us in that this is how we will defeat the enemy. He begins to taunt him and tempt him. This is the same thing you and I face whether we know it or not. There is a war going on around us all day long. The devil trying to find an entrance into our lives and God and His holy angels are protecting us and hoping we will have enough sense to not give in.

Everyone that is not born again has at least one evil spirit or they have the spirit of the world, which is the spirit of Satan really and there is a possibility that they may have many, many devils. This is found in Ephesians 2:1-5. *"And you hath he quickened, who were dead in trespasses and sins; Wherein in time past ye walked according to the course of this world, according to the prince of the power of the air, the spirit that now worketh in the children of disobedience: Among whom also we all had our* conversation *(Greek = Lifestyle) in times past in the lusts of our flesh, fulfilling the desires of the flesh and of the mind; and were by nature the children of wrath, even as others. But God, who is rich in mercy, for his great love wherewith he loved us, Even when we were dead in sins, hath quickened us together with Christ, (by grace ye are saved;)."* There are a couple of things I want to point out here. First of all, before we are born again we walked according to the course of this world. This world is filled with hatred, but what does Jesus say? *"If any man loves the world the love of the Father is not in him."* In Mark 4 it speaks of the *"lust of the flesh."* And in other places it speaks of the pride of this life, the cares of this world, the deceitfulness of riches, etc. That is what it means by the *"course of this world."* Unfortunately, we really didn't have anything to do with the entrance of sin into this world, but we were born into it. Then he goes on and says *"according to the prince of the power of the air"* realizing we were under the control of Satan. Next He says *"the spirit that now worketh in the children of disobedience."* So there is a spirit working in every heathen whether they like it or not, and it's a demon spirit. So who is it that whispers to Cain to kill his brother Abel? Obviously it was Satan who was *"a murderer from the beginning."* So it is racism that causes people to do vile acts against somebody else just because of the color of their skin or because of their culture. Where did he get that from? It originated in the spirit of racism.

In 1John 3:8-11 the Bible says, *"He that committeth sin is of the devil; for the devil sinneth from the beginning. For this purpose the Son of God was manifested, that he might destroy the works of the devil. For this purpose the Son of God was manifested, that he might destroy the works of the devil."* What are the works of the devil? Well, the works of the devil or Satan, you can really say are found in Galatians chapter 5, plus those things I mentioned earlier, the lust of the flesh, the cares of this world, the deceitfulness of riches, the lust of other things, etc. *"If any man loves the world the Father is not in him."* (1John

2:15) He that loveth the world, the pride of life, and all that stuff is controlled by Satan. So he exploits us and it is for this reason that Jesus came. The Son of God was manifested to destroy the works of the devil. Now listen to the next part of this passage. *"Whosoever is born of God doth not commit sin;"* How do we reconcile this statement? It is simple because we are born again in our spirit. Our spirit once we are born again will never sin again, but our soul and mind are a different story. This is a part of our three-fold salvation. Let's continue," *for his seed remaineth in him: and he cannot sin, because he is born of God. In this the children of God are manifest, and the children of the devil: whosoever doeth not righteousness is not of God, neither he that loveth not his brother. For this is the message that ye heard from the beginning, that we should love one another."* So the separation from those that love God and those that do not is determined how? It is determined by one, and one factor alone, if you love your brother as Jesus loved you. There's no other way. How many white southern Preachers led countless hundreds and thousands to Jesus all the while hating an entire race of people? You ask yourself, how could God put up with it? How could God put up with the likes of Hitler, Stalin, Bin Laden, Idi Amin, and countless other men that tried to destroy entire races? Even today, look at all the tribal wars in Africa, where ethnic cleansing is taking place. People are killing one another, trying to wipe each other out because they're of another tribe. It still exists today and maybe even worse now than in years past. In Somalia, hundreds of thousands of people have been murdered because they are of a certain tribe, or maybe they are Christian rather than Moslem. Yet the world just stands by and really doesn't do anything. It was the same attitude that prevailed when Hitler rose to power in Germany. Everybody just said well he's not going to eventually do this and he ended up doing everything they thought he wouldn't do. By the time they got their act together he had built a juggernaut of an army. He would have won World War II had he not made mistakes. Evil is always looking to control somebody. It is always looking to dominate someone. That is the whole purpose behind racism. It dominates; it despises, and looks to exalt one over another. It wants to have someone under them. Racism is truly an evil spirit.

Now in 1 Corinthians 2:12 it says, *"Now we have received, not the spirit of the world, but the spirit which is of God; that we might know the things that are freely given to us of God.* So there is a spirit of the world. It lives, it exists, it thrives in the heart of the heathen and it is obvious it is a spirit of hate. After Cain killed Abel the Bible says that men began to grow and expand and whatever came into the imagination of their hearts they did. It was so evil that God destroyed the earth with a flood. It didn't take any time at all for man to become so corrupt and so evil that God wanted to destroy them. When that destruction took place and God saw that all men were drowned in the waters, he said He would never destroy the earth again by a flood. But what do we find just from Genesis 6 to Genesis 11? Babylon begins to be built. Mankind doesn't need a lot of help to be evil and get off track. God has to come down again and this time he confuses their language and scatters them over the earth. When you think about it, how in Christianity, in less than 70 years after Jesus had been resurrected, we see Him in Revelation 3 on the outside of the Church knocking on the door and telling them if they would open the door He would come in and sup with them. *"...man at his best state is altogether vanity."* (Psalms 39:5) If man lives in the world, he is going to have and be led by the spirit of the world. He will walk in the course (lifestyle) of this world (age) and have demonic influences in his life.

So what do we do about this? There is only one thing we can do. We have to cast him out. First of all we have to be born again, washed in the blood of Jesus. Then every one of us needs to be baptized in water, but more so, be baptized in the Holy Ghost. In my own life, I look back over the almost 40 years I have been saved, and I realize that every person needs to have several moments or experiences in their walk with God, through their early years of deliverance. When I say that, what do I mean? In my life, I had been saved less than 3 months, I had been baptized in the Holy Ghost, a couple came out of nowhere. I don't even remember their names, but I ended up one night at a girl's house that was a friend of mine, and they took me up into this attic that they had redone, and for hours this man and woman cast demons out of me. I mean literally hours. That is how many demons I had in me. Then, a couple of years later I'm living in Jacksonville and a dear old friend of mine, George Wingate, who was a demon hunter, if you burped in front of him he would always say, "Um hm." If you coughed he would give you a look as if a devil had escaped from you. Even though he got to a point where he was overbalanced, he was still used mightily in my life. There was a time a little later that we were together at my spiritual father's house, Dan Duke, and he began casting demons out of me as I was choking Dan. So my thinking is that every child of God needs this in their life. We don't realize how damaged our chambers are. How many of our chambers are filled with demons. I thought I had a certain personality, but it wasn't me at all. Your personality is the sum total of all the chambers in your soul. When your soul is full of genetic defects, things handed down to you from your fathers and mothers, and their fathers and mothers, and so on and so on, these things have demons in them, and that is not the real you. I can honestly say that I didn't know the real me until I had been in the ministry for several years.

So racism is an evil spirit and stems from Satan, the father of it. Secondly, I want us to talk about how we were born into sin. We came into this world as sinners. We didn't have anything to do with the time, or place we were born. We didn't get to choose our parents or their economic status. Do you ever remember someone asking your input before you entered your mother's womb? I know I didn't. Here we are. We are born into this world, innocent and pure, part and parcel of our parents and all our ancestors. This is what we are made up of. We inherit certain things, certain personality traits, and generational curses. There are a lot of people who may disagree with me and what I am about to say, but I have been Pastoring for over 33 years now and I feel I have counseled with enough people to make this statement. I don't think people are born gay, but they can be born with certain inclinations to perversion. There's no question that we receive and are handed down many traits. In my own life, my father beat my mother, he was a murderer, and he raped my sisters, and constantly beat me and my brother and sisters. Some of the first books I ever looked at were of naked women. I was born into a very perverse environment. I battled pornography devils, lust devils, and all forms of sexual devils for years. I just wished that other ministers would be truthful with their sheep. Ministers are men, not gods. They have made mistakes and their congregations and disciples need to see that in them because they are probably dealing with some of those same issues. By telling the truth I know I am exposing myself, but at the same time maybe, I can help someone. Even after I was in the ministry, I would have seasons of peace and then all of a sudden, out of nowhere, here it would come again. Only by the grace of God, the divine influence upon my heart was I able to keep going. Thank God we have a Father in heaven that loves us and knows our hearts. Can you imagine if King David were in the ministry today? He would be kicked out of the ministry and forever put to shame. What a scandal it would be if what happened then happened now. God knew his heart. David loved God and wanted to be a righteous man, but he made a mistake and was in the wrong place at the wrong time. In everything he did wrong it was still said of him that he was a man after God's own heart. God even took the product of his wrong doing and made Solomon the wisest man ever to live. How wonderful and gracious our God is. He always tries to bring something good out of the dealings of God we go through.

Let's talk a little about the unredeemed man and even man after he gets saved. First of all, in Psalms 58:3, *"The wicked are estranged from the womb: they go astray as soon as they be born, speaking lies."* And how about Psalms 51:5,*"Behold, I was shapen in iniquity; and in sin did my mother conceive me."* So what happens here? Well, the passage in Romans 7:14-25 gives us great insight. Now I have already addressed the evil man, the spirit that works in him is the spirit of Satan or the spirit of the world. But now let's look at Christians who have the same background as the rest of the world. In sin I was conceived, but in hearing the gospel of Jesus I was saved, I was born again. I became a new creation (species) in the realm of the Spirit. Justification is for you spirit. Remember the three-fold plan of salvation. When I get saved, that is a spiritual experience known as Justification. When Jesus returns at the end of the last days our bodies are saved or glorified. The time in between Justification and Glorification is the period we know as Sanctification, or the saving of our souls or our minds. At the beginning, Justification makes your spirit forever right with God. Paul writes, *"For we know that the law is spiritual: but I am carnal, sold under sin. For that which I do I allow not: for what I would, that do I not; but what I hate, that do I. If then I do that which I would not, I consent unto the law that it is good. **Now then it is no more I that do it, but sin that dwelleth in me**"*. What is Paul saying? He is saying that some things we are immediately delivered from, but there are some things, sin, that remain in me. Sin remains in my soul, not my spirit. *"For I know that in me (that is, in my flesh,) dwelleth no good thing: for to will is present with me; but how to perform that which is good I find not. For the good that I would I do not: but the evil which I would not, that I do. **Now if I do that I would not, it is no more I that do it, but sin that dwelleth in me**. I find then a law, that, when I would do good, evil is present with me. For I delight in the law of God after the inward man:"* This flesh of ours, this soul is the problem. Evil is present within me. *"But I see another law in my members, warring against the law of my mind, and bringing me into captivity to the law of sin which is in my members. O wretched man that I am! who shall deliver me from the body of this death? I thank God through Jesus Christ our Lord. So then with the mind I myself serve the law of God; but with the flesh the law of sin."* My spirit is full of Jesus. My spirit is willing, but this body, my flesh is so weak. Why? There are in every one of us thousands of chambers in our soul. Remember when Jesus asked the demon in the Gadarene man what his name was? The demon answered that his name was Legion. This was the only time Jesus asked a demon to reveal his name and was for the soul purpose to show us how many chambers we had in our soul. Your soul is made up of thousands of chambers that are either filled with a spirit of Satan, or something that happened in your past like abuse or rejection, or something genetically handed down from generation to generation, or they are filled with the Spirit of God. Most people are not racists, they don't know why they act the way they do towards other races. It is because it has been handed down from their ancestors.

So the only way to deal with these issues is through Jesus. It is through His word. He said if you continue in my word then you will be my disciples. Through searching the scriptures you will come to know the truth and the truth will make you free. So the main ingredient in getting these chambers delivered is not having hands laid on you, it is becoming a disciple and a student of the scriptures. It will reshape and remake and it will force you to confront the things in those chambers. This is why a lot of people don't want come to a church that truly teaches the word, because affliction arises for the words sake. You can't come to this kind of church and skate by. At some point, something is going to be said that will jolt you and cause one of those chambers to open, because God wants to deal with it. Here is the thing. God opens them up not to condemn you, but to get you delivered from them. We have got the whole thing backwards. We think judgment is a bad thing. Actually, it is the best thing we could have happen to us. So he opens that chamber on jealousy, or ambition, or you name it. Then we have the choice to make, whether we are going to deal with it or not. Is our revelation going to be married to our situation or not? Sadly, a lot of people decide to move on and not deal with the issues. They just suppress them and move to another church. Therefore they live in that state with sin in their members because they willingly chose to. They will never be able to attain to bride ship because they are not going on to perfection. (Hebrews 6:1) They're not allowing the Word of God to sanctify them. Sanctification is a life long process that if allowed will change us into His image.

What do the scriptures say about racism and hatred? 1 John 3:15 says,"*Whosoever hateth his brother is a murderer: and ye know that no murderer hath eternal life abiding in him.*" I saw this very familiar show on television with this white Preacher dressed in Klu Klux Klan garb, preaching against black people and he is a Baptist Pastor. You can't love God and hate your brother. If you do than God says you are a murderer. 1 John 4:20 God says, "*If a man say, I love God, and hateth his brother, he is a liar: for he that loveth not his brother whom he hath seen, how can he love God whom he hath not seen?*" What a shock that is going to happen to a lot of white people when they see God. I think when we appear before God for a review of our history at the judgement seat of Christ and people look and see that Moses was black. They are going to say that Moses can't be black. And what are they going to say when they find out that white people don't even come on the scene until later in history. The people of the earth in the beginning were brown, reddish, or black for the most part. How can you love God who you can't see and hate your brother who you can see? Don't be going around saying you love the Lord and you despise your black brothers, and Mexicans, and Orientals, and other races of the world. 1 John 2:9-11 says, "*He that saith he is in the light, and hateth his brother, is in darkness even until now. He that loveth his brother abideth in the light, and there is none occasion of stumbling in him. But he that hateth his brother is in darkness, and walketh in darkness, and knoweth not whither he goeth, because that darkness hath blinded his eyes.*" The world says ignorance is bliss. So many people receive from authority figures and never challenge what they say. We ask why would they lie to us? Therefore our thought processes are forever shaped. All the things we go through in life shape us and make us who we are. Leviticus 19:17 says, "*Thou shalt not hate thy brother in thine heart...*" Can God be any clearer that that? Speaking of our brothers in 1 Thessalonians 4:6-10, the word says "*he therefore that despiseth, despiseth not man, but God...*" Let's consider this word despise. There are two words in the Hebrew for despise. The first one is buwz, which means to disrespect or to condemn. The second one is bazah, which interpreted means to disesteem, disdain, and think to scorn, or count someone as vile. In the Greek there are three words. The first is atheteo which means to set a side, disesteem, or to violate. The second word is kataphroneo which means to think against or a low opinion of someone. The third word is exoutheou which means to make utterly nothing or set at naught. Maybe a simpler definition would be tossed aside. What about Proverbs 11:12? *"He that is void of wisdom despiseth his neighbor..."* What were all those preachers in the south doing when they preached slavery? It is totally incomprehensible how they were able to sleep after ministering. This next passage really does shed light on men and the masks they wear. Proverbs 26:24-26, *"He that hateth dissembleth with his lips, and layeth up deceit within him; When he speaketh fair, believe him not: for there are seven abominations in his heart. Whose hatred is covered by deceit, his wickedness shall be shewed before the whole congregation."* How many people that are racist have spoken fairly in the presence of white people, or black people, or Hispanic people? But when they are alone and away from them they say what they really feel about them. God hates prejudice and racism. God doesn't despise anyone. He created all men and He created them equal. God gave His son Jesus to the whole world. He didn't send him to one race. He doesn't want to see any of His creation perish. He wants us all to live in peace and harmony.

Black Messengers Of God
Chapter 11

In this chapter, I would like to look at the messengers of God in the Bible who were black. Black people have been great messengers throughout the Scripture and have had the glory and anointing of God upon them. The more I study this subject, the more I have to make certain that what I write here is not only true Biblically, but historically. Let me preface this chapter by saying much of what is written here might be very new to you and you might even have a struggle believing some of it. This is why I have extensively researched this subject. But one of the first things I found during my research is most of the history and commentary of the Bible was written by white men and I have to say many were prejudiced. To even find this out took a lot of research as well. On the other hand, there are many Black theologians who go in the complete opposite direction and what they have to share is out of balance as well. Through my research, I am trying to declare to you things I know I can prove scripturally, historically, and genealogically. Above all, it shouldn't even matter to us what color Jesus was, what color the prophets were, and so on. It is not an issue to God nor should it be for us. But the job God has given me as a teacher and scribe is to search those things people do not want to search out. Even though color is not an issue to us, we should always have an answer to everything we believe to convince any gainsayers. We should be able to prove everything we believe in the Scriptures. In this book, I am trying to lay down a Biblical revelation that is not only true, but awesome when you see the myriad of the people that God uses. It is true our Kingdom as Christians is a spiritual kingdom, but because we live with people on the earth who want to have answers to earthly questions, we need to be like Peter exhorted, *"be ready always to give an answer to every man that asketh you a reason of the hope that is in you with meekness and fear"* (I Peter 3:15). Even in researching this book, I have learned quite a bit. At the same time, I've found that I have had no reservations in believing what I am seeing in the Scripture and I pray this is true for you also.

Before we look into God's Black messengers, I want to begin by looking at two words, Cush and Ethiopia. The first thing to notice is that both of these words are the same word in Hebrew. They are interchangeable. They mean black, burnt black in the face, sun burnt. In the Greek, the word for Ethiopia is *Aithiops* and means "an Ethiopian, as a black moor, sun burned faces, a black countenance, region of burnt faces" and comes from two words (*aitho* and *ops*). The first word (*aitho*) means "to scorch" an the second word (*ops*) means "the face. This is obviously saying Cush and Ethiopia speak of black people. The shocking thing is some Bible commentaries draws their conclusions not on clear evidence in the Bible. They twist things by not using the Scriptures but by following men who wrote history about the Bible hundreds and hundreds of years after the Bible. But what they don't understand and what we need to understand is the Bible is our plumb-line for everything. We don't put the opinion of some church father above the Scriptures. Josephus might have been a great man, but I don't get my true information of revelation from him. Even the translators of the King James Bible were prejudice many times not only against color but also against women. They leave glaring holes out of the Bible leaving out the word women and replacing it with something else. We need to then be able to look at the original transcripts (the original Hebrew, Greek, writings) that came from the mouth of God. II Peter 1:21 says *"For the prophecy came not in old time by the will of man: but holy men of God spake as they were moved by the Holy Ghost."* Every word of God is inspired. This is what we want and thank God we have the ability to trace these words on our own and find out the real meaning of them. For instance, many books that have the definitions of names in them won't even have the name "Cush" in them and it is a word in the Scriptures. They refuse to define it for some reason. I believe this could be a subtle prejudice. The main thing many try to say to try to prove that all the Old Testament figures were Caucasian is the following. Noah's sons again were Ham, Shem, and Japheth. Every scholar would believe that Ham is the father of all black groups. Cush is the son of Ham and all of the sons of Ham founded 4-5 different lands (all of them being in Africa). What they try to say is this. They don't use Scripture, but they pull out somebody's writings that said they found archeological evidence of pictures that made people look like they were Caucasoid. But there are just as many archeological findings that show that all the older Egyptians were black. But the commentators tend to lean on the Caucasoid side and say that there is a Lower Egypt and a higher Egypt. They say the Lower Egypt was the black Ham-ites and the upper regions were Japheth-ites (or white people). They even have to add that they have some color to them, but they say they weren't "black". I had to search through hundreds of these books and comb through their subtle racism where they try to be "educational" with their lies. I also read around 50 Black theological books, and then looked at Black liberation theology which say's every Biblical figure (even Jesus) was black. When you read these books, you can't even tell white people are even on the earth. They were much less subtle in their racism. So to try to hew out of the rock these truths found in this book were difficult and required a lot of research. The Word declares "a false balance is an abomination to the lord." I have sought to be balanced in all things. To not let my personal opinion come into play; I have honestly tired before God to let the scriptures speak for themselves.

Here are some things to note about the terms Cush & Ethiopia. First of all, Cush was the son of Ham. We see this in Genesis 10:6. We all know that the flood had destroyed the then-known earth, the earth had to be repopulated, and there were only three sons of Noah, Shem, Ham and Japheth. Everybody agrees that Shem became the royal seed and the lineage of Israel. Japheth was the father of all white races and Ham was the father of all black races. In Genesis 11 when the Lord scattered all of the people upon the face of the earth because they built the Tower of Babel, these three groups of peoples went to certain places. Ham and his descendents stayed around where the Garden of Eden was, which I believe was in Africa and not Iraq. Civilization as we know it was birthed in Africa.

Genesis 10:6, *"And the sons of Ham; Cush, and Mizraim, and Phut, and Canaan."* Ham was pretty prolific. He had a lot of sons. His sons had a lot of sons and they became a lot of the tribes Israel would face. This is the struggle I had during my research when considering Canaan. We know Canaan was the one who received the curse. Ham was not cursed, but Canaan was because he was the one who committed the homosexual act on his father. The Canaanites turned out to be the vilest and most perverse people in the Bible. But the question I have difficulty answering is, were the Canaanites black or of a different color?

Mizraim is simply Egypt. Mizraim and Egypt are the same thing like Cush & Ethiopia. Ham's name means heat, hot, warm, black, dark. He was father of all black people groups. Whether he was actually black or not is an interesting question. How does a man (Noah) have three sons, all of different color? I believe as time progressed and people moved to different places, the melanin in different people changed as they became acclimated to different geographical locations. So Ham might not have been black. But Ham is considered to be the first black man. Each of Ham's sons founded a nation: Cush = Ethiopia, Mizraim = Egypt, Phut = Libya, Canaan = Palestine and all of the area around there. All of these nations were founded by black men.

Let us look at a passage in Isaiah 11 that I think is beautiful about the black race. God is speaking of the last days starting in verse 10, *"[10]And in that day there shall be a root of Jesse, which shall stand for an ensign of the people; to it shall the Gentiles seek: and his rest shall be glorious. [11]And it shall come to pass in that day, that the Lord shall set his hand again the second time to recover the remnant of his people, which shall be left, from Assyria, and from Egypt, and from Pathros, and from Cush, and from Elam, and from Shinar, and from Hamath, and from the islands of the sea. [12]And he shall set up an ensign for the nations, and shall assemble the outcasts of Israel, and gather together the dispersed of Judah from the four corners of the earth."* A few years ago there was a great big push to get all of the black Ethiopian Jews freed to go to Israel. Black people are so associated with the Hebrew people. Instead of saying our "Judeo-Christian" heritage, we should really say our "African-Judeo-Christians" heritage. There is no way to say it any other way because all of the people in the Old Testament were people of color. There weren't white people in the Bible really until Cornelius in the New Testament comes along. Isaiah 11 tells us that God is going to recover His remnant in the last days and some of them are going to be coming out of Egypt and Cush. This is a revelatory Scripture about the last days which basically says among the remnant are going to be precious black saints!

We already saw in another chapter about the river flowing out of the Garden of Eden (Genesis 2:10-14). And flowing over the whole land of Ethiopia *"¹⁰And a river went out of Eden to water the garden; and from thence it was parted, and became into four heads...¹³And the name of the second river is Gihon: the same is it that compasseth the whole land of Ethiopia..."* This river is flowing out of the garden and is symbolic of the presence of God or His Holy Spirit. Therefore Genesis 2:13 symbolizes God sending His presence and Holy Ghost to encompass the entire land of Ethiopia. This tells me the blessing of God is on the black race. The Spirit of God is calling unto them like it is calling to everyone else.

In Psalms 68:31-32 it says *"Princes shall come out of Egypt; Ethiopia shall soon stretch out her hands unto God. ³²Sing unto God, ye kingdoms of the earth; O sing praises unto the Lord; Selah."* This is saying to us prophetically that leadership is going to come from the black race. Also, Ethiopia (black people) are going to stretch out their hands to God in intercession, in worship, and in hunger for the things of God. Psalms 87:2-6 says, *"²The LORD loveth the gates of Zion more than all the dwellings of Jacob. ³Glorious things are spoken of thee, O city of God. Selah. ⁴I will make mention of Rahab and Babylon to them that know me: behold Philistia, and Tyre, with Ethiopia; this man was born there. ⁵And of Zion it shall be said, This and that man was born in her: and the highest himself shall establish her. ⁶The LORD shall count, when he writeth up the people, that this man was born there. Selah."* This Psalm is about Zion. Naturally, Zion is an actual mountain in Israel. Spiritually, it speaks of the Kingdom of God and a place in God that we reach in the height of worship where we become one with heaven. In speaking of God in Psalms 80:1 it says *"thou that dwellest between the cherubims, shine forth."* Psalms 50:2 says, *"Out of Zion, the perfection of beauty, God hath shined."* Zion is when God comes done in the midst of us, His people, and is enthroned upon our hearts. Exodus 15:2 says, *"The LORD is my strength and song, and he is become my salvation: he is my God, and I will prepare him an habitation; my father's God, and I will exalt him."* Ephesians 2:22 talks about God's people being God's habitation, *"In whom ye also are builded together for an habitation of God through the Spirit."* So there comes a place where God Himself becomes seated in Zion, or God Himself sits upon the thrones of the hearts of His people. This is the same seat I believe where the antichrist will sit on. I don't believe this is a natural seat in natural Israel because antichrist is first and foremost a spirit. Therefore the abomination of desolation is when Satan sits upon the throne of people's hearts rather than the Lord. But when Jesus sits on the throne of His people's hearts, this is Zion. This can happen personally or corporately, when a person or people go through the outer court, then slip on in the holy place in worship, only to then to go into that third dimension, the most holy place, where God's glory rests upon His people. Psalms 132:13-14 says, *"¹³For the LORD hath chosen Zion; he hath desired it for his habitation. ¹⁴This is my rest for ever: here will I dwell; for I have desired it."* How else is God going to have a habitation with man, except with Zion? To us, Zion is not a natural place, but it is a spiritual place we reach. It is the same thing as the secret place (Psalms 91:1). It is the most holy place of God. Well, I said all this about Zion to bring out what we read in Psalms 87 about Zion, *"³Glorious things are spoken of thee, O city of God. Selah. ⁴I will make mention of Rahab and Babylon to them that know me: behold Philistia, and Tyre, with Ethiopia; this man was born there. ⁵And of Zion it shall be said, This and that man was born in her: and the highest himself shall establish her. ⁶The LORD shall count, when he writeth up the people, that this man was born there. Selah."* I already proved in another chapter that Rahab was a black woman. What this passage is saying is when God counts up the people who are Zion, Rahab and Ethiopia are a part of those written down who will be in Zion.

Next, let us look in Zephaniah 3. In verse 8, the Lord is talking about how He is going to come and judge the earth, but then in verse 9-10 we read, *"⁹For then will I turn to the people a pure language, that they may all call upon the name of the LORD, to serve him with one consent. ¹⁰From beyond the rivers of Ethiopia my suppliants, even the daughter of my dispersed, shall bring mine offering..."* Let me read another translations of verse 10, *"From beyond the rivers of Cush, those who pray to me, the daughters of my dispersed people will bring and present my offering"*, and *"From beyond the rivers of Ethiopia, my worshippers, my dispersed one..."* First, in the Hebrew "suppliants" means "incense, a worshipper" and comes from a root word that means "to burn incense in worship". This word really means a great deal of smoke or a great deal of incense. In other words, when God brings forth the last days, we see very clearly, that Ethiopia is going to be present as well. So is it any wonder that black people are great worshippers of the Lord. They are called here His suppliants and the word literally means a great smoke of incense. This is a revelation of Scriptures about the black race. The second thing I want to look at in Zephaniah 3:9-10 is the phrase, *"⁹For then will I turn to the people a pure language..."* When was language changed? At the tower of Babylon in Genesis 11 up to the point in history in Genesis 11 everybody looked the same and everybody spoke the same. It wasn't until God saw their unity was a Babylonish unity (trying to find their way to heaven on their own and rejecting Him), He came down and scattered the nations. Once the people began to scatter, languages changed and skin color changed. Isn't it interesting this was all due to Babylon? Babylon brought about the separation of races. This is

143

why in Acts 2, on the day of Pentecost, there were people present from every nation of the earth, and we pointed out previously many of these nations were black nations. After the Holy Ghost fell on the day of Pentecost, Peter said, *"For the promise is unto you, and to your children, and to all that are afar off, even as many as the Lord our God shall call"* (Acts 2:39). This pure language that God in Zephaniah 3:9 prophesied that His people will turn to is speaking in tongues, God's heavenly language.

Now let me begin by naming God's black messengers. First of all, turn to II Samuel 18 and I want to look at a black messenger called Cushi. This is the story when Absalom tried to usurp David's kingdom from him and David had to flee the capital to go hide until God fixed the situation and he could go back. Well, they are fighting the deciding battle and David is waiting to hear a word about what happened, so we pick up the story in verse 19, *"Then said Ahimaaz the son of Zadok, Let me now run, and bear the king tidings, how that the LORD hath avenged him of his enemies..."* Now let me say before I go on there were many black men in the mighty men of David. David's army had black men in it. Ahimaaz we find here is a bit ambitious, *"[20]And Joab said unto him, Thou shalt not bear tidings this day, but thou shalt bear tidings another day: but this day thou shalt bear no tidings, because the king's son is dead. [21]Then said Joab to <u>Cushi, Go tell the king what thou hast seen</u>..."* Cushi was a black man. Now why would Joab let Cushi go and tell the news to David and not Ahimaaz? The answer is simple – trust. Cushi was a proven and faithful soldier. Ahimaaz was not. This is important because Cushi was a black man in the army of David which is a type of the army of God, and David is a type of Jesus. So that within the army of God there are faithful and proven black messengers! Hallelujah! Cushi was told to *"Go tell the king what thou hast seen"*. This is an amazing principle. You and I can't give what we don't have nor share what we haven't seen. I believe this not only is speaking about reporting about the day of this battle, but when you and I share revelation and share the mysteries of God; we can only do that if we've seen them. Cushi was able and this says a lot about this man.

The story continues, *"...And Cushi bowed himself unto Joab, and ran. [22]Then said Ahimaaz the son of Zadok yet again to Joab, but howsoever, let me, I pray thee, also run after Cushi. And Joab said, wherefore wilt thou run, my son, seeing that thou hast no tidings ready?"* Ahimaaz is full of ambition. This brings in the principle of waiting on the timing of the Lord to minister, especially somebody like Ahimaaz, who was even a son of Zadok can be out of order. Jeremiah said, *"It is good for a man that he bear the yoke in his youth"* (Lamentations 3:27). Well, Ahimaaz said, *"[23]But howsoever, said he, let me run. And he said unto him, Run. Then Ahimaaz ran by the way of the plain, and overran Cushi..."* This principle here is many times spiritually young and ambitious people can maybe run faster than others, play better, sing better, preach better, prophesy better, and do a whole lot of things better than others, but God's not in it and the truth is these ambitious people do not have anything to share from Him. Ahimaaz in this story didn't have any tidings. It doesn't matter what Ahimaaz thought he could do. It was obvious he had yet to prove himself to the King. Cushi had.

"*²⁴And David sat between the two gates: and the watchman went up to the roof over the gate unto the wall, and lifted up his eyes, and looked, and behold a man running alone...*" I underlined "*a man running alone*" on purpose because it is the truth. We now have in the Body of Christ so many mature believers running alone not accountable to anyone, not submitted, not in a flow, not listening to leadership, and not sent from God. "*²⁵And the watchman cried, and told the king. And the king said, If he be alone, there is tidings in his mouth. And he came apace, and drew near. ²⁶And the watchman saw another man running: and the watchman called unto the porter, and said, Behold another man running alone. And the king said, He also bringeth tidings. ²⁷And the watchman said, Me thinketh the running of the foremost is like the running of Ahimaaz the son of Zadok. And the king said, He is a good man, and cometh with good tidings.*" Here is the thing. You can be good and the king knows your future, that one day you will have great revelation, great gifts, and a great minister ahead of you, but watch happens to Ahimaaz. "*²⁸And Ahimaaz called, and said unto the king, All is well. And he fell down to the earth upon his face before the king, and said, Blessed be the LORD thy God, which hath delivered up the men that lifted up their hand against my lord the king. ²⁹And the king said, Is the young man Absalom safe? And Ahimaaz answered, When Joab sent the king's servant, and me thy servant, I saw a great tumult, but I knew not what it was. ³⁰And the king said unto him, Turn aside, and stand here. And he turned aside, and stood still...*" First of all, Joab didn't send Ahimaaz. He went on his own. Second, Ahimaaz saw a great tumult and didn't have anything else to say. You and I can see something, but not understand the message. We see the king then telling Ahimaaz to turn aside and stand still. Ahimaaz should have been standing still from the beginning but he ran and ended up disappointing the king.

"*³¹And, behold, Cushi came; and Cushi said, Tidings, my lord the king: for the LORD hath avenged thee this day of all them that rose up against thee. ³²And the king said unto Cushi, Is the young man Absalom safe? And Cushi answered, The enemies of my lord the king, and all that rise against thee to do thee hurt, be as that young man is. 33 And the king was much moved, and went up to the chamber over the gate, and wept...*" Here we finish Cushi, a faithful black messenger, bearing tidings for the king!

Next, let us look at the first few words in Zephaniah 1:1, "*The word of the LORD which came unto Zephaniah the son of Cushi...*" Zephaniah was a black

145

man and a messenger of God! His name means "hid of the Lord, protected by the Lord, concealed of the Lord, whom Jehovah hid", Hallelujah!

The next messenger I want to address is found in Exodus. I have wrestled with this person for a couple of weeks but I don't think there is any way other than to say it like it is. Moses, the great man of God, I honestly believe was a black man and I'll show you why I believe this. Here is Exodus 2 we read, *"[1]And there went a man of the house of Levi, and took to wife a daughter of Levi. [2]And the woman conceived, and bare a son: and when she saw him that he was a goodly child, she hid him three months. [3]And when she could not longer hide him, she took for him an ark of bulrushes, and daubed it with slime and with pitch, and put the child therein; and she laid it in the flags by the river's brink. [4]And his sister stood afar off, to wit what would be done to him. [5]And the daughter of Pharaoh..."* Now, this daughter of Pharaoh was black. You can say it no other way. Pharaoh's daughter was black and his children were black. It is funny how Genesis ends with Joseph dying and the tribes of his two sons, Manasseh and Ephraim, lay him in a coffin in Egypt. We already saw that Manasseh and Ephraim were mixed children, sons of a black woman. Joseph married a black woman, who was the daughter of a black prince. Not only this, what do you think happened when only 70 souls came of Jacob's family down to Egypt and when they left, there was at least somewhere between 2-3 million of them. How do you go from 70 to 2-3 million, except you intermarry with the people you are living with? In Moses life, he is found by the daughter of Pharaoh, she has compassion on him, takes him as her own, and Moses grows up and lives in the house of Pharaoh for all of his young life. *"...[10]And the child grew, and she brought him unto Pharaoh's daughter, and he became her son. And she called his name Moses: and she said, Because I drew him out of the water."* Now, Moses might not have been as black as the ace of spades, but I am telling you Moses was able to pass for a black man in Pharaoh's house and look like a son of Pharaoh. This may sound radical to some, but it doesn't bother me at all. We can still revere Charlton Heston when he starred in the famous move about Moses called "The Ten Commandments", but Moses definitely wasn't white like him. I do give credit to Steven Spielberg which made Moses a man of color (not making him white) in the animated movie "The Prince of Egypt", It is said he wrestled, with the fact about what was the true color of Moses.

Now, holding our place in Moses' story in Exodus, let us look at Act 7 and see a companion verse about Moses. Acts 7:20-23, *"[20]In which time Moses was born, and was exceeding fair, and nourished up in his father's house three months: [21]And when he was cast out, Pharaoh's daughter took him up, and nourished him for her own son. [22]And Moses was learned in all the wisdom of the Egyptians, and was mighty in words and in deeds. [23]And when he was full forty years old, it came into his heart to visit his brethren the children of*

Israel." Now, Moses was a prince in Egypt. How could a man live in a black man's house for 40 years and his daughter try to say Moses was her son? This could only work if Moses had some characteristics that made him fit in this place. Moreover we see this is true when Moses was 40 years old. At age 40 Moses visits his brethren the children of Israel and kills an Egyptian and Pharaoh wants to kill Moses. Let us continue reading in Exodus 2:15, *"¹⁵Now when Pharaoh heard this thing, he sought to slay Moses. But Moses fled from the face of Pharaoh, and dwelt in the land of Midian: and he sat down by a well. ¹⁶Now the priest of Midian had seven daughters: and they came and drew water, and filled the troughs to water their father's flock. ¹⁷And the shepherds came and drove them away: but Moses stood up and helped them, and watered their flock. ¹⁸And when they came to Reuel their father, he said, How is it that ye are come so soon to day? ¹⁹And they said, An Egyptian delivered us out of the hand of the shepherds..."* These daughters of the priest of Midian mistook Moses for an Egyptian. Moses looked like an Egyptian, which proves this point further.

Next in Moses' story, let us look in Exodus 4. Moses is 80 now. God here is dealing with Moses about going and being His minister and Moses is trying to think of every reason not to go. This is unlike Ahimaaz which we just read who couldn't wait to run. This is what 40 years on the backside of a desert will do to you. Moses spent 40 years in the desert and the Lord destroyed all ambition out of him. Moses didn't want to go. I personally don't believe God truly sends anybody until He deals with their ambition. When people do not want to go, usually only then are they ready to go, because God doesn't need a bunch of ambitious people in the ministry. What He needs are broken men and women of God. Men and women who have spent time on the backside of a desert having all manner pride, ambition, etc, destroyed out of them, so whatever they do from that moment on will not be for them, but for Jesus and His Kingdom! So in Exodus 4, let us watch as Moses is arguing with the Lord, starting in verse 6, *"And the LORD said furthermore unto him, Put now thine hand into thy bosom. And he put his hand into his bosom: and when he took it out, behold, his hand was leprous as snow. ⁷And he said, Put thine hand into thy bosom again. And he put his hand into his bosom again; and plucked it out of his bosom, and, behold, it was turned again as his other flesh."* All I want to point out from this story is obviously Moses hand was not white, if it could be turned white. Now even after all I presented here and you want to believe Moses was white like the movie, it's your choice. I certainly don't believe this. All I know is when the Lord told me to research and write this book, these were the reasons. First of all, He told me He wants to encourage and release His precious Black people (though God doesn't see the outward appearance), but He knows we do. He told me to show them through the Scriptures who they really were, how they are to be honored, and what the calling on their life is. Secondly, the purpose of this book is to destroy racism in His people.

Hopefully, as people read this book, they will see that God does not judge after the outward appearance, but according to the heart. God told Peter that he should call no man common or unclean (Acts 10:28). The truth is there is no difference between Jew or Greek, bond or free, male or female, etc. God is the Father of His whole family in heaven and in earth. And I love the passage in Acts 17:26, *"And hath made of one blood all nations of men for to dwell on all the face of the earth, and hath determined the times before appointed, and the bounds of their habitation."* All the peoples of the earth come from one blood. The blood that runs through an Asian person's body is the same as everyone else. Color is a matter of pigmentation in the skin.

We saw in another chapter that the author of the racist theories that are so prevalent today that encouraged people like Hitler and others was Darwin's Theory on Evolution. This was the main source, because as a scientist, he basically was saying there are different races and he even went on to say the Australian Aborigines were the missing link and were inferior people. The inference is people of color haven't "evolved" or can evolve into a higher realm of thinking. Where do you think Hitler got his ideas from? This is the result of these types of teachings. This is why evolution is a lie from the pit of hell. The ironic thing is every liberal black democrat doesn't even know that the father of much of what they believe in had racist tendencies. I'm sure Darwin was sincere, but he believed there were races inferior to others and tried to prove this scientifically. But science has only proven there is no difference. If a white man is dying and needs a liver, a black man's liver will work just fine! The only difference between people groups is cultural difference. Darwin's work was all a theory. All racial prejudices were birthed by a spirit of racism and it is learned theory. Everyone on the earth has been racist in some form or fashion in their life. Sometimes, we don't even know how we got this way. It was passed down from our parents and culture. My heart in writing this book is to allow the Scriptures and the Spirit of God to expose the racism in His people with hopes of being completely delivered and seeing every body around us as God sees them. Well, God's Word is full of black messengers, and Moses was one of them, like it or not.

Another one of God's messengers the black race has produced is found in Mark 15:21, *"And they compel one Simon a Cyrenian, who passed by, coming out of the country, the father of Alexander and Rufus, to bear his cross."* In other words, Simon a Cyrenian bore the cross and helped Jesus carry the cross to Golgotha where He was crucified. Cyrene was an ancient city in North Africa which would later become Libya. Most scholars realize Cyrene was a black nation and Simon was a black man and this black man carried the cross. The revelation of this passage is that black people are to assist in the salvation of the world! I am going to take it a few steps further. Simon went on to father a boy named Rufus whom Paul in Romans 16:13 made a note of saying,

"Salute Rufus chosen in the Lord, and his mother and mine." Even theologians know that Rufus was the son of Simon the Cyrenian. So once again we see another black messenger, Rufus, chosen in the Lord. Glory to God!

The next passage I want to look at is in Acts 13:1, *"Now there were in the church that was at Antioch certain prophets and teachers; as Barnabas, and Simeon that was called Niger, and Lucius of Cyrene, and Manaen, which had been brought up with Herod the tetrarch, and Saul."* Here we see two black messengers, Simeon called Niger (Niger is very close to another name black people call each other nowadays) and Lucius of Cyrene. The word Niger means black we just saw with Simon that Cyrene was a black nation. Here are two black prophets and teachers, Simeon and Lucius, who were there in the church.

In Acts 11 we see more black messengers in the early church, starting in verse 19, *"¹⁹Now they which were scattered abroad upon the persecution that arose about Stephen travelled as far as Phenice, and Cyprus, and Antioch, preaching the word to none but unto the Jews only. ²⁰And some of them were men of Cyprus and Cyrene (a black nation), which, when they were come to Antioch, spake unto the Grecians (a white nation), preaching the Lord Jesus. ²¹And the hand of the Lord was with them: and a great number believed, and turned unto the Lord."* God had some black evangelists here in Acts 11 that were leading white men (a great number of them it says) to Jesus. Isn't it ironic that black slaves in our country were told everyday of their life by white men that they were to be servants and were born to serve other peoples of the earth? They might have told them about Jesus but perverted the Scriptures. Many blacks even believed this doctrine. What a horror white people did to blacks. All people groups have done horrible things, but sometimes I see, having lived among black people for a long time, I realize the damage that was done. Slavery in our country was for several hundred years. Even the very men who founded our country and wrote the Declaration of Independence, had slaves. Thomas Jefferson evidently was in love with one of his black slaves and just recently they just found out genetically that a whole group of black people that were a part of his family and they wanted in on the inheritance. It was proven to be true. Even Abraham Lincoln, and I am sorry to be the one to say this, was not the great deliverer of slavery that we thought he was. The war in the south was not really to free black people. It was to get those southerners in line because all of the produce that was coming out of the south was bringing in money to America and if they succeeded, America was going to be without a lot of products to sell between them and other nations, particularly, cotton. There are historical records where Abraham Lincoln even makes statements that it wasn't really about black people, but about bringing the union back together. This is the truth. Now I have stood at the Lincoln Memorial at night with my hand on Lincoln's hand. I revere him and love him. I am as patriotic as anybody. I love America and would die for it. I always cry when I hear the "Star Spangled Banner". I cry when I sing "God Bless America". I love my country but it doesn't blind me to the things that are wrong. We of all people (as Christians) should be to America like Paul said in Philippians 2:15, *"That ye may be blameless and harmless, the sons of God, without rebuke, in the midst of a crooked and perverse nation, among whom ye shine as lights in the world."* We need to shine the light of our precious Lord Jesus. We are the only Jesus people are ever going to see. Jesus said, *"By this shall all men know that ye are my disciples, if ye have love one to another"* (John 13:35). It wasn't even until the mid-1960's that many of the white preachers in the south stopped preaching this racist doctrine about blacks. This wasn't too long ago. Black people didn't even get to vote until the 1960's. I was alive in the 1960's. I was alive when black people couldn't vote, had to eat sometimes in different restaurants, or use different bathrooms.

Another messenger is found in I Samuel 30:10-17. This is the story of David in Ziklag and his army was attacked by the Amalekites and their wives, sons, and daughters were taken captive along with all of their possessions. So David is going after them and in verse 10, *"David pursued, he and four hundred men: for two hundred abode behind, which were so faint that they could not go over the brook Besor. [11]And they found an Egyptian in the field, and brought him to David, and gave him bread, and he did eat; and they made him drink water; [12]And they gave him a piece of a cake of figs, and two clusters of raisins: and when he had eaten, his spirit came again to him: for he had eaten no bread, nor drunk any water, three days and three nights. [13]And David said unto him, To whom belongest thou? and whence art thou? And he said, I am a young man of Egypt, servant to an Amalekite; and my master left me, because three days agone I fell sick. [14]We made an invasion upon the south of the Cherethites, and upon the coast which belongeth to Judah, and upon the south of Caleb; and we burned Ziklag with fire. [15]And David said to him, Canst thou bring me down to this company?"* This chapter is about black people used by God as messengers and helpers of the Kingdom of God. *"And he said, Swear unto me by God, that thou wilt neither kill me, nor deliver me into the hands of my master, and I will bring thee down to this company. [16]And when he had brought him down, behold, they were spread abroad upon all the earth, eating and drinking, and dancing, because of all the great spoil that they had taken out of the land of the Philistines, and out of the land of Judah. [17]And David smote them from the twilight even unto the evening of the next day..."* An Egyptian man, a nameless black man, led David to be able to recover all that was taken from them. Previously when David inquired of the Lord whether to pursue the Amalekites the Lord answered in verse 8, *"Pursue: for thou shalt surely overtake them, and without fail recover all."* This tells me the Lord knew there was a black man who would guide them.

150

Another black man is found in II Samuel 6:9-13. This is the story of David bringing back the ark (a type of the manifest presence of God) to Jerusalem. David doesn't do it after the due order the first time, so God smote Uzzah who tried to touch the ark when it stumbled. David didn't search the Scriptures to know how you handle the manifest presence of God. The manifest presence of God should never be carried on an earthen cart pulled by oxen. It is only to be carried on the shoulders of holy priests. And so David didn't know what to do, *"⁹And David was afraid of the LORD that day, and said, How shall the ark of the LORD come to me? ¹⁰So David would not remove the ark of the LORD unto him into the city of David: but David carried it aside into the house of Obed-edom the Gittite."* Gittites were descendents of Ham. Now how black Obededom was, we do not know, but his ancestry was black. Watch now what happens to Obededom, the black man that had the manifest presence of God (the ark) in his house, as we continue reading this story, *"¹¹And the ark of the LORD continued in the house of Obed-edom the Gittite three months: and the LORD blessed Obed-edom, and all his household. ¹²And it was told king David, saying, The LORD hath blessed the house of Obed-edom, and all that pertaineth unto him, because of the ark of God. So David went and brought up the ark of God from the house of Obed-edom into the city of David with gladness..."* This is so beautiful. What is the revelation found here? David said previously, *"How shall the ark of the Lord come to me?"* He was asking how the manifest presence of God shall abide with him. Obviously Obededom was a man who knew how to keep the manifest presence of God. Later in I Chronicles 15:22-24, when David is building the Tabernacle of David, this same man (Obededom) is made one of the guardians of the doorkeeper of the ark of the Lord. This says to us, that God is raising up black people who can be trusted, not only to carry the ark or the glory of God, but know how to do it after the due order. Obededom was made a care taker (a guardian) in the Tabernacle of David just like the Cherubims. Cherubims guard the glory. This signifies to us that black people are destined for the most holy place and destined to be men and women surrounded and covered by the manifest presence of God.

Even David the king did know how to carry the ark at first, but when it came into the hands of a black man, he learned because he saw the blessing of the Lord upon the house of Obededom. This says to us as well that when black people get a revelation of the glory the blessing of the Lord will be upon them. The glory is what we are called to. We need to all stop living in our own culture only worshipping like our culture dictates. Now I might ruffle some feathers here, but I want to say the truth. Many times we are too busy worshipping culturally calling it worship of God and it is not. I don't care how loud it is or how much you shake and how much you dance, but if it doesn't bring the glory, it is a mistake. Most people mistake noise for anointing and mistake and all kinds of charisma for manifestations of the glory. If there is no glory, I always wonder if it is really a true manifestation of how to worship God.

I remember years ago being invited to a church to minister in Virginia. It was an all black church in Richmond. When I got there, I was asked to sing and I didn't want to do it. Well, the worship was being led by a young black blind man who I found out later wasn't even saved. I was surprised by this and in my experience have found that many churches do this. They hire musicians (sometimes being unsaved) to come in and play. This is definitely not the due order (this is strange fire). Well, the blind guy ended up getting saved in the meeting and wow he could play. Up to that point he was playing, leading worship, and he wasn't even saved. I tell you for an hour as worshipping was being led everyone was jumping, dancing, and moving. Then when all of the noise was over, they turned it over to me and said this white man is going to sing now. So I am standing in front of 300-400 people, the only white person there except for my wife, with only a guitar and I am singing just a simple chorus the Lord gave me over the years. Well, we just had an hour of maybe praise with no glory. And before I started singing my chorus before the Lord I said this, "I acknowledge to you I am a white man and I am about to sing in a way that you haven't sung thus far in this meeting and it doesn't make me better or worse. But I am believing God for His presence to fall." I tell you those precious black people in that church became silent and as I began to sing my little chorus the Lord gave me, the glory of God descended in that place. The word that the Lord gave me to share during the meeting was about dancing unto the Lord. Now they had danced in the first hour, but it wasn't the kind of dancing the Scripture talks about. So, during my word, I did a demonstration, made them play a song, and asked them if anyone wanted to be delivered and set free into a new realm of worship and glory, come up. Well, three-fourths of the people came up, even grown black men. I told them to lift their hands (that was easy) and begin to be expressive to the Lord. Then I had them twirl around. Then I had them use their legs, and I tell you it was the most glorious thing I ever seen. I peeked open my eyes in the middle of it and I saw how the Spirit of God had arrested some of them and they were beginning to worship the Lord in spirit and in truth. They were dancing before the Lord after the due order! Psalms 45:10 says, "*Hearken, O daughter, and consider, and incline thine ear; forget also thine own people, and thy father's house. [11]So shall the king greatly desire thy beauty: for he is thy Lord; and worship thou him.*" Now if something will get you into the glory, I am all for it. I had to repent one day when I was hearing a song on TV that was southern gospel (I do not personally like southern gospel music) and the anointing fell. This just proves God can anoint what ever he wants, if the glory is on it, we must respond.

I believe in writing this book that it is a piece of the Lord bringing us all together like in Ephesians 4:13, "*Till we all come in the unity of the faith, and* of the knowledge of the Son of God, unto a perfect man, unto the measure of the stature of the fulness of Christ." This corporate man will be made up of every color, every ethnic tribe, nation, and people. As God's army is depicted in Joel 2, "*they shall not break their ranks*", but flowing together with the "*love of God is shed abroad in our hearts by the Holy Ghost which is given unto us*" (Romans 5:5). They will no longer see after the flesh, but will see as God sees. It doesn't say in Romans 8:19-22 that the white man is groaning and travailing for the manifestation of the sons of God, but it says "*the whole creation*" is. I pray now that if there is anything in you that the Lord may have put His finger on. Maybe it is not your fault and you were raised up to believe a certain thing. Ask God today to deliver some chamber in your soul that harbors some dark racism and causes you to think a certain way that you know now is unbiblical. We want to be as Paul said of himself; "*to have always a conscience void of offence toward God, and toward men*" (Acts 24:16).

We recently had a minister come to our church and during the service made all of us look each other in the face. Can you imagine a day when God's people can all look into each other's face and not see color anymore and see each other as trees walking? Diversity is not an enemy. It could be the greatest thing when we begin to appreciate each other.

Let me pray now dear reader, "Father, we come before the throne of grace now. I thank You for Your Word. You said "*the truth shall make you free*" (John 8:32). Make us free dear Jesus. Let all of the chambers of our soul that is filled with stuff we never asked for. We didn't asked to be raised up in a certain way and be told the things we were told as children. Lord, we want to speak the truth in our heart today. We want deliverance from any attitude or prejudice or racism! I bind the spirits of racism and prejudice! Every judgmental, self-righteous devil, and every spirit of pride, I bind you and command you to get out and be gone in Jesus' name. We don't want you living in us anymore! Loose Your people O God!" Now begin to pray and let the glory fill your soul and touch you. Make a covenant before the Lord to not judge people after the outward appearance anymore!

God's Beautiful Black Bride
Chapter 12

Let us begin this chapter by looking in Song of Solomon chapter 1. First and foremost, we know that the Song of Solomon is not really a story about two people, Solomon and his wife, but it is a picture of Jesus and the bride of Christ. But yet God uses natural stories to portray spiritual truths. We thank God for the natural story because as we look at it, it gives us great revelation and helps us understand the spiritual truths hidden within. The Song of Solomon is called the Song of Songs which means this is the Word of all Words as far as God is concerned. Hebrew priests were not even allowed to read it until they were 30 years old. Even to this day there is great misunderstanding about this book. So many people share so many different things about it that creates a lot of confusion. Some people use it as a guide book for marriage. Well, I guess it can be used for that, but that was not God's intent. Anybody with any kind of revelation knows it is speaking of the Song of all Songs or is the greatest love song expressing the love relationship between Jesus and His bride.

We will look at the main places in the Bible in type at how certain black women were married to certain major figures in the Scripture and these men are a type of the Lord Jesus. We will see this truth multiple times in the Scripture. II Corinthians 13:1 says, "*...In the mouth of two or three witnesses shall every word be established*". It is amazing how that some of the major Biblical characters who really represent Jesus to us were married to black women. Of all the people, groups, and nations on the earth, God chooses a black woman as a type of the bride of Christ many times in Scripture. Who would have ever imagined this? This was an amazing truth to me as the Lord unfolded it before my eyes. This word to me is the crowning message for this book as we have been talking about the presence of black people found throughout the Scriptures. My heart's desire (and I believe God's heart as well) is that black people would be encouraged, blessed, and see their proper place in the Kingdom of God and that white people and all other kinds of peoples would acknowledge and give credence to this. It is just another part of all of us coming together in unity as Ephesians 1:10 tells us "*that in the dispensation of the fulness of times he might gather together in one all things in Christ...*" ultimately culminating in Ephesians 4:11-13, "*And he gave some, apostles; and some, prophets; and some, evangelists; and some, pastors and teachers; [12]For the perfecting of the saints, for the work of the ministry, for the edifying of the body of Christ: [13]Till we all come in the unity of the faith, and of the knowledge of the Son of God, unto a perfect man, unto the measure of the stature of the fulness of Christ.*" There are not two knowledges or three knowledges of God, but there is only one real knowledge of the Lord and the remnant or the watchmen *"shall see eye to eye"* (Isaiah 52:8). I don't know if the entire body of Christ will come into it, but I know Hebrews 8:11 says *"...all shall know me, from the least to the greatest."* So I am confident that all of the remnant (there will be no more hierarchy in the body of Christ) will know their part walking in unity. So open your heart to hear the Word of God regarding this subject beginning in Song of Solomon 1.

"¹The song of songs, which is Solomon's. ²Let him kiss me with the kisses of his mouth: for thy love is better than wine. ³Because of the savour of thy good ointments thy name is as ointment poured forth, therefore do the virgins love thee. ⁴Draw me, we will run after thee..." Verse 4 should be the story in all of our lives. When God draws us, we bring others with us. *"...the king hath brought me into his chambers: we will be glad and rejoice in thee, we will remember thy love more than wine: the upright love thee..."* The bride begins now to speak in verse 5, *"⁵I am black, but comely, O ye daughters of Jerusalem..."* This is interesting. Who is the bride speaking to? She is speaking to the daughters of Jerusalem. To us this would be the rest of the body of Christ. This lets us know immediately that the bride of Christ is not everyone in the body of Christ. Within the body of Christ there are different ranks of believers. Song of Solomon 6:8-9 brings this out more. *"⁸There are threescore queens, and fourscore concubines, and virgins without number. ⁹My dove, my undefiled is but one; she is the only one of her mother, she is the choice one of her that bare her. The daughters saw her, and blessed her; yea, the queens and the concubines, and they praised her."* The bride is the *"undefiled"* and the *"choice one of her that bare her."* Queens, virgins, concubines, and daughters are all the other different ranks within the body of Christ. Jesus said in Matthew 13:8 in the parable of the sower, *"some an hundredfold, some sixtyfold, some thirtyfold"* which represent at least 3 ranks within the body of Christ. Concubines are people who love to have an experience with the Lord but are not "married" or close in their relationship with Jesus. These are those who only come to church but never enter into an intimate and daily relationship with the Lord. Queens are those who have some authority in their life, but are like Queen Vashti in the book of Esther who ultimately refused to come at the King's commandment. Virgins represent the multitudes in the body of Christ. The daughters of Jerusalem are those who love the Lord, are sincere and are part of the family of God, but at some point can't seem to break through into all that God has for them. I believe these daughters whom the bride is speaking to in Song of Solomon 1:5 are the 60-fold Christians who don't seem to break through to be the 100-fold bride. Another picture of this is in the Tabernacle of Moses (outer court, holy place, most holy place). The outer court represents the 30-fold Christians. This represents the all of Christendom who don't really progress past the born-again experience (brass altar) and knowing a little Word in their lives (brass laver). The holy place represents the 60-fold Christians. This is where we find the

lampstand (those who are baptized in the Holy Ghost and move in the gifts of God, etc.), the table of shewbread (those who operate in a revelatory or proceeding Word), and the golden altar of incense (which was made of gold over wood representing God's character or nature over our humanity). The golden altar of incense is the place of high levels of worship and intercession which prepares us to go through the veil into the most holy place (100-fold believers) where the bride will ultimately go to have communion with her Husband, Jesus.

So back in Song of Solomon 1:5, we find the bride speaking to the daughters of Jerusalem. These daughters of Jerusalem hang around in the story quite a bit. In these first few verses, the bride has to tell these daughters something as if she is defending herself. She says again, "*⁵I am black, but comely, O ye daughters of Jerusalem, as the tents of Kedar, as the curtains of Solomon. ⁶Look not upon me, because I am black, because the sun hath looked upon me...*" Let me stop here and read a few other translations. I read many commentaries about these two verses who said that this woman was really just a deeply tanned white woman. This is very ludicrous to me because as we have been seeing, there was never anybody white in Israel at this time. Many of the commentators go to great lengths to hide their racism just like Miriam did in Numbers 12 acting like she was really mad at Moses for supposedly lording over God's people. The truth was Miriam was mad at Moses for marrying a black woman. But let us look at other translations of this verse: "*Dark am I, and comely...fear me not, because I am very dark, because the sun hath scorched me.*" Why would a black woman be saying "*fear me not*"? We see in our culture and lives that many times white men have a problem with black men marrying white women. They don't have a problem necessarily marrying a black woman, but there is a real problem I have found when it is reversed. Subtly many have a fear of the black man. You and I should not be afraid that God would use a black woman as a type of the bride of Christ. I personally think it is absolutely lovely that the Lord did this. We will see later that the Scriptures are clear that Solomon did indeed marry a black woman. He married the daughter of Pharaoh. Maybe Solomon was using this relationship to form this revelation in Song of Solomon.

Another translation also reads, "*I am black but lovely...do not stare at me because I am swarthy*". Swarthy means a skin color that is darkish. Another reads, "*Dark am I but lovely...do not stare at me because I am dark, because I am darkened by the sun.*" Now this brings out what I said in an earlier chapter about how all of us have a certain ingredient in our skin called melanin and it varies according to the geographical place we live in. The difference in skin colors should be no big deal. I love this next translation, "*I am weathered but still elegant...weather darkened like Kedar's desert tents, time softened me like Solomon's Temple hangings. Don't look down on me because I am dark, darkened by the sun's harsh rays."* Why would anybody hate somebody whose skin had to be protected because of the burning hot sun raining down on them day after day? What about albino people? The only difference they have is they have no melanin operating in their skin, but again there should be no reason to think anything less of them for this.

Another translation reads, *"I am dark tanned but beautiful...it's the sun that tanned me."* I question this translation. I left it in on purpose. If black is supposedly so bad to many people, my question always is why are white people constantly trying to tan themselves and turn brown? They must love the color or the look. Other translations read, *"For the sun has burned my skin"*, *"Don't look at how dark I am, at how dark the sun has made me"*, *"Do not consider me that I am brown, because the sun hath altered my colour"*, and lastly, *"Don't look down on me because of my color, because the sun has tanned me."* God help us to see this "Don't look down on me because of my color..." This is the Word of God my friend. We are not allowed to look down on anyone's skin color, especially those in the "Bride of Christ".

Again, the Song of Solomon is a story and a type of Jesus' bride and the words *"black, but comely"* make it very clear that Solomon had in his mind a black woman or else he wouldn't have gone into the tents of Kedar which we will see in a moment. But the bride here says *"I am black, but comely"*. What does this really mean? The revelation is that the bride is not really speaking as much about her skin color but acknowledging that she is not yet everything she is supposed to be, but yet she recognizes the beauty that God has begun to create in her. Paul says in Romans 7:18 *"For I know that in me (that is, in my flesh,) dwelleth no good thing..."* But everything that God has done within us is beautiful. II Corinthians 4:7 says, *"But we have this treasure in earthen vessels"*. Philemon 6 reads, *"That the communication of thy faith may become effectual by the acknowledging of every good thing which is in you in Christ Jesus."* If you and I have any good thing in us, it came because of Jesus and when you witness to people, your witness will be much more effective when you concentrate on the good things Jesus did in you. This should be how we evangelize. We ought to be telling people about the good things Jesus has done in us. The day I got saved, I came to the Lord not out of a fear of hell. Somebody preaching about hell and trying to scare me to get saved never worked for me. It never ministered to me because I was already living in hell. I'd seen people killed, beaten within an inch of their life. I'd personally been beaten and knocked out taking my face a week or two to heal. I'd seen things done to people that are unspeakable. So to me as a teenager, the subject of hell never moved me. But when an old bald-headed hippy came to my high school and shared about the love of Jesus and how God loved me, I got saved. So this bride is acknowledging she is not perfect yet, but she has left and is on her journey.

157

I love the fact that this bride says she is "*black, but comely*". I was alive during the time when this phrase came out. I remember James Brown's funk song in 1968, "Say it loud - I am black and proud". I used to sing this along with the other dudes I was hanging out with as a little white boy. And then the saying came out "Black is beautiful". Why did this happen? Aren't white people or caramel colored people beautiful too? Of course, but black people were so beaten down for so long, their self-esteem withered to almost nothing being told by many they weren't even human beings, not being allowed to read or write, and not being told they could be something because they are inferior. Something had to change! You know, when something happens in our world in the natural, something is happening in the Spirit realm of God. It is like with the women's movement. Whatever happened in the natural with women, I know God was trying to liberate His women. This was the same with black people. Laws were signed to allow integration and stop segregation, allow blacks to vote, etc. and in the heavenlies God was saying "let my people go"!

Then the bride continues, "*I am black, but comely, O ye daughters of Jerusalem, as the tents of Kedar, as the curtains of Solomon.*" First of all the name Kedar means in the Hebrew "powerful, dark skinned man, black skinned, to be dark". Based on this definition again, I don't see how we can interpret anything other than this bride being a black woman. So let's establish that Kedar means dark. This is a double affirmation of her color. When God says something twice, He is establishing it as a fact. Joseph told Pharaoh in Genesis 41:32, "*And for that the dream was doubled unto Pharaoh twice; it is because the thing is established by God...*" II Corinthians 13:1 says, "*In the mouth of two or three witnesses shall every word be established.*" Now who was Kedar? He was one of the sons of Ishmael (Genesis 25:13). Ishmael came from Abraham's wife Hagar, the Egyptian. The story of Abraham taking Hagar to wife is found in Genesis 16:1-3. Kedar's people were a traveling tribe of men (black people) who were sojourners who never really stopped in one place and they had tents that were very, very dark.

In Isaiah 60:1-7 we find something about the last day great outpouring of the glory and we see some of the people that will be involved in receiving this and walking in it: "*¹Arise, shine; for thy light is come, and the glory of the LORD is risen upon thee. ²For, behold, the darkness shall cover the earth, and gross darkness the people: but the LORD shall arise upon thee, and his glory shall be seen upon thee. ³And the Gentiles shall come to thy light, and kings to the brightness of thy rising. ⁴Lift up thine eyes round about, and see: all they gather themselves together, they come to thee: thy sons shall come from far, and thy daughters shall be nursed at thy side. ⁵Then thou shalt see, and flow together* (Israel and all of the nations of the earth – every color!), *and thine heart shall fear, and be enlarged* (we need our hearts enlarged to receive

158

everyone); *because the abundance of the sea shall be converted unto thee, the forces of the Gentiles shall come unto thee.* ^{6}*The multitude of camels shall cover thee, the dromedaries of Midian and Ephah; all they from Sheba shall come: they shall bring gold and incense; and they shall shew forth the praises of the LORD.* ^{7}*All the flocks of Kedar* (black people!) *shall be gathered together unto thee, the rams of Nebaioth shall minister unto thee: they shall come up with acceptance on mine altar, and I will glorify the house of my glory.*" In other words, in the last great outpouring of God's glory, black people will be part of those who will come and be gathered in and will be accepted in that remnant company (the house of the Lord) and will bring great offerings of gold and incense. This means they will be worshippers and they are going to have the character of God in their lives.

Let us look at the story of Hagar so we can see Kedar's family tree in Genesis 16:1-3, "^{1}*Now Sarai Abram's wife bare him no children: and she had an handmaid, an Egyptian, whose name was Hagar.* ^{2}*And Sarai said unto Abram, Behold now, the LORD hath restrained me from bearing: I pray thee, go in unto my maid; it may be that I may obtain children by her. And Abram hearkened to the voice of Sarai.* ^{3}*And Sarai Abram's wife took Hagar her maid the Egyptian, after Abram had dwelt ten years in the land of Canaan, and gave her to her husband Abram to be his wife.*" The son of this union was Ishmael (Genesis 16:11). In Genesis 25:12-13 we read, "*Now these are the generations of Ishmael, Abraham's son, whom Hagar the Egyptian* (God keeps repeating this – can He make it any clearer!), *Sarah's handmaid, bare unto Abraham...*" Why have we read this all these years and have never seen this? There are more truths to come in Scripture. Things that we have read thousands of times, but have gone right by them and not even noticed, God is beginning to point these truths out to us. The thing about searching the Scriptures and you having a love for the Word of God and a love for truth, is that suddenly these little things tucked about in Scripture become illuminated to us. I never thought about Hagar as a black woman, even though I read this thousand of times knowing she was Egyptian. This may seem small, but it is very important because of the prejudices against black people all of these years and the need to give them credence. Some of these commentaries that I have read during the research of this book will say things like, "this is obviously not talking about the Negro's". It is highly offensive. But continuing in Genesis 25, "*And these are the names of the sons of Ishmael, by their names, according to their generations: the firstborn of Ishmael, Nebajoth; and Kedar, and Adbeel, and Mibsam.*" Now Ishmael is a mixed race, the union of Abraham and a black woman. But anytime we see anybody with any black color, we always associate them as black. And we see that Kedar comes from this black family.

Back in Song of Solomon when the bride mentions the curtains of Solomon, what does this mean? I believe since she is associating them with the tents of Kedar, the curtains of Solomon are dark as well, just like the veil that is used to bring a separation between those who are ready to enter into the glory and those who are not. Solomon is a type of the Lord Jesus. Job 26:9 says God *"holdeth back the face of his throne, and spreadeth his cloud upon it"* letting us know that now everybody is allowed through. Not everybody can go through the curtains of Solomon (the curtains of the husband Jesus) unless they have been allowed to do so. This is just like Esther. In the story of Esther, the king's scepter was held out to her allowing her to draw near the king (Esther 5:2, 8:4) and come into his chamber. So the curtains of Solomon form a separation from the place of deep fellowship and intimacy with God and only those who are prepared can go through those curtains.

Now let us look in I Kings and see that Solomon did in fact marry a black woman. I Kings 3:1 says, *"And Solomon made affinity with Pharaoh king of Egypt, and took Pharaoh's daughter, and brought her into the city of David, until he had made an end of building his own house, and the house of the LORD, and the wall of Jerusalem round about."* Egypt was a land of black skinned people. Many commentators like to say that they weren't black, but they were. We see this again in I Kings 9:16, *"For Pharaoh king of Egypt had gone up, and taken Gezer, and burnt it with fire, and slain the Canaanites that dwelt in the city, and given it for a present unto his daughter, Solomon's wife"* and in verse 24 as well, *"But Pharaoh's daughter came up out of the city of David unto her house which Solomon had built for her..."* In other words, Solomon's wife was a black woman. Now, some people think that when Solomon wrote the Song of Solomon he was either writing about his black wife or he was thinking of his mother. But I believe Solomon drew this story from his own personal life, namely from his relationship with this black woman.

What a tremendous thing that God would use a black woman to be the type of His bride! Why would He do this? Because I guess He knows the end from the beginning and He knows the hearts of men and that the least and the despised one (or the last) shall be first. He does this on purpose to show that God is no respecter of persons and that he loves all the nations of the world. It has even become very dangerous now in the charismatic movement with this emphasis on Messianic/Jewry Christianity as if to say Messianic Jews are better than Christians. It is a subtle thing and if you see to the heart of it, it is really racist and wrong because it violates the Scriptures when it says there is neither Jew nor Greek anymore (Galatians 3:28, Romans 10:12, Colossians 3:11). How do people get around this? In the Old Testament all things were for natural Israel. Yes Jesus participated in this because He lived in natural Israel and participated in their culture, but He Himself ministered to Gentiles constantly. He ministered to women constantly which Rabbis were not allowed to do. This was a big deal back then. In John 4, Jesus not only talked with a woman, but a Samaritan woman which was very radical. In John 4:27 it says the disciples *"marveled that he talked with the woman"*. In the Jewish oral law, a man was not supposed to be talking to a woman in public anyway. Also, the Jews hated the Samaritans because they were half-breeds (inter-married with other nations during the history of their captivity). Jews hated Samaritans because of the little bit of blood in them that came from another nation. Jesus in His story of the "good Samaritan" used a Samaritan on purpose to try to expose their racism.

Next, let us look at other examples in Scripture where we see a black woman as a type of the bride of Christ. Turn to Genesis 41. Is there anybody in the Old Testament that is more of a type of Jesus than Joseph? I don't think so. For instance, Joseph was the favored son who had the coat of many colors. All of his brothers would have to bow down to him (including his father). Moreover, Joseph in his life would later become the savior of the then-know world. The whole earth was in famine and because of what Joseph did, he saved the entire region because of his life. When the Pharaoh of Egypt had Joseph brought to him after all of the suffering Joseph went through and Joseph interprets Pharaoh's dream, the Egyptian name Pharaoh gave Joseph is so powerful that it proves beyond a shadow of a doubt that Joseph is the number one type of Jesus in the Old Testament. Now when Joseph interprets Pharaoh's dream and Pharaoh receives it, Pharaoh gives Joseph his daughter to marry.

Let us read in Genesis 41:37-45, *"[37]And the thing was good in the eyes of Pharaoh, and in the eyes of all his servants. [38]And Pharaoh said unto his servants, Can we find such a one as this is, a man in whom the Spirit of God is? [39]And Pharaoh said unto Joseph, Forasmuch as God hath shewed thee all this, there is none so discreet and wise as thou art..."* Let me stop here for a second. As I was considering this passage, the irony came very strongly to me how this is happening in Africa, especially in Egypt. The Egyptians were the people who built the pyramids and if you have ever read anything on the pyramids they hold a prophetic timeline till the end of time within them. These people invented the alphabet and so much came out of Africa and yet to find thousands of years later in our modern history how blacks were not allowed to be taught to read and write is sadly ironic. The very alphabet they invented was taken from them because of racism. This is the reason why God has the bride typified as a black woman). Reading again in verse 39, *"And Pharaoh said unto Joseph, Forasmuch as God hath shewed thee all this, there is none so discreet and wise as thou art: [40]Thou shalt be over my house, and according unto thy word shall all my people be ruled: only in the throne will I be greater than thou."* It is interesting how black people acknowledge the wisdom in white people. Black people in the Scriptures seem to have no prejudice whatsoever. *"[41] And Pharaoh said unto Joseph, See, I have set thee over all the land of Egypt. [42]And Pharaoh took off his ring from his hand, and put it upon Joseph's hand, and arrayed him in vestures of fine linen, and put a gold chain about his* neck; *[43]And he made him to ride in the second chariot which he had; and they cried before him, Bow the knee: and he made him ruler over all the land of Egypt."* Does this sound familiar in describing Joseph as a type of Jesus? Philippians 2:10-11 says that every knee shall bow to Jesus. Also, who sits at the right hand of the Father in heaven? Jesus does. This further proves Joseph as a type of Jesus. *"[44]And Pharaoh said unto Joseph, I am Pharaoh, and without thee shall no man lift up his hand or foot in all the land of Egypt. [45]And Pharaoh called Joseph's name Zaphnath-paaneah..."* This name is so outstanding it shows how God honored Joseph for all that he went through (betrayed by his brothers, sold as a slave, thrown into a pit, and falsely accused and thrown in prison for years). Joseph just happened to be the chosen one with the coat of many colors. *"...and he gave him to wife Asenath the daughter of Poti-pherah priest of On. And Joseph went out over all the land of Egypt."* Joseph's wife was an Egyptian or a black woman.

Joseph's Egyptian name (Zaphnath-paaneah) means "savior of the age, savior of the world, giver of the nourishment of life, revealer of secrets, treasury of the glorious rest". If this isn't Jesus in type, I don't know who is. Now it is interesting that born of Asenath, Joseph's Egyptian wife, were Manasseh and Ephraim who went on to replace Levi and Joseph in the twelve tribes of Israel. Manasseh and Ephraim were a mixed color, but we would call them today, black.

In Genesis 48 when Jacob was dying, he does what so many patriarchs did, he prophesied over his children before he passed on and we find him doing that to Joseph and his sons. *"[1]And it came to pass after these things, that one told Joseph, Behold, thy father is sick: and he took with him his two sons, Manasseh and Ephraim. [2]And one told Jacob, and said, Behold, thy son Joseph cometh unto thee: and Israel strengthened himself, and sat upon the bed. [3]And Jacob said unto Joseph, God Almighty appeared unto me at Luz in the land of Canaan, and blessed me, [4]And said unto me, Behold, I will make thee fruitful, and multiply thee, and I will make of thee a multitude of people; and will give this land to thy seed after thee for an everlasting possession. [5]And now thy two sons, Ephraim and Manasseh, which were born unto thee in the land of Egypt before I came unto thee into Egypt, are mine; as Reuben and Simeon, they shall be mine. [6]And thy issue, which thou begettest after them, shall be thine, and shall be called after the name of their brethren in their inheritance."* Jacob is saying here that he is receiving these mixed race children as his own sons. These sons, Manasseh and Ephraim are going to get the inheritance that everybody else got in the twelve tribes and they were basically black sons.

In Deuteronomy 33 we find Moses giving his prophecy to the twelve tribes and in verse 13-17 we find him prophesying over Joseph, *"[13]And of Joseph he said, Blessed of the LORD be his land, for the precious things of heaven, for the dew, and for the deep that coucheth beneath, [14]And for the precious fruits brought forth by the sun, and for the precious things put forth by the moon, [15]And for the chief things of the ancient mountains, and for the precious things of the lasting hills, [16]And for the precious things of the earth and fulness thereof, and for the good will of him that dwelt in the bush: let the blessing come upon the head of Joseph, and upon the top of the head of him that was separated from his brethren. [17]His glory is like the firstling of his bullock, and his horns are like the horns of unicorns: with them he shall push the people together to the ends of the earth: and they are the ten thousands of Ephraim, and they are the thousands of Manasseh.*" We find here the inheritance passing on to two black boys who become a mainstay throughout Scripture. Many times throughout Scripture God uses the names Manasseh and Ephraim when He is speaking to the whole nation of Israel. God doesn't do this with other sons like Rueben. Glory to God! For example in Hosea 6:4 the Lord says, "*O Ephraim, what shall I do unto thee?*"

Next, let us look in Numbers 12. Let us consider another figure in the Old Testament that was a type of the Lord Jesus. How about Moses? Didn't Moses deliver the nation of Israel? Didn't he bring them out of bondage? This is what Jesus did for us. Moses delivering the nation of Israel was simply a picture of what the Lord Jesus did for us. So Moses himself also is a type of the Lord Jesus. As was with the two examples already (Solomon and Joseph), so also was Moses. We see in Numbers 12 that Moses was married to a black woman. God, I believe, did this to try to make all things equal, like the lesson Peter learned in Acts 10, "*And he said unto them, Ye know how that it is an unlawful thing for a man that is a Jew to keep company, or come unto one of another nation; but God hath shewed me that I should not call any man common or unclean.*" (Acts 10:28).

We begin in verse 1 of Numbers 12, "*And Miriam and Aaron spake against Moses because of the Ethiopian woman whom he had married: for he had married an Ethiopian woman. [2]And they said, Hath the LORD indeed spoken only by Moses? hath he not spoken also by us? And the LORD heard it...*" Miriam and Aaron were upset with Moses because he married a black woman, but as we see in verse 2 this is not what they accuse him of. But they really did it because of the Ethiopian woman. This happens a lot with people. They will get upset at people and come up with a different reason to get upset because they are embarrassed to say the real reason (usually because it is either racist, foolish, or extremely petty and they know they will be made a fool of). But God exposes them for their racism. I remember years ago eating in a booth in a restaurant that was next to another booth that was separated by a partition and as I was sitting there, all of the sudden I hear my name. Two sisters on the other side of the partition that I couldn't see were literally running me down. Now they didn't see me and rather than getting upset, I began to chuckle because I knew that when I would see these two people again, they would smile, give me a hug like they always do as they say "love you brother!" Let us not be people like this. Even if we have a problem with somebody, let us go to the person to resolve the issue. Let us not gossip and go to another behind their backs to justify ourselves. But really, the reason why people still do this is because they know what they really believe or are feeling is petty, stupid, wrong, and shameful and it will be obvious once they open their mouth. So they have to find another reason to make them look good. This is what Miriam did and she didn't like Moses marrying an Ethiopian woman.

Continuing in Numbers 12, "*3(Now the man Moses was very meek, above all the men which were upon the face of the earth.) *4And the LORD spake suddenly unto Moses, and unto Aaron, and unto Miriam, Come out ye three unto the tabernacle of the congregation. And they three came out. *5And the LORD came down in the pillar of the cloud, and stood in the door of the tabernacle, and called Aaron and Miriam: and they both came forth. *6And he said, Hear now my words: If there be a prophet among you, I the LORD will make myself known unto him in a vision, and will speak unto him in a dream. *7My servant Moses is not so, who is faithful in all mine house. *8With him will I speak mouth to mouth, even apparently, and not in dark speeches; and the similitude of the LORD shall he behold: wherefore then were ye not afraid to speak against my servant Moses? *9And the anger of the LORD was kindled against them; and he departed. *10And the cloud departed from off the tabernacle; and, behold, Miriam became leprous, white as snow: and Aaron looked upon Miriam, and, behold, she was leprous.* We looked at this story in detail in another chapter, but I like to point out the fact again (and I have never heard anyone say this before) that a sign of God's displeasure is Him turning somebody white. "*11And Aaron said unto Moses, Alas, my lord, I beseech thee, lay not the sin upon us, wherein we have done foolishly, and wherein we have sinned.* It is foolish and a sin for criticizing somebody for marrying a black woman. "*12Let her not be as one dead, of whom the flesh is half consumed when he cometh out of his mother's womb. *13And Moses cried unto the LORD, saying, Heal her now, O God, I beseech thee. *14And the LORD said unto Moses, If her father had but spit in her face, should she not be ashamed seven days? let her be shut out from the camp seven days, and after that let her be received in again. *15And Miriam was shut out from the camp seven days: and the people journeyed not till Miriam was brought in again.* God left Miriam outside the camp to deal with her about this issue for seven days. On the eighth day she was allowed to come back in the camp. Eight in the Scriptures is the number for new beginnings. Seven is the number for perfection. God had her stay out until she was changed and perfected in that area and ready for a new beginning. God had finally delivered her of her critical spirit and her racism. Just like he will deliver all of us who truly repent.

164

The last example of God's beautiful black bride is found in Joshua 2. This black woman's name in this story is Rahab. Rahab was an Egyptian woman. Her name means "proud, quarrelsome", but in the definition of her name it means "applied to Egypt". Rahab was a black woman. The story in Joshua chapter 2 goes like this. Joshua sent two spies into Jericho and they enter into Rahab the harlot's home. She had heard about what the God of Israel had been doing for Israel and she believes in Him. She says she doesn't want to be part of her nation being destroyed so she offers to help in hopes of being spared. So Rahab hides the two spies and tells them what to do and the two spies in return promise her and her household will not be harmed when they come. The two spies tell Rahab to hang a scarlet thread outside her window so when they come back, they will know which house to spare. This scarlet thread is a type of the blood of Jesus. So in Joshua chapter 6, when Israel invades the place, he tells the Israelites to spare and not touch the house with the scarlet thread. Rahab was a harlot. God will use anyone and receives anyone. Nothing we do disqualifies us from being used by the Lord. You can even be a harlot like Rahab was. The city is taken and Rahab goes on to become a part of Israel. She is allowed to live and be joined to Israel. God said in Exodus 23:9, "*Also thou shalt not oppress a stranger: for ye know the heart of a stranger, seeing ye were strangers in the land of Egypt.*" So Rahab was invited in and Israel received and treated her as one of their own.

But interestingly enough, in Matthew 1:5-6, in the lineage of Jesus, Rahab is mentioned. Once she joined the children of Israel, she eventually got married to a man named Salmon, "*[5]And Salmon begat Booz of Rachab; and Booz begat Obed of Ruth; and Obed begat Jesse...*" The name Rachab is the same name as Rahab. "*[6]And Jesse begat David the king; and David the king begat Solomon of her that had been the wife of Urias...*" Rahab the harlot was allowed to marry and included in the genealogy of one of the parents of Jesus. This says to us God used this black woman to save His people. He used a black woman as a type because God always cares for the least among us, the despised ones, or the ones nobody cares about.

"*Black but comely*" is God's beautiful bride. Thank you heavenly Father for driving out racism from all of us that call ourselves a true disciple and that we would be able to look one another in the eye from this day on knowing that we are neither male nor female, Jew nor Greek, Black nor White, but we judge a man as Martin Luther King said by the content of their character and not by the color of their skin.

As Christians We Are A New Species
Chapter 13

We have been looking in the Scriptures at the presence of Black people throughout the Bible. So far we have looked at the origin of man, what color Adam was, the influence black people have had, and much more. As we have opened the Word of God, we have found some tremendous things because we desire the truth. So much of what is written in history, even in Christian history, is biased against black people and women and we need to discover what God himself has said, and not let our beliefs be founded upon men's ideas or their explanations; we want what we believe to be founded on the Rock.

But as we are coming down to the last few chapters, I want to look at what color we really are now that we are born again. What color will we be in the ages to come and even what color God is? My prayer is that the answers to these questions will revolutionize how people think about the Scriptures and stir them to search the Scriptures to see if the things they had been hearing were so (Acts 17:11). How much have we believed in the past because somebody just said it? Hollywood tells us all the people in the Bible were evidently white (consider a movie such as "The Ten Commandments"). I just watched on TV the stories of Abraham and Moses and I noticed that everybody in Egypt was white and it is just not true. We know that people in Egypt were a people of color. It is important that we know this. It is important for black people to know it. It is important for pastors and leaders to speak the truth in love and to bring correction where lies have been told for years. I do not want to stand before the judgment seat of Christ and be shown all the things I believed that were wrong and be asked why I never searched them out.

But in this chapter, before we look at our true color (or the color we will be for the ages to come) I want to look at who we are, now that we are born again. I Corinthians 15:47 says *"The first man is of the earth, earthy: the second man is the Lord from heaven."* The first Adam was the fallen Adam. We've searched the Scriptures and saw he was made of the earth and was a reddish clay color. He was neither white nor black. Then after the flood, Noah's sons, Shem, Ham, and Japheth formed the three fathers over all the races in the earth. Shem was the father of all the Semitic peoples. Ham was the father of all the Black nations and Japheth was the father of all the white or Caucasian peoples of the earth. We hear so much today about the most segregated time of the week being Sunday morning at church. I hate this statement because I do not believe it is true at the church where I pastor, or in many others. God is bringing forth many racially mixed congregations in the earth now. This is a new day, this new generation of spirit filled believers God is bringing forth no longer want to live in the past, or in half truths. They simply want reality in God. God is preparing his church for the last great move of God and racism will not be a part in this move.

First of all, let us begin in II Corinthians 5:14-19, "*[14]For the love of Christ constraineth us; because we thus judge, that if one died for all, then were all dead: [15]And that he died for all, that they which live should not henceforth live unto themselves, but unto him which died for them, and rose again. [16]Wherefore henceforth know we no man after the flesh* (this means by color of their skin as well!)*: yea, though we have known Christ after the flesh, yet now henceforth know we him no more. [17]Therefore if any man be in Christ, he is a new creature* (Greek for "*new creature*" = "*new species*")*: old things are passed away; behold, all things are become new. [18]And all things are of God...*" Once you and I come to a saving knowledge of the Lord Jesus and are washed in His precious blood, we are a new species. Moreover Revelation 5:9 says (speaking of Jesus) "*...and hast redeemed us to God by thy blood out of every kindred, and tongue, and people, and nation*". He has made us all one out of every kindred, tongue, nation, ethnic group, etc, and has washed all of us in the blood of Jesus Christ and brought us into unity and into a new species. This is so very important.

So after God made man, the first Adam, He fell and since we were all in Adam (I Corinthians 15:22), his sin applies to us. David said in Psalms 51:5, "*Behold, I was shapen in iniquity; and in sin did my mother conceive me.*" We didn't ask for it, but we were born into this world a sinner needing redemption. God sought for a man that would stand in the gap and there wasn't anybody who could do it. He did find in Abraham a man willing to kill His son and God said "*Now I know*" and it sealed it in His own heart (though the Lamb was slain before the foundations of the earth). In Abraham, God found a person who was willing to sacrifice to the uttermost. Therefore the Hebrews, the Jewish nation that came out of Abraham ultimately pointed to a Messiah that would come and cause us to have the ability to be "born again".

Man is a three-fold being. We have been created in the image of God. Since God is three fold, so are we. The three-fold God (Father, Son, & Holy Spirit) created a three-fold man (spirit, soul, & body) and for man (after his fall), gave a three-fold salvation (justification, sanctification, and glorification – each pertaining to each aspect of his being). Justification is when our spirits are born-again (washed in the blood of Jesus). Sanctification is God's daily salvation and redemption for our soul. Glorification is our future salvation for our body. In another chapter, I will look at glorification as we find out what our color is going to be throughout the ages to come. So now, even though we are living in the flesh in the world, we are really not of this world (John 17:16). Even though we live still with the flesh we were born with, our human spirit is perfect before God. Hebrews 12:23 says, "*To the general assembly and church of the firstborn, which are written in heaven, and to God the Judge of all, and to the spirits of just men made perfect."* There is nothing unclean in our spirit because as believers, God lives there now. We can't get a demon in our human spirit. The only place a demon can get into is our soul or body. We've been washed in the blood of the Lamb, born again and made into a new species! God help us to get this revelation. I am not the old Sam Greene. We're the new man in Christ Jesus. Colossians 3:9-10 says, *"⁹Lie not one to another, seeing that ye have put off the old man with his deeds; ¹⁰And have put on the new man, which is renewed in knowledge after the image of him that created him."* If you and I want to continue to live in the old Adamic nature, we will still be wrestling with racism, jealousy, hatred, violence, lust, etc.

We need to teach people we are a new creation. If all our emphasis is just one getting people saved and stop there, we're not doing enough. Heaven is just the beginning. The goal and calling as a Christian is to be transformed and conformed to the image of Jesus Christ. This is perfection. This is our heritage and the only reason why this isn't happening is because nobody is teaching and talking about it. But it is a new day.

For every reader of this book, I don't care what color you are, what nationality you are, or what culture you came from, it does not matter anymore, because *"if any man be in Christ, he is a new creature: old things are passed away; behold, all things are become new"* (II Corinthians 5:17). "All" means everything, even the color of your skin. All things became new when we became a Christian. We're a new species and even though we are still living in this earth with the body we were born with, we know that Philippians tells us that the day is coming when the Lord is going to fashion this old dead body like unto His glorious body and we shall be changed (Philippians 3:21). This is glorification of which many people do not know because it is not taught enough (the body of Christ desperately needs true shepherds and teachers). At the church where I pastor, we are laboring to disciple Christians who will be able to Pastor as well as teach (line upon line) and lift up the truth of the Word of God. So much of the body of Christ is about bigness and numbers, but in the Scriptures Jesus only had a church of around 70 people. He taught them constantly. So should we. Jesus taught the scriptures daily, and so did the Apostle Paul. Jesus said "make disciples of all nations not just convert. In Matthew 28:19 the word teach in the Greek means to disciple, to instruct, enroll as a scholar, a pupil.

So we are a new species which means that even though I have a pinkish white skin color, this is not me anymore. As you look in the mirror at your skin color, know that is not you anymore. The minute you and I pass on through to the other side, do you know what is going to happen? You see, all that is taking place right now as we finish the plan of God out (Revelation 10:7 says the mysteries of God will be finished) and when that end comes (Jeremiah 29:11

says the Lord has an expected end for us), what is going to happen is our bodies are going to be transfigured. This is exactly what happened to Jesus in Matthew 17:1-2. Jesus received His glorified body while He <u>was a man</u> on the earth. This tells me men can and will get their glorified body on the earth when Jesus returns. Paul said he was taken to paradise (II Corinthians 12:4). You see, our spirit and soulish man that is tied together and Hebrews 4:12 says the only thing that can separate it is the Word of God. Our spirit is where God lives and where God is always trying to get to us. Our soulish man fights against this. Galatians 5:17 says, *"the flesh lusteth against the Spirit, and the Spirit against the flesh: and these are contrary the one to the other: so that ye cannot do the things that ye would."* Jesus said in Matthew 26:41, *"the spirit indeed is willing, but the flesh is weak."* When the Bible speaks of our flesh, it comprises our physical body and our soulish man (our thoughts, affections, emotions, intellect, etc). Sanctification is the process after salvation where we allow God to change our soulish man and conform it to His image.

The first and most important way God changes us is through His Word. Jesus said in John 8:31-32, *"<u>If ye continue in my word</u>, then are ye my disciples indeed; And ye shall know the truth, and the truth shall <u>make you free</u>."* John 17:17 says, *"<u>Sanctify them through thy truth</u>: thy word is truth."* Psalms 119:9 reads, *"Wherewithal shall a young man cleanse his way? <u>by taking heed thereto according to thy word</u>"*, and Ephesians 5:26 says, *"That he might sanctify and cleanse it with the washing of water by the word."* The Word of God is God's greatest sanctifying agent. Secondly, the Holy Ghost was given as one called along side of us to help and sanctify us, convict us of sin, and turn us and help us become the righteous beings we really are. We are *"partakers of the divine nature"* (II Peter 2:14). This means we have God's nature in us. Peter said we were born again of *"incorruptible seed"* (I Peter 1:23). Your spirit, as you allow God to sanctify you through His Word, and His Spirit, and as you overcome the dealings of God when His revelation is being married to a situation in your life, you grow in authority, grace, and in the knowledge of Jesus. Eventually, whether you come to die or it comes during the catching away of the saints in the last days, I Corinthians 15 tells us *"we shall be changed"* (verse 52). Changed into what, you may think. You will be changed into your <u>new bodies</u> and what is going to determine what your new body will look like will be according to the degree you allowed God in your lifetime to transform your soul. I Corinthians 6:20 says our spirit and our body belong to the Lord. The only thing you and I have any control over is our soulish man. David said in Psalms 25:1, *"Unto thee, O LORD, do I lift up my soul"* and said in Psalms 119:109, *"My soul is continually in my hand..."* Many times I will say like David, *"Bless the Lord, O my soul"* (Psalms 103:1) because there are times when my soul doesn't want to bless the Lord. There are times when our soul wants to sin and lead us down a path that is not godly, perverse, unclean, unrighteous, and unholy. But yet, if we can just allow the Word of God to work, set our face like flint that we want to be holy as He is holy, be perfect as He is perfect, we can and will make it. But at that moment of change, the amount of glory that we've allowed to work into our lives will be the degree of glory we will shine. Romans 8:18 says, *"For I reckon that the sufferings of this present time are not worthy to be compared with the glory which shall be revealed in us."* Our color for the ages to come is going to be the color of God Himself and the Scriptures are very clear about the color of God (which we will look at in another chapter).

So in II Corinthians 5:17 we see that as Christians we are a *"new creature"* or a *"new species"*. Galatians 3:27-29 says, *"27For as many of you as have been baptized into Christ have put on Christ. 28There is neither Jew nor Greek, there is neither bond nor free, there is neither male nor female: for ye are all one in Christ Jesus. 29And if ye be Christ's, then are ye Abraham's seed, and heirs according to the promise."* Jesus puts an end to the law. Jesus puts an end to racism and Jesus puts an end to what Babylon did to us so many years ago. If you and I can allow God to purge our soul of the teachings we've grown up listening to, than when we look at somebody of another color or somebody of the other gender, we see them as God sees them, which is a son of God. To think like this will take a revolution. Our minds need to be renewed because we have been taught from birth that black people are like this, white people are like this, don't let women do anything because they are controllers, and the list of prejudices is endless that have been engrained in our soul.

Psalms 139:14-15 says, *"14I will praise thee; for I am fearfully and wonderfully made: marvellous are thy works; and that my soul knoweth right well. 15My substance was not hid from thee, when I was made in secret, and curiously wrought in the lowest parts of the earth."* I remember reading this passage years ago and the revelation hitting me. It was like walking into a bright room. I realized that my earthly father was not my true father, but my true father was Father God. Moreover, I realized I did not have to carry the defects and issues that were passed on to me through my parents and ancestors and that they could end with me. My children are not going to have this garbage that I was given in the way I was brought up. My father was a murderer and a rapist and child abuser. He was completely vile and very racist. As a child, I didn't want this in my life and any chances of me being like my earthly father later on in life ended when the blood of Jesus washed me as a teenager. But we hear things all the time like, "She's just like her mother". Well the next time somebody sees a weakness in you and says that to you, your response should be, "No I'm not. What you are seeing now is being transformed because I am not staying like this. I'm becoming transformed into the image of my Father in heaven." II Corinthians 3:18 says, *"But we all, with open face beholding as in a glass the glory of the Lord, are changed into the same image from glory to glory, even as by the Spirit of the Lord."* What color

170

is the glory? It is the color of amber. It is bright and full of light and beholding it is like walking out into bright sunshine. This light the Bible says is unapproachable in the flesh. This is the color of God and this is the color of our spirit and when you die or get caught up to be with the Lord this will be your color.

Stop looking at your brother and sister in earthly terms. In Mark 8:22-25 when Jesus was praying for a blind man, the first time Jesus touched the man, He asked him what he saw and he said, "*I see men as trees, walking*". Jesus then touched him again and asked again what he saw and the man said he "*saw every man clearly*". I don't want to see all men clearly anymore. I want to see my brother and sister as God sees them, as trees walking and as "*trees of righteousness, the planting of the Lord, that He might be glorified*" (Isaiah 61:3). Seeing "every man clearly" is a mindset we all have to be delivered from.

In Matthew 12:46-50 Jesus' mother and brothers tried to interrupt Him while He was ministering and Jesus' response must have broken Mary's heart when He said, "*Who is my mother? and who are my brethren?...*" You see this is a question we must all answer. Jesus continues, "*[49]And he stretched forth his hand toward his disciples, and said, Behold my mother and my brethren! [50]For whosoever shall do the will of my Father which is in heaven, the same is my brother, and sister, and mother.*" I remember right after I graduated from high school getting on a Trailways bus for 27 hours to move from Washington D.C. to Jacksonville, FL into a house of a man I barely knew to go on with God. I left everything I knew, but I knew deep down in my heart (even though I had only been saved 3 years), that I could never walk with Jesus if I stayed at home. None of my brothers and sisters (whom I all led to the Lord and prayed for them all to receive the Holy Ghost) were interested in going on with God and I couldn't hang around that environment anymore, so I left. And for 25 years my brother and sisters were upset with me and would say hurtful things to me over the years about leaving home. But what they didn't understand was I knew the only way I could ultimately help them was to go on with God myself and by me pressing through into God, that it would somehow bless them. It wasn't until my mother passing and I did her funeral that my brother and sisters saw me minister for the first time. In all those years of pastoring, ministering, and leading worship, my brother and sisters did not know me at all. But after that funeral, one by one, they came to me and said "now we understand why you left". It may take people 25 years to understand, but it doesn't matter. God knows what you are doing. I am no longer a part of the "Greene" family. I am a son of the living God. This is why I wrote an entire chapter on forgetting your own people and family. We see this clearly in so many places in Scripture, especially in Psalms 45:10-11, "*Hearken, O daughter, and consider, and incline thine ear; forget also thine own people, and thy father's house; [11]So*

171

shall the king greatly desire thy beauty: <u>for he is thy Lord</u>; and <u>worship thou</u> <u>him</u>." The inference here is our families lord over our lives instead of Jesus. Moreover Jesus said in Matthew 23:9, *"And call no man your father upon the earth: for one is your Father, which is in heaven."* Jesus even took it deeper when He said in Luke 14:26, *"If any man come to me, and hate not his father, and mother, and wife, and children, and brethren, and sisters, yea, and his own life also, he cannot be my disciple"* and in Matthew 10:37, *"He that loveth father or mother more than me is not worthy of me: and he that loveth son or daughter more than me is not worthy of me."* Now does God want us hating our mother and father? Of course not, for that would be contrary to His Word; Deuteronomy 5:16, *"Honour thy father and thy mother, as the LORD thy God hath commanded thee; that thy days may be prolonged, and that it may go well with thee, in the land which the LORD thy God giveth thee."* But He is saying to His people that their priorities are out of order when you let your family rule your life because our true father is God Almighty and our true brother is the Lord Jesus Christ and the men and women around you that are pressing in everyday, love God's Word, and are true worshippers. They are your family. Haven't you found in your life that the people in the body of Christ are closer to you than your natural family? It is this way in my life.

We are no longer a part of this world's structure. You see a picture of this in Ruth 1 when Naomi is returning to Bethlehem-Judah after backsliding with her husband and two sons and she is trying to ditch her two daughters in law from Moab (Orpah and Ruth). Orpah said she is going back to her home in Moab, but there was something about Ruth that wanted to forsake Moab. Moabites were Gentiles that served the God Chemosh (I Kings 11:33) where they scarified little children and burnt them in the fire. Ruth grew up in this culture. But she saw something in backslidden Naomi. And Naomi wanted Ruth to go home like Orpah and tried three times to get her to leave, but Ruth wouldn't hear it an she said beautifully, *"And Ruth said, Intreat me not to leave thee, or to return from following after thee: for whither thou goest, I will go; and where thou lodgest, I will lodge: <u>thy people shall be my people</u>, <u>and thy</u> <u>God my God</u>...."* (Ruth 1:16). You and I need to have this revelation and this kind of dedication. The people of God are my people now! Do you understand this? We are no longer of this world. Culture, nationality, heritage, color, and family is over with and done. We are now citizens of the Kingdom of God. We are all sons of God. We no longer carry the seed of Adam, but the seed of God. We are no longer the color of Adam, but are now being transformed into His likeness and soon our bodies will be changed into His color!

Our minds need to be transformed that we start thinking like the Word of God says and not how the world thinks, especially in relation to who we are now and who our true brothers and sisters are. My father is God and the earthly leadership He has placed in my life. My brothers and sisters (my family) are the people of God and when I look at them I do not see color and I don't see gender. I don't see social strata or culture. Black people try to make white people worship like they do (white people can't do it – they don't have rhythm so have mercy on them – ha ha!). I'll never forget being in Virginia and being asked to minister at a pretty large black church. God told me to put on my guitar and sing one of the songs the Lord gave me over the years and we had just gone through an hour of some serious Pentecostal worship. Have you ever been in a meeting like this? People were dancing like crazy, falling down, etc. It was all flesh, was mostly praise, but never touched into the realm of true worship. So the Lord tells my lily white self to get up there and sing a song called "Wrap Your Holy Arms Around Me". It is a worship song. Then the Lord told me to put on my guitar and lead them in a dance. Now they had just danced for an hour, but it was a cultural dance. But the wonderful thing about that precious church was their hearts were open. So I began to teach them about true worship (John 4:22-23) according to the Scriptures and God as my witness, we began to dance before the Lord (not the charismatic bunny-hop, but the prophetic dance). Three hundred black people with their arms raised until to Lord, eyes closed in worship, began to twirl around and the glory fell. These people saw something that day that they never saw before. The enemy tried everything to not make me teach this, but somebody has to stand up. We are a family now! We as white people have tried to make black people worship like us. It's not going to happen. We need to simply show people in the scriptures about true worship, and let them grow from there.

Let me quote some passages now to seal this truth that we have a new father now, namely God the Father. Jeremiah 31:1 says *"At the same time, saith the LORD, will I be the God of all the families of Israel, and they shall be my people."* Matthew 6:9 says *"After this manner therefore pray ye: Our Father which art in heaven, Hallowed be thy name."* He is our Father, not only white people's father or black people's father, but <u>our</u> father. Matthew 23:9 says *"And call no man your father upon the earth: for one is your Father, which is in heaven."* II Corinthians 6:18 reads *"And will be a Father unto you, and ye shall be my sons and daughters, saith the Lord Almighty."* Ephesians 3:14-15 says *"[14]For this cause I bow my knees unto the Father of our Lord Jesus Christ, [15]Of whom the whole family in heaven and earth is named."* Just these few passages should hammer this truth to our hearts. As Christians, we are a new species, in a new family with no culture, color, origin or identity from what we were before, but are now part of the Kingdom of His dear Son. We are brothers and sisters and are no longer male, female, black, white, Jew or Gentile. We are now all the color of God. Hallelujah!

As Christians now, people of the Kingdom of God, we are being changed into something. Philippians 3:21 says, *"Who shall change our vile body, that it may be fashioned like unto his glorious body..."* Where we are headed is being changed into the image of God. II Corinthians 3:18 says, *"But we all, with open face beholding as in a glass the glory of the Lord, are changed into the same image from glory to glory, even as by the Spirit of the Lord."* Romans 8:29 says He wants to conform us to the image of the Son. This is what is taking place now. God is not preparing you to be a great minister, a prophet, bishop, apostle, etc. He is preparing you to bear the image of the heavenly. Paul prayed in Galatians 4:19, *"My little children, of whom I travail in birth again until Christ be formed in you."* He even took it deeper in Ephesians 3 and said, *"that ye might be filled with all the fulness of God."* Think of it. He said in Ephesians 4:13, *"Till we all come in the unity of the faith, and of the knowledge of the Son of God, unto a perfect man, unto the measure of the stature of the fulness of Christ."* This means the exact measure and stature of the Lord Jesus. We are not going to be God, but we are going to look like Him, talk like Him, think like Him, and have His heart. The earth will finally be able to say they see a true representative of Christianity on the earth. You see, who would want to join a church that is full of racism? Who would want to join a church where people say one thing to your face and say something else behind it? Isn't the body of Christ riddled with this? The only reason why people are like this, I believe, is that leaders are like that. Until the leadership changes and starts acting like God, the people will never do. We are what we eat. We are who we behold and if the god we are beholding is a racist god or only caters to rich or beautiful people, than the people will be just as shallow. God wants to transform us now and prepare us for a heavenly body.

I Corinthians 15:39-44 says, *"[39]All flesh is not the same flesh: but there is one kind of flesh of men, another flesh of beasts, another of fishes, and another of birds. [40]There are also celestial bodies, and bodies terrestrial: but the glory of the celestial is one, and the glory of the terrestrial is another. [41]There is one glory of the sun, and another glory of the moon, and another glory of the stars: for one star differeth from another star in glory..."* Now before we read verse 42, do you understand what Paul is saying here? He is saying there is earthly flesh and there is a heavenly body. The sun, moon, and stars all have different degrees of light, brightness, and glory. Therefore now, let's read the next verse, *"[42]So also is the resurrection of the dead. It is sown in corruption; it is raised in incorruption: [43]It is sown in dishonour; it is raised in glory: it is sown in weakness; it is raised in power: [44]It is sown a natural body; it is raised a spiritual body..."* On a clear night (especially out in the country), you will see thousands of stars in the sky. Some shine more than others. Some are very bright and others have just a little light. Paul is using this natural description to talk about the glory in the resurrection of the dead. When our bodies are resurrected, our vile bodies will be fashioned like unto His glorious body (Philippians 3:21). What did Jesus' body look like? Initially, he still looked like a man, but we find Him 40 years later in the book of Revelation being described as, *"[14]His head and his hairs were white like wool, as white as snow;*

and his eyes were as a flame of fire; [15]*And his feet like unto fine brass, as if they burned in a furnace; and his voice as the sound of many waters."* (Revelation 1:14-15). What happened to Jesus? The change that took place in Jesus was the same thing that happened to Moses when he was in the glory. When he came down from the mount after being in the glory it says "[29]*And it came to pass, when Moses came down from mount Sinai with the two tables of testimony in Moses' hand, when he came down from the mount, that Moses wist not that the skin of his face shone while he talked with him.* [30]*And when Aaron and all the children of Israel saw Moses, behold, the skin of his face shone; and they were afraid to come nigh him"* (Exodus 34:29-30). The children of Israel were so afraid of Moses, they told him to put a veil over his face. The principle is this: the longer you stay in the manifest presence of God (the glory), the more you're changed into that same image! This is why we worship a long time at the church I pastor. This is why we take our time in the glory. We worship until God is satisfied. Every time we go into the glory (like Moses did), we're being changed. Therefore, in the resurrection, you and I are going to shine to the degree that we allowed God to deal with us and change us during our life. Some people are going to be so bright, as Daniel 12:3 puts it, they *"shall shine as the brightness of the firmament"*.

In our lives as Christians, we are being prepared to be changed into His image. This is the race we are running (I Corinthians 9:24, Philippians 3:14). Did you know that? Colossians 1:27 says *"To whom God would make known what is the riches of the glory of this mystery among the Gentiles; which is Christ in you, the hope of glory."* What does this mean? This means the glory of God coming upon our person and transforming us. Daniel 12:3 again says, *"And they that be wise shall shine as the brightness of the firmament; and they that turn many to righteousness as the stars for ever and ever."* This is what we are going to look like – as the brightness of the firmament and of the stars! II Thessalonians 1:10 says, *"When he shall come to be glorified in his saints, and to be admired in all them that believe..."* Jesus when He comes is going to glorify His saints by doing exactly what God the Father did to Him in Matthew 17 when He went up to the top of the mountain and was transfigured before the disciples. It said of Jesus, *"his face did shine as the sun"*. Upon seeing this, Peter, James, and John fell on their face and didn't know what to do. God is preparing us to be changed into His glorious image. Colossians 3:4 says, *"When Christ, who is our life, shall appear, then shall ye also appear with him in glory."* Jesus has to be our life. For many Christians, Jesus isn't their life. He is only part of their life. I Peter 5:1 reads, *"The elders which are among you I exhort, who am also an elder, and a witness of the sufferings of Christ, and also a partaker of the glory that shall be revealed."* To get an idea what will happen, let us look at II Chronicles 5. When the Temple of Solomon's foundation was laid it says when the glory fell like a cloud, *"So that the priests could not stand to minister by reason of the cloud: for the glory of the LORD had filled the house of God*" (II Chronicles 5:14). This is what is going to happen in us as people. We are God's house. We are going to be transformed and changed by that beautiful, fiery, and amber colored glory. Like Moses burning bush, though we look like fire ourselves, we will not be consumed (Exodus 3:2)!

II Corinthians 4:17 says, *"For our light affliction, which is but for a moment, worketh for us a far more exceeding and eternal weight of glory."* Are you allowing God to change you into His image? I John 3:2 says *"Beloved, now are we the sons of God, and it doth not yet appear what we shall be: but we know that, when he shall appear, we shall be like him; for we shall see him as he is."* I love David in Psalms 17:15 when he said, *"As for me, I will behold thy face in righteousness: I shall be satisfied, when I awake, with thy likeness."* The Hebrew word for "face" is the same word for "presence" and it means "the turning of the face towards". David longed to be like the Lord and behold His face. The Lord told Moses in Exodus 33:20, *"Thou canst not see my face: for there shall no man see me, and live"* so He hid Moses in the clift of the rock because the brightness of the purity and dazzling brilliance of His overshadowing glory would have killed Moses. He wasn't prepared to see God's face. It would have kill him. This is why in Revelation 6:16 we see many saying, *"And said to the mountains and rocks, Fall on us, and hide us from the face of him* that sitteth on the throne..." His face blazes with glorious light and perfect beauty. It is like the brightness of the natural sun magnified a million times. But the revelation is you and I are being changed to look into His face because you and I are going to look like that as well. Revelation 22:4 says of a remnant, *"And they shall see his face"*! There is going to be a people who are going to be able to look directly into His face and because everything in them has already been burnt up (every bondage broken, sin covered, issue dealt with, and every chamber in their soul taken over by the Word of God and the glory). They will be able to behold Him as He is! Everything God is doing in His people's lives is to prepare them for this moment. Numbers 14:21 says, *"But as truly as I live, all the earth shall be filled with the glory of the LORD."*

Lastly, I want to look at Isaiah 60 because eventually we are going to hear this Word come to us. Before we read this, I just want to review what I have said. As Christians, we are no longer human beings like we were but we are a new species with a new Father and a new family. Our culture, identity, ethnicity, and gender, is being enveloped now in a haze of glory and the blood of Jesus Christ. We are all now the sons of God hoping to be the bride of Christ. When we look at each other, we are to look at each other as trees walking. We should never judge each other after the color of the skin, gender, or any such thing, but look at each other as God sees us. Everything in me prays to God that He would impart this truth to your heart and that you would live like this. Eventually, all of us are going to have the same color for we will all be changed into the color and brilliancy of our Father in heaven. We will look at the color of God in another chapter.

But the day is coming when the voice of the Lord will say what Isaiah 60 declares, *"¹Arise, shine; for thy light is come, and the glory of the LORD is risen upon thee* (this should be personal to you). *²For, behold, the darkness shall cover the earth, and gross darkness the people: but the LORD shall arise upon thee, and his glory shall be seen upon thee. ³And the Gentiles shall come to thy light, and kings to the brightness of thy rising..."* I pray this word is sealed to your heart dear reader.

The Color of Our God
Chapter 14

In this chapter, let us investigate what the color of our God really is as revealed in Scripture. The whole purpose for this book as the Lord showed me is that we as a people are no longer a part of this world. We are a new species. We are a new creation and, in a sense, we are to forget our own families as our source of origin or personal and cultural identity. Jesus said in Matthew 23:9 *"call no man your father upon the earth: for one is your Father, which is in heaven."* We have a new father, and new brothers and sisters. All of our culture, our color, and our ethnicity mean nothing anymore. We are all starting at the same fresh point. Hallelujah! We are all the same in the eyes of God. Galatians 3:28 tells us that *"There is neither Jew nor Greek, there is neither bond nor free, there is neither male nor female: for ye are all one in Christ Jesus."* It matters not if we are black, white, brown, red, yellow, or pink. Once we are born again and have been washed in the blood, we are now in the Kingdom of God and not of this world. Colossians 1:13 *"Who hath delivered us from the power of darkness, and hath translated us into the kingdom of his dear Son".*

Without a doubt, it is very clear that the original color of man when he was created out of the dust was a reddish, clayish color. Once the flood came, the Bible teaches us that it was through Shem, Ham, and Japheth, the three sons of Noah, that the rest of the earth was populated and the races were separated. So we see that from Shem came the Semitic race, from Ham came the Black race, and from Japheth came the White or Caucasian race as they went to Europe.

In Ephesians 1:10 it says "That in the dispensation of the fulness of times he might gather together in one all things in Christ, both which are in heaven, and which are on earth; even in him". We rejoice in diversity, but more than that we need to begin to see that when someone begins to speak, that it is not a black person or a white person, it is a child of God. When someone sings, plays and instrument, or does anything that we do not see color. See, it is so important for us, the children of God, to leave culture behind. All of us have to leave our ethnicity, our culture, everything that we have grown up learning, because a lot of it has been racist. There is a great lack of trust between peoples and races. There's always this thing deep inside us that says; "Can I really trust a white man?" or "can I really trust a black man?" On and on it goes and it is something that has been developed in us. This is why this is the only book that I am going to have a picture of my lily white face on, because I want it to be known that a white man wrote this book about God's precious black people. I don't hate my race, because I don't have a race anymore. I'm in the only kingdom that I want to be in, and that is the Kingdom of God. Who is my mother and who are my brothers? They are them that "hear the word of God and keep it." Matt 12:48-50 " [48]*But he answered and said unto him that told him, Who is my mother? and who are my brethren?* [49]*And he stretched forth his hand toward his disciples, and said, Behold my mother and my brethren!* [50]*For whosoever shall do the will of my Father which is in heaven, the same is my brother, and sister, and mother.*

We mentioned before, how we are a new species in Christ and that we are not like other human beings anymore. We are now going to look at, as the Scriptures clearly show us, what the actual color of God is. People get real quiet when I talk about this. I wonder if it's because they are afraid to talk about it. That is the very reason that we need to get it out. People are bound up and they shouldn't be. God, as He manifests Himself to us, is Spirit. When He manifests Himself and appears to mankind, as He has over and over again, the scriptures confirm his true appearance. There are at least 30 scriptures we can look at to define what His color is; and we only need three, for in the mouth of two or three witnesses shall every word be established (II Corinthians 13:1). Understanding God's color is so important because, as He is, so are we in this world. II Corinthians 3:18, says " *but we all, with open face beholding as in a glass the glory of the Lord, are changed into the same image from glory to glory, even as by the Spirit of the Lord.*" We are being conformed to the image of the Son. Now this is a revelational truth and I pray that we allow the word of God to change how we perceive Him.

All of us, when we pray, probably have a picture in our minds of what God looks like; but I want to say that we don't realize that much of what we believe, know, and do, is not based many times on the Scriptures. For example, we picture Moses looking like Charlton Heston, because of the movie The Ten Commandments. Before this book, I would picture something like this big white man with a big white beard; like something I saw in a Star Trek movie. That's the kind of face that I've always seen when I prayed; but not anymore (John 8:32 "*And ye shall know the truth, and the truth shall make you free.*").

Let us turn to Ezekiel Chapter One. Ezekiel is having a visitation here and he is seeing God and the cherubims that surround him. Ezekiel 1:25-28 "[27]*And there was a voice from the firmament that was over their heads, when they stood, and had let down their wings.* [26]*And above the firmament that was over their heads was the likeness of a throne, as the appearance of a sapphire stone: and upon the likeness of the throne was the likeness as the appearance of a man above upon it.* [27]*And I saw as the colour of amber, as the appearance of fire round about within it, from the appearance of his loins even upward, and from the appearance of his loins even downward, I saw as it were the appearance of fire, and it had brightness round about.* [28]As the appearance of the bow that is

179

in the cloud in the day of rain, so was the appearance of the brightness round about. This was the appearance of the likeness of the glory of the LORD. And when I saw it, I fell upon my face, and I heard a voice of one that spake."

Ezekiel is seeing God in the Spirit in what is called a theophane; which means a divine appearance in the scripture. When he looks at the one upon the throne; he says *"I saw as the color of amber as the appearance of fire."* Fire and amber are alike. You could say it's like copper, burnish brass, fire, amber, goldish, brightness, light. All of these words make up what God Himself looks like. And again I read verse 28, *"As the appearance of the bow that is in the cloud in the day of rain, so was the appearance of the brightness round about. This was the appearance of the likeness of the glory of the LORD. And when I saw it, I fell upon my face, and I heard a voice of one that spake."* Ezekiel tells us in this scripture that this is God the Father, and this is what His color is.

Let us look now at Daniel 7:9 *"I beheld till the thrones were cast down, and the Ancient of days did sit, whose garment was white as snow, and the hair of his head like the pure wool: his throne was like the fiery flame, and his wheels as burning fire."* To understand this passage, we need to know that colors in the Bible are always speaking typically of something. For example, you will find that the color red or scarlet symbolizes "blood or suffering" and blue speaks of that which is "heavenly." Likewise, the color yellow, gold, and amber symbolize the color of the "glory."; and so many times the color white symbolizes everything "pure" and everything "clean". This is interesting, because if you read a dictionary definition you can understand why I think black people have been tormented by this reference of "white" being related to everything pure and clean, whereas the word "black" always symbolizes something dark or evil. I am reminded of the movie about Malcolm X, when he is in prison and is approached by this Muslim who begins to show him all these things. There is no question that a lot of it is true. All races and peoples have used colors to divide and separate. God doesn't do that, and He is all about including everyone. God is about drawing people together, not separating them.

I just watched a movie called "The Express" about Ernie Davis who was the first black man to win the Heisman Trophy. It showed that even when he was playing and went to Texas, he was pummeled with curses, bottles, rocks, and trash. The black players weren't even allowed to stay in the same part of hotel where all the other players stayed. They had to go way down to the basement to this dirty place to sleep. Yet he was the star of the team and took them to the championship. Even his own coach saw him looking at a white girl and he told him, "None of that here." He then said, "I'm not a racist. But that's just the way things are." Well, let me tell you about the way things are. The way things are, are the way the Bible declares them to be! Not some society, or some government. Our own government kept black people in bondage, and wouldn't even let them vote until the last 40 years. Now if you don't like it, I'm sorry. But that is the reason God had me bring this out. We need to repent for some of the things we've done. We don't need to get mad at people for the things they have done, because they are only doing it out of a reaction. Consider if you were cursed for four hundred years and treated like a slave and a dog. Do you think you might have an issue with your master? Do you think you may have trouble trusting somebody?

Joe Lewis, the greatest heavyweight fighter ever, who became the American Champion when he knocked out that German Max Shmelling, Hitler's pet little bully. All of America rejoiced about Joe Lewis, and yet his manager was taking three fifths of all his earnings. Even when he went in the army, and held free shows all over during WWII, the government and the IRS constantly harassed him, even until the day he died. The double standard has got to stop at the doors of the house of God. If anyone is going to walk in liberty and freedom, let it be in our House. We have to say "not here!"

I remember the first day I had moved to Alabama to start a work there. I love Alabama, it's called "Alabama the beautiful" for a reason. I had moved into my house and I went down to get my hair cut at a local barber shop. So I'm getting my hair cut and I'm telling them about my church and how it is a new work there. They're listening to me, this new young Pastor, and everything is going great; and then a black man passes the barber shop. He looks in, seems a little uncertain, and then comes through the door. Not a word was spoken, but the animosity was so thick you could feel it. It would have taken a jack hammer to break through it. You could see the confusion turn to embarrassment and then he quickly left the building. Then the remarks began, but I waited until he finished cutting my hair. You have to use wisdom; be wise as a serpent, gentle as a dove, because he could have "missed" and cut across my throat, or ruined my hair. So I waited until he was done and putting a little clubman talc on, and then I could say my peace. I said "I just want to make a statement, and I want everyone here to know it. I think that what you just did and said here is ungodly and awful. This will be the last time that I will ever dart the door of this barber shop, because you are racists. I don't know how you can call yourself Christians and act the way you do." Then I walked out the door. Now that probably didn't help my church in Alabama too much, but I would rather live in the light than in the darkness. I mention all of these stories to help shed light upon the real condition of our society, and to say that we need change.

When we hear the word "white" we always associate it with something good; and when we hear the word "black" we always associate it with something bad. We have been trained that way on purpose. Black is just a color. Black doesn't kill anybody. My Bible is hunter green and it's my favorite color. I wish God was hunter green. I'd like to be that color and then you could call me the "green hornet", but it is just a color. So when we see in the scriptures that He has a white garment, or His hair is white as snow, it has nothing to do with anything about race. It is simply saying that God is purer than any being in the universe. Let's look at Daniel 7:9 again, *"I beheld till the thrones were cast down, and the Ancient of days did sit, whose garment was white as snow, and the hair of his head like the pure wool: his throne was like the fiery flame, and his wheels as burning fire."* The colors in scriptures are just there to signify something. It is not a treatise on race. Just because black in scripture may be a type of darkness etc., God is not talking about black people. It would be unrighteous and error to try to use the types and symbols in scriptures to use them as a way to put down a race of people. God himself will judge all who do. Because it would be evil and it would misrepresent God and his word. You would be holding the truth in unrighteousness.

Here are a few scriptures showing us that when we shall see Him, and when He appears, He will look like fire, the color of amber; a burning shining bronze.

Ezekiel 8:2-4 states, " *²Then I beheld, and lo a likeness as the appearance of fire: from the appearance of his loins even downward, fire; and from his loins even upward, as the appearance of brightness, as the colour of amber. ³ And he put forth the form of an hand, and took me by a lock of mine head; and the spirit lifted me up between the earth and the heaven, and brought me in the visions of God to Jerusalem, to the door of the inner gate that looketh toward the north; where was the seat of the image of jealousy, which provoketh to jealousy. ⁴ And, behold, the glory of the God of Israel was there, according to the vision that I saw in the plain."* So when the God of Israel appears, He is in the likeness and as the appearance of fire. Matthew 17:1-2 says, *"¹And after six days Jesus taketh Peter, James, and John his brother, and bringeth them up into an high mountain apart, ² And was transfigured before them: and his face did shine as the sun, and his raiment was white as the light."*

Mark 9:2-8 has a little extra revelation to tie in with this account, " *² And after six days Jesus taketh with him Peter, and James, and John, and leadeth them up into an high mountain apart by themselves: and he was transfigured before them. ³ And his raiment became shining, exceeding white as snow; so as no fuller on earth can white them. ⁴ And there appeared unto them Elias with Moses: and they were talking with Jesus. ⁵ And Peter answered and said to Jesus, Master, it is good for us to be here: and let us make three tabernacles; one for thee, and one for Moses, and one for Elias. ⁶ For he wist not what to say; for they were sore afraid. ⁷ And there was a cloud that overshadowed* them: and a voice came out of the cloud, saying, This is my beloved Son: hear him. [8] And suddenly, when they had looked round about, they saw no man any more, save Jesus only with themselves." The word transfiguration comes from the word "metamorphoo"; which means to transform, to change shape, or to fashion like unto. In the Old and New Testament, when it says that we were created in the image and likeness of God, it really means "an exact duplicate in kind." When we are conformed to the image of Christ Jesus, we are going to look like Jesus. Matter of fact, we will be an exact duplicate in kind. A mate scripture to Mark 9 is Matthew 17:2 which says that Jesus *"was transfigured before them: and his face did shine as the sun, and his raiment was white as the light."* This is what He looked like in the glory and this is what we are going to look like in the glory.

Looking back at Mark 9:2-3, the word "raiment"(or garments) speak of our righteousness. We see this truth in Revelation 19:7-9, *"[7] Let us be glad and rejoice, and give honour to him: for the marriage of the Lamb is come, and his wife hath made herself ready. [8] And to her was granted that she should be arrayed in fine linen, clean and white: for the fine linen is the righteousness of saints. [9] And he saith unto me, Write, Blessed are they which are called unto the marriage supper of the Lamb. And he saith unto me, These are the true sayings of God."* This passage is speaking of the Bride, and shows that our clothes represent who we are and how far we have grown in God. What does it say about the Bride? Her clothing is of fine linen, clean and white representing light and brightness. Likewise, Psalms 45:13 says the bride is *"all glorious within: her clothing is of wrought gold."* She is wrought in gold which represents God's fire, light, and brilliancy.

Let us look now at Revelation 1:12-16, *"[12] And I turned to see the voice that spake with me. And being turned, I saw seven golden candlesticks; [13] And in the midst of the seven candlesticks one like unto the Son of man, clothed with a garment down to the foot, and girt about the paps with a golden girdle. [14] His head and his hairs were white like wool, as white as snow; and his eyes were as a flame of fire; [15] And his feet like unto fine brass, as if they burned in a furnace; and his voice as the sound of many waters. [16] And he had in his right hand seven stars: and out of his mouth went a sharp two-edged sword: and his countenance was as the sun shineth in his strength."* In the movie Malcom X or Spike Lee brought it out in that movie and tried to use this to say that Jesus was a black man. This is simply the glorified Jesus. With a complete unveiled face and open mind, I have searched the scriptures and have concluded that Jesus was neither black nor white. He was of the Semitic race. He had olive colored skin when he was here on earth. So all the lily white pictures of Jesus you and I have in my office aren't really true, but I love them anyway. You know Jesus will be a black man or white man to you, whatever you need him to be. If you're a redneck, He probably has a cowboy hat on; and if you're from the ghetto, He probably has some hip hop get up.

The word for brass in the Greek means "burnish copper, whiteness or brilliancy, an alloy of copper or gold and silver, having a brilliant luster". Are you beginning to get the image in your head of what we're talking about? So in this picture of Jesus here in Revelation chapter one, you are looking at the resurrected Jesus, the one who has been in the glory for forty years! What happened every time that Moses went into the manifest present of God and came out? He had to put a veil over his face, because the people couldn't look at him. The glory was so bright, so shining, so full of light and glory that the people couldn't look at him and were afraid to come near him. Well, what do you think Jesus looks like now? I'm just telling you what the scriptures say, not what I say.

Now let us look at a few more scriptures describing the color of our glorious Father. Revelation 2:18 says, "And unto the angel of the church in Thyatira write; These things saith the Son of God, who hath his eyes like unto a flame of fire, and his feet are like fine brass". In Acts 26:13-16 it says, " *At midday, O king, I saw in the way a light from heaven, above the brightness of the sun, shining round about me and them which journeyed with me. [14] And when we were all fallen to the earth, I heard a voice speaking unto me, and saying in the Hebrew tongue, Saul, Saul, why persecutest thou me? it is hard for thee to kick against the pricks. [15] And I said, Who art thou, Lord? And he said, I am Jesus whom thou persecutest. [16] But rise, and stand upon thy feet: for I have appeared unto thee for this purpose, to make thee a minister and a witness both of these things which thou hast seen, and of those things in the which I will appear unto thee;"* In this passage, Paul is telling the king about his visitation by the glory of Jesus. For Paul, it took a visitation of the glory to knock him off his horse high of religion.

Let us turn now to Psalms 50:2 *"Out of Zion, the perfection of beauty, God hath shined."* God has shined! The word "shine" in Hebrew means "to be light." Another translation says, "He blazes forth." The picture here of God when you see Him, is like a burning fiery flame. He was the burning bush that Moses spoke to that did not consume itself. So if you are wondering what we are going to look like and what God looks like, I promise you this, as we see in I Corinthians 15:41, *"[41] There is one glory of the sun, and another glory of the moon, and another glory of the stars: for one star differeth from another star in glory. [42] So also is the resurrection of the dead..."*. Some of us are going to be burning fiery flames, and some will be like the children's song, "this little light of mine, I'm gonna let it shine." We each determine how bright the glory of God will radiate in us by the way we live our lives now. You have got to walk with Jesus to get some brighter light. You have to be changed into His image, and you certainly can't be walking around holding grudges against other races.

Now I'm going to be honest with you, because I don't know how else to be. When I was really searching out the ancestry of Moses, I began to realize that there was no way that Moses was not a man of color. Something in me moved and my mind was saying; "Search again. That can't be true." Like I mentioned earlier, I see Charlton Heston standing at the Red Sea, as a white man. And the Lord whispered ever so gently to me, "Um hum." And I said, "What?" "Um Hum." Then I replied, "I don't have any racism in me. No way, devil." "Um Hum." I realized then that I was confronting something that was in my own soul, and I don't even know why. Moses could have been blue, but why would it make a difference? Then the Lord spoke to me, "From the time you were a baby, all you heard every day and every night was how horrible black people were." I know every ethnic slur that people use to call other races. I know what Polish people are called, what Jewish people are called, what Mexican people are called, what Black people are called. I know all the names given everybody. My father never had any names for white people though. Isn't it funny how ignorant people talk like they are professors? Ignorant people want to expound and give the world their wisdom and they don't know "jack" about anything. I can remember my father screaming about how the black people won't work, and yet he's just sitting there with no job and passing judgments on everybody else. See I went to school every day with nothing but black people and I didn't see the things that my father was saying; on the contrary, we were actually the ones on welfare. We hear these feelings from the day we wake up and we can't help but develop similar attitudes. If the authority figures in your life, like your mother or father, are racists, I'm sorry but you are going to have some racism in you too. And the only way that you're going to get rid of it is through Jesus and living on the other side of it for a while. I realized that I had to deal with that thing. Some of us need to deal with some things.

People despise someone who is truly free. I can say to you, if nothing else, that what this study has done for me; I am completely delivered and free. I have no stones to throw at anybody. I judge no man. And I tell you that I love what the Reverend Martin Luther King said; "I long for the day when man will be judged by the content of his character and not by the color of his skin." It is so distasteful to me, and I don't see how a person can call themselves a Christian with all the racism that came from pulpits in this country, even up until about 1965. How they could stand and sing "Amazing Grace", a song written by a man who got saved and was repenting for the horrors of racism in his life. Before he was saved, he was about to go crazy because he was a ship master that carried captive slaves. They don't even know the person that wrote the song they are singing.

185

Let us continue now with looking at some more powerful scriptures describing the color of our God. Revelation 22:16 says *"I Jesus have sent mine angel to testify unto you these things in the churches. I am the root and the offspring of David, and the bright and morning star."* Habbakuk 3:3-4 says, *"³God came from Teman, and the Holy One from mount Paran. Selah. His glory covered the heavens, and the earth was full of his praise. ⁴And his brightness was as the light."* Next we see in II Thessalonians 2:8, *"And then shall that Wicked be revealed, whom the Lord shall consume with the spirit of his mouth, and shall destroy with the brightness of his coming:"* Psalms 104:1-2 reads *"Bless the LORD, O my soul. O LORD my God, thou art very great; thou art clothed with honour and majesty. ²Who coverest thyself with light as with a garment: who stretchest out the heavens like a curtain:"* Exodus 24:16-17 says *"¹⁶And the glory of the LORD abode upon mount Sinai, and the cloud covered it six days: and the seventh day he called unto Moses out of the midst of the cloud. ¹⁷And the sight of the glory of the LORD was like devouring fire on the top of the mount in the eyes of the children of Israel."* Psalm 84:11 says *"For the LORD God is a sun and shield:"* Zechariah 2:5 says *"For I, saith the LORD, will be unto her a wall of fire round about, and will be the glory in the midst of her."* Finally in Psalms 80:1 we read, *"Give ear, O Shepherd of Israel, thou that leadest Joseph like a flock; thou that dwellest between the cherubims, shine forth."*

God when He appears is like fire, He looks like burnish brass, and He is the color of amber. We have to build this foundation of what the scripture says about God's color, so we can get to what God really wants and that is this. He wants us to think like Him and wants us to see like Him. He wants us to stop criticizing and belittling our brothers and sisters; and stop holding entire groups of people in bondage because of what one person did to you. I can say to you that I have seen things done to white people that are unspeakable. I've also seen things done to black people that are unspeakable. No one has a premium on goodness. There is no race that has not been a slave master. Blacks have held slaves just like others. The pendulum has swung way out, and that is why you have to have a little bit of compassion for some blacks who teach "black nationalism." But just try to understand that if you had been in oppression for 400 years, don't you think that you would be encouraged that there is some truth and validity to the fact that there were black people in the Bible? And actually, that black people were some of the greatest ministries in the Old Testament? The pendulum swings out, but don't be mad because the pendulum will finally swing back into the middle and into the proper balance. The balance is this: God is neither black nor white, He's the color of fire. You and I are no longer black or white, blue, green, Jew, Gentile, male, or female. We are the sons of God, and by the Spirit of God living inside of all of us we have been made a partaker of the divine nature. As Colossians 1:27 says, "Christ in us is the hope of glory!"

I believe God wants you to do something that will cause those old brain synapses in your head, which are real slow and don't like to learn new stuff when you get up there in age, to change. We are going to see a picture and an image that is about as close to God as we can get. And I want you to look at it and absorb it and perhaps then we can begin to see as God sees. Just consider a burning flaming fire. I want you to get that picture in your head. That's a pillar of fire, that's the fire and the glory of God. From now on, when you pray, stop seeing Charlton Heston, Jim Caviezel. Fire is the color of God, and I want you to close your eyes with that picture of God's consuming fire. Lord Jesus, burn that image into our hearts, that you look like the color of burnish brass or copper and that the brightness, light and glory of your presence is astonishingly golden. Help us to see you as you are, and when we look at our brothers and sisters, from this day forward, that we no longer see them as shapes, sizes, and colors; but we know that inside them is a seed, a holy burning fiery seed of fire that will ultimately over shadow it, in Jesus Name. Remember our God is a consuming fire. Heb 12:29

The Color Of God's People
Chapter 15

Let us begin this chapter by looking in Romans chapter 8 and Genesis chapter 1. We've looked so far at the color of God and in this chapter we are going to look at the color that you and I are going to be throughout eternity. All of this may seem rudimentary and nonsensical, but it is important that the principles that we will look at in this chapter be put in writing. I think if we can all receive this revelation, than we would all not have a problem with racism again because we would see ourselves and others as God see us and not how men see others. This has been the problem since the beginning. We see ourselves after men. When Jesus touched the blind man in Mark 8:22-26, the first time He touched him, Jesus asked him if he saw anything, and the man's answer was *"I see men as trees, walking"*. Now this was an interesting statement. Then Jesus touched him again and he said he *"saw every man clearly"*. I believe in this story, Jesus allowed this blind man to first see into the realm of the Spirit and what he saw were men as God intended them to be, *"as trees walking"*. All you have to do is pull out your concordance and do a study of the word "trees" and you will find over and over again the Bible describing men as "trees". The word "tree" in the Hebrew and Greek is the word "oak tree". Oak trees are very strong and have a great root system. So this is type is what God wants us to see in each other. I don't know about you, but I don't want to "see men clearly". I am tired of seeing their short-comings, their failures. I am tired of seeing my own failures and it can be very discouraging at times, but if we have this revelation, we will begin to see others differently.

This has been the whole purpose of this book, that we see each other with God's eyes and see men as He sees them (not as how our parents taught us, or how history taught us), but how the Word of God declares them to be. At some point in every subject in every part of our lives, we need to go to the Word of God to see what the Word says about it. I have been a minister since 1975 and I tell you, I have taught on thousands of subjects, but yet little did I know that God would speak to me to write a book about the presence of black people in the Bible. My initial response to the Lord was why did He want me to write about this? But the answer is simple. We are still bound many times by racism, elitism, etc. Even recently Senate Majority Leader Harry Reid stated that our new president Barack Obama could be a successful candidate because he is "light skinned" and that he speaks with "no Negro dialect". Well many responded to this and said he just slipped up. Yes he did, but he also showed us what he was really thinking. What he was really thinking was Obama is a black man who doesn't talk like a black man and acts like a white man so I can vote for him then. This is the truth and this is in the Senate of the United States.

Now this is just one example, but the truth is, lying hidden deep within many of us is this kind of thinking. People that confess to be believers in Jesus Christ cannot think like that. This is not the way God thinks or the way God sees Barack Obama or anybody else. We as believers need to begin to look, act, and walk out the Kingdom of God.

In the beginning in Genesis 1:26-27 it says, *"[26]And God said, Let us make man in our image, after our likeness...[27]So God created man in his own image, in the image of God created he him; male and female created he them."* We are looking in this chapter what our new color we'll have for the ages to come as God's people and we see in Genesis we were made in the beginning in God's image. Then in Genesis 2:7 is says, *"And the LORD God formed man of the dust of the ground, and breathed into his nostrils the breath of life; and man became a living soul."* Man in His original state was formed (or molded) out of the earth. The first Adam was made of the earth, but he was created in the image of likeness of God. This means he was in the image of God not in his physical characteristics like color per say, but he was molded from the earth in the likeness of God such as other attributes. God has eyes, fingers, ears, etc, and so does man. God laughs, cries, etc, and so does man. All that we are, He is. So in the beginning God created man and the original man had both male and female characteristics within him. When there was none to complement man, God took the female characteristics out of man (rib or "alter ego") and made a woman. That is why when a man and woman come together in marriage, they become one. We saw in another chapter that this original man was a reddish grayish color and more than likely stayed that way until we come to Noah's sons (Shem, Ham, and Japheth) which were sent to repopulate the earth after the flood creating three main classes of races that sprung into many others. Shem was the father of the Semitic peoples. Ham was the father of the Black peoples, and Japheth was the father of the Caucasian peoples.

Next in the New Testament in Romans 8:28-29 we read, *"[28]And we know that all things work together for good to them that love God, to them who are the called according to his purpose. [29]For whom he did foreknow, he also did predestinate to be conformed to the image of his Son, that he might be the firstborn among many brethren."* Now if we were created in the image and likeness of God, why would we need to be conformed to His image as Romans 8 tells us? The answer is simple – because man fell. Man went into sin. Because Adam fell, humankind became a fallen being and so humankind must be formed again. Well, God is not going to form man again in his physical body. But He is now reforming (or conforming man) into His image in the soulish realm (the image, likeness, or exact duplicate in kind of His Son) that has been lost.

Now today, if you ask Christians what our job is, most will say to preach the Gospel to every nation. This is absolutely true. But our number one job in ministry is not just getting people saved, but being conformed to the image of Jesus. Paul, in writing to the Galatians said, *"My little children, of whom I travail in birth again until Christ be formed in you"* (Galatians 4:19). Our minds need to be renewed to be like Jesus. In I Corinthians 15, we read, *"[45]And so it is written, The first man Adam was made a living soul; the last Adam was made a quickening spirit. [46]Howbeit that was not first which is spiritual, but that which is natural; and afterward that which is spiritual..."* Now before I go any further in the passage, we need to understand something. The first creation of man was a physical being to live on the earth as we know it (in the mineral and plant garden that had trees etc). Now there is another garden of God by the way that is the real garden of God that still exists as far as I am concerned in heaven where Lucifer was kicked out of. Lucifer (one of the three arch-angels) ruled the worship in heaven and covered the glory of God. He was called the *"anointed cherub that covereth"* (Ezekiel 28:14). Lucifer's story is found in Isaiah 14 and in Ezekiel 28. But it also talks about Lucifer trafficking in the earth in Ezekiel 28:16-18. This I believe took place between Genesis 1:1 and Genesis 1:2. Genesis 1:1-2 reads *"[1]In the beginning God created the heaven and the earth. [2]And the earth was without form, and void; and darkness was upon the face of the deep. And the Spirit of God moved upon the face of the waters."* Something happened between verse 1 and 2 because God does not create anything *"without form, and void"*. Many scholars agree with this. And the condition we find the earth in verse 2 was the result of God's judgment upon the earth at the time. To me, this causes science and the Bible to agree completely. I believe it is pretty foolish for people to say the earth is only 7000 years old. It makes Christians sound ignorant and foolish when scientific facts easily disprove this. The earth may be billions of years old. The Bible does not tell us the time from between verses 1 and 2. The Bible doesn't tell us how long Lucifer trafficked in the earth. Now there are many theories as to who lived on the earth during this period. But one thing that I believe that is pretty obvious is there were many different types of animals that we don't have today. The Bible mentions them (such as unicorns) and fossil records prove they once existed (such as dinosaurs). When somebody finds a dinosaur bone and says it is 2 million years old, I have absolutely no problem with this. I just say this fits right there between Genesis 1:1 and Genesis 1:2.

So after creation, God then kicked out Lucifer from the third heaven because iniquity was found in his heart and into the second heaven. In Job 1:7 when Satan is presented himself before the Lord and the Lord asked him where he came from, Satan responded and said, *"From going to and fro in the earth, and from walking up and down in it"*. Well, it seems that when God kicked him out of the third heaven, Satan made his throne in the second heaven, but his place where he used to rule was the third heaven. I believe when God showed the angelic host what was in His heart to create a man in His image, Lucifer couldn't stand this and got jealous because he saw himself as beautiful and he couldn't believe what beauty could come from the dust of the earth that would be better than him. When this happened, Lucifer was cast out of the third heaven. The earth was destroyed and God re-created the earth. This is easily proven in the Hebrew. The first word used when God created the heaven and the earth means in Hebrew creating something out of nothing. Every other time the word create is used it is a word that means like baking a cake (using pre-existing things to create something else). So God re-creates the earth and places Adam in it. Adam is the image of the earthy. Now God, as we already saw in another chapter, is a bright shiny being. His color is bronze and amber which is the color of glory. Maybe Adam looked like this, but as I pointed out in another chapter, the Scriptures give evidence of his color being a reddish-gray color. The amber bronze color of God maybe is depicted more in Adam's spirit than in his body. So once Adam fell, he needed to be redeemed, therefore Jesus came, became a man (a son of man) even though He was the Son of God, died, and rose again, so mankind could once again have the ability to have the image of God. But this time, not an earthy one, but a spiritual one as we see as we read on in I Corinthians 15.

"[47]The first man is of the earth, earthy: the second man is the Lord from heaven. [48]As is the earthy, such are they also that are earthy: and as is the heavenly, such are they also that are heavenly. [49]And as we have borne the image of the earthy, we shall also bear the image of the heavenly. [50]Now this I say, brethren, that flesh and blood cannot inherit the kingdom of God; neither doth corruption inherit incorruption." So man now is being prepared for something which is called in Colossians 1:27, *"Christ in you, the hope of glory"*, which is the second Adam, spiritual Adam, or the heavenly body that is going to be ours for the ages to come. Now we have pictures of this in the book of Revelation and Ezekiel with the living creatures. Those living creatures are not a form of angels, but they are representative of human beings. I believe this because in describing them, the Bible says they have the face of a man. So now that we are fallen beings, our earthy bodies represent corruption. As Christians now, we are looking for the incorruption to come upon us. Romans 8:23 says the Spirit of God that is inside us now groans within us for the redemption of our body. In our natural body, the older we get, the worse we seem to get. Our body develops more pain, disease tries to overtake us, bruises take longer to heal, etc. Getting old is a trip. And the older I get, the more I am looking for and can't wait for my new resurrected and glorified body. II Corinthians 3:18 says *"But we all, with open face beholding as in a glass the glory of the Lord, are changed into the same image from glory to glory, even as by the Spirit of the Lord."* As we behold the glory of the Lord we are being changed into the image of the second Adam which is the Lord Jesus!

We all know that God is threefold (Father, Son, and Holy Spirit). Since we were made in His image, we are threefold as well (spirit, soul, and body). When we are born again, we are born again of incorruptible seed I Peter 1:23 tells us. This incorruptible seed comes into our spirit. Hebrews 12:23 defines our salvation this way, *"the spirits of just men made perfect"*. Our spirit then upon salvation is made perfect and is just like God. I Corinthians 6:17 says *"he that is joined unto the Lord is one spirit"*. Every Christian then has the glorious shining seed of God inside of them, making them then a partaker of His divine nature. Our spirit is completely perfect and golden after salvation. So what happens after we are born again is our soul and body (which are still corrupted because of the fall) need to be changed. Jesus resurrected our spirit at salvation. This is called justification. This is the first aspect of our salvation. The second aspect of our salvation is called sanctification where the Lord takes our mind, emotions, intellect, feelings, etc (all of the aspects of our soul) and conforms it to God's mind and image. This takes a lifetime, but once this happens, the third aspect of our salvation comes forth which is for our body. The third aspect of our salvation is called glorification. Justification is the first aspect of our salvation (for our spirits and happens instantly when we are born again – we become a new species as we saw in another chapter). Glorification is the third aspect where our bodies will be changed in the twinkling of an eye and as Philippians 3:21 puts it, *"Who shall change our vile body, that it may be fashioned like unto his glorious body"* and is instantaneous as well. This is what we are waiting on. Sanctification is where God works on us everyday to change our soulish man and conform it to the mind of Christ.

It is of the utmost importance that you understand the three aspects of our salvation. This is where many miss it by saying we can lose our salvation. They confuse sanctification with justification because they do not understand glorification. Heaven is God's gift to mankind. John 3:16 says *"For God so loved the world, that he gave his only begotten Son, that whosoever believeth in him should not perish, but have everlasting life."* Jesus offering Himself once 2000 years ago in one place for all mankind was sufficient. This again is justification. Our spirits upon being born again are completely filled with God and made perfect because of the blood of Jesus Christ, bless His holy name! This makes us just like Jesus when He walked with earth. His spirit was all God just like ours is now that we are born again (although immature that has to grow, but yet full of God). But our soul, which comprises of thousands of chambers, is not perfect and still needs to be changed. The chambers in our soul are filled with all kinds of things: wounds, experiences, different emotions, good things, bad things, etc. Each chamber can be filled with God, the devil, inherited defects, or experiences (all the aspects of our psyche). This is why we have to be careful to certain aspects of psychology. Psychologists can open up our soul and expose certain chambers in our soul and cause harm. Deep inside of us are hurts, insecurities, wounds, and as we have been discussing in this book prejudices and racism. Many people carry in their soul deep and hidden racial prejudices and God wants to deal with all of these things and change us on the inside. Sometimes we don't know some of this exists in our soul until a situation arises to expose it. Therefore sanctification is the process where the Spirit of God and the Word of God invades every chamber in our soul until we are completely conformed to the image of Jesus. Until this completely happens, we will still be incomplete. When we consider our own heart, we may think this can never happen, but Jesus did command us to be perfect as He is perfect. Many times when I teach or talk about perfection, people look at me like I am crazy and say it can never happen. Well, I beg to differ. What about Enoch in Genesis 5? Genesis 5:24 says *"And Enoch walked with God: and he was not; for God took him."* This is why Jesus came as a man and became like one of us to show us it is possible. Hebrews 4:15 says of Jesus that He *"was in all points tempted like as we are, yet without sin."* Jesus was just a man with the Spirit of God in Him, just like we are now that we are born again. If Jesus did not come like we are, then He could've never redeemed us.

So while we want to preach the gospel to everything that moves or breathes, know that the greatest and deepest message that God has for His creation is for us to be completely redeemed, spirit, soul, and body. God wants us to regain what was lost in the garden and for us to have His image. This is what God wants for all of us. So right now, as we saw in II Corinthians 3:18, we are being changed right now in our soulish man from glory to glory. This takes time. Sanctification takes a lifetime. Justification is instantaneous. When we got saved, it happened just like that. I remember the day I got saved. I immediately got delivered from drugs, cursing, and a few other things. But I still wasn't perfect. I still wanted a cigarette later on in the day and at first this bothered me. I thought why didn't God deliver me from everything when I got saved? Every believer probably asked this same question in their heart as well. Dear reader, was everything cleansed in your heart the day you got saved? I don't think so. But a bunch of stuff was. God gives us a head start. So after our salvation experience (justification), the process of sanctification begins, chamber by chamber, where our soul is conformed to the image of the Son. I have been at this for 40 years now, and am not perfect yet, but I believe what I preach. I believe that there is going to be a people who will have allowed God total access into their life, where no chamber in their heart is left hidden, unturned, and unchanged. I John 3:1-3 say *"¹Behold, what manner of love the Father hath bestowed upon us, that we should be called the sons of God: therefore the world knoweth us not, because it knew him not. ²Beloved, now are we the sons of God, and it doth not yet appear what we shall be: but we know that, when he shall appear, we shall be like him; for we shall see him as he is..."* Consider all the way back to Moses in Exodus where he says to God, *"I beseech thee, show me thy glory"* (Exodus 33:18). God's response to Moses was *"Thou canst not see my face: for there shall no man see men, and live"*

(Exodus 33:20). Well, Moses seemed to look at a part of God and live. So did Paul. The point is this: Man, in his earthy state, cannot look upon God and live. But a man who is in the image of the Son can look directly into the eyes of God because when he looks into the eyes of God and God looks back, they are seeing the same thing! God is looking for this level of intimacy with His people. Revelation 22:4 says *"And they shall see his face; and his name shall be in their foreheads."* Somebody somewhere is going to have every chamber filled to where they can stand in the very presence of God and not be burnt to a crisp. Every time Moses would go up the mount and into God's presence, he would receive more glory. Moses began to change so much that the Israelites begged Moses to put something over his face because he was changing. Paul talks about this in II Corinthians 3:7-18, *"[7]But if the ministration of death, written and engraven in stones, was glorious, so that the children of Israel could not stedfastly behold the face of Moses for the glory of his countenance; which glory was to be done away..."* In other words, this is the Old Testament glory and it was so glorious that the people could not stand that. *"[8]How shall not the ministration of the spirit be rather glorious? [9]For if the ministration of condemnation* (i.e. that Law) *be glory, much more doth the ministration of righteousness exceed in glory. [10]For even that which was made glorious had no glory in this respect, by reason of the glory that excelleth..."* This means the Law had some glory. But he is saying since Jesus has come and brought righteousness to us, Moses glorious face can not even be compared to that which excels in glory. We don't want just our face to shine. We want our whole body to radiate with the glory of God. So he is saying the glory of righteousness far excels the glory of Moses that it isn't even comparable because of how great it is. *"[11]For if that which is done away was glorious, much more that which remaineth is glorious. [12]Seeing then that we have such hope, we use great plainness of speech. [13]And not as Moses, which put a vail over his face, that the children of Israel could not stedfastly look to the end of that which is abolished..."* In describing our hope of glory, Paul is trying to use as much plainness of speech as possible. Paul wasn't trying to use some fancy prophetic terminology. He says it pretty plainly and says basically, "Do you remember Moses when he came out of the glory and he had to cover his face? You think that was powerful? Wait until you see what's coming! Wait until you see what the resurrected Jesus is going to bring forth in His people!"

Let us now look back at I Corinthians 15, starting in verse 35, *"[35]But some man will say, How are the dead raised up? and with what body do they come? [36]Thou fool, that which thou sowest is not quickened, except it die: [37]And that which thou sowest, thou sowest not that body that shall be, but bare grain, it may chance of wheat, or of some other grain..."* In other words, when you put a seed of wheat into the ground it doesn't look like what it will ultimately going to be. Everything in the Kingdom of God and life in general begins with a seed. That is why Gabriel said to Mary *"And the angel answered and said unto* her, *The Holy Ghost shall come upon thee, and the power of the Highest shall overshadow thee: therefore also that <u>holy thing</u> which shall be born of thee shall be called the Son of God."* Like begets like. The seed is planted and everything that we are ever going to be and need to have is in the seed. Glory to God! We are constantly saying, "God come down". But the incorruptible and glorious seed (the divine nature) of God has already been place inside of us. We have to let it grow and bring it up. Jesus said in John 7:38, *"He that believeth on me, as the scripture hath said, <u>out of his belly</u> shall flow rivers of living water."* We have to stir up the gift of God within us, because the glory will be flowing out of a people in the last days.

Continuing in verse 38, *"But God giveth it a body as it hath pleased him, and to every seed his own body. [39]All flesh is not the same flesh: but there is one kind of flesh of men, another flesh of beasts, another of fishes, and another of birds. [40]There are also celestial bodies, and bodies terrestrial: but the glory of the celestial is one, and the glory of the terrestrial is another. [41]There is one glory of the sun, and another glory of the moon, and another glory of the stars: for one star differeth from another star in glory..."* When we walk out in the sun light, we have to guard our eyes or wear sun glasses. At night I don't need to wear sunglasses, but I can still see to walk around because a lesser light is shining. In the country at night is always the most beautiful where you can get away from a city. The stars and the moon shine. Different stars shine at different levels. Paul is using this plainness of speech to describe an important principle that he brings out in verse 42, *"<u>So also is the resurrection of the dead</u>..."* When the resurrection comes, we will be changed (when our vile body is made like unto His glorious body) according to the degree of light we've allowed God to work in us in our life. This is very simple. The greater we've allowed God to sanctify us throughout our lives, when glorification comes, we can expect a more glorious body. Some will shine like a dim star. Others brighter, and the bride will be like the moon. I Corinthians 3:12-15 says, *"[12]Now if any man build upon this foundation gold, silver, precious stones, wood, hay, stubble; [13]<u>Every man's work shall be made manifest</u>: for the day shall declare it, because it shall be revealed by fire; and the fire shall try every man's work of what sort it is. [14]If any man's work abide which he hath built thereupon, he shall receive a reward. [15]If any man's work shall be burned, he shall suffer loss: but he himself shall be saved; yet so as by fire."* Everything is going to be tried by fire. If we don't build upon the foundation of our salvation experience, no reward will remain. God is a consuming fire. When you walk into the presence of God, you walk into the consuming brilliance of His glory and everything that is impure and unholy will be burnt. If you do nothing after you are saved, you won't be able to stand there. The only thing that will remain will be your initial born again experience. But others, who build upon their foundation gold, silver, and precious stones, a reward remains upon after entering into God's consuming fire. I pray when it is my turn to face God's judgment, there is not one thing in me that can be burnt off. God's fire is going to try every man's work of what sort it is (not what size). Forget about size and bigness. God is after quality in our lives, not quantity. Understanding this principle of glorification and the resurrection, we can then begin to understand what we are going to all look like. I don't know how we are going to see and communicate, but it is going to be awesome. I John 4:17 says, *"Herein is our love made perfect, that we may have boldness in the day of judgment: because as he is, so are we in this world."* This is what God wants for His precious people.

I want to spend some time in this chapter talking about our clothing. Many things in the Bible represent something other than themselves. For instance, if we do a study on colors, we find that the color red can have several interpretations or meanings. We also find that many numbers in Scripture have specific meanings. How can we find these meanings? Well, we take the color red, look in our concordance where every time the word red is used. Looking at the compilation of the Scriptures where red is used, we will find some sort of repeating revelation or association of red to something. Therefore you can say red means this and that. For example, consider the word "water". Water in Scriptures can mean many things such as a type of the Holy Ghost, a type of the Word of God, a type of many, many peoples, etc. We can also do this for numbers, colors, names, directions, objects, or anything in the Bible. We allow the Word of God to define for us their definition and we find that they can mean something other than themselves. So when it comes to clothing in Scripture we can do the same thing. Proverbs 6:27 says *"Can a man take fire in his bosom, and his clothes not be burned?"* This is in context to adultery. In other words Proverbs 6:27 is using the terminology of clothes to describe a spiritual principle. Revelation 19:7-8 says, *"[7]Let us be glad and rejoice, and give honour to him: for the marriage of the Lamb is come, and his wife hath made herself ready. [8]And to her was granted that she should be arrayed in fine linen, clean and white: for the fine linen is the righteousness of saints..."* We find in Psalms 45:13 speaking of the bride, *"The king's daughter is all glorious within: her clothing is of wrought gold."* Clothing not only speaks of our righteousness, but what is seen outwardly in our person because of what we have allowed God to do on the inside. What is going to shine (as we saw earlier) is going to be our body. So the Scriptures use the terminology of "clothes" to represent our righteousness and what we've attained to in God. As we read in Proverbs 6:27, when a person commits adultery, their clothes are burned. This means their reward or what they have gained in God has been burned. Now they can gain it back, but any person that commits adultery loses something. You can't take fire in your bosom (adultery) and not have your clothes be affected by it. You can repent and tell Jesus you didn't mean to and He will forgive you, but you lost something and you have to work to regain it. Psalms 45:13 says the bride's clothing is of wrought gold. Wrought means to

196

be worked in. So the bride of Christ's clothing is of worked in gold. This isn't telling us she is going to have a fancy gown on. This is what she looks like! Our clothing is our body in the ages to come.

In continuing with the idea of clothing, let's consider God's clothing. Psalms 104:1-2 says, "*¹Bless the LORD, O my soul. O LORD my God, thou art very great; thou art clothed with honour and majesty. ²Who coverest thyself with light as with a garment: who stretchest out the heavens like a curtain*". How is God clothed with honour and majesty? Is the psalmist talking about a shirt called honour and some pants called majesty? I don't think so. The psalmist is speaking on the character of God or who really He is. Our clothing reveals who we really are on the inside. Moreover, in verse 2, a garment is not a piece of cloth we put on, but it is light. There are hundreds of Scriptures talking about clothing. Daniel 7:9 says "*I beheld till the thrones were cast down, and the Ancient of days did sit, whose garment was white as snow, and the hair of his head like the pure wool: his throne was like the fiery flame, and his wheels as burning fire.*" Why was His garment white as snow? White in this sense in the Scriptures speaks of spiritual purity. Fine linen speaks of spiritual purity. In Ezekiel 44:17-18, the sons of Zadok (the priests) we told by God to only wear linen garments because every other kind of garment causes sweat and sweat comes from the works of the earth (the works of men and not the grace of God).

Let us look at some more Scriptures about our clothing. In Proverbs 31:22 and 25 in describing the bride it says, "*²²She maketh herself coverings of tapestry; her clothing is silk and purple...²⁵Strength and honour are her clothing; and she shall rejoice in time to come.*" Now, when you got up this morning and thought about what you were going to wear, you probably chose the clothing appropriate for the day's activity. If you don't have to meet anybody important, you will dress more casually. If you may run into somebody that you need to look half descent, you will dress better. Clothing reveals our physical appearance. Our physical appearance will show what has happened to us in our soulish man. So Proverbs 31 gives us insight to the bride's clothing or the nature of the bride in her soul. In Matthew 22:2-13 we find Jesus speaking on a parable about a wedding and in verse 11-12 somebody was at the wedding without having a wedding garment, so he was kicked out of the wedding. This reveals to us that to be in the wedding, you have to have the right garment or clothing on. In other words, to be in the wedding, you have to grow up and allow the sanctification process to take place to where you shine brightly. Revelation 3:5 says, "*He that overcometh, the same shall be clothed in white raiment...*" Revelation 4:4, in speaking of the 24 elders, we find them "*clothed in white raiment*". Revelation 7:9 says "*After this I beheld, and, lo, a great multitude, which no man could number, of all nations, and kindreds, and people, and tongues, stood before the throne, and before the Lamb, clothed with*

197

white robes, and palms in their hands;" Revelation 10:1 says *"And I saw another mighty angel come down from heaven, clothed with a cloud: and a rainbow was upon his head, and his face was as it were the sun, and his feet as pillars of fire:"* This is speaking of a mighty messenger in the last days. Angel in the Greek simply means messenger and I believe this mighty angel is a person who is alive on the earth today having an open book in his hand (Revelation 10:8). I believe that God is raising up many teachers all over the earth who look like a cloud and have a rainbow round about their heads. The cloud represents the glory or being full of the Holy Ghost. Having a rainbow around their heads mean they have a complete understanding of the covenant they have with God. You see, we can be that messenger ourselves, that when we are enveloped in the glory, we are God's messenger able to bring people into the glory, reveal the Word of God to them (the open book) and show them and live before them the covenant that they have with God is forever sure and true. This is what we are aspiring to be. Anything less is superfluous and worth nothing. But it says also that this mighty angel's face was as it were the sun and his feet as pillars of fire. This is where we are headed. Proverbs 27:19 says, *"As in water face answereth to face, so the heart of man to man."* Our face or countenance reveals who we really are. Have you ever looked into somebody's eyes and knew the struggles that they had on the inside? I have many times. Other times you can look into somebody's eyes and see their gentleness and meekness. In the years to come, God is going to have a people that is going to radiate so much glory, that it will be like they are walking in a cloud. I pray that the day comes when you are so filled with the glory of the Lord and as Peter was in Acts 5:15, he was enveloped in a haze of glory. The word overshadow in Acts 5:15 means "to envelop in a haze of glory or brilliancy". Peter's shadow healed the sick. There is something about that overshadowing anointing and glory that can be upon God's people. Our calling is to be enveloped in God's glory. We might not see it with our eyes, but we can feel it and know when it is there. The day is coming when God is going to raise up a messenger company whose face is like the sun. There is no impurity in them. There is no uncleanness in them. Many may think this impossible. But Jesus came as a man, was tempted in all points as a man, to prove that it can be done! In Matthew 17:1-2 Peter, James, and John, saw Jesus being transfigured before them (as a man). It says, *"his face did shine as the sun, and his raiment was white as the light"*. Because Jesus had no sin, He could immediately step into His glorious body. We are not there yet, but a day will come! The same thing God was after from the beginning, He is after today. He wants a man to fellowship with; a man that can sit across the table from Him and not be destroyed.

Lastly it describes the messenger in Revelation 10 having feet like pillars of fire. This means that this last days company of messengers will be like those described in Romans 10:15 and Isaiah 52:7, *"How beautiful are the feet of them that preach the gospel of peace, and bring glad tidings of good things!"* This company is going to have feet like pillars of fire. Where ever they tread their feet, as God told Joshua, it will belong to them. For example, if they walk into another nation (and it doesn't matter if anybody has been there before), when their foot steps down into that country, who they are in God begins to have dominion everything around them. They will not have to pray for hours anymore if they are walking in the light as He is in the light and they've allowed the truth to make them free, they will literally be the sons of God, like when Jesus walked the earth. Revelation 1:15 describes Jesus feet as, *"his feet like unto fine brass, as if they burned in a furnace"*. When they walk into a room, they don't have to pray down every devil. No, when they walk in their authority, it demands demons to leave. When they walk into a foreign country, it doesn't matter what devils have been reigning for thousands of years, they have to move because one of greater authority has come! When their feet like pillars of fire step into a place, they are saying they are not leaving until God gets Him a home in that place. We need to have this vision for our lives. We need to have a vision for what is coming and prepare the people of God to see what is coming. What is coming is glorious! Do you want to be like this messenger in Revelation 10? Their face is like the sun! They walk with a cloud all the time, a rainbow is around their head, and their feet are like pillars of fire! They bring God's glory, authority, and covenant wherever they go. Wherever they go they have in their hand an open book and people's eyes are opened and revelation begins to flow when they speak. True proceeding words come out of their mouth and they stand as an oracle of God to people! I look forward to the glorious day when we are completely changed (spirit, soul, and body). But until that day, we say to our Father in heaven: "sanctify us!", "purify us!", "cleanse us!", "mold us!", and "conform us!" into the men and women we were born to be. We were born to be sons of the Living God! We can walk in the glory all the day long. Don't let anybody rob you from the glory. The longer you and I stay in the glory, like Moses, we are going to be changed!

God wants you to be like that messenger in Revelation 10. As far as I know, there are only a few ways to get there. First, you have to be saved. Secondly, you have to be water baptized. Thirdly, you have to be baptized in the Holy Ghost. Then you have to fall in love with the Word of God and give your life to it. You have to devour the Word of God. Then you have to begin to pray and spend time in the presence of God and understand what He is like. In the glory, you can feel His heart and feel His different moods and what He is thinking. You need to be a radical worshiper and be delivered from the opinions of men. You can't worry about what other people think about you. What is the greatest thing a person can do in his life and what can this legacy be, but that he or she brought Jesus to others? When I am gone, I want to be remembered for one thing. If someone would mention my name after I am gone, I would like others to hear, "You know Brother Sam, one thing about him is he knew the Word of God, he opened my eyes, brought the glory wherever he went, and was a door opener". That is what you are called to be. We are not called to just preach or prophecy. We are called to be those that when they enter a room they literally bring the Lord Jesus into the room! May God grant this for all of us and that we change the generation in which we live. As David fulfilled the will of God in his generation, let this be said of you and I. We can't do anything without Jesus! We have proven in our lives that we can not do anything without Jesus! Philemon 6 says, "*acknowledging every good thing which is in you in Christ Jesus*". I John 4:4 says "*greater is he that is in you, than he that is in the world.*" Job 6:13 says "*Is not my help in me?*" Jesus said in John 7:38, "*He that believeth on me, as the scripture hath said, out of his belly shall flow rivers of living water.*" Out of us should flow that "*pure river of water of life, clear as crystal, proceeding out of the throne of God and of the Lamb*" (Revelation 22:1)! Out of us should flow rivers of Glory and revelation to change this world!

Next, I want to look at the principle that if we were created in the image of God and that our God is a consuming fire, then that will make us a flame of fire. Psalms 104:4 says, "*Who maketh his angels spirits; his ministers a flaming fire.*" Therefore, for the ages to come, we are going to be that fiery color (that amber or burnt bronze). But before I get into passages of Scripture about our future color, I want to bring up something David said in Psalms 17:15, "*As for me, I will behold thy face in righteousness: I shall be satisfied, when I awake, with thy likeness.*" Have you said this about yourself, "*As for me*", not caring what others think? We can't make decisions for others. We can't make decisions for our spouse, children, brothers, or sisters whom we love dearly. We can lead a horse to water, but if they don't drink, they will die and there is nothing we can do about it. We can only make decisions for ourselves and when it comes to our family, Jesus comes first. So in Psalms 17:15, David is talking about beholding the face of God. Many may think this was not possible for David with all the issues and sins during his life. God, in His Word, doesn't leave any of this out. He always shows the weakness in men and never leaves them out because there are no super-men. Every one of us has issues, weaknesses, etc, but there must be that one resounding cry in our hearts, "Jesus is everything to me!" This is what spared David. The Lord knew his heart. After David committed adultery and had a man (Uriah) killed, what was the first thing out of Nathan's mouth after he exposed David and said "*thou art the man*" (II Samuel 12:7) and David immediately repented? "*...And Nathan said unto David, The LORD also hath put away thy sin; thou shalt not die*" (II Samuel 12:13). Well, I wonder how Uriah's family felt about this? God does things we wouldn't do because He is able to look beyond what we see and sees the heart of a man. In David's heart, he was a true psalmist and was a man after God's own heart. Even if he did have failings in his life (this doesn't excuse sin), God sees beyond this. David says in Psalms 17:15, "*...I shall be satisfied, when I awake, with thy likeness.*" David is saying we will behold God's face in righteousness and this was the longing of his heart. Chamber by chamber, God is dealing with us until He fills every part of our soul. Stop for a second and get out of your weak filled mind and get this mind set. You are a partaker of the divine nature. Right now as you read this, in the eyes of God, you are pure, perfect, clean, and holy. Yes He knows how far you still have to go, but He has already counted the cost and was willing to pay the price to get you where you need to be. All He asks of us is that we have this kind of cry in our hearts. I want to be able to look into God's face without any sin in my life whatsoever. I want to be able to behold Him as He is and I want His likeness instead of mine. Like Paul said in Galatians 2:20, "*I am crucified with Christ: nevertheless I live; yet not I, but Christ liveth in me: and the life which I now live in the flesh I live by the faith of the Son of God, who loved me, and gave himself for me.*"

Next, let us turn to Job 23 as we look at some passages related to our color for the ages to come. Job 23:8-10 says, "[8]*Behold, I go forward, but he is not there; and backward, but I cannot perceive him: [9]On the left hand, where he doth work, but I cannot behold him: he hideth himself on the right hand, that I cannot see him...*" Have you ever been in this position? You didn't know where God was. But Job says as we continue in verse 10, "*But he knoweth the way that I take: when he hath tried me, I shall come forth as gold.*" Once again, we see the term gold. Gold always speaks of the divine nature of God. So you and I, as we go through the issues in our life as Job was going through his, must know deep in our heart, that this is a trial of our faith and, as Peter said, "*That the trial of your faith, being much more precious than of gold...*" (I Peter 1:7). Your faith is not what is much more precious, but the "*trial of your faith*". Jesus said in Revelation 3:18 to the church, "*I counsel thee to buy of me gold tried in the fire, that thou mayest be rich; and white raiment, that thou mayest be clothed...*" You can only get the gold by going through the fire.

II Timothy 2:20-21 reads, "[20]*But in a great house* (keep in mind we are the house of the Lord) *there are not only vessels of gold and of silver, but also of wood and of earth; and some to honour, and some to dishonour. [21]If a man therefore purge himself from these, he shall be a vessel unto honour, sanctified, and meet for the master's use, and prepared unto every good work.*" This is similar to I Corinthians 3 that we read earlier. You see, there are many vessels and ranks in the house of God. Some are of wood and of earth, and some are going to be of gold and silver. What will determine what kind of vessel you and I will be, we have to do what verse 21 says, "*If a man therefore purge himself from these...*" Wood speaks of humanity. Earth speaks of flesh. So God is asking us to purge ourselves from the Adamic nature and the flesh so that we can become gold and silver vessels in the house of the Lord. So when we stand before the Lord, we will immediately appear as the fire of God burns everything away from us, and in the ages to come, all that will remain is the gold, silver, and precious stones that you and I have built upon that foundation.

Isaiah 60 is one of the most powerful Scriptures in the Bible about the end time sons of God, *"[1]Arise, shine; for thy light is come, and the glory of the LORD is risen upon thee..."* This verse is talking about God's glory being on these last days sons of God. *"[2]For, behold, the darkness shall cover the earth, and gross darkness the people: but the LORD shall arise upon thee, and his glory shall be seen upon thee."* God's glory shall be seen upon them. What does God's glory look like? Ezekiel 1:27-28 describes the appearance of the glory of God as the color of amber or bright fire. *"[3]And the Gentiles shall come to thy light, and kings to the brightness of thy rising."* This is the manifestation of the sons of God. There is going to come a time when a voice from heaven is going to cry *"Arise and shine!"* You see many have been waiting for God's glory to come down upon us. But what I am writing to tell you is the seed is already in you and I. Paul says in Colossians 1:27, *"...Christ in you, the hope of glory."* Christ, or the anointed one, is in you and I right now and He is growing and when the day comes when the Spirit of God says "I am now ready for my many-membered son throughout the earth to come forth", the Spirit of God is going to simply say, *"Arise"* and then He is going to say *"Shine"*. Well, how do you and I shine? We shine by turning on the switch ourselves. We have the ability and the understanding on how to bring and to draw out the glory within us. We are not asking it to come down. God has given us already everything we need. It is already in us. When an egg is fertilized in a mother's womb, everything that the baby is going to be is already there in seed form. It just needs to grow up. Well, we have been in great and long times of hibernation, but anybody who is a true disciple on the earth feels something is different now. We are moving into something, like Joel 2 says, that the earth has never seen before. Do you know how to bring out the glory that is within you? Do you know how to draw out the river of life that is within you? One of the greatest ways is by praying in the Holy Ghost and as you do, out of your belly will flow rivers of living water and the anointing of God will rise out of you and upon you. It is going to be so apparent in the last days who are the remnant, and who are not by they way that they shine. Their life, their character, and their whole countenance and being, when they walk in a room, they are going to demand the attention of everybody in the place without even trying. They are going to affect everyone around them because of the glory that is shining in and through them. So *"Arise, shine; for thy light is come, and the glory of the LORD is risen upon thee."* It is our time to shine! The word for shine in the Hebrew in this passage means "to be luminous, to show light, or to set on fire". Are you getting the color we are going to be?

I have been teaching this for over 30 years now. I am hungry to see the manifestation of the sons of God! Something in me is crying out to see the manifestation of the things I've taught and believed. Have we entered into this to a degree? Yes. There have been times when the glory has been so real, so very prominent, and so very heavy that it affected the atmosphere of wherever I was. Literally, change came because of the glory! The day is coming when the sons of God will literally bring change wherever they go. If they get on a bus, everyone on the bus will begin to get convicted of their sins because of the righteousness and purity that just came on that bus. Glory to God! The sons of God are going to walk into God's house and there is going to be weeping and wailing. People that have been hiding sin (especially ministers), they are going to be screaming because their sin is going to be uncovered. It is so important and I beg of you dear reader, I don't care what you have done up to this moment, stop now! Please stop now please because if you go on any further, you are going to get exposed. We have all made mistakes and have done bad things, but let's get it dealt with and move on. It is time to arise now. Leave the earthly foolishness. What is sex to us now? We need to be beyond the lusts of the flesh. There is no sex in heaven. This is earthy and flesh. The marriage bed is honorable and praise God for all of that, but don't be caught up in the nonsense of the lusts of our flesh that the devil tries to throw our way. The devil is going to try to tempt us with sex, power, money, etc. We have to be determined to say no! We can't sell out now! We have to be determined not to be bought by anybody or anything. We have to be able to stand up and declare what we believe without fear or hesitation. Jesus wants us free and *"delivered from the bondage of corruption into the glorious liberty of the children of God"* (Romans 8:21).

The people who God is raising up in the last days are a people that are not racist. They will be full of the love of God, full of the glory of God, full of the Word of God, and full of the compassion of God. They will not judge after gender, after color, or anything like this. They will see all people as God's beautiful creation and their job will be to minister to them purely. We are not to be building kingdoms for ourselves or trying to get rich. Our job is to build the Kingdom of God. Especially in leadership, God in these days wants to deal with their hidden sin. This is the dangerous thing about the anointing. The glory and the anointing is the greatest and most beautiful commodity in the universe. Somebody can look outwardly ugly, but under the anointing, people will find them beautiful. People want to be next to people who are under the anointing. The danger is if somebody is weak in a certain area and because they have an anointing, great temptation can come. This is why the sons of God have to be purified because God doesn't want leadership in the last days to carry the glory for their own glory anymore. God truly cannot trust many people because too many have used the anointing on their life for their own gain and they have destroyed the character of the Lord and caused the people of God to despise the way of the Lord. Just because a person has an anointing, doesn't mean they are a person of character. Jesus said you will know them by

203

their fruit. For a true ministry of the glory, the dealings and the process involved will cost you everything. This is why Paul said of himself, *"He counted me faithful, putting me into the ministry"* (I Timothy 1:12).

Looking again in Isaiah 60, let us read verse 2 again, *"For, behold, the darkness shall cover the earth, and gross darkness the people: but the LORD shall arise upon thee, and his glory shall be seen upon thee."* Now consider this for a moment. Remember Lucifer? He was called the *"son of the morning"* (Isaiah 14:12). Lucifer was *"the anointed cherub that covereth"* (Ezekiel 28:14). Please hear this. This is why we will go through the dealings of God because Lucifer walked up and down in the midst of the stones of fire, the place right before the actual throne of God. These stones of fire are the last defense of God before His actual throne where He sits. It is a like a liquid pure fire that nobody can get through to get to God. But Lucifer walked up and down in the midst of it and we don't know for how long. It could have been millions of years, but one day, he saw he was beautiful and he forgot who made him so. But he was so convinced himself and was able to deceive a third of the angelic beings. Therefore, God is not going to allow anybody into those stones of fire that He feels can fall like Lucifer. Just because somebody has an anointing, doesn't mean that much really. Lucifer had more glory than we have and look what he did. We have to see then that the trials we go through are so important for us. This is why it will be only a remnant that makes it (not everybody). God has got to weed out the bad seed and weed out those who are in it for themselves, doing things for ulterior motives. He is going to shake everything that can be shaken and burn everything that can be burnt so that when it is all said and done, there is purity in a people standing before Him that loves Him and would never betray Him like Lucifer. So Isaiah 60 is saying there will be a people where the glory of God will be seen upon them.

I remember being sent to Chicago in the late 1970's to pastor my first church. I was sent to a church of about 150 people. It was a cult and when I got there, I realized nobody was really saved. Over my time there, God moved mightily, the people got saved, filled with the Holy Ghost, and their lives were transformed. Well, after pastoring there, I remember asking the Lord what was next in my life. This was around 1980 and I never forgot what He said to me. He said to me, "Son, your anointing far outweighs your character". This was 30 years ago. What the Lord also said to me was He was going to do something with me and that I wouldn't like it. He told me He was going to pull me back and told me to take the back seat in everything I do. He told me to never push myself forward and told me I had a choice. He said He had given me a great anointing, but He told me my character was weak and that it would take me most of my life to make me to be able to handle the glory that He wants me to carry. Thirty years later now, I can't begin to explain everything I have been through. But in this last hour, I can say it is worth it because I can behold His face now. The Sam Greene that then-was has been broken and crushed by the hand of God so that instead of me, it is now Him. The glory will be seen upon a people in the last days when their character is in line with their anointing. This is why it is a remnant.

One of my mothers in the Lord had a dream one time that she shared with me. It was a dream about all of God's people coming before the Lord and making their entrances into heaven and all the great evangelists and great men of God from history were coming in. They all had this great following, but were told to go and sit in the corner. And then one by one all these little old ladies would come and stand before the throne of grace and the angels would come and minister to them while God spoke very highly of them before the whole of heaven and great glory was given unto ones none ever thought much about. It is not the man who preaches the greatest, but the man who lives the life of God, whose faith follows the end of their conversation.

Isaiah 60:3 then continues, "*...And the Gentiles* (or nations) *shall come to thy light, and kings to the brightness of thy rising.*" In other words, when the sons of God come to a place, the atmosphere will change because they will be a burning light. John 5:35 said of John the Baptist, "*He was a burning and a shining light: and ye were willing for a season to rejoice in his light.*" Psalms 104:4 says God makes "*His ministers a flaming fire.*" This is what we have to be. If you and I sit under the Word of God long enough, day and night, and we get so much Word in us, we will not have to every worry about what to say. Wherever we go, we can have the Word of the Lord. Moreover, kings and the nations are going to come to the "*brightness of thy rising*". As we begin to walk in God's fiery flame anointing and begin to become a manifested son of God in the earth, we will speak as an oracle of God. It is very treacherous ground, but we can handle it if your heart is right and you are accountable. We have to remain accountable to somebody somewhere. Somebody has to know our secrets because if they don't, we are going to be in trouble. Those little secrets (or foxes) will spoil our vine. How do I know? I have been through 40 years of the dealings of God. I used to be great at hiding but our precious God is the hound of heaven. The Holy Ghost will always find us out. The best thing we can do is just repent and ask for the Lord's mercy. I have no problem with the men of God over me calling me up on the phone and asking me if I am staying pure, staying faithful and committed to my wife, or involved in any foolishness. We should all have this kind of accountability in our lives, especially as leaders. Why should we not want this, unless we are hiding something? Everything that God the Father does is about relationships and family. It is so important that we stay pure and clean, vessels of honor. Would you please think of yourself this way from now on? You are a vessel of honor. Don't mess around with wood, clay, and darkness. You are better than that. You are called to much higher things than that to get involved in foolishness. If you want the people to ultimately come to the brightness of your rising, that is only going to happen as you yield and walk with God.

Daniel 12:2-3, speaking of the last days, says, *"²And many of them that sleep in the dust of the earth shall awake* (this is speaking of resurrection), *some to everlasting life, and some to shame and everlasting contempt. ³And they that be wise shall shine as the brightness of the firmament; and they that turn many to righteousness as the stars for ever and ever."* So this is what we are going to look like! We are going to look like the brightness of the firmament and we are going to shine like stars.

Psalms 45, speaking of the bride of Christ says, *"⁹Kings' daughters were among thy honourable women: upon thy right hand did stand the queen in gold of Ophir..."* The word for gold in Hebrew means "something carved out or pure gold". The queen came out of all the other daughters. Song of Solomon 6:8-9, *"There are threescore queens, and fourscore concubines, and virgins without number".⁹ " my dove, my undefiled is but one; she is the only one of her mother, she is the choice one of her that bare her. The daughters saw her, and blessed her; yea, the queens and the concubines, and they praised her."* Continuing in Psalms 45, he begins to talk about the bride of Christ, *"¹⁰Hearken, O daughter, and consider, and incline thine ear; forget also thine own people, and thy father's house..."* I have tried to warn all of us (black, white, brown, red, etc) throughout this book to forget our own people. All of us need to forget our father's house because our people are the people of God now. We have to be leaders and people of purity, character, full of faith, who know God, know His glory, know His Word, and can convey His love and mercy to people without any hint or racism towards anybody. We have to show that Christianity is not a white man's religion or anybody's religion, but it is a way of life. There is only one way that is true and it is Jesus! You and I have an opportunity, so while we have it, let's give ourselves to the Word of God. Then His Word will become us and we will be a living epistle, known and read of all men.

Jesus was able to say of Himself in John 14:30, *"for the prince of this world cometh, and hath nothing in me."* Don't you want to be able to say that about yourself? I know I do. The holier we live (I'm not talking about rules and regulations – but living a life where we stay in the glory and do nothing to displease the Lord), every time we stretch forth our hands toward somebody, the greater the impartation will be for them. This is all I care about. Malachi 4:1-2 promises us, *"¹For, behold, the day cometh, that shall burn as an oven; and all the proud, yea, and all that do wickedly, shall be stubble: and the day that cometh shall burn them up, saith the LORD of hosts, that it shall leave them neither root nor branch. ²But unto you that fear my name shall the Sun* (speaking of the brightness and glory of God) *of righteousness arise with healing in his wings...*" We are going to see the greatest dispensation of healing and deliverance that the earth has ever seen before come through a remnant of people. Obadiah 17 declares "*But upon mount Zion shall be deliverance, and there shall be holiness...*" We will be able to stand up to someone, despite if people struggled with demons for 30 years, and bring deliverance to them. It is like when Jesus came down from the mount of transfiguration and helped the disciples who couldn't cast a demon out. Jesus reveals His heart a bit and lets us know how He really felt that the disciples couldn't cast out the demon in Matthew 17:17, "*Then Jesus answered and said, O faithless and perverse generation, how long shall I be with you? how long shall I suffer you? bring him hither to me.*" Jesus was saying how long does he have to put up with their unbelief. The disciples didn't get it yet. Three of them just came from seeing Jesus in the glory on top of the mountain. Jesus explains in verse 21 about casting out the demon, "*Howbeit this kind goeth not out but by prayer and fasting.*" What He was trying to say was "Haven't you watched me over the last 3 ½ years of my life and there are times when I don't eat? I do that purposely for when I meet a devil like that, I live a fasted life. The devil then has to leave." When Jesus died, the disciples weren't even sure Jesus was going to be resurrected and they saw all the miracles Jesus did. They saw blind eyes open on a daily basis and they didn't have a revelation on how He really was.

Something deep inside of me cries out for the ministry Jesus had. I remember a story R.W. Shambach told about A.A. Allen years ago. A.A. Allen had lots of weakness when he lived, but if weaknesses disqualify us for the ministry, nobody would be in the ministry. I am not trying to justify what he did, but I want to share a story told by Shambach about the ministry of A.A. Allen. Shambach told of a story when a mother with her baby came to a meeting one night. The baby had like 15 major physical afflictions. The child's tongue was sticking out, he had no eyeballs, his legs and body was twisted, to name a few. The mother and child had no money. She had hitchhiked with her child to this meeting that A.A. Allen was having. R.W. Shambach was A.A. Allen's associate minister serving in an "Elijah/Elisha" ministry at the time. When Shambach saw the woman and child coming to A.A. Allen, he ran to them because he wanted to see what would happen. A.A. Allen was not moved by the deformities. A.A. Allen took that little baby and asked the woman if she believed that God would heal this child. The woman had no money, and had lost much in her life, and she said "yes, I believe". Shambach said the first thing that happened after A.A. Allen prayed was he saw a whirlwind begin in the eyes of the child until eyeballs formed. Then he heard snapping and popping sounds as hands, joints, legs, and feet all turned correctly. Then there was a loud sound like a rubber band snapping and his tongue went back into his mouth and within another minute that baby was completely made whole! Shambach said he saw it with his own eyes. Then as she stepped down from the platform, thousands of people came up to her and stuffed money into her pockets. Do you think this mother's life was changed? Do you think she believes in Jesus? Glory to God – of course! Unto you that fear His name, shall the sun, that bright, glorious, burning, and fiery flame, is going to rise up in the sons of God because like a great eagle, we are the wings of God. We are representatives on the earth for Him.

Let me tell you another story which actually happened to me. I am telling you the absolute truth without exaggeration. My sister got saved before I did. She watched a Billy Graham meeting on T.V. and got born again. I got saved about a year later and then my sister backslid. At this point she hadn't received the baptism in the Holy Ghost. I was full of innocence in my faith. And during this time many had just begun the "leg lengthening" thing back in the early 1970's. So I told my sister, if God did something miraculous today, would she give her heart back to the Lord and return to Jesus? She said yes. I told her to hold out her arms and put her hands together. One of her arms was slightly shorter than the other one. So I said, "Jesus, you know my sister got saved before me and tried to tell me about you, and now I am saved. Would you do a miracle here to bring back my sister to You?" And God (and my sister) as my witness, her fingers in the one hand that was shorter began to grow (just her fingers), and they kept growing. And they kept growing that it scared me so much, I started screaming, "Jesus, stop!" My sister was in a state of shock, her face ashen white. Then her fingers started to recede and they came right back to where they were. Of course, she gave her heart to the Lord right then and there, but really, it was more for me than her. Job 42:5-6 says, "*I have heard of thee by the hearing of the ear: but now mine eye seeth thee. Wherefore I abhor myself, and repent in dust and ashes.*" I have never forgotten this story. God is a miracle God! God can fix anything. I determined years ago that I want to be a manifested son of God.

Now that we know the hope of our calling, let us look at some more Scriptures as we consider the future color of the people of God as the Scriptures declare. The image that we will be for the ages to come we find in the Scripture is one of fire, brightness, and light. Psalms 50:2 reads "*Out of Zion, the perfection of beauty, God hath shined.*" Another translation of "*God hath shined*" is "*God blazes forth*". Now who is Zion? Zion in the natural we know is an actual place, but Zion also is a people. Most importantly however, Zion represents the place in our hearts that enthrones the Lord in worship. But we, a last day company of people, could also be called Zion. Out of this company Zion, as Psalms 50:2 said, comes the perfection of beauty and God is shining through them. What a wondrous thing to behold! When God found us in the beginning, just like in Ezekiel 16:1-14, we were nothing lying by the side of the road. God found us all messed up, but He wants to do something mighty in us and then through us! Let us read this story in Ezekiel 16, "*¹Again the word of* the LORD came unto me, saying, *²Son of man, cause Jerusalem to know her abominations...*" Now when we see in Scriptures (both in the Old and New Testaments) the place or term "Jerusalem" God is not just speaking to the Jews, but He is speaking to His people everywhere. "*³And say, Thus saith the Lord GOD unto Jerusalem; Thy birth and thy nativity is of the land of Canaan; thy father was an Amorite, and thy mother an Hittite. ⁴And as for thy nativity, in the day thou wast born thy navel was not cut, neither wast thou washed in water to supple thee; thou wast not salted at all, nor swaddled at all. ⁵None eye pitied thee, to do any of these unto thee, to have compassion upon thee; but thou wast cast out in the open field, to the lothing of thy person, in the day that thou wast born...*"

Now this is not everybody's story, but it is the story of many and certainly this is a true picture of our soulish man. Some people were born with a silver spoon in their mouth with everything they needed, while others were born in abject poverty or others just in middle class. But all of us have inherited, by virtue of Adam, the Adamic nature which is filthy, sin-filled, and our souls and bodies are corrupted. So Ezekiel is saying God's people, upon their birth, were lying in an open field and loathing themselves. I consider the state I was in before I came to know Jesus and it wasn't good. Even though I tried to live my life in the world as best as I could, my heart cried out. So many people passed me by and rather than help me, they spit on me because they looked at my outward appearance or situation. But Jesus helped me, just as verse 6 in this story reads, "*⁶And when I passed by thee, and saw thee polluted in thine own blood, I said unto thee when thou wast in thy blood, Live; yea, I said unto thee when thou wast in thy blood, Live...*" When we are in our worst condition, Jesus doesn't pass us by and reject us. He passes by to help and bring life to us and say "*Live!*".

As we keep reading the story in Ezekiel 16, look what God does to His people, "*⁷I have caused thee to multiply as the bud of the field, and thou hast increased and waxen great, and thou art come to excellent ornaments: thy breasts are fashioned, and thine hair is grown, whereas thou wast naked and bare.*" God gives a short synopsis of what He does for us. We thought we found Jesus, but really, He found us and called us "*out of darkness into His marvelous light*" (I Peter 2:9). Every Christian can say this was their testimony and share the glory of being saved and washed in the blood of Jesus. When Jesus passes by, He always has compassion like the good Samaritan. God wants us to be like this too to others.

"*⁸Now when I passed by thee, and looked upon thee, behold, thy time was the time of love...*" God sees us at our worst and to Him, it is a time of love. This is why I love Jesus so much. When I was at my worst, He loved me!!! Think of the worst thing you ever did or the worst situation you were ever in.

At that moment, He loved you! It is at those moments when the love of God is needed the most. It is only fair now that we give back what He gave us as we love others. "*...and I spread my skirt over thee, and covered thy nakedness: yea, I sware unto thee, and entered into a covenant with thee, saith the Lord GOD, and thou becamest mine...*" When nobody else wants you, Jesus does. Glory to God! This verse represents our salvation experience. "*⁹Then washed I thee with water; yea, I throughly washed away thy blood from thee, and I anointed thee with oil.*" This verse represents not only our justification, but the process of sanctification, water baptism, and the baptism of the Holy Ghost in our lives. And then, "*¹⁰I clothed thee also with broidered work, and shod thee with badgers' skin, and I girded thee about with fine linen, and I covered thee with silk.*" Fine linen is the righteousness of the saints (Revelation 19:8). This one in the story who was out lying there, loathing themselves, is now beginning to become righteous. "*¹¹I decked thee also with ornaments, and I put bracelets upon thy hands, and a chain on thy neck.*" These are the gifts and fruits of the Spirit to do the works of the Lord. "*¹²And I put a jewel on thy forehead...*" This is having the mind of Christ. "*...and earrings in thine ears, and a beautiful crown upon thine head. ¹³Thus wast thou decked with gold and silver; and thy raiment was of fine linen, and silk, and broidered work; thou didst eat fine flour, and honey, and oil: and thou wast exceeding beautiful, and thou didst prosper into a kingdom. ¹⁴And thy renown went forth among the heathen for thy beauty: <u>for it was perfect</u> through my comeliness, which I had put upon thee, saith the Lord GOD.*" Psalms 50:2 said again, "*Out of Zion, the perfection of beauty, God hath shined.*" Zion will reach perfection through Jesus!

It may not look like this now in the body of Christ as a whole. But you see, there is a people within a people, a wheel within a wheel, where God is really moving and changing them. It is happening in a people who aren't religious and the things of God aren't a Sunday morning thing or a Wednesday night thing, but Jesus is their whole life. These people try everyday to walk the Word of God out and the more Word they put in them, the more God can marry that Word to a situation in their life, causing them to overcome, and become a living epistle. This takes a lifetime. I have been at this for 40 years now. The more you and I overcome, the more authority we gain, the more anointing we will have, and the more we grow in God. Don't let anybody feed you that horrible lie that we are always going to be a sinner. I <u>was</u> a sinner and now I am saved by grace. Not only was I saved by grace, but Romans 8:29 tells me I was called according to His purpose to be <u>conformed</u> to the image of the Son. How does this happen? II Corinthians 3:18 says, "*But we all, with open face beholding as in a glass the glory of the Lord, <u>are changed</u> <u>into the same image</u> from glory to glory, even as by the Spirit of the Lord.*" So God's highest desire is not for us to go to heaven. Heaven is not the goal. The goal is to dwell in the living fiery presence of God. Isaiah 33:14 says "*Who among us shall dwell* with the devouring fire? who among us shall dwell with everlasting burnings?" Our God is a consuming fire. As I consider God in my mind, I don't think of an old man with long white beard and long white hair anymore. I just see now an absolutely raging fire! God is preparing a people to walk right into that fire, right into His brilliant presence, and not be burnt ourselves! This is our calling and our goal! The Bible says God makes "*his ministers a flaming fire*" (Psalms 104:4). At some point it will be truly fulfilled as I John 4:17 puts it, "*as He is, so are we in this world.*" Jesus taught us to pray and say, "*Our Father which art in heaven, Hallowed be thy name. Thy kingdom come. Thy will be done in earth, as it is in heaven.*" (Matthew 6:9-10). At some point, somebody somewhere is going to receive all that God promised! They are going to walk in everything that God said they could have. Paradise was stolen from us, but Jesus came to give us paradise back! This means Jesus conquered sin, sickness, death, you name it! Jesus came to the earth as God, but also <u>as a man</u> and showed us that <u>as a man</u> (flesh and blood), we can live a life without sinning. Jesus taught us we can live a life, despite being tempted at all points, and say like Him in John 14:30 "*the prince of this world cometh, and hath <u>nothing in me</u>.*" Let us get rid of anything the devil can find in us to cause us to fall. Jesus said to Peter, "*Simon, Simon, behold, Satan hath desired to have you, that he may sift you as wheat*" (Luke 22:31). Satan looks for something in us to exploit. Satan is not omniscient. He doesn't know anything about us unless we tell him or he sees it in our life. Demons are watching us all the time, and listening to us. But thanks be unto God we have angels too to help us! Hallelujah.

We've been lied to our whole life and have believed it. We've been told we can never be perfect and that we will always just be sinners. Well, no more! Jesus told us plainly in Matthew 5:48, "*<u>Be ye therefore perfect</u>, even as your Father which is in heaven is perfect.*" Perfect in the Greek simply means complete. It means we have finished and completed all that God wants us to complete. Paul said in II Timothy 4:7-8 "*I have fought a good fight, I have finished my course, I have kept the faith: Henceforth there is laid up for me a crown of righteousness...*" Paul did what he was supposed to do and graduated. You and I are running a race right now and at the end of this race, somebody is going to win something. I Corinthians 9:24 says, "*Know ye not that they which run in a race run all, but one receiveth the prize? So run, that ye may obtain.*" God wants us running with purpose knowing we are the called of God. At the end of this race is "*the prize of the high calling of God in Christ Jesus*" (Philippians 3:14). It is "*Christ in you, the hope of glory*" (Colossians 1:27). I am talking about real, fiery glory upon God's people! This glory followed the children of Israel. They had a cloud by day and a pillar of fire by night surrounding them. All of the other nations knew about them and were fearful. Romans 8:18 says God's "*glory which shall be revealed in us*". What will this people look like?

What color will we have for the ages and what color will we look like? Proverbs 4:18 says, *"But the path of the just is as the shining light, that shineth more and more unto the perfect day."* We just saw in Ezekiel 16 that a people will be made perfect through the Lord's *"comliness"*. Paul exhorts us in Hebrews 6:1, *"let us go on unto perfection"*. Jesus wants us to *"grow up into him in all things, which is the head, even Christ"* (Ephesians 4:15). So the path we are on is going to lead us to perfection and total light. At the end of this road is a great and marvelous light that we are going to be enveloped in. Philippians 2:13-16 echoes this calling, *"[13]For it is God which worketh in you both to will and to do of his good pleasure. [14]Do all things without murmurings and disputings: [15]That ye may be blameless and harmless, the sons of God, without rebuke, in the midst of a crooked and perverse nation, among whom ye shine as lights in the world; [16]Holding forth the word of life; that I may rejoice in the day of Christ, that I have not run in vain, neither laboured in vain."*

Haggai 2:6-9 says *"[6]For thus saith the LORD of hosts; Yet once, it is a little while, and I will shake the heavens, and the earth, and the sea, and the dry land; [7]And I will shake all nations, and the desire of all nations shall come: and I will fill this house with glory, saith the LORD of hosts...[9]The glory of this latter house shall be greater than of the former, saith the LORD of hosts: and in this place will I give peace, saith the LORD of hosts."* The Tabernacle in the wilderness was quite a thing and the glory would fill it. The same was true with Solomon's Temple which was quite a building. But what God is building now is not a temple made with hands, but it is a people, living stones, that are being made into His image. These will be stones of fire! The ultimate end for the true sons of God is to be filled with God's glory. Their end is full of light. Just like Jesus in Matthew 17 upon the mount was transfigured before three disciples and His face shone like the son, this is the appearance of the people of God in the last days.

Zechariah 2:5 declares, *"For I, saith the LORD, will be unto her a wall of fire round about, and will be the glory in the midst of her."* We are going to see this in reality in the sons of God as Joel 2 shows. In Joel 2, we find an interesting passage. Now there is a lot of theological arguments over who this is talking about, but I believe it is talking about the army of God in the last days. People who are locked into dispensational theology or locked into a word of faith kind of teaching, they can't believe that God would send an army that deals with his people. They think everything bad is of the devil. Afflictions come from 4 places. The first source is the devil. We can bind him, resist him, cast him out, and he must flee. The second source is ourselves. We reap what we sow. There is nothing we can do but repent and go on. The third source is just life. Situations in life just happen. I don't remember choosing what family I was going to be born in. I may just ask the Lord when I am in heaven why I wasn't I born in England in a palace instead of the ghetto in Washington D.C. I would have rather have been Prince Samuel. But the fourth source of affliction is God and there is nothing we can do about it except bow our head and ask the Lord to do it quickly. But look here in Joel 2, "*¹Blow ye the trumpet in Zion, and sound an alarm in my holy mountain: let all the inhabitants of the land tremble: for the day of the LORD cometh, for it is nigh at hand...*" So the premise of this chapter is "*the day of the Lord*" which is the last days. It is going to be "*²A day of darkness and of gloominess, a day of clouds and of thick darkness...*" This is just like the pattern expressed in Isaiah 60:1-3 (*1Arise, shine; for thy light is come, and the glory of the LORD is risen upon thee. ²For, behold, the darkness shall cover the earth, and gross darkness the people: but the LORD shall arise upon thee, and his glory shall be seen upon thee. ³And the Gentiles shall come to thy light, and kings to the brightness of thy rising.*"). While one is experiencing gross darkness, another will be experiencing the greatest dimension of light ever known to men!

We need to stop thinking of the anti-Christ as a person. He may be, but I don't care. I used to worry about that when I was young in the Lord. I John 2:18 talks about the spirit of anti-Christ and it is already here. The number 6 in the Scriptures is the number for man and Satan because man was created on the sixth day and so was the serpent. So 666 means, more than anything, man rising to his fullest capabilities (though fallen) together as Satan comes to the fullness of his own power. 666 simply mean the fullness of Satan in the fullness of unredeemed man. This is the spirit of anti-Christ. It hates Jesus. It hates the anointing, but they can do nothing against it. Why do you think those two witnesses in Revelation 11 can't be hurt until God says so? Many times the religious Pharisees tried to kill or do harm to Jesus before His time and it says Jesus would walk right out through the midst of them. Satan couldn't do anything to Jesus until the Father allowed him to be crucified. Satan can't do anything to us. He hates us because we love God. He used to love the Lord dearly until he fell and when he sees us crying, weeping, and pouring out our hearts in worship (he, as Lucifer, used to be the worship leader in heaven), it infuriates him.

But back to Joel 2 where we see darkness coming on the earth, but light upon His people. This is the picture of the last day saints as we continue reading in verse 2, "*...as the morning spread upon the mountains a great people and a strong; there hath not been ever the like, neither shall be any more after it, even to the years of many generations...*" This tells me the earth has never seen yet what God is going to do in the last days. This is a great people. Has anyone ever called you great? The Bible does. Has anyone ever called you strong? If you are going to be part of God's manifested sons in the last days, this will be your testimony. "*³A fire devoureth before them; and behind them a flame burneth...*" When the sons of God walk anywhere, a fire

213

not only comes, but it devours before them and a flame burns when they leave. They will look just like our God! This is why we go through the dealings of God. Everything in us must be burnt up so we can dwell with everlasting burnings. As we keep reading it says also, "...*the land is as the garden of Eden before them, and behind them a desolate wilderness; yea, and nothing shall escape them...*" Do you get the picture? Out of Zion, which is God's holy remnant and the perfection of beauty, God is shining through.

Let us see this picture in Acts 5:12-16. Previously in this chapter Ananias and Sapphira had just dropped dead because they kept back part of the price and lied to the Holy Ghost. Because of this, verse 11 says, "*And great fear came upon the church*". "*[12]And by the hands of the apostles were many signs and wonders wrought among the people; (and they were all with one accord in Solomon's porch. [13]And of the rest durst no man join himself to them: but the people magnified them...*" This means the people which saw them didn't want to go near the apostles because there was something wonderfully powerful about them. "*[14]And believers were the more added to the Lord, multitudes both of men and women.) [15]Insomuch that they brought forth the sick into the streets, and laid them on beds and couches...*" Now before we keep reading, I just want to say that I believe this is going to happen again. There will be no more controlled meetings. You and I are going to be at our job one day and all of the sudden we will be walking in the glory and somebody there that is sick or has an ailment, you and I are going to reach out our hand and the person will be healed and made completely whole! Word then will spread and people will bring their sick to your job where you are at. Church as we know it will change. Forget the buildings and the "system" of Christianity. This is why being a family of believers is so important and being in right relationships is so important because once the glory falls, it is going to be wild! They may be afraid of us, but they will know to come because the true power and glory of God is there. So in Acts 5, they brought the sick into the streets "*...that at the least the shadow of Peter passing by might overshadow some of them. [16]There came also a multitude out of the cities round about unto Jerusalem, bringing sick folks, and them which were vexed with unclean spirits: and they were healed every one.*" Not one or two were healed, but every one of them!

My life was transformed years ago when the Lord showed me something in this passage in Acts 5. In verse 15, the Greek word translated "overshadow" is the Greek word *Episkiazo* (Strong's number 1982) which means "to cast a shade upon". This means when we walk up to people, we bring something over them. This Greek word also means "to envelop in a haze of glory or brilliancy, to invest with preternatural influence, an effulgence, radiance, or shining forth of divine energy". This is beautiful. When we walk down the street, this is what is supposed to happen. This Greek word is also used in Luke 1:35 when speaking to Mary about Jesus, "*And the angel answered and said unto her, The*

Holy Ghost shall come upon thee, and the power of the Highest shall <u>*overshadow*</u> *thee: therefore also that holy thing which shall be born of thee shall be called the Son of God.*" The same thing happened to Mary, the mother Jesus, came upon Peter in Acts 5. And this is the same thing the army in Joel experiences. A fire devours before them and will heal all the sick people. If we really had a healing ministry, we should be going to the hospital and the insane asylums and healing those people! Well, a day is coming when we will be able to (Malachi 4:2).

Even in the church's early beginning, God gives us a picture because Peter would go on to make many mistakes in the Scripture. This story in Acts 5 is a little window into a picture of what could really be. This picture is that somebody who is so devoted to Jesus, so devoted to the Word of God, so in love with Jesus, so full of the glory, that God's divine energy streams out of them. They are like a burning and shining light! Glory to God! I am telling you, I see it, but I want to be it. We've touched into it a little bit, but not like we want to see it. For so long we have had such a Babylonish mindset when it came to the Kingdom of God. We haven't known and understood true purposes and calling of God upon His people. First, God wants us to be enveloped by His glory that we get so filled and full that the river and glory of God flows out from under the door (Ezekiel 47). Then, like Samuel, after growing up he opened the doors to the house of the Lord. All the glorious sons of God are going to step out into a dark world and they are going to shine as lights everywhere they go. To think people teach that the two witnesses is limited to two people is absurd. First of all, two people cannot handle the kind of glory God is going to send. It will take a company of people to handle it. Jesus is looking for a place to lay His head or lay His government. He hasn't found anybody strong enough yet. Like the lesson David learned when he first tried to bring the glory to Jerusalem and somebody died, we have to get things in order and find the proper priests who can bear the ark. God instructed the Israelites that the only way to carry the ark with them was to have it be carried on the shoulders of the priests. Priests had to be clean and sanctified. You and I cannot carry the ark if we are unclean. How many people are carrying the ark today and are unsanctified? And we wonder why we don't see the kind of glory and miracle power flowing. But this is not a word of discouragement. Everywhere I go and minister (all over the world), I see in the eyes of so many believers, the hunger for more of God. I see a people preparing themselves, giving themselves to the Word of God, being enveloped in the glory, and they are changing and Psalms 50:2 is going to be fulfilled which says again, "*Out of Zion, the perfection of beauty, God hath shined!*" Put your name in there! Out of YOU, the perfection of beautify, God will shine!!

I end with Romans 12:1-2 which says, "*I beseech you therefore, brethren, by the mercies of God, that ye present your bodies a living sacrifice, holy, acceptable unto God, which is your reasonable service. And be not conformed to this world: but be ye transformed by the renewing of your mind, that ye may prove what is that good, and acceptable, and perfect, will of God."* It doesn't sound reasonable, that we have to let go of everything in our soulish man that we like. But God is after a people that will be transformed and be like Him. This is the good, acceptable, and perfect will of God. *"For the LORD's portion is his people"*, Deuteronomy 32:9 says. I wonder how God the Father does it. He has waited so long for a people. He gave us everything we need and yet we do so many foolish things. We live so far below the level we are called to live and we are content to live like this. But the older I get, the hungrier I get for my mind to be completely transformed. I want to be like Jesus. Like David I declare, *"As for me, I will behold thy face in righteousness: I shall be satisfied, when I awake, with thy likeness"* (Psalms 17:15). Have you made this decision? You see, when I left my family 40 years ago, I couldn't make them walk with Jesus. I tried. They wouldn't do it so the longer I stayed; I was tempted too much, so I had to go. I knew the only way I would ever help them was to leave and become a man of God. You and I are being brought to a place where two ways meet. Have you decided to give everything to Jesus? God is watching, believe me. He is hoping that we will be like Job and retain our integrity. God wants to show Lucifer, who so hates God's creation (the highest thing He created was mankind, you and I), that a people will not be like him. Lucifer, I believe, rebelled because one day he saw in the heart of God that He was going to create a people out of the dust of the earth. He thought he was more beautiful than that which was formed from that reddish clay dust. Satan, in arguing against Job said to the Lord, *"Skin for skin, yea, all that a man hath will he give for his life"* (Job 2:4). In other words, Satan was saying man will do anything to survive, even deny the Lord to save his own skin. Satan was accusing to God that if He took Job's money and possessions away, or if you make him sick, or if you take away his family, Job will leave you. But we see what dear Job does, when even his own wife says to him, *"Dost thou still retain thine integrity? Curse God, and die"* (Job 2:9). He says *"Thou speakest as one of the foolish women speaketh. What? Shall we receive good at the hand of God, and shall we not receive evil?"* Job 13:15 says, *"Though he slay me, yet will I trust in him."* Later in Job 23:10 he says, *"But he knoweth the way that I take: when he hath tried me, I shall come forth as gold."* And Lucifer saw in one man by the name of Job, a picture of what a many-membered company is going to be. They will suffer the loss of all things. They like Abraham, will have to give up their Isaacs and their Ishmaels. They will have to survive the fire, wind, storms, and the rain as well as remaining true in prosperity. They will have to come through it all and as we see the precious bride, as Song of Solomon shows, coming out of the wilderness leaning upon the arm of her beloved. Jesus has brought the bride into the wilderness and one day will bring her out so she can shine!

The Color Of Angels
Chapter 16

We've looked at pretty much everything; the origin of man, the color of the first man, and civilization's beginnings in Africa. Instead of what we call the Judeo-Christian Principles we should call it the African Judeo-Christian Principles. There is no way around it, it is the truth. We've seen that people in the Old Testament were mostly people of color. Some of the greatest figures in the Old Testament were black men. This is revolutionary to most people, but I think it's just the last straw to break that camel's back of racism and cause the scales to fall from our eyes. You know Paul was a Pharisee of Pharisees, a doctor. He was a very learned man, but when he met Jesus on the road to Damascus the glory of God shined so brightly that it changed him. I don't care how intelligent or how ignorant you are, the glory of God is able to cause the scales (those things that we believe, that are not the truth) to fall off our eyes. The only way I know for that to happen is two ways: either by a visitation of the glory of God or by knowing the truth.

In this book we have looked at the color of God, and what color we are going to be in the ages to come. In this chapter, we will explore this last aspect of colors in the heavenly realm. I want to look at the color of angels and the living creatures. The importance of this is because they are spiritual beings, and we are going to be interacting with them for thousands and thousands of years. God Himself is the color of amber, fire, brass, burnished brass, brightness, lightening, and light. Not only Him, but His angels are the same; and then His redeemed sons are going to be the same.

We have looked at how God has asked us to forget our own people; to forget even our own cultures and embrace the kingdom of God. You cannot go on with God, until you do that. So many people are stuck in their cultures; white churches, black churches. Black people don't want to go to a white church, because they don't like the way white people worship. White people don't want to go to a black church because they worship forever. As long as you are staying in your natural estate, there will be a little bit of an issue to deal with. We, as the children of God, need to learn that we can ascend into the glory and be free. You can clap anyway you want to, and you can sing, not according to your personality, but according to whom God has made you to be. You must be confident in who you are in Jesus no matter where you stand!

As we grow, you have to understand that there are two natures that we need to operate in, according to what is needed at the time. There is the "lion" and the "lamb" nature. Sometimes, when you just minister to people, what you need is the lamb nature and bless them with a still small voice. Other times, you have to respond to the glory of God in our midst, with cries from the depths of our being. I remember years ago one of my mothers in the Lord, said something so precious to me. She said, "Brother Sam, there is something about that sound that you make when you get into the high and holy place. It is like a shofar in the spirit. It's a clarion call to worship." I am reminded of a meeting about ten years ago, when I was in a beautiful black church in Virginia. After the meeting, the pastor and his wife asked me, "What was that thing you were doing?" I didn't know what they were talking about, so I asked what they were referring to. They said, "That Shout! When you shouted like that something happened!" See, like David when he was out taking care of the sheep and when no one was around, he got free! He worshipped the Lord, and played that little harp and shouted experiencing the glory. He was free from people and gave himself freely to God in worship. People need leadership; they need someone to give that "clarion call" in the spirit, so they can respond to it. God wants human shofars!

We have seen God, and He is a consuming fire! If He is any color at all, it's amber, bright, gold, and burnished bronze. That's God! This revelation has totally changed the way I see God when I worship. I see Him now as the burning fiery flame. We as His Sons, the remnant, are going to shine like Him. Our glorified bodies are going to be radiant with light, brightness, and that glory, that amber color. Hallelujah! As we look at the color of angels, we see that in everything that God does there is continuity. Everything that He does is done in order to the last detail; nothing is different.

I want to share a very precious, personal experience with you. It happened when I was leading worship about fifteen or twenty years ago, and I was literally taken to heaven. I had been very ill before I got to the meeting and my Assistant Pastor wanted to take me home. But I told him "no" because you never know what God might do. When I stood up, as I played the first chord, I was immediately in the spirit. Even though I was physically standing in that place, in a little town called Lincolnton, I was actually in heaven; and no one knew what was happening. (You can never prepare for these things; it just happens and you step into them. Every time I've tried to seek for a sacred experience, I never got one.) I was coming up out of something into a tunnel of brightness, and I found myself standing on a big circular platform that was rising up into this great stadium. As far as the eye could see, on either side, were people dressed in white. I couldn't see faces because everything was just so dazzling and bright. In front of me, were all these beings, all kinds of colors that I don't believe we have ever seen here on earth. I agree with Paul, there are some things that you can't describe, and I couldn't begin to tell you what they are like. I saw glorious beings, beautiful and there was such peace and harmony radiated everywhere. There was such unity, goodness, and purity: this is heaven. I was not allowed to look behind me, but I could feel a heartbeat reverberating through my system. It was the heartbeat of God. In that moment, I realized that I was still singing. Now the people back in the meeting knew that something had happened. They had all fallen on their faces, because the glory fell in that place so strongly, and they told me that I continued to sing. Back in heaven, I realized that as I was singing, all of the people, hundreds of thousands, were singing the song that I was singing. It happened, and I will go to my grave knowing what I saw. It doesn't bother me what anyone else believes, I have seen the other side. Words cannot describe the freedom, the joy, and the complete deliverance from the earthly. It is so completely enjoyable and full of joy. I wanted to stay there, but then I felt like the platform was starting to sink back down and even though I continued to sing, my spirit was like "No, No, I don't want to go back." I wasn't in any kind of physical pain there in heaven, like I had been on earth. But I was saying; "Please, no I don't want to go back to that. Let me just stay here." Then the words of the Lord came to me in that booming voice that is like many waters. He said, "No, you've got to go back; I want you to tell my people that we (everything with God is about "we") are waiting for them." And I knew what He meant. He continued and said, "Son, if you can get the people to worship, to a level that we are worshipping here, there will be a Mahanaim experience (the place where heaven and earth will meet)". It is necessary that before we go through the veil that we learn to worship Him the way that heaven is worshipping Him now. As He is, so are we. Matthew 6:10, "*Thy kingdom come. Thy will be done in earth, as it is in heaven.*" You see at some point the Sons of God are going to literally step through the veil and worship, and the joint armies of heaven and earth will finally be together. Then the Lord said, "Go back and tell them, and teach them." Then instantly, I felt my pain returning and I realized that I was back in Lincolnton, NC. Such things we are going to see! So in this chapter we are just going to finish this off with a look at what angels look like.

Lets look at Matthew 28:1-3 which says, " *[1]In the end of the sabbath, as it began to dawn toward the first day of the week, came Mary Magdalene and the other Mary to see the sepulchre. [2] And, behold, there was a great earthquake: for the angel of the Lord descended from heaven, and came and rolled back the stone from the door, and sat upon it. [3] His countenance was like lightning, and his raiment white as snow:*" Now remember the term "white" simply means purity. It is the only word in the English language, or earthly language, that can be used to describe the brightness of God. It has nothing to do with the color "white" like this paper, but it is speaking of innocence and purity; the "brightest." Now looking at this angel's countenance, it was like lightening; think of that, like lightening. Now we all have at least one angel, and in Matthew 18:10 Jesus says that children's angels always behold the face of the Father. I believe that everyone who is born in the earth has one angel to watch over and protect them. But then as we grow and increase in God, we are given more angels to aid us in our calling. We know that Elijah saw his all of the time, and talked with him; same with Elisha. It was known about William Branham that without the angel of the Lord in the room he was nothing. Robert Thom told a personal story about his experience with William Branham at a meeting. Before the meeting, all of the ministers were gathered in a room before they went out onto the platform waiting for the man of God. In walked William Branham, a little wisp of a man who had a bald head and whose fingernails were all chewed up. He sat off in the corner, biting his fingernails and acting like he was scared and frightened. The ministers were all wondering, "Is this the man of God?" Then all of a sudden, William Branham turns and says "There he is." As soon as he said that, all those in the room about had a heart attack, because they could feel that something had come into room. It was the angel of the Lord that had visited William Branham years prior, that God had sent to tell him that he had a healing ministry. Also, he was told that this angel would be with him whenever he ministered, and would reveal to him what diseases the people had. Robert Thom said from that moment on, William Branham became a different man when he stepped out with the presence of the angel. Like lightening!

Now God will allow angels to change their physical form. Matter of fact, I believe that we entertain angels unaware. How many stories in all of our lives, can we say that someone appeared, out of no where, to help us and then when we looked to find them, they were gone. Believe me they were angels, and they are all around us; even right in our own rooms. You can't see them because you are living on a natural plain. If you are in tune spiritually, you can sense where they are, where they are standing, and what they are doing. If you want to see into the spirit realm, you will have to give yourself to the things of the Spirit of God. It has nothing to do what is in our mind, our intellect, but has everything to do with our spirit. God intimates with our spirit. God doesn't say, "Thus sayeth the Lord, Sam do this." No, it's a response from His heart to yours and you move immediately. If you doubt for a second, the moment passes and it's over.

I want to share with you one of the unforgettable experiences I had with angels. It was on a Thursday night, I was at my desk preparing to go minister, and all of a sudden five angels appeared right in front of my desk. When I saw them they were dancing and rejoicing, and so what do you think I did? I got up and danced with them! I don't know what people were thinking outside my office, but I was having a glorious time! Normally, we are all bound up when we dance, but I tell you when the angels danced they were leaping and jumping around. As long as I was connected to them, I was able to do it. The touch of those angels, when I intertwined my arm with theirs, I leapt and twirled with them. For some reason, God just wanted me to have fun that night. Out of nowhere they appeared; it's crazy but it actually happened! I know that I was given five angels to aid me. Then a few years after I moved to Jacksonville,

FL, the Lord spoke to me and said He was giving me three more angels because of the spiritual warfare I would be facing; so now I know that I have eight. This is not to boast, but to say that as you grow in God, and God begins to bring you into your calling, the warfare will be greater and so He has provision to aid you. No one can lay a hand on you, unless God allows them to. The Spirit Realm is just as real as you squeezing your fist together right now; it's even more real than that.

The color of those in the spiritual world is the color of brightness like lightening. Let us look over in Acts 1:9-11, "[9]*And when he had spoken these things, while they beheld, he was taken up; and a cloud received him out of their sight.* [10]*And while they looked stedfastly toward heaven as he went up, behold, two men stood by them in white apparel;* [11]*Which also said, Ye men of Galilee, why stand ye gazing up into heaven? this same Jesus, which is taken up from you into heaven, shall so come in like manner as ye have seen him go into heaven.*" So we see that there were two men in white apparel. I just want to take a moment, and say that we all describe things as we perceive them. Everyone perceives things differently. The writer here in Acts, wrote "white apparel", but I want to say that I don't believe that they necessarily had on a white shirt or white apparel. I believe that their whole being was bright. We describe what we think they look like, but it is hard for us, as humans, to describe the supernatural. We may say they looked like fine linen, white as snow, or like the sun shining. Here these men appear out of nowhere, standing there in white apparel. In other words, the brightness of God was upon them. We see in Luke 24: 2-3, "[2] *And they found the stone rolled away from the sepulchre.* [3] *And they entered in, and found not the body of the Lord Jesus.*[4] *And it came to pass, as they were much perplexed thereabout, behold, two men stood by them in shining garments:*" This is like the same thing, and the reason that I bring this out is because people always associate white with goodness and black with darkness. I want to stay away from that type of thinking.

When the Bible is describing something as white, what it means is brightness, purity, and the innocence of God. If you will look in your concordance, and you compare the word "white" and the word "black" you will find that white really speaks of a curse. In the book of Leviticus, it says that if you had a white hair on a wound, any kind of injury, or any kind of sickness, it meant that you were cursed and not allowed to come into the temple. On the other hand, if you had a black hair you were allowed in, because it meant that you were healed. So you see, we can't get caught up in what we have been trained to think. The whole purpose of this book is to emphasize to the races, especially to black people, their importance, their presence, their dignity, and their absolutely overwhelming part in what God has done from the beginning. We need to break these old shackles of thinking. We are moving into an hour when it is so important that we are liberated from what other people (and commentators & historians) have said regarding the races. We need the truth because we are coming to the end of all things, and as we prepare to step through that veil, into the glorious liberty of the Sons of God, we must go through it as women and men of truth. We must be men and women who are free from all of the earthly garbage.

Let us look back now at Luke 24, verse 5, which says, *"as they were afraid, and bowed down their faces to the earth, they said unto them, Why seek ye the living among the dead?"* Now this tells you something about these two men in shining garments. They radiated such power that it caused the disciples to bow down. However, when John tried to bow down to the "angel" mentioned in the book of Revelation, he said, "No! I am one of you." The word "angelos" here in the Greek means "messenger." Sometimes it's a spirit being, but sometimes it's a man or a messenger. You have to decide by the context of the passage. But here in Luke, these brothers did not say; "don't get up." Therefore, we can conclude that these two were greater than the one in Revelation. These men did not receive worship, but there was something about them that was on a far greater level, that made the disciples acknowledge them immediately.

Before we go on, remember the last passage in Luke 24, when it says that when they came looking for Jesus, all of a sudden these two men appeared in white apparel. Where did they come from? We need to start being aware of the world around us. The real world is the Spirit world, not this temporal world that we see. You can only live here about eighty years before your body decays and you have to go, but the Spirit world is eternal. It is constantly in tune with what is happening here. While they are looking for Jesus, and wondering what they are going to do, two men appear in dazzling garments and say; "This same Jesus is going to come"; (as if the disciples should know that, to shake them back to reality). What it says to me is that there are angels around us all the time. The Bible says that they are ministers, sent to help the heirs of salvation. If you need help in a situation, you have an angel that you can call on. Have you ever called on one? For example, there was a lady years ago who had a man brake into her house. She was in her bed, and as he was coming towards her, she sat up in the bed and began to pray in tongues. Miraculously, the angel of the Lord came; the man stopped, repented, and got saved all before the police even showed up. Hallelujah! We need to know that we are not alone, and to call upon the Lord and He will deliver us! I have had many personal experiences when God has sovereignly delivered me out of situations, and I know it was because of the presence of His angels surrounding me. In a similar story, many years ago, I walked into a Coffee House that was being robbed. A man had padded down everyone, and had everyone give him their money. As I walked in, he was standing there with a knife, and all of the people were cowering in the corner. I said; "Hey, what's going on?" When he tried to get my money, I pointed at him and said; "In the name of Jesus you drop that thing right now!" He muttered some things that he was going to try and do to me, and then suddenly something passed between us. He dropped the knife, and I said; "Now, go sit in the corner." I led him to Jesus while we waited for the police to come and pick him up.

Now I don't mention these things so that you will start worshipping angels. They have a job to do just like me and you; but their job is you and me. They are to minister for the heirs of salvation, and we need help. Let them help you! What do you think happens when you hear of people doing great feats that they couldn't normally do? What do you think is happening? I'm telling you an angel has stepped in. Someone is run over, the tire is on them, and you have to pull the car off of them. Suddenly, you get this supernatural strength and you are able to pull it off of them. Do you think that you did that all by yourself? No, you had help! Angels are here to help us with things that can be beyond us.

We are going to look now at a few more scriptures declaring the color of angels. This is simply to establish this principal, as it says "out of the mouth of two or three witnesses, let everything be established". Therefore, remembering that the color white simply means "brightness", let us look at John 20:11-12, which says, *"[11]But Mary stood without at the sepulchre weeping: and as she wept, she stooped down, and looked into the sepulchre, [12]And seeth two angels in white sitting, the one at the head, and the other at the feet, where the body of Jesus had lain."* Let's look also at Revelation 19:11-14, *"[11]And I saw heaven opened, and behold a white horse; and he that sat upon him was called Faithful and True, and in righteousness he doth judge and make war. [12]His eyes were as a flame of fire, and on his head were many crowns; and he had a name written, that no man knew, but he himself. [13]And he was clothed with a vesture dipped in blood: and his name is called The Word of God. [14]And the armies which were in heaven followed him upon white horses, clothed in fine linen, white and clean..."* Once again, white is the purity, the brightness. But look on down to verse 17, *"And I saw an angel standing in the sun; and he cried with a loud voice, saying to all the fowls that fly in the midst of heaven, Come and gather yourselves together unto the supper of the great God."* You can't stand in the sun unless there is nothing in you to burn. Hallelujah! So this is the color of the angels, the same burning brightness that we have seen everywhere else in the scriptures.

In Acts 10:30 Cornelius was fasting and praying in his house, and *"behold, a man stood before me in bright clothing"*. And in Revelation 18:1, John says *"after these things I saw another angel come down from heaven, having great power; and the earth was lightened with his glory."* I want us to be like this angel, so that when we walk into a room it is lightened with the glory. Hallelujah! In Ezekiel 40:3, we see Ezekiel seeing a man, or angel, *"whose appearance was like the appearance of brass..."*, once again we see that the angels appearance was as burnished brass.

I know as soon as this book comes out, it's going to be challenged unbelievably. It's going to be criticized, scrutinized and refuted. It's like I'm going to court to defend the presence of black people in the Bible. That's why I've spent thousands of hours making sure that everything I've written or said cannot be refuted. So it is very important that we be thorough in our study. If we are going to talk about the color of God, the color of the original man, the color of God's saints and the color of angels it's all important because it's all a continuum.

Daniel 10:5-6 says, *"[5] Then I lifted up mine eyes, and looked, and behold a certain man clothed in linen, whose loins were girded with fine gold of Uphaz: [6] His body also was like the beryl, and his face as the appearance of lightning, and his eyes as lamps of fire, and his arms and his feet like in color to polished brass, and the voice of his words like the voice of a multitude."* Now let's think about this. What does a face look like, that looks like lightening? Earthly lightening flashes, and then it's gone. But what if it stays? You're talking about a powerful brightness. The reason that they are like that, is because they are in the presence of God. The longer that you are in the presence of God, the more you are becoming like that image you behold. We become what we behold, so if you spend your time watching a television, doing all kinds of other stuff, then that's who you are going to be. But if you read the Word of God, that Word is going to make you into a living epistle. If you behold the face of God in worship, you are going to become like the angels that worship Him.

We are going to look now at what's called the living creatures. In Isaiah 6:1-5, we see, *"[1] In the year that king Uzziah died I saw also the Lord sitting upon a throne, high and lifted up, and his train filled the temple. [2] Above it stood the seraphims: each one had six wings; with twain he covered his face, and with twain he covered his feet, and with twain he did fly. [3] And one cried unto another, and said, Holy, holy, holy, is the LORD of hosts: the whole earth is full of his glory. [4] And the posts of the door moved at the voice of him that cried, and the house was filled with smoke. [5] Then said I, Woe is me! for I am undone; because I am a man of unclean lips, and I dwell in the midst of a people of unclean lips: for mine eyes have seen the King, the LORD of hosts."* Now the word seraphim in Hebrew mean "the burning ones." There is a lot of discrepancy in theological circles, because they say that there is a difference between the seraphims, cherubims, and the living creatures. They divide them, because in two places it says that they have six wings and one place it says that they have four wings. That doesn't change anything. All of that are just representative pictures to explain who these beings are. There's no Hebrew word for "cherubim." The closest you can come to it is that it is an illusionary being, something ethereal. They don't even know the root of the word. It can't be explained. But I believe that the cherubims, the living creatures, the seraphims are all the same. Now here in Isaiah, these two beings that are tied to the Mercy Seat, facing each other, are the cherubims. All they do, day in and day out is, behold the face and the glory of God. When Lucifer fell, he created a vacancy in heaven. There's a vacuum right now, and it's not going to be filled by one person, but there will be a many-membered company of people who will be able to behold God in His glory and see Him as He is. They will guard the glory, and we are to guard it with our life. We need to be like the sons of Issachar. We need to be men who understand the times in which we live. God gives everyone a season, or two, where He separates them from everything else in their life. They are like a "garden enclosed, a fountain shut up" Song of Solomon 4:12 calls it. In that season, you are to do nothing else but immerse yourself in the Word and presence of God. You live, breathe, and eat it. I remember before I went to Chicago in 1977 to Pastor my first church, I went to meetings seven days and seven nights. I worked a job that could fit around the meetings, so that I would be able to sit under the Word. My whole focus was the Kingdom of God. It was all about Jesus because it was the golden time that God had graciously given me to sit under the Word. So many people don't take that opportunity because they don't have the revelation that they are called to be these seraphims. The seraphims are the same thing as the living creatures and in Ezekiel 1:4-24 it says, *"they sparkled like the colour of burhished brass"*. Descriptions of these creatures can also be found in Ezekiel 10 and Revelation 4:6-9.

No matter what they are called, we see they all have the same color, and that is the color of amber. Amber in Hebrew means "bronze or a polished metal". We see that both these creatures and angels have the same color. They all reflect the brightness and glory of God, because they behold His face. We want to be like them, in that, by beholding Him we are changed and reflect His same brilliancy.

Racism Ends With Us
Chapter 17

We will begin this chapter by looking in two places, Galatians 3 and Colossians 3. As I was doing my studying of the presence of black people in the scriptures, the Lord quickened something to my heart that I feel is a finishing note upon all that we've talked about. Ending racism, ending prejudice is something that is not going to be done through legislation of laws. You cannot legislate morality. You cannot legislate the things of the heart. It must spring from within. The only true change the Earth will ever experience will come by having an invasion of the Holy Ghost and the Word of God in their lives. There have been great men and women who have tried to do wonderful things. We applaud them. But in the end, evil has seemed to always triumph. For even in the day in which we live, there is still slavery, still the buying and selling of human beings and it seems as if the whole world has gone to sleep. This is happening before us, the drumbeat of anti-Semitism is reaching throughout the world again, like in the days of Hitler and the world is so accustomed to it that now we tolerate hate and even try to make excuses for it. The only place that's going to see the end of racism, the end of prejudice is going to come out of the body of Christ. In this chapter, I would like to look at this principle of racism ending with us. This takes a revelation on our part that we are all the children of God. We cannot have any lingering prejudices even in our own lives.

Galatians 3:26-28 states, *"For ye are all the children of God by faith in Christ Jesus. For as many of you as have been baptized into Christ have put on Christ. There is neither Jew nor Greek, there is neither bond nor free, there is neither male nor female: for ye are all one in Christ Jesus."* A similar passage is found in Colossians 3:10. *"And have put on the new man, which is renewed in knowledge after the image of him that created him: Where there is neither Greek nor Jew, circumcision nor uncircumcision, barbarian, Scythian, bond nor free: but Christ is all, and in all."* This is true in the spirit, in the kingdom of His dear Son, the kingdom of God. The Bible doesn't say in John 3:16 "For God so loved the Caucasions, that he gave his only son..." But it says, *"For God so loved the world..."*

One of the things we need to understand is this word found in the Bible translated "nations," found both in the Greek and Hebrew. For example Revelation 5:9 states, *"And they sung a new song, saying, Thou art worthy to take the book, and to open the seals thereof: for thou wast slain, and hast redeemed us to God by thy blood out of every kindred, and tongue, and people, and nation."* This verse doesn't leave anything out concerning all the people groups in the Earth. The Greek word found here for "nations" is *ethnos*, where

226

we get the words ethnicity, ethnic, etc. This word means, *"a tribe, a foreign nation; anything other than the Jews."* This also reflects the Hebrew definition for the word "nation," which means, *"a foreign nation; a Gentile."* Many times when you find this word "Gentile" you can substitute the word "nations," anything other than the Jewish people. Notice that Revelation 5:9 is stating that out of every ethnicity, God's blood has been shed.

When Peter said in Acts 10:34 that *"God is no respecter of persons,"* he was defending the fact that God poured out the Holy Ghost upon the Gentiles. It's amazing how you can be a people of God, a Jew like Peter, born again, filled with the Holy Ghost, yet be so filled with racist attitudes towards Gentiles that you don't want them included in the joy that you have experienced. Just because you are saved and even filled with the Holy Ghost does not make you exempt from hatred and prejudice. God's people still need to be delivered from a lot of things. Even in Psalms 95:10 it states that, *"Forty years long was I grieved with this generation, and said, It is a people that do err in their heart, and they have not known my ways."* The Israelites there had a great preponderance to be rebellious and to stay in their own mindset that they lived in.

While they are always thinking of themselves, Psalms 66:7 states, *"his eyes behold the nations."* God had His eyes on the Gentiles long before the Jews ever did. So the Jews became just as racist if you will, as the world was towards them. To be truthful, they brought a lot on themselves by arrogance and pride. How many times did God allow them to be judged horribly because they assumed that just because they had the ark, they were protected. We see this principle in I Samuel 4 when the backslidden priests Hophni and Phineas were committing adultery with the women at the Tabernacle door. Just when the ark came into the camp everybody acted like they were going to win against the Philistines. However they were smitten before their enemies. You can have the ark of God in your midst but if you are not walking uprightly or holy before the Lord, you can still be judged horribly. The ark is not a protection just because you have it. The presence of God only becomes effective in our life when our lives are lined up with Him and His holy nature. Apart from that, the ark is just a box. Even the Philistines heard the shout and the cry and Israel's reputation of their God's great deliverance and power was known to them. Sad to say, there are still believers today who secretly hold racist thoughts. I read a saying today by a neo-Nazi group who was trying to be very respectable, but were black and Jew haters. He was making statements like, "Every white person who reads this, you know deep in your heart if all the Jews and all the blacks could be sent back to their own counties and leave, you would rejoice." I tell that man to speak for himself. Don't be lumping me into your groups. A lot of these white-groups today claim to be Christians. The height of foolishness is that Hitler said that he was a Christian.

It is amazing to me the Bible is so clear about how God in I Timothy 2:4 states, "[God] *who will have all men to be saved, and to come unto the knowledge of the truth.*" He hasn't chosen just a few. Acts 17 is another passage that confirms this truth when Paul is speaking to the people of Athens. He says in of God in Acts 17:26 that God, "*hath made of one blood all nations of men...*" How do race haters and even early Christian writers try to get around that? The only way they could is to say that black people were not men. They were beasts instead. You and I might look at that and say what a crazy notion, but I want you to know that that theology was well received and taught by many in the denominational world well into the 1960s. It was taught that black people didn't even have a soul. They were like animals, being called living creatures. If you can receive this without being offended, in truth the Anglo people have been very imperialistic in history. Everywhere they have gone, they have left traces of tragedy, murder, lands being stolen, conquering and all the while saying that God was on their side.

Do you remember when Israel was led by Joshua? Joshua was by Jericho and the Lord appeared to him (Joshua 5:13-15). Joshua looked at him and he wasn't sure of who he was and said in Joshua 5:13, "*Art thou for us, or for our adversaries?*" An interesting answer came back from the Lord who said neither. We like to say that God is on our side. We use God in a way to puff up and exalt ourselves but God is not partial. God is not a respecter of persons. He makes this plain throughout the scriptures. Even to Israel here in Joshua He was saying, "I'm not going to be on your side when you do wrong things."

For instance, we have a lot of people today who are called Zionists, who basically infer to us that everything that is Jewish is wonderful. And if you don't believe this then you are labeled an anti-Semite. I don't believe everything that is Jewish is wonderful. There are evil Jews. There are Jews today that slaughter Palestinians for no reason at all. I am not a Zionist. I am a Christian. I have no business interfering in the politics of men. If the son of God didn't do it, why should I do it? If none of the major apostles in the Bible didn't do it, why should we do it? The whole program of the religious right and the hatred that is spewed out against our president today is not of God. I also don't agree with a lot of stuff that is going on with our president, but I will tell you this. I am not going to stand by people who do nothing but accuse constantly and blaspheme the name of the president who we are supposed to be praying for and acknowledging as our leader. Proverbs 21:1 states, "*The king's heart is in the hand of the LORD, as the rivers of water: he turneth it whithersoever he will.*" So I have no desire to be a part of the religious right at all. There is no such thing in the Bible. There are Christians and heathens. I'm just sticking with Christians who portray Christian behavior. We've seen in the last few years how the very ones who scream the most about how we shouldn't have bad things on the internet, and passing laws against gay people, only to find these very men are gay themselves, living in sin themselves. So the hypocrisy has reached levels it has never reached before. All it has done is make a mockery of the things of God.

Recently, with the earthquake in Haiti, there have been those who say that the earthquake was the judgment of God upon them because they have made a pact with the devil. Those that say these things have done nothing but bring great shame upon the name of Jesus. And as a Christian, I have to try and explain what you've said to everybody. Do you know that many of these TV evangelists do not have a local church that they attend? Who are they submitted to? Who can speak into their life? It seems that the only people who can speak into their lives are the media. We are supposed to be presenting to the world a God of reconciliation, a God of love and mercy. Does God judge? Absolutely He does. But does God kill innocent people with an earthquake because somebody somewhere made a pact with the devil? Well, if you are going to say that, then you have to go all the way with your beliefs and say that the whole Jewish race is doomed. Because it says in Matthew 27:25 that the Jewish people said of Jesus death, *"His blood be on us, and on our children."* So you can say that the Jews brought the curse on themselves and that is why the Holocaust came. None of us in our right minds would ever believe that. But it would hold true if you follow that kind of thinking. What we need is Jesus.

Acts 17:26-27 states, *"And hath made of one blood all nations of men for to dwell on all the face of the earth, and hath determined the times before appointed, and the bounds of their habitation; that they should seek the Lord."* God wants everybody. And it's so amazing when the Holy Ghost is poured out in Acts 10 and even Peter realizes that you can't call something common or unclean that which God has blessed. And Peter has to stand before the leaders of the Christian church and say, "I'm sorry but the Holy Ghost bade me do it." The revelation there is that there were those that didn't want it done, didn't want the Gentiles to have the Holy Ghost. And for years, the Judaizers continued to bring in their racist superiority. The whole thing about racism is a thinking of superiority, thinking you are better that somebody else. If there is anything that God is saying to all of us, it is reflected in what is said in Romans 12:3, *"For I say...to every man that is among you, not to think of himself more highly than he ought to think..."* God himself came down and became like unto a man and made himself of no reputation. That is God's nature. His nature is one of mercy, love and reconciliation. Every person that has ever been born in this Earth was created by the Lord and deserves respect.

229

Racism is not going be ended until we as Christians start believing and living these truths. We need to show people by the way we live our lives that God is not a racist. God doesn't choose one race above another. He loves all of His people. God says to Abraham (which was before ever there was a Jew), "I am going to make of you a father of a multitude of nations. Not just one nation, but many nations. In the New Testament it is brought up very clearly that anybody who does the same thing that Abraham did, which was to believe God and it was counted to him for righteousness shall be saved. We ourselves are the children of Abraham by faith. Not just for the Jews, but you and I are the children of Abraham by faith.

One of the first steps, I believe, in ending racism is acknowledging that everyone that has ever been created was created by God and that there are no partialities or class distinctions in His mind. The second thing is that God commands us to preach the Gospel to everybody, to all nations, as Matthew 28:19 states, *"Go ye therefore, and teach all nations, baptizing them in the name of the Father, and of the Son, and of the Holy Ghost: teaching them to observe all things whatsoever I have commanded you."* He didn't just say to go to Europe. He said "all nations." Luke 24:47 echoes this command when it says, *"And that repentance and remission of sins should be preached in his name among all nations."* Moreover Revelation 10:11 states, after the messenger appears to John and tells him to eat the little book (which is the Word of God), *"Thou must prophesy again before many peoples, and nations, and tongues, and kings."* God wants us to have a world view as we minister. Zechariah 2:8 also states, *"After the glory hath he sent me unto the nations..."*

What are we to do when we go to the nations? We are to bring them the Gospel, the good news of Jesus Christ. The Gospel is liberation, as Isaiah 61:1 states, *"The Spirit of the Lord God is upon me; because the Lord hath anointed me to preach good tidings unto the meek; he hath sent me to bind up the broken-hearted, to proclaim liberty to the captives, and the opening of the prison to them that are bound..."* This is the good news of the Gospel. It's not getting people saved and them telling them that there is a difference between whites and blacks. Nobody will stand up and say that anymore, but they just make it known that you are not welcome here.

Racism has to end somewhere. Somewhere, one day, a remnant of people is going to come forth free from worldly chains of the ideology of racism and superiority. Nobody is superior to another. We have all come from one hand and in John 13:34-35, Jesus' great words proclaim, *"A new commandment I give unto you, That ye love one another; as I have loved you, that ye also love one another. By this shall all men know that ye are my disciples, if ye have love one to another."*

230

Isaiah 52:10 it says, *"The LORD hath made bare his holy arm in the eyes of all the nations; and all the ends of the earth shall see the salvation of our God."* God is interested in everyone coming to the Lord. Another scripture is in Mark 11:17 says, *"Is it not written, My house shall be called of all nations the house of prayer?"* God's house is not just a house of white people, but of all nations. Do you know that today there exists in my own home town a church that will not let a black person through its doors? It's just accepted and people just live with it. It is like a hidden secret. Like the day that I was in the barber's shop and a black man walks in and nobody will say anything to him. They then wait until He leaves. We have to be people that confront this kind of foolishness, only when it deals with Christianity. I am not going to mess with what one nation is doing to another nation. My concern is the Gospel. But if someone is purporting to be a Christian, and they do something that is racist, I'm honor bound by the Word of God to point out that iniquity. Did you hear what I just said? It's not enough for me just to later say that was terrible after I've walked away. I need to say something. I need to let it be known, that that wasn't scriptural and is not ministering the love of God. Rather what you did was minister hate.

If you are white, can you image being a black person, being held in subjection, sold naked in front of people, families separated, never to see one another again, completely told that you must obey what your white master does? Why do you think that there is hardly a black person in this country that doesn't have white blood in them? And not because a black person and a white person fell in love, but because a white master would just go and take any black slave he wanted and do what he wanted with her. What if you were in love with that black woman and your master did that? Can you image the heart break, the fear, the terror of thinking you might be separated from your children because they would be sold to someone else? We ought to sit in another man's seat. Like when Ezekiel said in Ezekiel 3:15, *"I sat where they sat."* We must get an idea of what injustice has taken place. Most white people don't really experience a lot of injustice. They don't know what it means to be denied something on the basis of your race. Unless we have lived in a situation of injustice, we can never understand the totality of it. So we look at a black person that seems to be angry and violent and we say to ourselves, "I haven't held any slaves. I've never done anything wrong to anybody. Why are you mad at me?" Well, they must think, "Why did you subject my race to 400 years of slavery, because the color of the skin was different than yours?

People don't want to hear these things. They say times are different and things have changed. Well, they are about as different when two weeks ago a senator stood up and said, "Barrack Obama was elected because He didn't have a Negro dialect and He was a light skinned Negro." Most black people do not want to be called Negroes anymore. It's a mentality that still

231

persists. What do we think in the recesses of our hearts about other races? Somebody has to tell the truth. Somebody has to stand up when an injustice is shown, especially where Christianity is concerned. Therefore John 13:35-36 means that people know we are of Jesus by our love we show one to another.

Jesus has broken down the middle wall of partition between us and hath made both one. All of us that are born again believers are together and are in a new family, in a new culture and have a new father, new brothers and sisters and we have to live this to the world. And when they see the kingdom of God on the Earth in a people, they will want to be a part of it. They will see that we are not phonies. They will see that we don't say one thing and do another. They will see that we don't speak with a forked tongue. We need to tell people that not everyone that calls him/herself a Christian acts like Jesus.

While I was meditating upon these truths, the Lord spoke to me that He wanted me to look at the parable of the Good Samaritan in Luke 10:25-37 in this study of how racism is going to end. When we look at this parable, my prayer is that God will bring new light on an old path. Most of us have read this parable and have been taught out of this parable a thousand times, but I am asking the Lord to open our hearts, eyes and ears to hear fresh revelation and not to be thinking of somebody else, but to examine our own hearts.

How is racism going to end, when it begins in the body of Christ? Luke 10:25-37 states, "*[25]And, behold, a certain lawyer stood up, and tempted him, saying, Master, what shall I do to inherit eternal life? [26]He said unto him, what is written in the law? How readest thou? [27]And he answering said, Thou shalt love the Lord thy God with all thy heart, and with all thy soul, and with all thy strength, and with all thy mind; and thy neighbour as thyself. [28]And he said unto him, Thou hast answered right: this do, and thou shalt live. [29]But he, willing to justify himself, said unto Jesus, And who is my neighbour? [30]And Jesus answering said, A certain man went down from Jerusalem to Jericho, and fell among thieves, which stripped him of his raiment, and wounded him, and departed, leaving him half dead. [31]And by chance there came down a certain priest that way: and when he saw him, he passed by on the other side. [32]And likewise a Levite, when he was at the place, came and looked on him, and passed by on the other side. [33]But a certain Samaritan, as he journeyed, came where he was: and when he saw him, he had compassion on him, [34]And went to him, and bound up his wounds, pouring in oil and wine, and set him on his own beast, and brought him to an inn, and took care of him. [35]And on the morrow when he departed, he took out two pence, and gave them to the host, and said unto him, Take care of him; and whatsoever thou spendest more, when I come again, I will repay thee. [36]Which now of these three, thinkest thou, was neighbour unto him that fell among the thieves? [37]And he said, He that shewed mercy on him. Then said Jesus unto him, Go, and do thou likewise.*

232

The first thing to notice about this parable is that the lawyer wasn't asking how to inherit eternal life because he really wanted to know. He was asking Jesus to tempt or trick the Lord. Notice, it says in verse 29 that the lawyer wanted to justify himself. Why did he feel the need to want to justify himself to the Lord? I believe because he didn't love His neighbor. Anybody can love God who they can't see but it is very difficult to love the person on Earth who they can see.

I will never forget years ago I was making an awesome vow before the Lord. I was telling the Lord that I will die for you and that I will be a martyr for your kingdom. I'll do anything. But as I was telling Him these things, the Lord whispered to my heart, "I'd rather you live for me." I then asked Him, "What do you mean by that?" And he said, "It's easy to die once, but I ever-live to make intercession for you." It's a noble thing to give your body to be burned, but it sometimes can be no more that a tinkling symbol and sounding brass because it is not done with a true love of God.

Who is our neighbor? Remember when Cain slew his brother Abel because his deeds were righteous and God asks Cain, "Where is your brother Abel?" And Cain responded to God, "Am I my brother's keeper?" The answer comes back to us, "Yes, of course we are our brother's keeper." How we respond to God's people and to the people He's created will determine what kind of disciples we are. They will know that we are His disciples if we have love one to another. How can any man say that he loves God and he hates his brother, John tells us? Most of us would respond to this and say, "Most of us do not hate our brother. What does hate mean anyway?" It can take many forms and manifestations.

The wonderful thing about Jesus is that He is always looking. I imagine that if Jesus ever walked into a party and He saw somebody sitting by themselves, even though He was the toast of the party, He would go and talk to that individual. Like when the prostitute who came into the Pharisees home while Jesus was sitting there and eating. Everyone in that place despised that she was there, but they were all afraid to say anything because Jesus was present. Isn't it amazing that Jesus engaged her. We must learn that too important lesson to show respect to every child of God. Always be watching and watchful for the one who is out of place. Always have a concern and care for the one that seems to be lost in the crowd and nobody cares about. It is done ignorantly and not viciously. We fellowship with those around us who are our close friends most of the time. But without knowing it, we can alienate ourselves from others who need our help. Not everybody can fit in easily with other people. Now I am not trying to justify their shyness because God has not given us a spirit of timidity. But you understand that some people just need a little help to be brought out. That means we invite people to our homes, we

233

invite people for lunch, we call and see people and we do our best to bless people who necessarily are not in our circle of friends. I just have had too many experiences personally of being treated unfairly. So many times I have had the feeling that even though I was in a place, nobody would even care or notice if I was there or not. Have you ever felt like that? Sometimes people would just rather you to hurry up and leave. Those things hurt deeply. Those are the kinds of wounds that go down to the innermost parts of the belly and deal with your self-esteem. Everyone of us should always be conscience of what is happening round about us.

Years ago, in 1978, as a young pastor, I walked inside of my church in Chicago, Illinois on a Sunday morning. I've always had to lead the worship and preach so I had a lot on my mind. I was praying, believing and thinking. As I walked through the front door, we had a long big foyer. There was a young lady whom I had just led to the Lord and prayed for her to receive the Holy Ghost about a month or so before. When I walked in, I felt a pull in my spirit, a nudge. God help us to be sensitive to the gentle nudging of the Holy Ghost. You may not have to take anyone out to lunch. You might just need to wrap your arms around them and tell them that you love them and ask them how they are doing. Not in some quick way, but with sincerity and care. You always know when someone is not being sincere with you.

I know what it's like to be completely insignificant and treated such. But it's amazing how soon we forget when we reach a place of some kind of strata or some place in our lives when people receive us and we are well-known.

Well, as I walked through that foyer, I felt a definite nudge towards that person. Yet, I was a minister and must be about the Father's business. So I ignored it and just went on and did my thing. The worship that followed was wonderful and there wasn't any sign that anything was wrong. I began to then preach the Word. Everything was going great. But right in the middle of that Word, I felt almost like a hand coming up inside of my soul and just yanking me back. I continued to preach, but yet God began to speak to me and say, "You need to repent." Could you imagine preaching on the baptism on the Holy Ghost and speaking in other tongues and all the while you are talking about it, God is telling you that you need to repent?

In my mind I'm asking the Lord, "What do I need to repent for?" Then He said, "You know very well." Then immediately I felt the nudge again and recognized that I had not obeyed the Lord by not greeting that person.

That experience really showed me something, how important the smallest thing is to God. It seems so insignificant to me, but so important to

Him. Please hear me. If you want to be a faithful shepherd, if you want to be a man or woman of God, then you need to be a man or woman of God to all people. And remember that the people are your main mission, not just preaching and teaching, but themselves!

So the Lord was asking me to repent. I was young and proud at that time. Nobody wants to be embarrassed when you are in your first pastorate. I had only been in the ministry for about a year and people started to like me and receive me. However, I stopped was I was doing and I said, "I'm sorry ladies and gentlemen, but I have to stop. The Lord has dealt with me." I turned to that sister and I said, "Sister, would you please stand up?" She then stands up and I said, "I have to apologize to you. This morning as I walked in the building, I felt the leading of the Lord to come over and greet you, but I disobeyed Him and He very seriously told me that I have to repent to you for not doing that." I repented to her in front of everybody from the pulpit. As she was standing there (and the place being in a state of shock), she said, "Brother Sam, I'll tell you what happened. As I was coming to church this morning, I prayed to God and asked that God would have you, Brother Sam, as my shepherd to just come over to me and give me a hug. I just wanted you to know who I was and that you remembered me and that you loved me." Well, I came down from the platform and hugged her in front of the entire congregation and learned one of the most tremendous lessons I have ever learned in my life. Nothing that the Holy Ghost says is insignificant. The slightest nudge can hold within it the greatest miracle. I have found that after pasturing for 35 years, that it doesn't take a thirty minutes sit-down conversation in my office but sometimes just a smile, an acceptance, a knowing, making eye-contact, and a welcoming knowing inside of you and always putting forth a spirit of being able to be approached as a minister. Never put off any arrogant spirit nor try to keep people from you but always have, as Jesus had, a welcoming and tender heart. Remember when the disciples even tried to keep the children from Him. Jesus said to them, "What are you doing? Let them come unto me."

So this lawyer in Luke 10 had to justify himself because he did not love his neighbor. So, he said in verse 29, *"And who is my neighbor?"* Jesus then put forth the parable of the Good Samaritan. What is a parable? It is a natural story told that hides a spiritual truth in it.

The first thing to notice about the parable is that the man in the story was going from Jerusalem to Jericho when he fell among thieves. He was going from Jerusalem, the house of God. The thief in this parable is the devil as John 10:10 states, *"The thief cometh not, but for to steal, and to kill, and to destroy."* Satan is always trying to steal from all of us and to tempt all of us. He stripped the man of his raiment, trying to steal his righteousness, or made him try not to feel very righteous. Notice I am looking at this story in an allegorical way.

This thief also wounded him as well. The Greek word for "wounded" means "to impose a calamity upon." The devil does try as well to tell people who are coming from the house of God, Jerusalem, the place of double peace, that they are not really the righteousness of God in Christ Jesus. Have you ever felt like that you weren't good enough? Have you ever felt that you didn't measure up enough or that you weren't holy enough? Well, that didn't come from the Holy Spirit. That came from the devil. God never condemns, but He convicts the world of sin. So Satan is always trying to steal our righteousness of God in Christ from us. Romans 8:35 states, *"Who shall separate us from the love of Christ?"* Satan wants to try to separate us from the revelation of who we are in God and remind us of things that we have done in our past, or not done. Satan wants to get us out of a place of union with Jesus. Anyone of us can be this man in the parable. If you think not, then you are crazy.

Satan wants to wound us. How many wounded soldiers are there in the body of Christ? How many people have had a calamity imposed upon them, which was maybe not of their doing? I know some ministers who, when they get up to preach, are very anointed and are great men of God. But after years of watching them I have seen that when they ever come across a person who has great needs or whose reputation is not very good, they don't get involved. To get involved means that their reputation, by even being with that person, might be darkened. But if we read the Gospels, what do we see Jesus doing constantly? He's with harlots, tax collectors, publicans, and sinners. He got more along with them than with the Pharisees and the elders. If I had a choice, I would rather be with the rankest sinner than with a Pharisee because I and that Pharisee are going to get into a fight eventually. There is nothing that I can't stand worst than a sanctimonious hypocrite who strains at a gnat and swallows a camel. Then we realize that we have done the same thing. How many gnats have we swat at and how many camels have we swallowed, pointing our fingers at the iniquities of others, while we ourselves were living with iniquities in our own lives. Beware putting forth of the finger because there are three pointing back at you. I don't care if you have a mote, a boulder, or a forest in you eyes. All you are going to get from me is mercy. Instead of throwing fire at you, I will throw mercy at you. You see, I've had a forest of motes in my eye. And you learn that the thing that the Lord can't stand is when you are being a hypocrite and judging someone else in the very thing that you are doing yourself!

Just like this man in the parable, when we are wounded (whether we were responsible or not) we need help. We need the body of Christ. The thief, after stripping him, wounding him, departed and left him half dead. Do we leave people when they are at their worst? How do you answer the question, is the glass half empty or half full? This man was called half dead, not half alive! So many people, when they see this man half dead, are pessimistic and say, "There isn't any point in helping that, they are half dead! Let them die!" But Ezekiel 16 states that when God passed by (in verse 6), *"And when I passed by thee, and saw thee polluted in thine own blood, I said unto thee when thou wast in thy blood, Live..."* Verse 8 of Ezekiel 16 also states, *"Now when I passed by thee, and looked upon thee, behold, thy time was the time of love; and I spread my skirt over thee, and covered thy nakedness."* What do you do when you pass by someone that has been found in open sin and has got all types of obvious problems? Do you think to yourself, "This is the time of love?"

When I think back when I was 15 years old, I can see myself sitting in the hallway of my school with my feet crossed smoking a cigarette on purpose. A female teacher passed by me and I defiantly took a puff and blew circles of smoke in her face and she told me to get up off the floor and get to class. What I then said to her, I shall never repeat. It was so horrible and wicked. When I think about that now, I think about what she must have thought about me. Do you know that that teacher went on to marry my music instructor and years later I went to visit him before he died of multiple sclerosis to repent to him for failing him in my final year of high school. I was able to repent to that woman as well. I told her that night that whether she knew it or not, inside of my heart as a 15 year old was a boy who was crying out to be loved and to be helped. I was a product of an environment of cruelty and my only response to violence was violence.

How many times have we seen people walk in and consider them half dead? But thanks be unto God that when He passes by us, it is the time of love. When we were polluted in our own blood, He said for us to live! He didn't pass by us and ridicule us, saying that we will never make it and will never survive. He doesn't move on and leave us half dead. He stops and has compassion upon us.

Verse 31 of Luke 10 states, *"And by chance..."* There is no chance in life. Everything is ordained of God. God brings situations into our lives to test us. The first man to pass by was a priest. A priest is to perform the functions of God. The priest is to act like God upon Earth. So this priest could be any man or woman of God. Paul said in I Timothy 1:12, *"And I thank Christ Jesus our Lord, who hath enabled me, for that he counted me faithful, putting me into the ministry."* He was put in the ministry to minister in the place of God. Malachi tells us that in the priests' mouths should be the laws of truth and the laws of kindness.

But look at this priest. What does he do? When the priest saw him, he passed by on the other side. Now, first of all, a couple things need to be said about this. He saw his condition and it didn't affect him. Why did it not affect him? It didn't affect him because it would require him to be personally involved with that person. As a pastor, it is not enough for a person to just come up during an altar call and get saved, filled with the Holy Ghost or get delivered from a demon. Most of the time, you have to go where they are! This means that you have to go to the "other side." It's like when Jesus said that these people draw nigh unto me with their lips, but their hearts are far from me.

Luke 18:9 describes this priest in the parable of the Good Samaritan. *"And he spake this parable unto certain which trusted in themselves that they were righteous, and despised others."* Remember what the Greek word for "despised" means. It means, "to set at naught." It's like throwing something in the corner because it is worthless to you. People are never unimportant. Please listen to me. People are never not-important. They are never to be despised and tossed into a corner. Isn't it awful when we see in churches these rich people paraded around in the front? The pastor is making lunch deals with all of the rich people, and fawning over them. When was the last time they took out just the middle class families to lunch with them and brought them into their inner circle as it were? We have to ask ourselves, "Do we trust in ourselves that we are righteous, or do we trust in the grace of God?"

Secondly, we have to ask ourselves, "Are we acting like Jesus? Or are we acting like people who despise others?" When Paul says in I Thessalonians 5:20, *"Despise not prophesyings,"* what he is really saying to us is to not despise the vessel who is prophesying. Isn't it interesting how God uses those very people so many times to bring us the Word of the Lord.

The parable in Luke 18:9-14 continues with verse 10 by stating, *two men went up into the temple to pray; the one a Pharisee and the other a publican. 11 The Pharisee stood and prayed thus with himself, God, I thank thee, that I am not as other men are, extortioners, unjust, adulterers, or even as this publican. 12 I fast twice in the week, I give tithes of all that I possess."* It was that the Pharisee was praying with himself. God had nothing to do with this man's prayer. You and I would never say a thing like this Pharisee said, but I wonder if subtly sometimes we actually think it. We pass by the man who is half dead and think, "I am glad I am not like that." How many times have I said that only to find myself licking the dirt my self? Save yourselves from years of the dealings of God. Micah 6:8 states, *"He hath shewed thee, O man, what is good and what doth the LORD require of thee, but to do justly, and to love mercy, and to walk humbly with thy God?"* We have to do justly in every area of our life. We have to love mercy and we have to walk humbly with God.

We must decide to live like that, like Paul, who said in Acts 24:16, *"And herein do I exercise myself, to have always a conscience void of offence toward God, and toward men."* If we do this day by day, chamber by chamber, Jesus will be taking control of our lives and we will become like Him. We don't want to be like this Pharisee in Luke 18 who despised the publican and was self-righteous.

The publican's prayer was different. Luke 18:13-14 states, *"13 And the publican, standing afar off, would not lift up so much as his eyes unto heaven, but smote upon his breast, saying, God be merciful to me a sinner. 14 I tell you, this man went down to his house justified rather than the other: for every one that exalteth himself shall be abased; and he that humbleth himself shall be exalted."*

I remember when I was in a hotel room one day as I was writing one of the books God had given to me to write. A lady knocks on the door of my room and I tell her that I don't need anything except for a few extra towels. As I closed to door, I felt that same nudge that I felt in 1978. Then I remembered that I only had a hundred dollar bill in my pocket and I wanted to change it to get some twenties. But the Lord said to me, "No. Give her the whole thing." I didn't know this woman from Adam. So I took the money and ran down the hallway and found her. I then said to her, "Excuse me, but what is your name?" I then told her that I was a pastor and that when she came and knocked on my door that the Lord had spoken unto me to give her something. So I gave her the money. She saw it and she started to cry. I then said to her, "Jesus Christ gave that money to you and He is calling you back home to Him. Never forget that He loves you." I then walked away. Months went by and one day I was pulling up to a gas station. As I was getting gas one afternoon, "by chance" as I was pumping the gas, I hear this woman say, "Hey!" She then comes running up to me and says, "Do you remember me?" I told her that I didn't. And she said, "I was the maid in the hotel that you sowed that money to." Then she went on to tell me how she had started going back to church and was now involved in a Spirit-filled church and was going on with God. Just think, a hundred dollars turned that life around. Listen to the gentle witness deep down in our spirits. If you can learn to hear those witnesses, the prophetic anointing is not far off. If you will just obey immediately, then you get accustomed to doing it and then God can use you more in those ways.

I'm not justifying the publican in Luke 18, and neither was Jesus. What I am saying is then when he prayed, he wasn't trying to be more than what he was. He knew where His heart was. I don't know about you, but the Bible says that the heart is deceitful and desperately wicked above all things. I know that apart from the grace of God I am capable of anything. That is not just talk but that is the truth. If I personally stay out of the Word of God for a week or two, I'm liable to hear some voices and to get involved in some things

239

I shouldn't get involved in. I can't speak for you. You may be rock solid all the time. But I know me. I can't go days without filling myself with the Word of God because it makes me open to things. If I don't keep myself, then one day an opportune time comes when I'll be tempted with something and end up falling. A couple of days not walking with Jesus, I might be tempted to do something, whereas when I am walking with the Lord, I don't even consider it. Take heed, lest you fall. I Corinthians 10:12 states, *"Wherefore let him that thinketh he standeth take heed lest he fall."*

Well, the priest, the man of God passes by on the other side. A good companion scripture is found in Mark 5:1-20 where Jesus went to the "other side" where there were demons that possessed a Gadarene man. Jesus goes where our flesh doesn't want to go. Really, we don't want to be reminded of who we were.

The next person to pass the man that fell among the thieves was a Levite. Now, Levite in the Hebrew language means "joined." The Levites were the chosen people out of the tribes of Israel. They were supposed to be "joined" of the Lord. Luke 10:32 states, *"And likewise a Levite, when he was at the place, came and looked on him, and passes by on the other side."* His eye also didn't affect his heart. How hard must your heart be if you can look at a situation like that and not be moved or not want to get involved and help. Once again, he passes by to the other side like the priest.

But verse 33 of Luke 10 states, *"But a certain Samaritan..."* In that day, Samaritans were counted as half-breeds. It's funny how Jesus always uses the half-breeds. The verse continues by saying, *"...as he journeyed, came where he was."* Jesus will always come where you are. *"And when he saw him, he had compassion on him."* Many times it says of Jesus that when Jesus saw something, that he was moved with compassion.

Now, let's relate this to racism. What if you were passing by a rapper. You know, a young man, showing his boxers and his pants hang down low and he has these brown boots and he is laying on the ground and you see his gun next to him. He's got dreadlocks and a t-shirt that says, "I hate everything white." What would you do? What would Jesus do? What did he do when He passed by you? Did he care what color you were? If the world is ever going to see an end of racism, it must begin in the body of Christ.

The Samaritan went to where he was and had compassion on him. Then he, according to verse 34, *"and went to him, and bound up his wounds, pouring in oil and wine, and set him on his own beast, and brought him to an inn, and took care of him."* He got personally involved with that person. Ministry means getting personally involved. Does it take a lot of time? Yes. Is it hard? Yes. Today, I was on the phone for almost two hours on an international call paid for by myself ministering to a situation in another country. I'm thousands of miles away and yet the need was real and I being their father in the Lord had to deal with it.

When you become a minister, your life is over. Your life belongs to another. And you can't select and choose the times when and where you'll be a minister.

The Samaritan then poured in oil and wine. This is a type of the anointing and the Holy Ghost. Then he set him on his own beast. This signifies that he gave that man the very best that he had. Are you living a life like that? Because this Samaritan is the Lord Jesus. Then he brought him to an inn, which is a type of the local church and took care of him.

Verse 35 of Luke 10 then states, *"And on the morrow when he departed, he took out two pence, and gave them to the host, and said unto him, Take care of him; and whatsoever thou spendest more, when I come again, I will repay thee."* How motivated are we to help others and get involved in their life and bless them, even those of another race when we know they can't pay us back, when they can't bless us in return. That's true ministry.

Finally, Jesus asked him in verse 36, *"Which now of these three, thinkest thou, was neighbour unto him that fell among the thieves?"* And the lawyer responded, *"He that shewed mercy on him."* Then Jesus said, *"Go, and do thou likewise."* Jesus was telling that lawyer, "You do everything right, but you hate your neighbor and you are not loving him.

So, where and when will racism end? It will come to an end when the body of Christ, whose image and nature has been so transformed into the nature of Jesus, begins to walk out and live these principles. The world will then know that Jesus is real.

Mixed Marriages In Scripture
Chapter 18

In this chapter I want to discuss inter- racial marriage according to Scriptures. I had no idea when I started writing this book, how it would all end up, but it has been marvelously illuminating to me. Now in looking at the term inter-marriage, I want to begin by telling a story of something that happened to me a few minutes after my salvation.

I was the only person that day in my high school to get saved. It was the third Thursday of September, 1971, on the stage of my high school during an assembly when I got saved. As I was walking down the stairs of the stage just having been born again, before I reached my seat, I was accosted by two ladies (each one had a bun on their head). One of them said to me that if I didn't cut my hair, I would lose my salvation. Mind you, I had just gotten saved minutes before and I was threatened I would lose it if I didn't do something about my hair. Right after that (I'm still not back to my seat) a second lady asked me if it was true that I was dating a black woman. I told her yes and she told me that if I continued dating her, that I was going to go to hell. I asked her why I would go to hell for dating a black person and she said because the Bible says that we are not to inter-marry. Have you ever heard this before? Most of us may have heard something about this subject but have never been shown in the scriptures where it talks of it. Now the goal of this whole book is to get to the truth and in this chapter I want you to see clearly what the Bible really says on this subject of inter-marriage.

Inter-marriage as we have known it has meant being married to someone of a different color. Let me state clearly that being married to someone of a different color, ethnicity, or race is not forbidden in the Scriptures. I want to prove this in the Scriptures in this chapter once and for all. Many reading this may say why is this important? It is important because this subject needs to be written down, in plain language, so people can see where in the Bible this subject is mentioned and what does it say about it. This chapter's goal is to prove conclusively what the Scripture say on this issue.

So here I was in 1971, just saved, and threatened about my hair and about dating the black person. At the time, I knew nothing about the Bible whatsoever. I never went to church growing up. As a teenager thumbing through the Bible later that week, God somehow and someway got me over to the Old Testament to a passage that we will see in this chapter. He supernaturally showed me that what He was saying to Israel was not that inter-marriage between people's was the issue, but what He was saying was do not marry outside of the Kingdom of God or our side of his covenant people. The second lady ended up inviting me to her church the following Wednesday night and I went. And I told her what I had discovered and she told me I was going to hell and sent me home. Well it is forty years later and I am still standing!

Why is it that people take the Scriptures to emphasis their petty prejudices? People want us to live in fear. People want us to believe what they say while never emphasizing to search the Scriptures for ourselves to see if what they are saying is actually true and Scriptural. Most of us, since the time we were born, if our parents believed something, we more than likely believed it. The irony in my family is my father was a terrible racist towards blacks and my brother ended up marrying a black woman and has been happily married for over 40 years now! So when God speaks of inter-marriage in the Scriptures, He is speaking of we, as God's people, are not to marry outside the people of God.

Now first, let us look at the warnings God gave about inter-marriage and see why He gave these warnings. Why does God not allow us to marry outside of the Kingdom? Exodus 34:10-16 says, *"10And he said, Behold, I make a covenant: before all thy people I will do marvels, such as have not been done in all the earth, nor in any nation: and all the people among which thou art shall see the work of the LORD: for it is a terrible thing that I will do with thee. 11Observe thou that which I command thee this day: behold, I drive out before thee the Amorite, and the Canaanite, and the Hittite, and the Perizzite, and the Hivite, and the Jebusite. 12Take heed to thyself, lest thou make a covenant with the inhabitants of the land whither thou goest, lest it be for a snare in the midst of thee..."* We cannot go playing in places that we are not supposed to go. *"13But ye shall destroy their altars, break their images, and cut down their groves: 14For thou shalt worship no other god: for the LORD, whose name is Jealous, is a jealous God. 15Lest thou make a covenant with the inhabitants of the land, and they go a whoring after their gods , and do sacrifice unto their gods, and one call thee, and thou eat of his sacrifice; 16And thou take of their daughters unto thy sons, and their daughters go a whoring after their gods, and make thy sons go a whoring after their gods."* What a warning by God. God gave a strong warning to Israel to not have their sons or daughters go into other nations because ultimately they would be a snare to them.

As we look at the passages and the numerous warnings to not marry outside the people of God, we find one of the wisest men, Solomon, who loved many strange women at the end of his life. He even worshipped and sacrificed to a false god. This always reminds me as I Corinthians 10:12 says, *"let him that thinketh he standeth take heed lest he fall."* The Lord gives us these warnings as a reason, not because He hates the Gentiles or the nations. It is what they do that He doesn't want entering into our hearts because they will become a snare to us. To this day when Joshua made a covenant to one of the nations they were to conquer (because they tricked Joshua), they thought it was fine until later they realized they were their enemies. When Joshua made a league with these people, you will still find today in Palestine the fight between the Jews and the Arabs, hating and fighting one another.

If we look at all of the gods of the nations mentioned in Exodus 34 that we just read we will find that many of them required child sacrifices. I read in the USA Today recently that in one foreign country (in Africa) one of the leaders used to be a witch doctor and he admitted that he had partaken in 34 child sacrifices including his own son. He said when he was a child, he was taken to a child sacrifice. The child they sacrificed was opened from the neck down and was placed upon this person (blood and all) for some demonic reason. This is what was happening with the nations around Israel. You see, you can't play in the devil's playground without getting dirty. God was simply warning Israel because He knew them and He saw what was going on in these nations. It reminds me when I was young in the Lord and was out evangelizing with some brothers around some bars. Well, there was one topless bar in particular that they wanted to go in and evangelize and I told them it wasn't a good idea. They went in anyway and I waited outside. Well, they didn't come out for hours and when they came out, they were ashamed and felt condemned because they fell. The principle is you and I are not to go into the devil's territory like this unless it is truly the Lord.

As a pastor, I can tell you the numerous stories of sisters saying they can find no men in the body of Christ that they can marry so they are just going to go to bars or look to the world to find a man and get him saved. These are famous last words I have heard too many times. This doesn't work. It comes down to this. We are a holy people and we are not to mingle our seed with that which is not holy. We are a partaker of the divine nature and God refuses to be joined with the devil. How many marriages can you think of right now that are full of torment because the woman is saved and the man is not (or vice versa)? God warned Israel about this. He had no problem with colors of skin because we are all His offspring (every nation, tribe, and tongue is made up of one blood the Bible says). It is not the physical characteristics of people that is the issue, but it is the things that people do and the spirits they entertain. So we have to be very careful about the people we hang around with. To Israel it meant the tribes around them but to us it is the people we have relationships with that are in the world. As parents, we need to be very careful with our children. Who are they hanging around with really?

Next, let us read a passage in Leviticus 19, "*[19]Ye shall keep my statutes. Thou shalt not let thy cattle gender with a diverse kind: thou shalt not sow thy field with mingled seed: neither shall a garment mingled of linen and woollen come upon thee...*" The issue here is mixture. God doesn't want mixture in His people. But if you hang around heathens you are going to have mixture. What is more surprising for us in the charismatic world is many churches hire heathens who play instruments to help lead the worship. How can a heathen lead God's people into God's presence?!! They can't. It is a wonder to me that lightning hasn't struck some of these churches. I personally would be afraid to do this at my church. Many who do this say they do it because hopefully the Holy Spirit will touch them. Well, what about their spirit touching you and polluting the pure stream of the river of God? I don't see how God's glory can fall when where there is strange fire. God doesn't want mixture when it comes to His glory. Later in this chapter we will see the definition of a mixed multitude or a mingled multitude. A mingled multitude is taking the godly seed and mingling it with the world. God doesn't care if you or I marry a black person, a red person, brown person, or a white person as long as they are in the Kingdom. Not all of the people of the earth are God's people and therefore because they are not, they serve *"the spirit that now worketh in the children of disobedience"*, Ephesians 2:1 tells us. Every person that is not born again is under the throes and power of Satan.

Deuteronomy 7:1-6 says, *"[1]When the LORD thy God shall bring thee into the land whither thou goest to possess it, and hath cast out many nations before thee, the Hittites, and the Girgashites, and the Amorites, and the Canaanites, and the Perizzites, and the Hivites, and the Jebusites, seven nations greater and mightier than thou; [2]And when the LORD thy God shall deliver them before thee; thou shalt smite them, and utterly destroy them..."* This may sound harsh by the Lord but the principle is we can't let anything live in us that is not godly. How many of us today are wrestling and living with fleshly problems because we did not smite the devil completely and let things that we know weren't of God live? We have allowed ourselves little privileges and they haunt us to this day. God is saying these things must be destroyed. The Lord gave me a word years ago that these 7 nations are a type of 7 major enemies we have to overcome as a New Testament Christian in our soul. Continuing in verse 2, *"...thou shalt make no covenant with them, nor shew mercy unto them..."* This can also speak of subjects about our business practices and going into business with a heathen. We are not to do that. *"[3]Neither shalt thou make marriages with them; thy daughter thou shalt not give unto his son, nor his daughter shalt thou take unto thy son. [4]For* (this is the reason God doesn't want mixed marriages) *they will turn away thy son from following me, that they may serve other gods: so will the anger of the LORD be kindled against you, and destroy thee suddenly. [5]But thus shall ye deal with them; ye shall destroy their altars, and break down their images, and cut down their groves, and burn their graven images with fire. [6]For thou art an holy people unto the LORD thy God: the LORD thy God hath chosen thee to be a special people unto himself, above all people that are upon the face of the earth..."* God is warning them that the other nations will turn them away from following Him and cause them to serve other gods.

Next, let us look at Joshua 23. Joshua is speaking to the children of Israel. Let us pick it up in verse 8, "*[8]But cleave unto the LORD your God, as ye have done unto this day. [9]For the LORD hath driven out from before you great nations and strong: but as for you, no man hath been able to stand before you unto this day. [10]One man of you shall chase a thousand: for the LORD your God, he it is that fighteth for you, as he hath promised you. [11]Take good heed therefore unto yourselves, that ye love the LORD your God. [12]Else if ye do in any wise go back...*" Let me stop here before we go forward. If you and I love the Lord your God, you and I will in no wise go back. I John 2:15 says "*Love not the world, neither the things that are in the world. If any man love the world, the love of the Father is not in him.*" I used to think this passage meant if we love the world we are void of the love of God. But now I understand what this means. John was writing to Christians. You and I have to love God the Father more than the world, flesh, and the devil. And when we give into the world, flesh, and the devil, the love that we have towards God the Father will fade into silence.

Many times during my years of pastoring I have heard countless people say to me "Brother Sam, I'm not really backsliding. I'm just not really pressing on". Well my Bible tells me we are either going on to perfection or drawing back unto perdition. There are only two directions. There is no middle ground. You are backsliding the minute you begin to turn your heart from the Lord. Consider the bride in Song of Solomon 5:2-6 when the Lord comes to meet with her. When He comes to her door she doesn't respond but says to herself "*I have put off my coat; how shall I put it on? I have washed my feet; how shall I defile them?*" (verse 3). This means she has stopped walking with the Lord and when He called upon her to have intimacy with her, she refused because she later in verse 6 says "*my soul failed when he spake*". The principle is never take off your shoes if you want to be the bride of Christ. Don't stop walking with Jesus.

It is similar to Ephesians 4:22-27 which says, "*[22]That ye put off concerning the former conversation the old man, which is corrupt according to the deceitful lusts; [23]And be renewed in the spirit of your mind; [24]And that ye put on the new man, which after God is created in righteousness and true holiness...*" The context here is as Christians, we have to put on the divine nature and walk in the newness that God has brought us into. "*[25]Wherefore putting away lying, speak every man truth with his neighbour: for we are members one of another. [26]Be ye angry, and sin not: let not the sun go down upon your wrath: [27]Neither give place to the devil.*" Now I have actually heard preachers teach that verse 26 is saying that it is okay to be angry as long as the sun doesn't go down. This is not what Paul is saying. He is telling us to be angry at sin. If we have righteous indignation, we won't sin. We can't let our righteous indignation cease in our heart because verse 27 says if we do, we will give place to the devil. This is all Paul is trying to say. The minute we stop in our relentless pursuit and passion for Jesus, we are opening the door to the enemy. It is "*the little foxes, that spoil the vines*" (Song of Solomon 2:15). Ecclesiastes 10:8 says "*whoso breaketh an hedge, a serpent shall bite him.*" God doesn't want us to give place to the devil, but Israel on a large scale was giving place to the devil, especially by marrying the people of these godless nations. Everything in our life is important to God, especially our relationships.

Going back to Joshua 23, we continue back in verse 12, "*¹²Else if ye do in any wise go back and cleave unto the remnant of these nations, even these that remain among you, and shall make marriages with them, and go in unto them, and they to you...*" This was Israel's mistake. They allowed some of these nations and people of these nations to remain among them. Now there are instances in the Bible, like the story of Rahab and Ruth, where they are welcomed by God into the household of God and even allowed to marry. But these were exceptions where they came under the direction and believed in the Lord themselves. "*¹³Know for a certainty that the LORD your God will no more drive out any of these nations from before you; but they shall be snares and traps unto you, and scourges in your sides, and thorns in your eyes, until ye perish from off this good land which the LORD your God hath given you.*" This doesn't have to be, but God is warning them what would happen if they don't take heed to this.

Numbers 36:5-10 says, "*⁵And Moses commanded the children of Israel according to the word of the LORD, saying, The tribe of the sons of Joseph hath said well. ⁶This is the thing which the LORD doth command concerning the daughters of Zelophehad, saying, Let them marry to whom they think best; only to the family of the tribe of their father shall they marry. ⁷So shall not the inheritance of the children of Israel remove from tribe to tribe: for every one of the children of Israel shall keep himself to the inheritance of the tribe of his fathers.*" The point is this (as we look also at Genesis 24): if we allow our sons or daughters to marry outside the Kingdom of God, we are going to lose our inheritance as a child of God. In Genesis 24 we see what Abraham commanded his servants, beginning in verse 1, "*¹And Abraham was old, and well stricken in age: and the LORD had blessed Abraham in all things. ²And Abraham said unto his eldest servant of his house, that ruled over all that he had, Put, I pray thee, thy hand under my thigh: ³And I will make thee swear by the LORD, the God of heaven, and the God of the earth, that thou shalt not take a wife unto my son of the daughters of the Canaanites, among whom I dwell: ⁴But thou shalt go unto my country, and to my kindred, and take a wife unto my son Isaac.*" Abraham didn't want his son to marry any of the daughters of the Canaanites because these people worshipped false gods. They sacrificed their children and did unspeakable and abominable things in the eyes of God.

But let us look at what happens when God's people inter-marry with people outside the Kingdom of God. Once again, all of these passages are not talking about not being able to marry someone because of their skin color. In I Kings 11 we read, *"[1]But king Solomon loved many strange women, together with the daughter of Pharaoh, women of the Moabites, Ammonites, Edomites, Zidonians, and Hittites; [2]Of the nations concerning which the LORD said unto the children of Israel, Ye shall not go in to them, neither shall they come in unto you: for surely they will turn away your heart after their gods: Solomon clave unto these in love..."* How many times have I heard from someone that they were "in love", when I knew and they knew that they were "in lust"? I've seen it too many times. Six months later they are sitting in my office (after I told them not to get married) seeking marriage counseling from me. It is true that there should and will always be a physical attraction with the person God wants us to marry, but you don't marry somebody only because of physical attraction. I remember years ago a brother in the church I was part of fell for this gorgeous model and told everybody he was in love and it wasn't too much time after that that he wanted to marry her. All of us tried to tell him he is only marrying her for her looks, but he didn't listen. We even thought that when she received the Holy Ghost that she faked speaking in tongues. We tried to tell him, but he wouldn't listen. The day after they got married I didn't see the brother for ten years. Ten years later he walked into my office and said his wife was committing adultery with the deacon at another church and he wanted a divorce. I didn't want to say to him "I told you so", but I asked him what happened. He said the day after they got married she said to me that she will never go to a charismatic church and neither will you. The marriage cost him ten years of his life. So I counseled him and told him he had a right scripturally to get divorced, but I told him he wasn't allowed to date anybody for one whole year to purge himself from his foolishness. The bizarre thing about this was when I was counseling him before his divorce God showed me who his wife was (while he was still married to his first wife). I called my pastor and told him what the Lord showed me and he told me to just keep quiet and see what happens. Well, he divorced the woman who was a model and a year later I had a get together at my house. I invited many people, one of them being this brother and the other being this sister whom the Lord showed me a year previous was to be his wife. Well, wouldn't you know it before the night was out, they were sitting together on a love seat engrossed in conversation, obviously smitten by each other. Six months later I performed their marriage and they have been married now 25-30 years, and have had several children. This story has a great ending, but ten years of this brother's life was ruined because he was dazzled by outward beauty. You see if what we do is of the world and birthed of the flesh, it will die and be a snare to us. It will be as

Joshua said, *"snares and traps unto you, and scourges in your sides, and thorns in your eyes"* and it will cause us to bring shame to our lives and to the Lord Jesus Himself. And we definitely don't want to do that. The scriptures declare *"that which is born of the flesh, is flesh."* God help us to walk and live in the Spirit of God.

Continuing in Solomon's story, *"³And he had seven hundred wives, princesses, and three hundred concubines: and his wives turned away his heart. ⁴For it came to pass, when Solomon was old, that <u>his wives turned away his heart</u> after other gods: and his heart was not perfect with the LORD his God, as was the heart of David his father. ⁵For Solomon went after Ashtoreth the goddess of the Zidonians, and after Milcom the abomination of the Ammonites. ⁶And Solomon did evil in the sight of the LORD, and went not fully after the LORD, as did David his father."* Solomon's story reminds us of Samson's story. Samson's parents tried to stop Samson from marrying a Philistine, but they couldn't (Judges 14:3), *"Then his father and his mother said unto him, Is there never a woman among the daughters of thy brethren, or among all my people, that thou goest to take a wife of the uncircumcised Philistines? And Samson said unto his father, Get her for me; for she pleaseth me well."* Samson didn't care and only cared for what pleased him, but it created a lot of destruction for his life. Proverbs 6:27 says, in context to adultery, *"Can a man take fire in his bosom, and his clothes not be burned?"* You and I can't take strange fire into our bosom and not expect to receive some kind of judgment from God for what we have done. Clothes in the Bible speak of our reward or what we have gained in Jesus, so if we do these things, we lose part of our reward. Now we can gain it back, but we will have lost precious anointing and authority because we embraced something that we knowingly knew was not of God.

What about David standing upon a rooftop when he should be out in battle? Satan is looking for a more opportune time in all of our lives. It may be women for some and it may be money for others. Money rules some. Power may rule others. All of us are different and some of us are tempted in all points.

So many people settle for less than God's best and they don't wait. They rush into things even as Christian. They rush into marriages that God didn't ordain and they end up going through literal hell. As a pastor, I can tell within three minutes whether a couple is going to make it or not, or if the couple was truly joined by God. The divorce rate in the church even supersedes the divorce of the world. Obviously, something is wrong. We are not teaching the people correctly before they marry somebody. It's important to be attracted on the physical level. But you have to have somebody with a personality that you like. Your spouse should be your very best friend. I can honestly say to you that if I had nothing but my wife ever in my life and we were the only two left on the earth, we would have an awesome time. I would be perfectly happy because not only is my wife attractive to me physically, but she has a tremendous soul, and intellect. I can engage her in conversation in many things. I've seen brothers marry these beautiful looking women with these gorgeous faces and then you ask the woman a question and she responds, "Huh?" How long are you going to be able to live with somebody who you can hardly have a decent conversation with?

The first thing we should go for is where their spirit is at. Do they have the same passion and love for the Lord Jesus? Do they have the same like precious faith? Are you both going in the same direction spiritually? Do they see the vision that you have? If not, then you need to let them go. It will only mean trouble. Better to not marry Paul said.

There are a lot of people married today, who would be a whole lot better off if they just plain and simply never married. Paul even says that you will have trouble in the flesh. "I thought marriage was to always be like heaven, Brother Sam?" Well, there are days where it is like heaven on earth, but then there are days where you have to work at it.

God doesn't care if you marry a Japanese woman, just don't worship a Japanese god. If the Japanese woman is a Spirit-filled Christian, loves to worship and search the Scriptures, then go for it. It has nothing to do with race. When you are born again, we are all a new species. We are a different creation than the world. That is why we can't mingle our seed with them. When we got born again, we became a partaker of the divine nature. We sully the wonderful glory when we marry outside Kingdom of God. We must guard the glory, guard the presence of God. You don't marry somebody without realizing that they are going to be with you, with your vision. They need to stand along side you and be a help mate. If the woman is the minister in the relationship, it's the same thing. Because if you marry somebody, even if they are Spirit-filled but don't have the same vision, then you are going to have trouble. They are going to want you to go to a church that you know that you don't belong at. How many people aren't coming to the church God called them to because of that issue?

So there are people who couldn't wait and they find out that their spouse doesn't want them going to a place of glory, a place of intensity. They wanted their minivan and two kids and the white picket fence. But it says that in heaven, they neither marry nor are given into marriage. Once we leave this life, all of that fades into oblivion. Those of us who are trying to be truly spiritual and have broken through into a heavenly sphere and a heavenly place know. That is why Paul said in some times and seasons that we will fast one from another from partaking in a sexual act because things like that aren't as important anymore like they were. The greater includes the lesser. I told my wife the day before I married her, "I cannot love two masters. Jesus will always be first. Don't ever challenge it and try to make me stop caring for the body of Christ. You know who you are marrying so if you can't deal with this don't marry me." God knows these years, how many days and nights I have been gone. But that is my wife's reward for the sacrifice that she gave.

Let's look what these women did with Solomon. Verses 4-5 of I Kings 11 states, *"For it came to pass, when Solomon was old, that his wives turned away his heart after other gods: and his heart was not perfect with the LORD his God, as was the heart of David his father. For Solomon went Ashtoreth the goddess of the Zidonians."* Solomon did this. The same Solomon that got upon the altar at the temple of Solomon, who placed himself upon the altar and prayed the prayer, "All I want is an understanding heart." God was so moved by Solomon's heart and that he didn't ask for anything for himself, God promised him anything that he wanted. I don't care how wise you are, how great you are. We can all be deceived. We cannot allow one little blade of worldliness to exist in our lives. If we have these secret things in our lives, they will one day rise up to cause shame in our lives and bring shame to the kingdom and the ministry.

Verses 6-7 continue by saying, *"And Solomon did evil in the sight of the LORD, and went not fully after the LORD, as did David his father. Then did Solomon build an high place for Chemosh, the abomination of Moab, in the hill that is before Jerusalem, and for Molech, the abomination of the children of Ammon."* These were the religions that sacrificed children. Verses 8-9 then state *"And likewise did he for all his strange wives, which burnt incese and sacrificed unto their gods. And the LORD was angry with Solomon, because his heart was turned from the LORD God of Israel, which had appeared unto him twice."*

God didn't want a mixed multitude among his people. The whole reason of not having a mixed multitude was the mixture it would bring among God's people, the body of Christ. Numbers 11:1-4 state, *"[1]And when the people complained, it displeased the LORD: and the LORD heard it; and his anger was kindled; and the fire of the LORD burnt among them, and consumed them that were in the uttermost parts of the camp. [2]And the people cried unto Moses; and when Moses prayed unto the LORD, the fire was quenched. [3]And he called the name of the place Taberah: because the fire of the LORD burnt among them. [4]And the mixed multitude that was among them fell a lusting."* In other words, it wasn't the children of Israel who went lusting, but the mixed multitude that traveled with them. When they came out of Egypt, there were many who came with them who were Egyptians. The word "mixed" in Hebrew means, "a collection, a rabble, a mongrel race." In other words, it's something that God doesn't want in our lives and that's mixture. Exodus 12:37-38 state, "*And the children of Israel journeyed from Rameses to Succoth, about six hundred thousand on foot that were men, beside children. And a mixed multitude went up also with them.*" God never wanted his people to have a mixed multitude. Hosea 7:8-10 even state, "*Ephraim, he hath mixed himself among the people; Ephraim is a cake not turned. Strangers have devoured his strength, and he knoweth it not: yea, gray hairs are here and there upon him, yet he knoweth not. And the pride of Israel testifieth to his face.*" Ephraim was unbalanced and that was an abomination to the Lord. You don't allow mixture in your life.

The two scriptures I want to look at are in Ezra 9 and Nehemiah 13. In Ezra 9, Ezra has come to the land with the king's commission along with the people of Israel, the priests and Levites and it says in verse 1 that they, "*have not separated themselves from the people of the lands, doing according to their abominations...*" When you don't separate yourselves from the people of the lands or the ungodly, you end up allowing them and their gods, idols and demons into your life. We see this principle in II Corinthian 6:14-18 which states, "*Be ye not unequally yoked together with unbelievers: for what fellowship hath righteousness with unrighteousness? And what communion hath light with darkness? And what concord hath Christ with Belial? Or what part hath he that believeth with an infidel? And what agreement hath the temple of God with idols? For ye are the temple of the living God.*" The answer to these questions is nothing. God's people have nothing in common with the people of the world. We are another species, another race of beings. We are in this world, but we are not of the world. Do not yoke yourselves with unbelievers, in businesses, in marriage and even in friendship. Somewhere along the line, that seed will bring you down and cause you to depart from the Lord.

Ezra 9:2 continues... "*for they have taken of their daughters for themselves, and for their sons; so that the holy seed have mingled themselves with the people of those lands.*" Verse 3 then states, "*And when I heard this thing, I rent my garment and my mantle, and plucked off the hair of my head of my beard, and sat down astonied.*" Ezra was upset. He was really moved by his sheep. Ezra then goes off to repent for his brethren. In Ezra 10, all of the people repent for what they did. They realized what they did wrong.

Nehemiah gives a similar story in Nehemiah 13:1-3 which states, "*[1]On that day they read in the book of Moses in the audience of the people; and therein was found written, that the Ammonite and the Moabite should not come into the congregation of God forever; [2]Because they met not the children of Israel with bread and water...[3]Now it came to pass, when they had heard the*

252

law, that they separated from Israel all the mixed multitude." The Ammonites and the Moabites were two of the most heinous nations in their practices in religion. The word of God is the only thing that can bring the separation that is needed.

Nehemiah 13:23 then picks up the story which states, *"In those days also saw I Jews that had married wives of Ashdod, of Ammon, and of Moab: ²⁴And their children spake half in the speech of Ashdod, and could not speak in the Jews' language, but according to the language of each people. ²⁵And I contended with them, and cursed them, and smoke certain of them, and plucked off their hair, and made them swear by God, saying, Ye shall not give your daughters unto their sons, nor take their daughters unto your sons, or for yourselves. ²⁶Did not Solomon king of Israel sin by these things? ²⁷Shall we then hearken unto you to do all this great evil, to transgress against our God in marrying strange wives?"*

Let me finish by saying this. Some other marriages that ended in failure because they were not of God were the marriages of Naomi's sons. When Naomi and her husband left Bethlehem-Judah and went into Moab, what happened? They took wives of Moab and the husbands ended up dying.

The whole principle for inter-marriage is this. It has nothing to do with color, race, ethnicity, but everything to do with not being a part of the things of God, the people of God or having the nature of God. What did Ruth say to Naomi in Ruth 1:16? *"Entreat me not to leave thee, or to return from following after thee: for whither thou goest I will go; and where thou lodgest, I will lodge: thy people shall be my people, and thy God my God."* Moreover Rahab said that she knows that the Lord is with you all. And they allowed Rahab to come in and join. People believed she ended up marrying one of the princes of Israel. But God allowed it to happen because these women embraced God. We know in scriptures that Moses married a black woman. If God got angry it was only because Moses' sister and brother argued with him about it. And whose side did God take? God took Moses' side. This showed that there was nothing wrong with an Israelite marrying a black woman.

Don't marry outside of the Kingdom of God. I am going to even take it a step further. If you are in the tribe of Judah, you don't want to marry someone who is not a worshipper. You don't want to marry someone who is not sold out to worship. It's just going to cause you trouble. The marriage may be blessed. God blesses a lot of stuff that He never said to do. All things are lawful but not all things are expedient. Be not unequally yoked with an unbeliever.

So when some racist says to you that you are not supposed to intermarry, you can now tell them what the scriptures say. God wasn't talking about races, but marrying outside the nation of Israel, outside of the house of God, outside of the people of God and not mingling the holy seed with an unholy seed. God help us to recognize that we have a holy seed. What did Gabriel say to Mary in Luke 1:35, "*...that holy thing which shall be born of thee shall be called the Son of God.*" In everyone of us that is saved, we are born of incorruptible seed by the Word of God, partaker of the divine nature, and in our spirit God has placed himself in us. He lives in your spirits and how dare we mix the precious seed of God with that which is in the world.

Judging After The Outward Appearance
Chapter 19

As we have been reading, we now know without any doubt that we are a new species in a new kingdom, and we all have the same color, the color of Glory. In this chapter, I want to look at the subject that God does not want us judging after the outward appearance. When you and I see somebody for the first time, we have been trained by our human Adamic nature to judge them after the outward appearance. All of us without realizing it immediately compartmentalize and judge them upon seeing them. Then when they speak, we look at the way they act, how they sound, judge their intellect, etc, and we judge people without realizing it unrighteously. Most people, even though this thought process exists, do not want to be overtly evil. Much of the problem that creates this thinking is a lack of knowledge. I have known many white people that never met a black person growing up until they went to college. For many blacks, the only white people they have ever seen are like policemen, judges, teachers, or people who they think despise them, creating the idea that everybody in authority is against them. I grew up in this environment and I grew up thinking this same way. I despised authority, whether it was good, bad, or indifferent. I really grew to despise the fallacies of my own race because I saw through what I thought to be very phony. You see, I spent most of my childhood as a white boy in an all black environment. When my family moved to an all white neighborhood, it was very hard for me. I did the very same things I accused other people for doing when I lived in an all black environment. I judged all the white people around me as phonies, hypocrites, and snobbish, when the truth was, there may have been some like that but most of them were not. The first time we meet someone, it is very important because many people say it leaves a lasting impression. I believe it leaves an indelible impression on you and you have to be careful not to peg somebody the wrong way. The point I believe the Lord wants to put upon our hearts in this chapter is that we recognize our Adamic nature thinks like this, so we must allow our minds to be renewed to where we don't see our brother or sister after the outward appearance, but we see them as God sees them.

Years ago a friend of mine introduced another brother to me and he said, "this is backsliding Joe". And God as my witness, every time I ran into that brother, what do you think was the first thought that went into my mind? It was "hey, there is backsliding Joe". "Backsliding Joe" sat under the Word for years, gave himself to the things of God, moved to Arkansas to be part of a sister church of ours and the day came where I had to participate in ordaining him into the ministry. But even as I am getting ready for the ordination, I'm thinking "backsliding Joe". So I went to him before the service and said I never understood the power of words until today. His life spoke louder than the words that defined him in my head all those years. He was and still is a tremendous brother who has certainly proved his worthiness and faithfulness to the Lord. Don't let anybody define you with their perceptions. Let your faith follow the end of your conversation. You be Jesus to everybody you come into contact with. When I think of Jesus, I think of just a cool person. I think of somebody you can sit down with and pour your heart out to. Some people you meet, you feel like you've known them for years and feel like you can tell them anything. This is who Jesus is. He is not arrogant. He doesn't put people off. So many ministries today are full of that unseemliness. We are to be like Jesus. I don't care if I become the most famous minister in the world, I will still be Brother Sam and my sheep will still have my cell phone number and be able to call me. What kind of an attitude are we putting off? What kind of atmosphere surrounds us when we interact with God's precious people? This is important to God. Let me tell you I learned years ago that God is a wonderful being that He loves to laugh, and is approachable. I also learned as a minister that if you can make people laugh, it breaks down the walls of their heart and makes them more open to receive an arrow of truth.

All of us judge people unjustly. I think all of us can agree to that, but many times we do it unconsciously. It is like now young men need to be trained how to look at a woman. From our early age, we can't seem to help ourselves. Our Adamic nature trains us to look at a woman unrighteously. We need to seriously train young men how to look at a woman because even in the church this is a problem. We judge people after the outward appearance. How many times in your life alone have you met people and upon meeting them, you judged them incorrectly? Never believe anything people say about someone. Always remember, what you hear coming from a person is that person's perception of that person and doesn't make it solid fact. Even if it comes from somebody you trust. I don't believe we should ever form an opinion based on what one person said. The Bible says *"He that answereth a matter before he heareth it, it is folly and shame unto him"* (Proverbs 18:13).

I pray God would stamp this truth upon our hearts about no longer judging according to the flesh. Do not lump all black people into one pot. Do not lump all white people, brown people, etc. into one pot. I have to confess growing up that I memorized thousands of Polish jokes and if I met somebody with a Polish sounding name, I immediately judged them and started with the jokes. God had to help me and now I can't remember any of them. I can't help but wonder how many people have misjudged me? I wonder how many people that I know think something about me that is not even true. We judge people according to what we see with our natural eye.

We are talking about this subject because I want all of us to stop judging others on the basis of their skin color. I want us to stop judging black people because they are black or white people because they are white, etc. What does Jesus have to say about this? In John 7:24 He says, "*Judge not according to the appearance, but judge righteous judgment.*" So this means that if we judge according to the appearance, we are making an unrighteous judgment. Listen to what the Amplified Version says in this verse because it is beautiful, "*Be honest in your judgment and do not decide at a glance, superficially, and by appearances, but judge fairly and righteously*". In Isaiah 11:1-5 it speaks prophetically of the Lord and it says, "*...and he shall not judge after the sight of his eyes, neither reprove after the hearing of his ears...*" This means that the seeing of his eyes and the hearing of his ears may tell him the wrong thing, that the only true witness about anybody is not in the mind or through the sense gates, but it is the witness of the Spirit. I John 5:10 says, "*He that believeth on the Son of God hath the witness in himself...*" I John 2:20 says, "*But ye have an unction from the Holy One, and ye know all things.*" The word unction here means an umpire. So the Spirit of God that lives within a believer will always witness and be an umpire for the believer as to what is right or wrong and always make a righteous judgment. The Holy Spirit will always tell the truth. He does it by either a lack of peace or by a release of peace. We really don't need to pray much for the will of God in a given situation because we should immediately know because of the witness of the Spirit of God in us. I John 2:27 puts it this way, "*But the anointing which ye have received of him abideth in you, and ye need not that any man teach you: but as the same anointing teacheth you of all things, and is truth, and is no lie, and even as it hath taught you, ye shall abide in him.*" The anointing of God or the Spirit of God that lives within a believer is able to teach them God's will by giving a witness of peace or lack of peace in every given situation. Proverbs 20:27 says "*The spirit of man is the candle of the LORD...*" The sons of God are supposed to be led by the Spirit. This witness is what we need to learn to listen to and judge by. We have to un-train ourselves to judge with our natural eyes. We don't judge with our soulish man or with the outward appearance, but with the witness of our spirit.

Paul in II Corinthians 5:12 says, "*For we commend not ourselves again unto you, but give you occasion to glory on our behalf, that ye may have somewhat to answer them which glory in appearance, and not in heart.*" Paul here is comparing himself with other apostles. This is very important, especially in the day in which we live because everybody around us seems to have a title. Everybody seems to have an armor bearer and an entourage and it wants to make you think they are doing some great things. I'll never forget what one of my mother's in the Lord shared with me one day. She was ministering at a large conference in Washington D.C. Some of the greatest ministers in the body of Christ were there. While, she was standing in the wings, ready to be introduced standing by her were three very powerful and well known ministers. Now, we can't judge people for what they do before a meeting and there is nothing wrong about talking about stuff, but I share this to make a point. My mother in the Lord said as she stood there while she was praying in the Holy Ghost and preparing to minister, all the other men could talk about was how much their suits cost. They are all getting ready to go out and minister to the people of God, and yet they are comparing who spent more on their Italian suits and Italian leather shoes.

I'll never forget another person who every body was telling me was such a great revelatory teacher and that I just had to meet him. So I went to the place where he was ministering. I was introduced to him. He seemed like a nice fellow. I was asked to sit on the front row. The worship began and he was standing right in front of me on stage and was facing me. Rather than worship for 45 minutes with everyone else, he sat down and talked out loud to another minister he knew. I was hearing everything he was saying as the rest of the people (myself included) were trying to worship. This went on for the entire 45 minutes of worship and even went through the offering and everything else. When another man finally introduced him, he finally stopped talking, got up, and began to minister. That man was no more in the Holy Ghost than a man on the moon. He hadn't worshipped, hadn't been in the presence of God and as I began to listen to his so called heavy revelation message, I realized it was sounding brass and a tinkling cymbal. People were impressed by a name and assumed that he was such. But upon further investigation, I found there was really nothing there. How much are we moved by somebody else's title and outward show? How much are we moved by a man of God that comes in with an entourage of people or when he stands before us, with his rings catching the light and dazzling our eyes because there are so many diamonds? How intimidated have we allowed ourselves to be by so called men and women of God? Everything in me screams to be careful and not judge them and believe me I am not judging them after the flesh because this is unrighteous. But a man that does not worship with the people before he stands and ministers is <u>not</u> Biblical! A man that does not engage the congregation and the common people is <u>not Biblical</u>! A man that avoids any contact with any common person is wrong.

So Paul in II Corinthians 5 is saying some people glory in their appearance. I was in a meeting one time when a man was introduced as "Reverend Doctor..." I thought wow! Isn't it enough to be "Reverend" or "Doctor", but "Reverend Doctor"? And when he got up to speak, he didn't seem much like a Reverend and he sure didn't heal anything in me. He was a big name with a fancy title, but had no substance of God flowing out of him. You see, in the end Jesus said, "*Ye shall know them by their fruits*" (Matthew 7:16) or as we would put it, "the proof is in the pudding". You can tell me all you want about somebody, but I won't think anything until I taste and see the fruit myself. Job puts it this way, "*Doth not the ear try words? and the mouth taste his meat?"* (Job 12:11). So many of us are so mind controlled in the charismatic movement that we walk into a meeting and think everything is wonderful because everyone else says everything is wonderful.

I will never forget the meeting where there was a famous minister. And I happened to be with some of my friends sitting about 3 rows back. Well, I had just heard this great joke earlier that day and it was very funny to me at the time. So I told this joke to my friends before the service began and several of them started to crack up laughing. And moments later I noticed many people around us that didn't hear the joke but yet they started laughing as well. Then, like a wave, all the right side of the church started laughing and it moved all the way through the congregation and up on the platform and everybody was laughing for no reason. I was even acknowledged from the platform for starting this laughing revival. In a meeting with the minister's the next day, I was pointed out and thanked profusely for being used of the Lord and the whole time I wanted to get up and say the truth. All I did was tell a natural joke and because we are so mind controlled, people assume because I was laughing, that I was "in the river or in the spirit". They supposedly started laughing in the Holy Ghost, but it wasn't the Holy Ghost. Now I am not against laughing and the moving of the Holy Ghost. Anybody who knows me knows this isn't true in the slightest. I share this story to make a point that in our charismatic world, we have been trained to laugh, to fall down, and do things on queue.

II Corinthians 10:7 says, *"Do ye look on things after the outward appearance? If any man trust to himself that he is Christ's, let him of himself think this again, that, as he is Christ's, even so are we Christ's."* In other words, if someone thinks they are something in the Lord Jesus they need to think again, because so are their brothers and sisters. I don't care how great a person looks after the outward appearance; we are all just brothers and sisters in the Lord. Isn't it funny that we do things that are so opposite the Scriptures? We think men and women of God are supposed to dress up in ten thousand dollar suits, wear extravagant jewelry, and drive the fanciest cars, whereas in the New Testament we find John the Baptist being a health food nut while wearing only a loin cloth. Jesus had one nice robe probably and he didn't even have enough money to stay at an inn. He slept on the open ground many times. Jesus said Himself in Luke 12:15, *"Take heed, and beware of covetousness: for a man's life consisteth not in the abundance of the things which he possesseth."* A man's life consists of what he has done for the Lord and what kind of relationship he has with Him. Not the amount of jewelry he wears or how expensive his suits cost or if he's wearing American made or Italian made shoes.

Here are some Scriptures showing how we can be deceived by outward appearance. Proverbs 27:6 says, *"Faithful are the wounds of a friend; but the kisses of an enemy are deceitful."* Is every kiss a true kiss? How about Judas giving the Lord a kiss and Jesus response to him, *"Judas, betrayest thou the Son of man with a kiss?"* (Luke 22:48). In another place in II Samuel 20:9-10 Joab kills a man by the name of Amasa while kissing him. Beware of kisses because there may be a blade plunging into your stomach as you're being kissed. Outward expressions of love are most deceiving many times. I knew of a couple in my church years ago that showed a lot of public affection. So much so, that in a meeting they would be kissing each other (while I was ministering). It bothered me that they were doing that during the word, but what was worse was I knew, as their pastor, the real problems they were having in their relationship and family. I am not impressed by outward shows of affection between husbands and wives. Anybody can kiss their wife in public and abuse her secretly at home. So beware of what you see. The truth is many times the exact opposite of what you see is happening. Beware of flattery. Beware of the "Hosanna, Hosanna one day and Crucify Him, Crucify Him the next day" syndrome.

In Judges 3:16-25 Ehud comes to kill Eglon, king of Moab and in order to get to him tells him he has a secret message from God for him. So the king of Moab sends out all the people from the room so it is just Ehud and Eglon and Ehud comes close to Eglon and thrusts a dagger into his belly. This tells us that sometimes people come and say they have a message from God for us, but have ulterior motives. Do we think that everything that everybody who says they are from God is actually sent from God? Just because somebody comes to you with a prophetic word saying it is from God doesn't necessarily make it from God? It may be some trick of the enemy, especially in these charismatic days when it seems everybody has the word of the Lord. I don't despise prophecy, but if I look back on my life and if I believed every word of prophesy somebody came to me with saying it was the word of the Lord, I would be very confused. If I got all the money that was prophesied over me over 40 years, I would be a multi-billionaire! People prophesied to me that I would die at age thirty. The list of "so called" prophesies over my life is endless. Especially as a pastor for over 30 years, I have seen much pain brought into so many people's lives from being told false words. The lesson is everybody that claims to have a message from God isn't really from God.

Let's bring it back now. We are talking about looking at another person who is of another race. All we can go on is what we have been taught. The computer inside of us only prints out what it has been taught and knows or experienced. So if you are going to be a person who really wants to be used of God, first, you have to really love God's people. In spite of all of their stuff, you have to see the men as trees walking. You have to truly love all of God's people and you have to be able to see them as God sees them. As a minister, I have learned years ago to not put too much expectation on people because I would always end up disappointed. I would rather be expecting nothing and surprised and blessed when somebody does something.

How many people judge others when they get on an elevator with a person of another color? When are we, as the body of Christ, going to look at one another purely? This whole book has been about how as Christians we are to forget our own people, forget our own culture because we are a new species now. We are a new creation in Christ Jesus and we have our own kingdom and set of laws and guidelines, and most importantly, we have our own color now! And it has nothing to do with the world at all or the outward appearance. As long as we live in the realm of the soul, we will never be able to judge a righteous judgment. Until we can learn to live in the Spirit, we will be like the rest of the world judging after the outward appearance. I am not talking about being spooky people. For instance, a lady in my church came to me after I was away visiting another church and ministering elsewhere and she told me she was leaving the church. I asked her why and she told me I have no discernment whatsoever. So I asked her what was wrong. She complained about the person I allowed to minister while I was away. She said he was full of demons and not of God. So I asked her what was demonic about him? What did he say that was demonic when he ministered? She said it wasn't really what he said, but who he was. And I said what did he do that makes you feel this way? So she finally confessed and said she didn't like his black beard. She said his big black beard was demonic. Now this was a woman I had known for 20 years, and a woman that sat under the Word of God. Well, she ended up leaving the church because the man had a dark black beard and I had to rebuke her. Her pride wouldn't let her deal with it. Can you imagine such nonsense? Now I confess to you reader that I have had issues with anyone having a goat-tee and when I saw someone with a goat-tee, I would tell myself to be careful and not judge them. I had to put down the thoughts that came.

Appearances can be very deceiving. We can think somebody is very wonderful because they are beautiful. Jesus said this about the Pharisees in Matthew 23:24-28, *"24Ye blind guides, which strain at a gnat, and swallow a camel. 25Woe unto you, scribes and Pharisees, hypocrites! for ye make clean the outside of the cup and of the platter, but within they are full of extortion and excess. 26Thou blind Pharisee, cleanse first that which is within the cup and platter, that the outside of them may be clean also. 27Woe unto you, scribes and Pharisees, hypocrites! for ye are like unto whited sepulchres, which indeed appear beautiful outward, but are within full of dead men's bones, and of all uncleanness. 28Even so ye also outwardly appear righteous unto men, but within ye are full of hypocrisy and iniquity."* You and I can't judge by the outward appearance! It could be a wolf in sheep's clothing. In the charismatic realm, why are we so moved by bigness? Why are we so impressed by numbers, great choirs, and the finest luxuries? What is it about us that religious ornaments or creature comforts mean so much to us? Now if the substance in the place matches the beauty of the ornaments, than great! But if all you are doing as a Christian is sitting in a gorgeous building on a plush seat paid for by the blood of the saints while some man parades around like Nebuchadnezzar saying "what a great kingdom I have built", and there is nothing but dead men's bones everywhere (i.e. there is no life, no real discipleship, no glory, and no relationships), than you need to leave because it is simply not of God.

In I Samuel 16 is the story when Samuel has been told by God to stop mourning for Saul because God has rejected him from reigning over Israel and go and fill your horn with oil, and go to Jesse's house, *"for I have provided me a king among his sons."* Now Samuel was not just any prophet. He was a prophet whose words never fell to the ground. In other words, Samuel never prophesied a bad prophecy. But even Samuel, the great prophet, judged after the outward appearance as we will see.

Years ago, I remember sitting in the head elder's office of the church that I was on staff and we were in between pastors. They had just fired the former pastor. I remember one of the elders saying, "You just wait and see the new pastor that we contacted and has agreed to come". I asked him what he meant and these were his exact words, "He looks just like Hollywood!" My heart sank as I thought what does this have to do with Jesus? Have we fallen into a trap of appearance over substance or beauty over character? It is like somebody who gets up with a great singing voice but has no anointing or character or heart of worship. I have found that most people cannot tell the difference between anointing and talent. They will stand up and act like God is moving in a place, when they are just relishing in talent. It is amazing to me. I was around in the early 1970's when it used to be one lowly person standing in a church with one little guitar leading the people in worship as the glory descended. People didn't even have to look at a transparency because everybody knew the songs and had memorized the Scriptures we were singing. Everybody was not even conscious of the person playing, but was only conscious of Jesus and His wonderful presence and glory. Now we have to look at a screen because now we not only get words on a screen, but we get pictures behind the words of scenes of nature. Now it seems the new thing are props on stage as somebody ministers illustrated sermons. Well, they can try hard, but they can never produce the anointing or glory themselves. It may look good and seem good, but if God's glory and anointing are not present, it is nothing.

So Samuel goes to Jesse's house in I Samuel 16 and he tells Jesse he needs to see his sons and the sons are brought before him in verse 6, *"And it came to pass, when they were come, that he looked on Eliab, and said, Surely the LORD's anointed is before him..."* How many times has this been said about people who had no anointing? In many denominations when they are choosing a new pastor, they will allow a few men to "try-out" during their services and allow the people to pick who they like. The people end up voting on who their pastor will be. It has nothing to do whether the Holy Ghost wanted them to be there, but the people vote on them. This is the Laodicean church expressed in Revelation 3:14-22. Laodicean in the Greek means "opinion of the people, or majority rules". The church is not a democracy. It is a theocracy. This is akin to the disciples casting lots when they were deciding who should replace Judas as the twelfth apostle. But we do it in our modern church without any hesitation because that is the way we always have done it.

You see, even Samuel the great prophet judged after the outward appearance. We do not realize so much of what we do and how we think, especially when it comes to others, has been trained in us. For example, let us say your grandmother always said to you, "you know those black people are lazy, shiftless, and they never want to hold a job, and they will steal if you turn your eyes from them for a minute". In addition your mom and dad say similar things, maybe not as forceful, but they still push the point across too. What do you think your reaction will be when you meet or see a black person? You didn't ask for it, but it was dumped upon you and you were trained to judge black people as lazy, shiftless, and no good thieves. Worse than this is ministers for hundreds of years taught that black people were not human beings, that they didn't have a soul and that they are here to only serve white people. If you think I am lying, this is the true history of our country. Throughout the south, and even the north, this was taught. I even found a quote by Abraham Lincoln the other day that would blow your mind. What he said about black people in that quote is mind-boggling. He never started the civil war to free black people. It was over money. The south had money and the cotton. The North wanted all of that and so they used slavery as a quote. Now I love Abraham Lincoln. I am touched every time I stand in Washington D.C. at the Lincoln Memorial. But the truth is he did not free the slaves because he loved the slaves. He actually said in this quote that he thought that blacks were inferior to whites. And yet he wrote the Emancipation Proclamation. Well I guess the lesson is God will use anybody.

So in this story in I Samuel 16, even Samuel was judging after the outward appearance, "*7But the LORD said unto Samuel, Look not on his countenance, or on the height of his stature; because I have refused him: for the LORD seeth not as man seeth; for man looketh on the outward appearance, but the LORD looketh on the heart...*" Samuel ends up passing by all of Jesse's sons and not one of them were chosen even though they all looked the part and Samuel says to Jesse, "*Are here all thy children? And he said, There remaineth yet the youngest, and, behold, he keepeth the sheep. And Samuel said unto Jesse, Send and fetch him: for we will not sit down till he come hither...*" And when David

263

walks into the room where Samuel was at the witness of God spoke to Samuel and said, *"Arise, anoint him: for this is he."* The one nobody wanted and the one nobody expected anything from, was God's choice! This is our hope! Most of us are not going to be paraded around. Most of us are not invited to the big party. But like David, we are lucky to be working the grounds as the party is taking place. But Jesus knows what you are doing in secret. He knows and sees the faithful ones all over the earth. The scripture declares "His eyes are on the faithful of the land."

The last example I want to discuss is found in Genesis 27 which is the story of Isaac's sons, Jacob and Esau. Esau is the eldest son and was a hairy man. Isaac his father is old and about to die and wants to give his blessing to his firstborn son Esau. So he tells Esau to kill venison, dress it the way he likes, make for him that special meal he always does, and after he eats, he will give Esau his firstborn blessing. Well Rachel, his mother, overhears it and tells Jacob, the younger son, to get her two goats from the farm. So she kills the two animals and makes the same savory meal that Esau was planning on doing and she takes the skin of the animals and puts them on Jacob's hands and neck because Esau was very hairy and tells Jacob to go in to get the blessing. She tells Jacob to tell Isaac that he is Esau. Jacob's name means "supplanter, deceiver". He couldn't help himself and he was only doing what his mother told him. Now look what happens. Isaac, being old, had poor vision. Jacob goes in to where Isaac was waiting pretending to be Esau. He came with the meal and the skins on his hands and neck. Listen to Isaac, the old man of God, and Jacob's dialogue in Genesis 27:18-23, *"[18]And he came unto his father, and said, My father: and he said, Here am I; who art thou, my son? [19]And Jacob said unto his father, I am Esau thy firstborn; I have done according as thou badest me: arise, I pray thee, sit and eat of my venison, that thy soul may bless me. [20]And Isaac said unto his son, How is it that thou hast found it so quickly, my son? And he said, Because the LORD thy God brought it to me. [21]And Isaac said unto Jacob, Come near, I pray thee, that I may feel thee, my son, whether thou be my very son Esau or not. [22]And Jacob went near unto Isaac his father; and he felt him, and said, The voice is Jacob's voice, but the hands are the hands of Esau. [23]And he discerned him not, because his hands were hairy, as his brother Esau's hands: so he blessed him."* Isaac went with what he felt and not by the voice. How many of us are like Isaac? We go by what we feel rather than by faith. You see even though Isaac tasted the savory meat, felt the hairy hands of Esau, you can still hear in Isaac's voice doubt because something deep within him was troubling him. It was the inner voice! Three times Isaac asks Jacob if he was really his son Esau. Isaac ended up believing Jacob and went by what he felt rather than what he knew was the voice.

In the book of John in the garden we find Mary Magdalene at the tomb and the body of Jesus was gone and the disciples were already gone and she sees a man standing there, "*[14]And when she had thus said, she turned herself back, and saw Jesus standing, and knew not that it was Jesus. [15]Jesus saith unto her, Woman, why weepest thou? whom seekest thou? She, supposing him to be the gardener, saith unto him, Sir, if thou have borne him hence, tell me where thou hast laid him, and I will take him away. [16]Jesus saith unto her, Mary. She turned herself, and saith unto him, Rabboni; which is to say, Master.*" Mary supposed Jesus was just a gardener. I wonder how many times the Lord has appeared to us in the form of a human being and we didn't even know it. But listen, she spoke to him again and, he then simply says "*Mary*". When Jesus said "*Mary*" her spirit reverberated and leaped and she knew immediately it was Jesus and she said "*Master*". You see, it was the voice she went by and not the sight of the eyes.

Now for the rest of our lives, I pray that God will give us the grace to no longer judge people by the color of their skin, but on the content of their character. Let us give every person a chance to prove themselves before we make judgments. We are told to not respect persons in judgment or give place to rich people. We are told not to make hasty judgments. But we are told to make righteous judgments! Listen, just read the Gospels and pay attention to what Jesus did because He only said and did that which pleased the Father. He also said if you see Me, you have seen the Father. So everything Jesus did, it was what the Father was doing. Jesus talked to harlots, women, Samaritans, and everything the law said He shouldn't have done, He did it with grace, with class, and with mercy. Jesus never intimidated anyone. He was never arrogant nor put anybody off. He never acted like He didn't have time for people and He never judged anybody after the outward appearance.

As I close, picture Jesus carrying His cross. He is marred beyond recognition. As Jesus was at the end of His strength, bearing His cross down the road, the Roman soldiers saw He had no more strength left and at the same moment a black man, a Cyrenian, appears. I wonder how Jesus felt at the moment, when He looked up and saw that precious black brother lift His cross and carry it for Him. How dare anyone say anything against black people! They have been involved in the workings of God with man from the beginning. If anything, white people are simply a footnote and black people are the main characters. If you can't live with this, than you need to ask yourself if you have hidden racism in your heart. Please confront it, confess it, and allow the grace of God to change your heart today!

A Prophetic Look At Black People
In The Last Days
Chapter 20

In this chapter, I want to look at several different instances in Scripture where black people are concerned. Specifically, I want to look at these stories in an allegorical way as they reveal important aspects and roles that black people will play in the last days. Though these were natural and true historical stories, they have tremendous ramifications as we enter into the last of the last days as the sons of God come forth and enter into their inheritance. Moreover, these stories will help us see and know that black people are necessary for Jesus to come back. These stories will also help us see the importance of black people and how they are going to be a partaker of bringing in the manifestation of the sons of God. In addition, we can learn from what these black men in Scripture did and apply it to our lives. It is funny that we never have a problem looking at people like David, Isaiah, Peter, Paul, etc, but when we start mentioning the great tales of a black person in Scripture, offense seems to come to some. But they shouldn't be offended because all of us are brothers in the Kingdom of God. I thank God for these men that we will see because what they did leave a legacy for you and me. These people we look at, we will look at them as types. And by doing this we can apply it to our lives both now and in the future.

First, the young Egyptian in I Samuel 30 helps us to obtain our inheritance in God that was stolen from us. II Samuel 6, which is the story of Obededom the Gittite, teaches us how to live in the manifest presence of God, how to guard it, and to give our lives for it. Thirdly, the black man in Jeremiah 38 shows us how that in the last days God is going deliver a true prophetic company and release them from the leadership in the body of Christ that has put them in a dungeon. Fourthly, by looking at Simon, we see how to bear the burden of the cross of Jesus in the last days. Last but not least in Uriah, we see what it means to be a man of integrity, a man of loyalty having a warrior spirit, and a faithful man. In this chapter, we will look at many instances of how God will use black people in the last days. These stories will emphasise prophetic truth to us, for though these were actual stories, we can receive divine insight that speaks to us in our own lives. Plus see as a picture of who God will use in the last days.

I would like to start with Uriah, which is found in II Samuel 11. This chapter begins with David staying at home when he should have been out to battle. He ends up on a rooftop (when he should have been fighting the enemy) and then he ends up committing adultery with Bathsheba, Uriah's wife. After he commits adultery he conspires to have Uriah come home and sleep with

Bathsheba to try to cover up his sin. After Uriah refuses to go in unto his wife, David conspires to have Uriah murdered. I'm sure David would have never dreamed he would ever do this. The principle is when we get deceived, it is a progression. David on the rooftop never started out thinking he wanted to kill Uriah. But the longer we stay in our deception, the worse it gets and you can convince yourself you are okay doing what you are doing until at some point (and there always comes some point) your sin is exposed and the truth has to be dealt with. Would to God we would listen to the witness of the Spirit or look at the instruction of the Word of God or listen to the instruction of a leader. But if we refuse those, God leaves us to ourselves and our circumstances and if that doesn't work, God turns us over to Satan for the destruction of the flesh that the spirit may be saved. Nobody is ever exposed publicly who didn't have years to repent. Now get this picture. David is a wonderful type of Jesus in the Old Testament. He was a prophet, priest, and king. And yet David here commits a horrible sin, but the beautiful thing about this chapter is this story of Uriah the Hittite.

First of all, Uriah's name means "Jehovah is light, Lord of light, light of Jehovah". Uriah was walking in the light and exhibiting the light of God. He was a descendent of Ham. One of Ham's sons was Canaan and out of Canaan came the tribe of the Hittites. Ham was the father of all black races so many of the Canaanite tribes were black people. So it is important we get this in our spirit as we consider this man Uriah. Since the Hittites were part of the black families that came out of Ham, I believe Uriah was a black man. By the way in II Samuel 23, we also see that Uriah was one of David's mighty men. Uriah was not just any soldier in David's army; he was one of the mighty men. Black men have been part of the mighty men of God throughout history and we need to learn from their example and rejoice.

So David gets Bathsheba pregnant and she sends word to David asking what they should do. And so then David begins to move in a very strange and ungodly fashion. He calls Uriah home from the war as we read starting in verse 6, *"And David sent to Joab, saying, Send me Uriah the Hittite. And Joab sent Uriah to David..."* David here is also a type of leadership in the body of Christ who many times isn't doing what God wants them to do. Before we throw stones at David, we remember all of us have been outside the will of God at some point in our life and have done things that we are very regretful of. Yet God has glorious people who are full of integrity. There will be examples. We want to let them provoke us to love and to good works. We want to learn from their examples and be like them. Let us learn from Uriah as we continue the story.

David brings Uriah home from the war. Now David's soldiers loved David and esteemed him. But in the body of Christ right now there are men in leadership who like David aren't battling the enemy. Rather they are staying home, building kingdoms for themselves and have hidden sin in their life. So here comes Uriah who was sent for by David. *"[7]And when Uriah was come unto him, David demanded of him how Joab did, and how the people did, and how the war prospered. [8]And David said to Uriah, Go down to thy house, and wash thy feet. And Uriah departed out of the king's house, and there followed him a mess of meat from the king..."* David was doing everything he could to encourage Uriah to go home and have a connection with Bathsheba. Now who wouldn't be honored by all that David did for Uriah? Consider if you were in Uriah's shoes. You are out to war and all of the sudden the king calls for you personally. You are the one he asks to report to him what is happening. All of this is heady stuff. The lesson is, we can't let this kind of flattery move us. Leaders in the body of Christ will do things like this to make us feel good, give you positions, etc. But they have an ulterior motive that will ultimately kill you! Beware if someone flatters you with words, money, power, influence, and things that try to distract you from doing the will of God. Always follow the witness of the Spirit. Not everybody that hands you money is handing you a blessing from God. We need to ask ourselves if the gifts we receive have strings attached to them. Many times in my life I have put a check in my pocket without really watching the witness of the Spirit, and that ended up being a very destructive thing in my life. Not every gift comes from the Lord. James 1:17 says every <u>perfect</u> gift is from above. Are you impressed with flattery from leadership? Are you looking to be seen of men? From Uriah's point of view, meeting the king could have been a great opportunity for him. As you look in II Samuel 23, Uriah was part of David's mighty men, but he wasn't part of the elite three or even the top second three. Uriah at this point could have been thinking this was his opportunity to get promoted by David. But it was not what David wanted. Our hearts need to be in tune with only what God the Father wants.

So David sends a mess of meat to Uriah's house, *"[9]But Uriah slept at the door of the king's house with all the servants of his lord, and went not down to his house..."* What a slap in the face to David. Not only had David not gone out to war, he had committed adultery, and was living in his own luxurious palace. While David is sleeping in his finery, Uriah sleeps on the floor next to David's servants when he could have gone home and slept in his own bed with his wife. We are talking here about a man with real integrity! We are talking about a man who knew what it meant to be a part of an army of people. He knew that if you are a soldier, you are a soldier all the time (not just part of the time)! And when it is a time when kings should be out to battle, you don't go home to the comforts of your wife and home. It wasn't time for that. When Uriah's fellow soldiers were out there fighting (many perhaps dying) and sleeping on the hard ground, eating nothing, he did not think of receiving the king's mess of meat and being with his wife. A loyal and faithful man like

Uriah didn't even consider doing these things when there was war. He was a man of integrity! You see, David was a man after God's own heart but like all of us, he slipped. Let the life of Uriah provoke you and I today. Let the testimony of this precious black man provoke us. I don't care what everyone else is doing in the body of Christ. All I know is what God has called me to do and I am going to do it. It is a time to be fighting the good fight of faith in the body of Christ. It is not a time to be taking it easy. Lives are at stake all over the world.

"¹⁰And when they had told David, saying, Uriah went not down unto his house, David said unto Uriah, Camest thou not from thy journey? Why then didst thou not go down unto thine house? ¹¹And Uriah said unto David, The ark, and Israel, and Judah, abide in tents; and my lord Joab, and the servants of my lord, are encamped in the open fields; shall I then go into mine house, to eat and to drink, and to lie with my wife? as thou livest, and as thy soul liveth, I will not do this thing." The ark represents the manifest presence of God. This is the glory. You see, when you are not out there battling the enemy and have drawn back to perdition, you forget the glory. I wonder what was going through David's heart as Uriah was saying this. David was one of the most faithful people in the Bible. But he had allowed himself to be deceived. In the last days Paul says *"...perilous times shall come. For men shall be lovers of their own selves...lovers of pleasure more than lovers of God..."* (II Timothy 3:1-4). Don't be deceived, there is leadership that is more interested in what is happening with them than the Kingdom of God. But Uriah didn't think of himself at this moment. His heart was devoted to the ark, God's people, and God's Kingdom rather than escape for moments of pleasure with his wife. We looked at a whole chapter about forgetting your own family. Jesus said if you love your family more than me, you are not worthy of me (Matthew 10:37). In Mark 3:33-35, Jesus said *"Who is my mother, or my brethren? ³⁴And he looked round about on them which sat about him, and said, Behold my mother and my brethren! ³⁵For whosoever shall do the will of God, the same is my brother, and my sister, and mother."* Our spouses need to find their place in the plan of God for our lives. When kings are going out to battle, it is not a time to be having fun. It is time to be concerned with the Kingdom of God.

So David discovered Uriah wouldn't give in, *"¹²And David said to Uriah, Tarry here to day also, and to morrow I will let thee depart. So Uriah abode in Jerusalem that day, and the morrow. ¹³And when David had called him, he did eat and drink before him; and he made him drunk: and at even he went out to lie on his bed with the servants of his lord, but went not down to his house."* David even made Uriah drunk, but Uriah still didn't give in. David was trying to cover his sin by making Uriah drunk, but it still didn't work. The lengths people go to hide their deception and sin is unbelievable. David was hoping by making Uriah drunk, that would cause Uriah not to be faithful. In these last days, beware of leadership that isn't doing the will of God. If they are not out there fighting the battle of the Lord, what are they really doing? If they are building a kingdom for themselves, you need to leave that place because there is sin in that camp. I don't care how great the choir sounds and how many thousands of people they may have. If the glory, the manifest presence of God, is not there, then flee!

"14And it came to pass in the morning, that David wrote a letter to Joab, and sent it by the hand of Uriah. 15And he wrote in the letter, saying, Set ye Uriah in the forefront of the hottest battle, and retire ye from him, that he may be smitten, and die..." Now David, six months before this would have never dreamed of doing this. This is the progression of sin. It is amazing as well as frightening. It should make us all fear God. If a man like David, a man after God's own heart, can fall like this, we need to take heed because so can we. He is the greatest military leader the world has ever known. But this is the amazing thing. Uriah carries in his hand the letter that has his own death sentence. If you were Uriah, would you have been tempted to peak at the letter? But Uriah was faithful and David knew this. Joab obeys David and Uriah dies. If there is anyone that I want to meet when I get to glory, Uriah is one of them. Proverbs 20:6 says *"a faithful man who can find?"* Well, we find one here by the name of Uriah, a black man. In these last days, we need more than ever, faithful men and women of God who are full of integrity and are willing to die for what they believe in. We need men and women of God like Uriah who are willing to sacrifice to do the will of God and put the Kingdom of God and the glory of God above their own life and desires. Also, these are perilous days we live in, but we have an example of how to live. When everybody else is backsliding and giving in to their baser inclinations, you and I can draw strength from Uriah and say I would rather be loyal, faithful, and a man of integrity than to have all the pleasure and provision in the world.

Next, let us look at a story in Luke 23. If there was ever a time we need some teaching on the cross, it is now because in the midst of all of the cacophony of voices that we listen to on Christian TV that we are supposed to be rich and blessed, there is not a lot said about the dealings of God or bearing the cross of Christ. People have not been prepared to deal with tribulation, suffering, and affliction. We have spent the last 25 years being told that we can be rich, increased with goods, and have need of nothing. We are truly a picture of the Laodicean church in Revelation 3. And now, we are going to see what we have produced in the body of Christ, much of it being shallow, substance-less believers who are going to start crying and backsliding and a great falling away will happen because the men of God over them did not prepare them with the truth. They might have gotten rich off the offerings that came in, but they never taught the people how to go through afflictions and the dealings of God. But here in this story in Luke 23, Pilate gave sentence and he delivered Jesus to be crucified and as they led Jesus away we read in verse 26, *"And as they led him away, they laid hold upon one Simon, a Cyrenian, coming out of the country, and on him they laid the cross, that he might bear it after Jesus."* Let me also read the account in Mark 15:21, *"And they compel one Simon a Cyrenian, who passed by, coming out of the country, the father of Alexander and Rufus, to bear his cross."* Now Rufus is found in Romans 16:13 and he is honored there by the Apostle Paul. So whoever this Simon was, who was just passing through, had an encounter with God by carrying the cross. So much so, that Simon's children got saved!

Consider now this man, Simon the Cyrenian. Cyrene was a city in Libya, from the descendants of Ham. There is no question that this Simon was a black man. Isn't it interesting that of all the people that God would choose to help carry the cross was a black man. What did the segregating white preachers do with this when they taught that black people didn't have a soul? Well, they lied like all the other commentators did. We can't believe all of history because it was written by white men and a lot of history was told according to what they wanted it to be like and not the way it was. If this offends you, I am sorry, but we need to not be naive but desire to know the truth. We need to change this in the body of Christ. For hundreds of years black people were looked down upon and demoralized because of the color of their skin. We need to change this. Jesus purposely had this man selected because on His journey to the cross, the only man that stood with him was a black man! Where was Peter, James, John, and the rest of the disciples? They were not there, but a black man is found faithful, just one who was passing through. Look who is killing Jesus here of the three races. The line of Shem, the Israelites, said, *"His blood be upon us, and on our children"* (Matthew 27:25). The line of Japheth, the white Roman soldiers, performed the crucifixion. So you tell me what race is blessed? A descendent of Ham carried the cross of Jesus. Can you imagine Jesus, tired and beaten, His body marred beyond recognition, and exhausted? All of His disciples had left Him and forsaken Him. Only the women and a black man stood with Jesus! The two most oppressed peoples in the earth were there when he was crucified. So many do not allow women to minister just as they have kept black people back for so long without giving them credence or honor.

So Jesus had fallen with the cross heavy on his back and the Roman soldiers knew Jesus couldn't carry it anymore because they had beaten Him too badly. So they grabbed this black man and compelled him to pick up the cross. Jesus lifted up His face with His hair matted upon him and through the haze, He saw a precious black man help Him who carried it to His final destination. In the last days a company of black men and women are going to show us the way to the cross. They are going to show us how to carry the cross and how to bear the burden of hard times. Many white people do not know what it is like to go without. Many have not missed a meal. My family was on welfare as a child

271

and I was embarrassed to walk with my mother to the place where we picked up our government cheese and powdered milk. All night long I would hear my father curse and put down black people saying they were shiftless, lazy, and all they wanted to do is be on welfare. But when I went to school, I found that most of my black friends were not on welfare, but as we were. This is the height of ignorance.

But the encounter with Jesus so moved Simon, that he obviously got saved on the hill of Golgotha and his son Rufus was pointed out by the Apostle Paul in Romans 16:13, "*Salute Rufus chosen in the Lord, and his mother and mine.*" Also, Simon's wife is mentioned here and Paul even calls her his mother too! I can tell you that there are many precious women of God in my life that have been more of a mother to me than my own natural mother. I know what Paul means here. We are going to need some examples, so God is raising up mighty black men and women to show us how to handle adversity. They have shown us in history as they were slaves in the hot sun, bent over and picking cotton with the weight of sorrow, oppression, and horror upon them, how a song would be birthed in them and they would sing and others would sing. They taught us that somehow in the midst of their horror, they lifted their spirits by the presence of God! Swing low sweet chariot! In the greatest affliction come the greatest songs of deliverance and who can sing those songs better than precious black people. Glory to God!

Moreover, "*Salute Rufus chosen in the Lord, and his mother and mine.*" For Paul to salute Rufus tells us he must have been important. All the commentators agree on this because Paul singled him out. Let me give you some other translations of this phrase, "*chosen in the Lord*" because it brings out more the kind of person Rufus was: "*who is one of the Lord's chosen people*", "*Rufus, eminent in the Lord*", "*Greet Rufus whom the Lord picked out to be His very own*", "*Say hello to Rufus, a good choice by the Master*", "*that outstanding Christian*", "*Give my love to Rufus, one of the Lord's selection*", "*that outstanding worker in the Lord's service*", "*Rufus, the elect in the Lord*", "*He is such a special person in the Lord and to his mother whose been like a mother to me.*" When Simon carried the cross, he obviously got saved and more than likely went home and told his wife and she got saved. Then their two sons came into the Lord, one of them being Rufus. Simon's wife, who was Rufus' mother, Paul says she is not only his mother, but mine as well. Paul is identifying himself with this black woman to say she is almost like his real mother. This is such a small verse of Scripture, but who has even seen before that Paul actually loved an old black woman and treated her like a mama. Glory to God!

The next account I would like us to consider is found in Jeremiah 38. The story is that God is wants Israel to simply go and be taken captive by

Nebuchadnezzar and has prophesied this through Jeremiah. God was telling Israel through the mouth of Jeremiah, don't fight them, just go. He said they will be in captivity for 70 years and it was His will for this to happen to them. Can you imagine a prophetic word like that? None of the leaders wanted to hear this, so they put Jeremiah in jail. Now watch this because this is absolutely tremendous. Zedekiah was the king (and a coward) and told the princes of the land to do with Jeremiah however they saw fit. So in Jeremiah 38:6, *"Then took they Jeremiah, and cast him into the dungeon of Malchiah the son of Hammelech, that was in the court of the prison: and they let down Jeremiah with cords. And in the dungeon there was no water, but mire: so Jeremiah sunk in the mire..."* Think of this. In Ezekiel 47, it says the only place the glory will not go is in the miry places. They tried to cut the prophet of God off from the glory. They will love you when you are prophesying smooth things, but when you tell them the truth, they will put you in a dungeon and it takes a black man (as we see in verse 7) to bring Jeremiah out of the dungeon and into the light. In the last days, a great company of prophets will be told to shut up and placed in a dungeon so their voices can't be heard because some don't agree with what they are saying. Many in leadership don't believe God would ever tell us to go into captivity or put us through hard places and they also mock people who teach on the dealings of God. They will point out that Jeremiah only has a loin cloth on but they have their rich attire. They then try to convince the people, who God really is blessing. But it will be a lie because they don't know the Word of God. Many try to teach that Jesus was rich and had the best robes, but it is simply not true. Oh how we must search the Scriptures!

Let us read now how Jeremiah gets out of the dungeon. *"⁷Now when Ebed-melech the Ethiopian, one of the eunuchs which was in the king's house, heard that they had put Jeremiah in the dungeon; the king then sitting in the gate of Benjamin; ⁸Ebed-melech went forth out of the king's house, and spake to the king, saying, ⁹My lord the king, these men have done evil in all that they have done to Jeremiah the prophet, whom they have cast into the dungeon; and he is like to die for hunger in the place where he is: for there is no more bread in the city. ¹⁰Then the king commanded Ebed-melech the Ethiopian, saying, Take from hence thirty men with thee, and take up Jeremiah the prophet out of the dungeon, before he die. ¹¹So Ebed-melech took the men with him, and went into the house of the king under the treasury, and took thence old cast clouts and old rotten rags, and let them down by cords into the dungeon to Jeremiah. ¹²And Ebed-melech the Ethiopian said unto Jeremiah, Put now these old cast clouts and rotten rags under thine armholes under the cords. And Jeremiah did so. ¹³So they drew up Jeremiah with cords, and took him up out of the dungeon: and Jeremiah remained in the court of the prison."* I tell you, what many consider are just old rotten rags, are our deliverance so many times. What other people think are old rags, really they are God's deliverance for us. This precious black man delivered Jeremiah the prophet.

Ebedmelech's name means "servant of the king". Ethiopia translated means "blackness". Notice in this story it keeps saying "Ebedmelech the Ethiopian", just like it said in Luke 23 "Simon the Cyrenian" or in II Samuel 11 "Uriah the Hittite". God leaves this in His Word on purpose because He wants us to know that these precious men were black! Ebedmelech was a black man and was one of the eunuchs which were in the king's house. Jesus says in Matthew 19:12, *"For there are some eunuchs, which were so born from their mother's womb: and there are some eunuchs, which were made eunuchs of men: and there be eunuchs, which have made themselves eunuchs for the kingdom of heaven's sake. He that is able to receive it let him receive it."* A eunuch is somebody who has given up the pleasures of this life to serve God completely. So this black brother was a eunuch, serving in the house of God. But the leadership did not step in and do what was right. This dear black brother goes to the king when he heard what they did to Jeremiah and stood for the truth and delivered Jeremiah out of the pit. It just maybe, dear reader that some black people is going to be the ones who are going to bring your deliverance to you. You may hate a black person, but if you are dying and you need a liver transplant and the only one available is in the body of a black person, what are you going to do? My advice is please take the liver. Trust me, the color of someone's skin won't matter then.

But look what happens in verse 15 of chapter 39 after Jeremiah gets his deliverance, *"¹⁵Now the word of the LORD came unto Jeremiah, while he was shut up in the court of the prison, saying, ¹⁶Go and speak to Ebed-melech the Ethiopian, saying, Thus saith the LORD of hosts, the God of Israel; Behold, I will bring my words upon this city for evil, and not for good; and they shall be accomplished in that day before thee. ¹⁷But I will deliver thee in that day, saith the LORD: and thou shalt not be given into the hand of the men of whom thou art afraid..."* Hear this black people! God will deliver you and you will not be given into the hands of men anymore, *"¹⁸For I will surely deliver thee, and thou shalt not fall by the sword, but thy life shall be for a prey unto thee: because thou hast put thy trust in me, saith the LORD."* All Israel was going into Babylon but Ebedmelech received a promise from God he will be delivered!

The sad thing is so many leaders today do not interact with their sheep. And those of you who desire to be in the ministry must know that you are going to have to love people to be in the ministry. If you don't love all people, you can't be a true minister of Jesus Christ. You are not going to be preaching at them, you are going to be preaching to them. You are going to have to embrace them and not just shake their hand on a Sunday morning, but embrace them into your heart, lives, and into your home. They have to know that you are their father and they are a part of your family. The days of not being able to get a hold of your pastor or shepherd are over with. The days of the emphasis on big churches are coming to an end because God is a Father Himself and He believes in His people being a family. Everything in the Kingdom is about family and being connected via fathers, mothers, sons, daughters, brothers, and sisters. This is the day we are moving into. How many prophets are in a dungeon right now where the glory can't reach them because the leadership over them have put them there and will not allow them to speak? How many leaders have betrayed us and sent us to our own death like David did to Uriah? And how can anybody not love the only race of people who stood with Jesus at the cross? God is emphasizing this precious revelation of His precious black people because He wants us to open our eyes and let the racial scales fall from all of our eyes. There are just as many white and Semitic men of God in Scriptures. Don't worry, it all evens itself out. We are all God's people. The pendulum is just swinging to get this truth into all of our hearts.

The next passage I would to look at in relation to important black people used by God with prophetic implications of the last days are found in Matthew 2, right after the birth of Jesus. We begin in verse 12 and read through verse 15, "*And being warned of God in a dream that they should not return to Herod, they departed into their own country another way. [13]And when they were departed, behold, the angel of the Lord appeareth to Joseph in a dream, saying, Arise, and take the young child and his mother, and flee into Egypt, and be thou there until I bring thee word: for Herod will seek the young child to destroy him. [14]When he arose, he took the young child and his mother by night, and departed into Egypt: [15]And was there until the death of Herod: that it might be fulfilled which was spoken of the Lord by the prophet, saying, Out of Egypt have I called my son.*" A couple of things to note before I get into this story: The meaning of Egypt is "black". Egypt's descendents came from Ham. Ham's sons founded Egypt. Herod here is a type of Satan and Mary and Joseph would represent to us a type of the church or the five-fold ministry. As I was studying this passage, what was really quickened to me was this: Out of Egypt (out of blackness), has God called His son. Jesus here would then represent to us the manchild. The manchild is the remnant or the overcomers in the last days. Where are the remnant and overcomers going to come from? They will come out of Egypt. So a great company of black overcomers is coming in the last days!

Let us look deeper into this passage. As we start in verse 13, we first realize them going to Egypt was very important because God sent a messenger. It wasn't just a little word. It was a command in a vision. They were told to flee to Egypt. They were told to flee where black people were. The church, especially the white church, needs to see the truth of black people in Scripture. Let me swing this pendulum of truth once more. I don't hate white people or anything crazy like that. I am just trying to bring balance so that we can move on from here not worrying about color or culture or anything like that. My point is that to get to this place in the body of Christ, we have to begin by giving honor where honor is due and we must first point out that there is without question been a total disregard for the truth in history and even in Christian history and doctrine concerning black people. For example, commentators seem to stretch the fact that these black people in the Old and New Testament were not really black people. We need to have a love for the truth and have an answer to deal with racism because in the church there is subtle racism in the hearts of men and women.

So God sends Jesus to be protected by black people. Hallelujah! I tell you I've been saved for 40 years and have extensively studied the Bible over and over again and I never seen this before, but it is revolutionary. God the Father wanted His Son safe and the safest place to Him was with black people. So hidden in the house of the Lord, hidden in the black church, lives the Lord Jesus. The precious thing about black people in many of these stories is they never seem to have a problem with receiving from others of another race. Consider the black eunuch in Acts receiving from Philip, or as we will see later in this chapter Pharaoh receiving Joseph, etc. In our history, especially in this country, this didn't seem to be true of white people receiving from black people. They didn't want to sit next to them in buses and things like that. Now I know we have come a long way, but this thinking still exists (no matter how small) hidden in many hearts and God wants to eradicate any traces of racism in all of our hearts. Even in writing this book I had to deal in my heart with the fact that Moses more than likely was a man of color. I don't know why, but I am trying to be transparent before you. Many of the readers of this book will find things disturbing or find things they don't understand, but rather than reject it, if they love the truth, they should bow to it. God is looking for people who will speak truth in their heart and not hide behind some racist thinking. Now, let me say that some Black Theologians are just as bad. As far as they are concerned, there is nobody in the Bible that is white and they can get very ridiculous in some of their claims. But who can blame them when they see so much evidence of their presence being denied. So I will cut them some slack there, but there is a militant black liberation theology that is not of God and is causing great problems in the black community and in the lives of Spirit-filled black people. There are many great black preachers and teachers bringing great truths. However, one of the black writers of one of these books said it is absolutely foolish for all of these young black men becoming Muslims because if they only knew their history they wouldn't leave Christianity. Moreover, it is a lie to tell these black men that Christianity is a white man's religion. Well we've been finding in this book that it is not a white man's religion at all.

What a beautiful illustration in Matthew 2 of black people receiving Jesus. As we continue considering this passage, Joseph was told to stay in Egypt until the Word comes. In a typical sense, consider Revelation 12. The first 5 verses describe a woman clothed with the sun and upon her head a crown of twelve stars. I have proven many times in other writings that this woman represents the church, and more specifically the 60-fold part of the body of Christ who birth the manchild or the overcomers. Jesus expressed in the parable of the sower His people bringing forth fruit, some 30-fold, 60-fold, and 100-fold. The manchild is the 100-fold believer. The woman is the 60-fold believer, and the rest of her seed spoken of in verse 17 is the 30-fold believer. The woman, the 60-fold believer, doesn't quite pay the entire price to pass through the veil into the most holy place, but the manchild does. This is why we see, as we keep reading in Revelation 12, that the manchild is caught up to God and to His throne and the woman is not. She is sent into the wilderness. But a manchild is birthed out of the woman. So back in Matthew 2, Mary and Joseph are likened unto the 60-fold church that is carrying with them the manchild of the last days, the Son revealed in the sons of God.

So there is a word coming very soon to the sons of God that is going to say like Isaiah 60:1, *"Arise, shine; for thy light is come, and the glory of the Lord is risen upon thee"*. When this word comes, deliverance is going to come. This says to me that God is going to send a word to the precious precious Black saints to arise and shine because the glory of God is rising upon them. I think it is safe to say that today God is moving more in Black churches than He is in white churches. Some of the greatest churches today are black churches where God is moving tremendously. So this tells me that hidden within the black part of the body of Christ is an overcomer waiting for the Word of the Lord while Herod (a type of Satan) wants to destroy them. He wants to destroy the overcomers just like we see in Revelation 12:4 where the dragon sought to devour her child as soon as it was born. Every time a manchild was born in Scripture, babies were killed. When Jesus was born, Herod killed all the children ages 2 and under. Before Moses came forth, what happened? All of the male children in Israel were killed. Even today, abortion is rampant. Moreover, how many young black men are in prison for the rest of their lives, locked up with the key thrown away? I don't have the percentage, but it is a great number. There is a great number of black men incarcerated for the rest of their lives. To me, this is just Herod trying to kill them. Herod, a type of Satan, wants to kill the manchild hidden in the black church, but he is not going to be able to do it. Bless the Lord!

So in the night (verse 14), Joseph took Mary and Jesus and fled to Egypt. What comes after night? Morning does and morning in the Scriptures always speaks of resurrection. So we may be in a night time season right now, but when that word comes to arise and shine, a people are going to come forth, especially out of black people. This will be fulfilled as verse 15 says which was spoken of the Lord by the prophet saying, *"Out of Egypt have I called my son"*. God wants His manifested sons of God to come out of the black race too!

This book was not just written to open white people's eyes, but more importantly, I wanted to bring the honor, the esteem, and the credence and self respect to every black person that loves Jesus. As Ephesians 1:18 says, my prayer is the eyes of black people's understanding may be enlightened, that they may know what is the hope of their calling, that *"out of Egypt have I called my son"*. The next time you or I find ourselves witnessing to a black person, let's quote this passage and explain how God wants them saved, brought out of bondage into His marvelous light, and bring them forth as true sons of God, full of His glory! It amazes me the sovereignty of God purposely putting this story in the Bible. He knows the end from the beginning and foresaw the racism that would come in the history books.

The next story I would like to look at is found in Acts 11:19-21. Prior to this story, God had to give Peter a vision for him to take the Gospel to the Gentiles. God had to deal with Peter about racism. But as we will see guess; who were some of the people that founded the church in Antioch? Black People! This is amazing to me! But let us read in Acts 11, starting in verse 18, *"When they heard these things, they held their peace, and glorified God, saying, then hath God also to the Gentiles granted repentance unto life. ^{19}Now they which were scattered abroad upon the persecution that arose about Stephen travelled as far as Phenice, and Cyprus, and Antioch, <u>preaching the word to none but unto the Jews only</u>..."* Now they just saw how God marvelously moved among the Gentiles, but they still only preached to the Jews. This is nothing but racism and elitism. What more evidence do we need? This is why I believe the Apostle Paul, next to Jesus, is the greatest figure in the Bible because that little man stood against the Apostles (the "pillars of the church") when it came to their racism. He had to even call Peter out in front of everybody because when Peter saw the Judaizers looking at him while he was eating with Gentiles, he quickly withdrew himself and stopped sitting with them. We can't be like Peter and have this racism in our hearts and we need to be strong like Paul to stand up against racism. In this story in Acts 11, why wouldn't they want the Gentiles to receive the Word of the Lord?

As we continue the story, *"^{20}And some of them were men of Cyprus and <u>Cyrene</u>, which, when they were come to Antioch, spake unto the Grecians, preaching the Lord Jesus..."* Cyrene again was a city that came out of Libya that was established by Phut, which was one of Ham's sons. Some of these brethren were black. Now consider this. In verse 19, some of the believers that were scattered only preached to the Jews, but isn't it interesting that evangelists in verse 20 (some of them being black) preached to the Greeks. They took the preaching of the Lord Jesus to the Greek people. So if anybody ever wants to think that black people cannot minister to white people, they need to read this story. Moreover, as we keep reading, "...*[21]And the hand of the Lord was with them: and a great number believed, and turned unto the Lord.*" The hand of the Lord being with somebody always means in Scripture the anointing, the power of God, or the ability to do the works of God. In verse 22 it continues, "*Then tidings of these things came unto the ears of the church which was in Jerusalem: and they sent forth Barnabas, that he should go as far as Antioch. [23]Who, when he came, and had seen the grace of God, was glad, and exhorted them all, that with purpose of heart they would cleave unto the Lord. [24]For he was a good man, and full of the Holy Ghost and of faith: and much people was added unto the Lord. [25]Then departed Barnabas to Tarsus, for to seek Saul: [26]And when he had found him, he brought him unto Antioch. And it came to pass, that a whole year they assembled themselves with the church, and taught much people. And the disciples were called Christians first in Antioch.*"

Once again these same brethren were there. I also believe these were the same brethren found in Acts 13:1, "*Now there were in the church that was at Antioch certain prophets and teachers; as Barnabas, and Simeon that was called Niger, and Lucius of Cyrene, and Manaen, which had been brought up with Herod the tetrarch, and Saul...*" Four men are mentioned as leaders of the Antioch church and two of them are black! And as we read in Acts 11:26, "*...the disciples were called Christians first in Antioch.*" Interesting that the place where we get our name as believers, was evangelized and started by black men preaching the gospel.

Next I want us to look at this Ethiopian eunuch again found in Acts 8. Let us begin in verse 25, "*And they, when they had testified and preached the word of the Lord, returned to Jerusalem, and preached the gospel in many villages of the Samaritans. [26]And the angel of the Lord spake unto Philip, saying, Arise, and go toward the south unto the way that goeth down from Jerusalem unto Gaza, which is desert...*" Before we continue, let's get this in our spirit. The Spirit of God sends an angel to tell Philip to go to one man, a black man! One man can change an entire nation. One man by the name of Moses delivered the entire nation of Israel. You could be that man in whatever city or place the Lord sends you. Why believe for anything less than this?

This must have been very important to God for Him to send Philip on a special mission, especially having to translate Philip. God took him right to this Ethiopian supernaturally, "*[27]And he arose and went: and, behold, a man of Ethiopia, an eunuch of great authority under Candace queen of the Ethiopians, who had the charge of all her treasure, and had come to Jerusalem for to worship, [28]Was returning, and sitting in his chariot read Esaias the prophet. [29]Then the Spirit said unto Philip, Go near, and join thyself to this chariot.*"

[30]*And Philip ran thither to him..."* This is remarkable. Philip is caught up supernaturally, dropped near the chariot, and has to run to catch up with it. And as he does, Philip *"heard him read the prophet Esaias, and said, Understandest thou what thou readest?* [31]*And he said, How can I, except some man should guide me? And he desired Philip that he would come up and sit with him.* [32]*The place of the scripture which he read was this, He was led as a sheep to the slaughter; and like a lamb dumb before his shearer, so opened he not his mouth:* [33]*In his humiliation his judgment was taken away: and who shall declare his generation? for his life is taken from the earth.* [34]*And the eunuch answered Philip, and said, I pray thee, of whom speaketh the prophet this? of himself, or of some other man?* [35]*Then Philip opened his mouth, and began at the same scripture, and preached unto him Jesus.* [36]*And as they went on their way, they came unto a certain water: and the eunuch said, See, here is water; what doth hinder me to be baptized?* [37]*And Philip said, If thou believest with all thine heart, thou mayest. And he answered and said, I believe that Jesus Christ is the Son of God.* [38]*And he commanded the chariot to stand still: and they went down both into the water, both Philip and the eunuch; and he baptized him.* [39]*And when they were come up out of the water, the Spirit of the Lord caught away Philip, that the eunuch saw him no more: and he went on his way rejoicing.* [40]*But Philip was found at Azotus: and passing through he preached in all the cities, till he came to Caesarea."* Can you imagine if you were the eunuch? This man Philip just appears to him, gets him saved, and then just vanishes.

First of all, let me point out a few things. Ham's son Cush founded the nation of Ethiopia. Ethiopia was a black nation. This black man appears to be the first non-Jewish convert to Christianity, excluding whoever might have gotten saved in Acts 2 when 3000 people got saved. But as far as any one person is concerned, this is the first convert to Christianity and it is a black man. Glory to God! I want you to know that history records that when this man went back to Ethiopia, he evangelized the entire nation. To this day a church he planted has a marker on it with his name on it. Philip, a Jew, led a black man to Jesus. There should be no animosity between Jews and blacks because of all the people that have suffered in the world, those two groups have suffered more than almost anybody. They have too much in common to hate each other.

This one black man changed an entire nation! First of all, we see he had great authority. This means he was a man of great importance in his country. Secondly, he served right under the queen. Thirdly, he was the secretary of the treasury for his nation. The image that people try to portray that black people are uneducated is obviously dispelled by this man. He had to be a trustworthy man to hold the positions he did. He also had to be highly educated. He must have had great mathematical skills to perform his job. He took care of the finances for the entire country. He obviously was able to read and write. I wonder how many of those white preachers in the south told black people that they were born only to be servants and that they didn't need to read and write? Oh the judgment of God that is going to come upon them. Jesus said in Matthew 18:6, *"But whoso shall offend one of these little ones which believe in me, it were better for him that a millstone were hanged about his neck, and that he were drowned in the depth of the sea."*

This eunuch somehow had gotten his hands on the scroll of Isaiah. Think of this. There wasn't a bookstore where he could've just picked one up. The Word of God was very precious and how he got his hands on a copy must have been a miracle. Moreover, he was already up to chapter 53. This tells us this eunuch was hungry for the Word of God. The Lord seeing this, He sends Philip to him. Obviously God wants black people saved. Not only this, but in the black community, there are people hungry for a true word from God, hungry to be taught the Word of God, and who are willing to pay the price to be whatever they need to be for the Kingdom of God.

Philip, after running up to the chariot, hears him reading out loud and asks the black eunuch if he understood what he was reading. Why haven't many preachers cared if black people understood the Scriptures? The body of Christ has so many ministries in Africa and other places around the world where people are evangelized, but our job is to not only get people saved, but make them disciples and teach them the Word of God. This story in Acts is a type of the black people crying out to be taught the Word of God and be disciples. Are you willing to sit down with black people and teach them the Word of God? This requires committing yourselves to people when you do that. It is too easy to fly in on a jet, have a nice hotel, where you step out from in your expensive suit, preach for a few hours and leave. Where are the men of God who are willing to get down where the people are at, put up a tent and teach morning and evening?

The black eunuch confessing to Philip he didn't understand the Scriptures saw his need to be taught says much about his character. He must have had a meek and teachable spirit. He also must have been very friendly and personable because he had no problem telling Philip to get into the chariot with him. He actually said to Philip to sit by him. As I said before, we have seen in many of these stories that black people never seem to have a problem receiving from and being near white people, but in our history, especially in America, this is sadly not true of Caucasian Christians.

So Philip preaches Jesus to this eunuch. He must have believed instantly because he wanted to be baptized in water immediately. This says to me that the hunger in the hearts of black people (especially in the last days) is like a river underneath them waiting for somebody to tap into it. I believe this is happening right now all over the earth. If anybody has a true hunger for God, when they come into contact with the presence of God, they will know it and respond. The grace of God is real and it is available to anyone of any color, anytime. But maybe you and I need to reach them with kindness and respect. We need to be like Barnabas as we read in Acts 11, "*who, when he came, and had seen the grace of God, was glad, and exhorted them all, that with purpose of heart they would cleave unto the Lord. For he was a good man, and full of the Holy Ghost and of faith...*" (Acts 11:23-24).

So Philip leads this black eunuch to Jesus and they pull over so Philip can immerse him in water baptism and it says the eunuch, "*went on his way rejoicing*". This says to me that after he got saved, water baptized, and went on his way, that this Ethiopian eunuch got the Holy Ghost as he was rejoicing. Let me read other translations of this, "*he went on his way happy as he could be*", "*he went on his way full of joy*", "*with a glad heart he resumed his journey*".

The finality of this story in Acts 8 is this. He went back to Ethiopia and the entire nation was evangelized because of one man. Even today, they remember and honor this man with a marker at a church that bears his name for the great work he did. How many precious black people are waiting for someone to go up to their chariot, sit with them, and teach them the Word of God? Hallelujah!

Next, let us look in Acts 13 again verses 1-3, "*[1]Now there were in the church that was at Antioch certain prophets and teachers; as Barnabas, and Simeon that was called Niger, and Lucius of Cyrene, and Manaen, which had been brought up with Herod the tetrarch, and Saul. [2]As they ministered to the Lord, and fasted, the Holy Ghost said, Separate me Barnabas and Saul for the work whereunto I have called them. [3]And when they had fasted and prayed, and laid their hands on them, they sent them away.*" Simeon was called Niger. The word Niger means "black". Simeon's name means "hearkening, hearing with acceptance, hearing and obeying". This says to me that this black prophet and teacher was a man who wanted to hear the Word of the Lord and obey it. He hearkened with acceptance, meaning he readily wanted to receive the Word of God. Lucius came from Cyrene, which was a place from the North African black nation of Libya. Lucius obviously was a black man. Lucius' name means "of the light, luminous, a noble". These two black men were prophets and teachers who had authority and were in leadership in the local church at Antioch. They ministered to the Lord. Ezekiel 44 talks about the sons of Zadok ministering to the Lord compared to the backslidden sons of Levi who couldn't and were only allowed to minister to the house. I Samuel 3:1 says "*Samuel ministered unto the Lord*". There is a tremendous calling on all of us to minister to the Lord, where we don't pray or ask for things, but we are simply in God's presence to take care of His needs and minister to Him. The word minister means to be a servant or somebody who does menial tasks. Ministering to the Lord means caring first and foremost for the needs of our Lord Jesus as a servant and ministering to His heart in worship. As you minister to His heart, you will have His heart and see His great love and care for His people. A true minister loves God's people and teaches and cares for them as a father would. This was the leadership at Antioch and two of them mentioned were black men. They were able to listen and hear the Holy Ghost. They were chosen enough to be able to lay hands on Barnabas and Saul (the Apostle Paul) and send them out into the ministry. We see Lucius mentioned by Paul in Romans 16:21, *"Timotheus my workfellow, and Lucius...my kinsmen, salute you."* In the preciousness of this scripture we see so many black people involved that we have never before seen. Only God can open our eyes to the truth of what the Scriptures clearly say.

Recently, as I was just spending my time in the Word of God one morning, the Lord spoke very clearly and then I realized how could I have not thought of this all along? What He said was a black Pharaoh saved the then known world by preparing before the seven years of famine to feed the entire earth. The earth would have been destroyed through famine and hunger had it not been for the graciousness of a black Pharaoh seeing the Spirit of God in Joseph and releasing him to it. When God whispered this to my heart, it was profound to me that nobody ever thinks about the great things that black people have done in the scriptures and gives them honor for what they did. When the Lord spoke this to me, I just stopped in astonishment, thanking the precious Holy Spirit for being free to reveal that to me. I don't know if I could have heard this a month ago. But the Word of God has a way of sanctifying us, changing us and preparing us for the next level of revelation. In this chapter, I would like to look at this story in the book of Genesis. Only God in His greatness can open the Word of God to us.

Let's begin the story in Genesis 41:1. *"And it came to pass at the end of two full years, that Pharaoh dreamed..."* Pharaoh is the ruler of Egypt, whose name means, "black." Egypt was a black nation. Pharaoh was a black man. To try to say anything differently would be, as far as I am concerned, erroneous. First of all, God gave Pharaoh this dream. He may have been a heathen, but God still uses heathens. I tell you the presence of God can be on stuff that we ourselves may question. It's like with music. Somebody that we perceive is worldly, how do we know that at some point in their life they didn't invite Jesus to come into their heart. Maybe they messed up and aren't walking with Jesus like we think they should. But does that mean that God might not use them in certain situations?

I remember in 1988 Jesse Jackson's speech at the Democratic Convention. I remember watching it. It was the famous "Keep Hope Alive" speech. There was an absolute anointing on him that night in that room. I remember a reporter asking one of the leaders of the Democratic Party what he thought of it and these were his words, "All I can say is that Jesse was under the anointing tonight." Glory to God!

What have we done in our meager little lives? What lives have we changed or affected? Yet we are going to sit and judge a man's personal life like Martin Luther King Jr. who finally was able to through his tenacity, faith, and his continuing dream of moving in nonviolence, affect a generation. I was there in the sixties, living in the ghetto of Washington DC. There were black voices crying out for violence. But Martin Luther King Jr. kept with his nonviolent ways because he said they were biblical, despite the shortcomings of the man's life. This is the Glory and the Grace of God. God will use even a donkey to speak His Word.

Who would ever think that history recorded that a black Pharaoh delivered not only just Egypt, but the then known world? Genesis 41:56-57 states, *"And the famine was over all the face of the earth: And Joseph opened all the storehouses, and sold unto the Egyptians; and the famine waxed sore in the land of Egypt. *[57]*And all countries came into Egypt to Joseph for to buy corn; because that the famine was so sore in all lands."* Then in the next chapter, the Patriarch Jacob sends his sons to be fed by a black Pharaoh. Glory to Jesus!

Here is the story of Pharaoh in Genesis 41, *"[1]And it came to pass at the end of two full years, that Pharaoh dreamed: and, behold, he stood by the river. [2]And, behold, there came up out of the river seven well favoured kine and fatfleshed; and they fed in a meadow. [3]And, behold, seven other kine came up after them out of the river, ill favoured and leanfleshed; and stood by the other kine upon the brink of the river. [4]And the ill favoured and leanfleshed kine did eat up the seven well favoured and fat kine. So Pharaoh awoke. [5]And he slept and dreamed the second time: and, behold, seven ears of corn came up upon one stalk, rank and good. [6]And, behold, seven thin ears and blasted with the east wind sprung up after them. [7]And the seven thin ears devoured the seven rank and full ears. And Pharaoh awoke, and, behold, it was a dream. [8]And it came to pass in the morning that his spirit was troubled; and he sent and called for all the magicians of Egypt, and all the wise men thereof: and Pharaoh told them his dream; but there was none that could interpret them unto Pharaoh. [9]Then spake the chief butler unto Pharaoh, saying, I do remember my faults this day: [10]Pharaoh was wroth with his servants, and put me in ward in the captain of the guard's house, both me and the chief baker: [11]And we dreamed a dream in one night, I and he; we dreamed each man according to the interpretation of his dream. [12]And there was there with us a young man, an Hebrew, servant to* the captain of the guard; and we told him, and he interpreted to us our dreams; to each man according to his dream he did interpret. [13]And it came to pass, as he interpreted to us, so it was; me he restored unto mine office, and him he hanged. [14]Then Pharaoh sent and called Joseph, and they brought him hastily out of the dungeon: and he shaved himself, and changed his raiment, and came in unto Pharaoh. [15]And Pharaoh said unto Joseph, I have dreamed a dream, and there is none that can interpret it: and I have heard say of thee, that thou canst understand a dream to interpret it. [16]And Joseph answered Pharaoh, saying, It is not in me: God shall give Pharaoh an answer of peace. [17]And Pharaoh said unto Joseph, In my dream, behold, I stood upon the bank of the river: [18]And, behold, there came up out of the river seven kine, fatfleshed and well favoured; and they fed in a meadow: [19]And, behold, seven other kine came up after them, poor and very ill favoured and leanfleshed, such as I never saw in all the land of Egypt for badness: [20]And the lean and the ill favoured kine did eat up the first seven fat kine: [21]And when they had eaten them up, it could not be known that they had eaten them; but they were still ill favoured, as at the beginning. So I awoke. [22]And I saw in my dream, and, behold, seven ears came up in one stalk, full and good: [23]And, behold, seven ears, withered, thin, and blasted with the east wind, sprung up after them: [24]And the thin ears devoured the seven good ears: and I told this unto the magicians; but there was none that could declare it to me. [25]And Joseph said unto Pharaoh, The dream of Pharaoh is one: God hath shewed Pharaoh what he is about to do. [26]The seven good kine are seven years; and the seven good ears are seven years: the dream is one. [27]And the seven thin and ill favoured kine that came up after them are seven years; and the seven empty ears blasted with the east wind shall be seven years of famine. [28]This is the thing which I have spoken unto Pharaoh: What God is about to do he sheweth unto Pharaoh. [29]Behold, there come seven years of great plenty throughout all the land of Egypt: [30]And there shall arise after them seven years of famine; and all the plenty shall be forgotten in the land of Egypt; and the famine shall consume the land; [31]And the plenty shall not be known in the land by reason of that famine following; for it shall be very grievous. [32]And for that the dream was doubled unto Pharaoh twice; it is because the thing is established by God, and God will shortly bring it to pass. [33]Now therefore let Pharaoh look out a man discreet and wise, and set him over the land of Egypt. [34]Let Pharaoh do this, and let him appoint officers over the land, and take up the fifth part of the land of Egypt in the seven plenteous years. [35]And let them gather all the food of those good years that come, and lay up corn under the hand of Pharaoh, and let them keep food in the cities. [36]And that food shall be for store to the land against the seven years of famine, which shall be in the land of Egypt; that the land perish not through the famine. [37]And the thing was good in the eyes of Pharaoh, and in the eyes of all his servants. [38]And Pharaoh said unto his servants, Can we find such a one as this is, a man in whom the Spirit of God is? [39]And Pharaoh said unto Joseph, Forasmuch as God hath shewed thee all this, there is none so discreet and wise as thou art: [40] Thou *shalt be over my house, and according unto thy word shall all my people be ruled: only in the throne will I be greater than thou. [41]And Pharaoh said unto Joseph, See, I have set thee over all the land of Egypt. 42And Pharaoh took off his ring from his hand, and put it upon Joseph's hand, and arrayed him in vestures of fine linen, and put a gold chain about his neck; [43]And he made him to ride in the second chariot which he had; and they cried before him, Bow the knee: and he made him ruler over all the land of Egypt. [44]And Pharaoh said unto Joseph, I am Pharaoh, and without thee shall no man lift up his hand or foot in all the land of Egypt. [45]And Pharaoh called Joseph's name Zaphnath-paaneah; and he gave him to wife Asenath the daughter of Poti-pherah priest of On. And Joseph went out over all the land of Egypt. [46]And Joseph was thirty years old when he stood before Pharaoh king of Egypt. And Joseph went out from the presence of Pharaoh, and went throughout all the land of Egypt. [47]And in the seven plenteous years the earth brought forth by handfuls. [48]And he gathered up all the food of the seven years, which were in the land of Egypt, and laid up the food in the cities: the food of the field, which was round about every city, laid he up in the same. [49]And Joseph gathered corn as the sand of the sea, very much, until he left numbering; for it was without number. [50]And unto Joseph were born two sons before the years of famine came, which Asenath the daughter of Poti-pherah priest of On bare unto him. [51]And Joseph called the name of the firstborn Manasseh: For God, said he, hath made me forget all my toil, and all my father's house. [52]And the name of the second called he Ephraim: For God hath caused me to be fruitful in the land of my affliction. [53]And the seven years of plenteousness, that was in the land of Egypt, were ended. [54]And the seven years of dearth began to come, according as Joseph had said: and the dearth was in all lands; but in all the land of Egypt there was bread. [55]And when all the land of Egypt was famished, the people cried to Pharaoh for bread: and Pharaoh said unto all the Egyptians, Go unto Joseph; what he saith to you, do. [56]And the famine was over all the face of the earth: and Joseph opened all the storehouses, and sold unto the Egyptians; and the famine waxed sore in the land of Egypt. [57]And all countries came into Egypt to Joseph for to buy corn; because that the famine was so sore in all lands."*

As we take a look at Genesis 41 concerning Pharaoh, the first thing we notice is that God gave Pharaoh the dream. Joseph tells Pharaoh that God gave it to him twice because He wanted Pharaoh to know it came from Him and that it will shortly come to pass. In II Corinthians 13:1, *"In the mouth of two or three witnesses shall every word be established."* Many of us, when we hear something, maybe we ought to wait for a second confirmation. There are many voices in the world. Three years ago I thought God wanted me to leave the city I pastored. I was just absolutely convinced that my time had ended here. I've labored and I thought it was time for me to move on to my next . Then one of my fathers in the Lord, Derrick Kuhn walks into my office, looks me in the face and says, "No!" I said, "What are you talking about?" He responded,

"Absolutely not! Don't even think about it. You know exactly what I am talking about. Don't even think about leaving here. This is the time for you to begin receiving the rewards of your labor. Why would God send you away now?" But I was convinced it was of God for me to leave. Even men of God mess up. That is why we need accountability in our lives. Once he said that to me, my spirit immediately witnessed to it and all heaviness lifted off of me. Now I am committed to stay in this city until Jesus himself appears to me in a burning bush.

The other thing that it says in this chapter is what a black Pharaoh sees in Joseph in Genesis 41:38, *"Can we find such a one as this is, a man in whom the Spirit of God is?"* This means that black leadership will recognize the anointing. Joseph tells Pharaoh to put a man over the collection of food over against the days of famine. Then Pharaoh basically says, "Who can be such a one with wisdom as you." Then Pharaoh does this. To a man just five minutes earlier had been in his own prisons, Pharaoh then sets Joseph over the entire country. Not only that, but Pharaoh tells Joseph that he will be as him and everybody in this nation will bow to him. He also tells him that he will ride in the second chariot next to him. He gave him his ring, which meant all of the authority in the nation of Egypt was given to Joseph. Anything Joseph did was as if Pharaoh himself did it. He totally yielded to Joseph, which means to me that there wasn't a racist bone in Pharaoh's body. Later there came a Pharaoh that knew not Joseph and was threatened by Israel. But you can't generalize peoples and say all Pharaohs were black and bad. Not all of them, however. Not this one in Genesis 41. Moreover, Pharaoh gave his daughter to be Joseph's wife. Joseph himself just came out of prison. Certainly this says about this black man that he had the ability to recognize the Holy Ghost, to recognize true leadership and to recognize the anointing and authority on Joseph's life. And he turned everything over in the kingdom to him and he also gave him his daughter to wife. Finally, Pharaoh gave Joseph a new name which means, "Savior of the age." In typology, Joseph is a type of Jesus and Pharaoh is a type of God the Father in this story.

Next in our study of a symbolic look at important black people, we want to talk about Simon the Canaanite. Matthew 10:1-4 states, *"And when he had called unto him his twelve disciples, he gave them power against unclean spirits, to cast them out, and to heal all manner of sickness and all manner of disease. Now the names of the twelve apostles are these; the first, Simon, who is called Peter, and Andrew his brother; James the son of Zebedee, and John his brother; Philip, and Bartholomew; Thomas, and Matthew the publican James the son of Alphaeus, and Lebbaeus, whose surname was Thaddaeus; Simon the Canaanite, and Judas Iscariot, who also betrayed him"*. The Jewish custom during this time was that if you made the list of names, the most honorable wcre listed first and the least honorable were listed last. Simon the Canaanite was a black man. First of all, why are people upset about this? Most commentaries take a circuitous route about this topic and write that they really don't know who Simon the Canaanite was. The answer is right in front of us. Simon was a Canaanite but people don't want to admit he was black, or partially black. Nevertheless, he was a man of color.

Mark 3:16-19 also states the list of apostles as follows. *"Simon he surnamed Peter; and James the son of Zebedee, and John the brother of James; and he surnamed them Boanerges, which is, The sons of thunder: and Andrew, and Philip, and Bartholomew, and Matthew, and Thomas, and James the son of Alphaeus, and Thaddaeus, and Simon the Canaanite, and Judas Iscariot..."* Now, notice in both listings of the apostles, where Simon the Canaanite was listed. He was next to last. John 6:70 states, "Jesus answered them, *Have not I chosen you twelve, and one of you is a devil?"* Who do you think the other Apostles in this verse thought was the devil? They thought Simon the Canaanite was the devil. Abraham told his family to not let my son marry a Canaanite. Isaac said the same thing to his sons. This was a strict rule because they were a perverse and godless people. Canaanites had a history with the Israelites of being commanded by God to have nothing to do with them. That is why when Jesus talked with Canaanites, it was a big deal. Every time Jesus talked to a woman it was a big deal too. Jesus was such a revolutionary, controversial figure of his day. So, the history of the Canaanites was not good and he was named second to last. The one who did betray Jesus, however, was a Jew and Simon was not. Simon was a Canaanite who converted to Judaism.

Simon was a member of a fanatical sect of zealots who wanted to overthrow Rome. He is also called in another place, *"Simon Zelotes"* (Luke 6:15). These zealots vowed suicide rather than to submit to Rome. They wanted to destroy Rome by any means necessary. He had obviously come to the Jewish faith and have been circumcised but he was not a Jew naturally.

Let's consider this fact that Simon was a Canaanite. Remember on the night before he was betrayed, Jesus knelt and washed all of the disciples feet. What an act of mercy Jesus did and he was saying by washing Simon's feet that even the worst person that we think is awful, no good, etc..., Jesus is not listening to your rhetoric. He is down there washing their feet. He is saying that His forgiveness is for everyone. Oh that God would give us the heart of Jesus that we could love like that and forgive people and empower them. All authority and power He also gave to a Canaanite.

Acts 1:13 also states the listing of those in the upper room. *"And when they were come in, they went unto an upper room, where abode both Peter, and James, and John, and Andrew, Philip, and Thomas, Bartholomew, and*

Matthew, James the son of Alphaeus, and Simon Zelotes, and Judas the brother of James." All of the apostles were in the upper room waiting for the Holy Spirit to be poured out. Simon the Canaanite obviously received the baptism of the Holy Ghost soon thereafter.

Moreover, in Revelation 21, when the new Jerusalem was being described, it says in verse 14, *"And the wall of the city had twelve foundations, and in them the names of the twelve apostles of the Lamb..."* One of the foundation stones in the new Jerusalem is going to be occupied by the name "Simon the Canaanite," a black man.

At the end of his life, history doesn't say much about Simon's life. However, there are four accounts in church history of how Simon the Canaanite was martyred. He was martyred either by crucifixion in Judea but others say he was tortured horribly in another city. Others say he was dismembered and still others how he was tortured. Nonetheless, Simon was martyred for the kingdom of heaven's sake.

Why would someone be upset that one of the twelve apostles was a black man? When you think about it, why should it matter at all? But we need to give honor to where honor is due.

The next Scripture we want to look at in our symbolic look at important black people is in I Samuel 30. In this story, David was coming back to where he was living in Ziklag and he finds out that the Amalekites had invaded and stolen all that he had, burned everything and stolen all the women and children. David is very discouraged in verse 3 and 4 in discovering all of their families were taken. In verse 6 the people also spoke of stoning David because they were so grieved at what happened. So David encouraged himself in the Lord, got a linen ephod and sought the Lord. God then told David to pursue them and without fail to recover all.

This story has typological truths that can speak to where we are at today. The enemy comes in to the house of God, to the people of God, (obviously for us the enemy being Satan, the thief that comes to kill, steal and destroy) and steals not only our prosperity, but our children and our families. This is going on today like never before. Families are being ripped apart because Satan is whispering in men and women's ears to leave their husband or their wife and to move on to bigger and better things as it were. Granted, some marriages need that. However, there is more divorce in the church than in the world. A lot of people right now are under attack financially. So this story can speak to you and me.

When this happens in our lives, rather than asking God what we should do like David did and get the ephod (which means to go and worship the Lord), we sit around and listen to our own minds and we place blame on others. Our soul is never going to tell us something godly. Our souls are going to put blame on David saying, our family and money is gone because David didn't take care of it. These reasonings are ridiculous. We always seem to need to have an answer because we can't deal personally with the issues facing us. What we ought to do is get an ephod and seek and worship God and get the answer.

I believe in the last days, in this whole season that the earth is in right now, we are experiencing situations like this story in I Samuel 30. And I believe that despite all that the enemy tries, you and I will prosper no matter the adversity that comes our way. We may go through tough times. But we will come out of these times leaning upon the arm of our beloved and we are not going to lack anything we need to live this life because God promised it. He said that if we would seek first his kingdom and his righteousness, then all of these things would be added unto us.

One day I was driving down a street in the early 1980s and the Lord spoke to me about a couple I was ministering to. I didn't know where they lived but the Lord told me where to turn and I found their house. I pulled in to their house and walked up to the screen door. As I looked inside, lying on a couch was this sister with a bottle of pills in her hand. Their four kids were also in the house just screaming and yelling and the lady had passed out from trying to kill herself. I called 911 and the ambulance came and ultimately saved her life. When she came out of the hospital, I asked her why she tried to kill herself and she said it was because she couldn't take life anymore. Her husband only makes about 150-200 dollars a week and it was not enough to provide for the family. She was tired of being poor. Well, after ministering to them and allowing them to live with me for a short season, I asked the sister, "Do you have any kind of trade or education?" Then she said, "Yes, I have a master's degree in nuclear medicine." Then I said, "Why aren't you getting a job in your field?" She then responded with the answer that the woman was supposed to stay at home and raise the kids. She felt she would be disobeying God by getting a job. Obviously she had the anointing to be the working one in the relationship and the father could be at home raising the kids. This theory that women belong in the home might have been true a long time ago, but we are living in a day where that just isn't the answer for everybody. Do you think God is going to hold people responsible when a woman needs to work? In this society, it is almost an absolute neccessity in households for both husband and wife to be working. I then told the sister to put her resume out and see what happens. Within a very short time, she got a job making six figures. With the money she made, she ultimately put her husband through school and they found peace and deliverance in their lives. Their answer was right in front of them.

That is why people need pastors to speak into people's lives, to give them a different perspective on the Word of God.

God will always answer us when we seek him. God told David to pursue after the Amalekites. Consider this as your and my situation. Who did God use to be the eyes of God and deliver David's men, bring back everything that was lost and even everything the enemy had as well? Who did God use? An Egyptian. I believe in the last days, we are going to see black people being the eyes of God for the body of Christ showing us where to go to defeat the enemy and how to get our inheritance.

As the story goes in I Samuel 30, David and his men in verse 11 found an Egyptian in the field. The field in scripture represents either the world or your place of ministry. They brought this black man to David and they gave him bread and water to eat and drink. If we as leadership (like David here) are doing our job and are giving the Word of God to black people and we are giving them the Holy Ghost symbolic of the cake of figs with the raisins which are a type of the fruit of the Spirit, gifts of the Spirit, then we will get a response from them. In verse 12, it says that the Egyptian's spirit came again to him. What does this mean? He was resurrected spiritually. He was born again in a sense.

Then in verse 13 it states, *"And David said unto him, To whom belongest thou? And whence art thou?"* David was asking about his heritage. Leadership needs to be involved with their congregation. Leadership needs to be involved with black people. If we will persevere and keep doing the will of God, then I believe black people (despite any rejection) will ultimate respond and receive. If we keep coming and showing our fellow black brethren the love of God, keep giving them bread and water and a cake of raisins, then they will respond. The Egyptian then responded and said in verse 13, *"I am a young man of Egypt, servant to an Amalekite, and my master left me, because three days agone I fell sick."* I wonder how many people in leadership have forsaken or have not included black people in their thinking when they minister. Years ago I heard a preacher say, "I want to build a church and reach only the Yuppees of my city." Does Jesus only want to reach the Yuppees? It is interesting to note that the people who came to Jesus and those he ordained to be with him were unlearned and ignorant men. But we are trying to surround ourselves with rich people who can help build our kingdom!

This Egyptian then relays the story of what the Amalekites have done and David asks him in verse 15, *"Canst thou bring me down to this company?"* The black man was in the company that burns Ziklag with fire but he didn't want to be. He was a slave to a system that he couldn't get out of. If wasn't until he became so sick that he was of no use to them, that the master left him. How many people are in Babylon today in the old church system, who if they had their chance, would never do some of the stuff that is being done. How can any tongue-talking Spirit-filled believers go to a place where they tell you that you can't speak in tongues during the meeting? They then tell you that you can do that at the end when others have left and have your little time of worship. As Psalms 137:4 states, *"How shall we sing the LORD's song in a strange land?"*

This Egyptian didn't like what they were doing, but he was a slave to it. Babylon is written on their foreheads. When you finally come out, it still takes a couple of years to get it rooted out of you or you will go right back into another Babylon. Then years later, you look back and realize how much time you wasted there in Babylon. But God in His greatness and in His mercy brought you out to ultimately take you in to His plans and purposes for your life.

This Egyptian was sick and they left him. Let me tell you something. Babylon will use you until there is nothing left they can get out of you. When your talent is no longer worth it to them, they forsake you. Saul had David play on his harp to get his demons out but as soon as people were saying that Saul has slain his thousands but David his ten thousands, he was cast out. When you begin to touch their glory and their power, then you are headed out the door.

In response to David's question, the Egyptian tells David in verse 15, *"Swear unto me by God, that thou wilt neither kill me, nor deliver me into the hands of my master, and I will bring thee down to this company."* The Egyptian only wanted assurance that he wasn't going to be a slave anymore nor die. We can tell those coming out of Babylon that they are not going to die or be slaves to a church system but begin to live. We can tell people that they will not be in bondage and slavery but they will be freer than they have ever been.

I Samuel 30:16-19 then states *"And when he had brought him down, behold, they were spread abroad upon all the earth, eating and drinking, and dancing, because of all the great spoil that they had taken out of the land of the Philistines, and out of the land of Judah.* [17]*And David smote them from the twilight even unto the evening of the next day...* [18]*And David recovered all that the Amalekites had carried away: And David rescued his two wives.* [19]*And there was nothing lacking to them, neither small nor great, neither sons nor daughters, neither spoil, nor anything that they had taken to them: David recovered all."* How did David recover all? Because of a young black Egyptian who by the Grace of God was the eyes of God for the nation of Israel.

Now let us turn to II Samuel 6 as we look at the man Obededom the Gittite. In this chapter, David has gone to get the ark of the Lord to bring it to Jerusalem. He did it not according to the *"due order"* as the book of Chronicles tells us and he allowed men who were not Levites to carry the ark on a wooden cart (which speaks of everything of earth and humanity and religion). God doesn't need anything to carry His presence except the shoulders of priests. So a man by the name of Uzzah was killed in the process. David said it was such a big deal that he called it a breach. Then David was afraid of the Lord and asked the Lord in verse 9 of 2 Samuel 6, *"How shall the ark of the LORD come to me?"*

Then verse 10 of the same chapter says, *"So David would not remove the ark of the LORD unto him unto the city of David: but David carried it aside into the house of Obed-edom the Gittite."* The first thing to notice here is that David carried the ark aside. Many times we need to go sideways to go onward with God. You may have to go to a side that nobody wants to go to in order to find the manifest presence of God. This place was not in Judah, but at a black man's house, to a man named Obed-edom.

Verse 11 then states, *"And the ark of the LORD continued in the house of Obed-edom the Gittite three months: and the LORD blessed Obed-edom and all his household."* This same story is also found in I Chronicles 13:12-14. The only difference in the two accounts is in verse 14 where it states, *"And the ark of God remained with the family of Obed-edom in his house three months..."* It says here that the ark remained with the *"family"* of Obed-edom which to us would speak of the family of black people.

First of all, when you look at these stories, how do you determine whether someone was black or not? I am sure there will be a host of people who will try to say that Obed-edom was not a black man. But this is what the Lord gave me. Whoever was a descendent of Ham, was of the black race. There is really no way to get around it. They were people of color, no matter what you say. There are no white people in the descendents of Ham. Where did Obed-edom come from and the term "Gittite?" The term Gittite means, "inhabitants of Gath, which is the winepress." This is important to us because anybody that's going to carry and have within its house and within one's own being the ark, the manifest presence of God, will have had to be pressed out of measure. This is another picture, just like Jesus in the garden of Gethsemane. Gethsemane means, "olive-press." This means that the dealings of God have so pressed you to the place where you can handle the glory of the God to the glory of God.

These Gittites were from Gath or Gath-Rimmon. But where did they come from? Ham's son, Mizraim, who's basically Egypt, had seven sons. One of his sons was named Casluhim (Genesis 10). Out of Casluhim was born Philistim, who was the father of the Philistines. There were then five great lords of the Philistines. One of these was the Gittites (Joshua 13:3). Obed-edom was a Gittite.

293

How do we justify him being a Levite, where he is later called? He obviously converted to Judaism. But his heritage was simply from Ham. He is one of Ham's descendants.

The name Obed-edom is really made up of two words, which basically means, "serving Edom." Obed means "serving" and Edom means "red; red earth." In many dictionary definitions, then, Obed-edom means, "serving Edom; a servant; a servant who worships; worshipping God or laborer of the earth." You cannot be around the manifest presence of God without being a worshiper.

During the days of Samuel, the Philistines kidnapped the ark (I Samuel 4) and the ark remained among these five lords of the Philistines and their cities. Then in I Samuel 5 when the ark was among them, the Philistines ended up getting hemorrhoids to such a degree that they didn't want the ark around them. They were so moved by the ark that they made golden emerods to try to sacrifice to and to even honor God. They wanted that ark as far away from them as possible.

Then the ark of God stayed for a season with a man named Abinadab. After that we see Samuel challenging the people of Israel to put away their false gods and in I Samuel 7:10, God has the Philistines and Israel meet together and God then thunders upon the Philistines. Israel was able to subdue the Philistines. I Samuel 7:14 states, *"And the cities which the Philistines had taken from Israel were restored to Israel, from Ekron even unto Gath; and the coasts thereof did Israel deliver out of the hands of the Philistines. And there was peace between Israel and the Amorites."* The city of Gath, where the Gittites were from, was restored to Israel.

Between I Samuel 7:14 and II Samuel 6 is a period of twenty years. Twenty is the number for expectancy in the scriptures. The religion in Jerusalem went on as usual without the presence of God (because the ark was not in Jerusalem at that time). Finally, then David says in 2 Samuel 6 that he wants the ark, the glory of God back into Jerusalem. However he doesn't do it the right way and God smites Uzzah and there is a breach. That was when David said, *"How shall the ark of the LORD come to me?"* (II Samuel 6:9) Well, the only way to have the ark is to bring it after the "due order."

What happened to Obed-edom at this time? Obviously, Obed-edom, a descendent of Ham, through the line of the Gittites converted to the nation of Israel. He also would have had to have been circumcised so that he would have been allowed into the Israeli congregation. Otherwise, he wouldn't have been allowed to obtain custody of the ark. The only reason I point this out is because that is a very terrible surgery for an older man. Obviously, something in Obed-edom hungered to be with the people of God. So much so, that he converted to Israeli and Judaism and began to worship the one true God. Not only that, he proceeded along so well that he was eventually invited into the congregation of Israel. Remember, they were commanded to never allow strangers into the congregation, unless they were willing to be circumcised. So it was a big deal for Obed-edom to get into this story in 2 Samuel 6.

David wanted the ark to come back to Jerusalem and his heart was right. But is says in verse 10, *"So David would not remove the ark of the LORD unto him into the city of David: but David carried it aside into the house of Obed-edom the Gittite."*

This is then something that we have to see. Later on in Obed-edom's life, he would become a guardian of the ark of the LORD. His children, even up to like 62 grandchildren all had to do with caring for the presence of God. This is powerful because we are talking about this subject in relation to black people and how precious the presence of God is to black people.

I know that there is a Pentecostal order in black worship that falls far short of the true. But, within the heart of black people, as was in Obed-edom, such a yearning, such a hunger to do whatever it took, even to personal suffering, is to get that presence of God. That heart is within the hearts of black people even today. Even when we sit through forty-five minutes of basically rhythm songs and people acting out in the flesh, you'll find that at some point, somebody will sing and as they begin to sing, the glory begins to trickle down. That precious presence that means everything to them, comes and manifests itself.

So as I was meditating on this passage of Obed-edom, just as the white charismatic churches or the white southern Gospel churches fall so far short of the due order of worship, so do the black Pentecostal churches. There is a lot of shouting, a lot of jumping and a lot of moving around and very little substance and very little manifest presence.

But because deep within the heart of black people, who suffered horribly under the hands of white people, they found, as Israel found under the bondage of Egypt, that as they began to sing unto the LORD, God would meet them. So hidden within the black church is the ark of God. But what needs to happen is a resurrection, a revolution for Obed-edoms to come forth in the black church. Throwing off the old culture and saying we acknowledge and appreciate you, but you've allowed this stuff to come and be in the house of God. Listen folks, there are black churches where the people who are playing in the worship band aren't even saved. I mean, they aren't even trying to be saved. That's strange fire. That's not even God.

So God cannot manifest Himself the way He wants to until that is dealt with. That needs to happen in white churches as well. We have a whole association of churches now that hire skilled musicians to play who are not saved under the guise of "Let these people play to try to reach them." No, they cannot play because it blocks the Glory from falling. They can come to church, but they are not able to sing the song of the Lord. All you are doing when you do that is diluting what is of God.

Within the black church lies the very manifest presence of God. Once that presence is released, like in Obed-edoms house, "...*and the LORD blessed Obed-edom, and all his household.*" Then verse 12 of 2 Samuel 6 states, "*And it was told king David, saying, The LORD hath blessed the house of Obed-edom, and all that pertaineth unto him, because of the ark of God.*" This blessing reaches to everything in Obed-edom's life.

Why did David let it go to Obed-edom's house? I believe because David wanted to see what would happen. Let's see if the black man can handle it. I'm not bringing it home to me, so let the black people handle it for a season. David waited three months and when he hears how God is prospering everything that Obed-edom is and has and his family as well, David wanted to bring up the ark again. Prosperity comes when you live in the manifest presence of God. If black people would stop all of this praise and start actually worshiping and allowing the Glory to descend in their meetings, transformation would take place like never before. Those days are over, where people come up at an altar call and are never changed. It is time for people when they come into the very presence of God to be changed. If leadership is living in sin, don't you dare put your hands on those people. There is something called transference of spirits.

I want my family blessed with the manifest presence of God. I want all that pertains to me to be blessed because of the manifest presence of God. This is the revelation for the black peoples all over the world. If they will give themselves to the manifest presence of God, leave behind all those dead works of religion and embrace whatever it takes and whatever you have to do (because others will resist it and challenge it) and break through into the Glory, then millions are going to follow and be blessed.

So David went up and brought back the ark of God from Obed-edom's house when he was sure. He tested it on black people first to make sure. Later on in his life, Obed-edom in I Chronicles 15:24, became a door keeper in the house of the Lord, protecting the ark. That's why there are so many wonderful, black Gospel singers that have the anointing that they have.

Obed-edom had eight sons, I Chronicles 26:6-8 states. Out of them came sixty-two descendents, which were black people. It says that they were mighty men of valour, able men for strength and service. I Chronicles 26:15 shows Obed-edom and his son's place was guarding the ark. Now remember David pitched a tent for the ark (Tabernacle of David). Now the old Tabernacle of Moses was still standing at this time. People still went to the Tabernacle of Moses all the time, even the manifest presence of God, the ark, was no longer there but at David's camp. Obed-edom and his sons were called to guard the south side of the Tabernacle of David. I love that, because south in the Scriptures speaks of prosperity. Moreover, one of the names of the house was called the house of Asuppim. Asuppim means "collection of offerings, storehouse". In other words all of his sons were treasurers in the house of the Lord.

Last but not least, when Israel would be taken over and destroyed and the ark taken from them, in II Chronicles 25:24 we find that Obed-edom was there protecting the ark of God, defending it, and is taken hostage by the enemy. But still he fights all the way to the end!

Let us look at some other passages as we consider the prophetic implications of black people in the last days. Isaiah 60 is a very familiar passage about the glory being revealed in the last days. It is interesting what we find there as the Lord in the last day is revealing His glory. We begin in verse 4 as we see God's people gathering together, *"Lift up thine eyes round about, and see: all they gather themselves together, they come to thee: thy sons shall come from far, and thy daughters shall be nursed at thy side. ⁵Then thou shalt see, and flow together, and thine heart shall fear, and be enlarged; because the abundance of the sea shall be converted unto thee, the forces of the Gentiles shall come unto thee. ⁶The multitude of camels shall cover thee, the dromedaries of Midian and Ephah; all they from Sheba shall come: they shall bring gold and incense; and they shall shew forth the praises of the LORD. ⁷All the flocks of Kedar shall be gathered together unto thee, the rams of Nebaioth shall minister unto thee: they shall come up with acceptance on mine altar, and I will glorify the house of my glory."* So the context from Isaiah 60:1-7 is God's glory being revealed during the day of the Lord (the last days), which is during the time of the revealing of the sons of God. God's glory is being poured out and God is bringing His sons and daughters from all over the earth and gathering them together. Then it happens to mention in verse 7, the flocks of Kedar. Kedar, as I have already said elsewhere, means "black, dark skinned man, blackness, swarthy". In Song of Solomon 1:5 we see the bride of Christ *"as the tents of Kedar"*. So the flocks of Kedar are the flocks of black people. In Ephesians 1:10 God says *"That in the dispensation of the fulness of times he might gather together in one all things in Christ, both which are in heaven, and which are on earth; even in him."* This is what God is doing in the last days and in verse 7 of Isaiah 60, we find that one of those mentioned whom the Lord is gathering together are the flocks of black people. Kedar was the son of Ishmael, who was the son of Hagar the Egyptian, a black woman (Genesis 25:13).

Another passage where Kedar is mentioned is in Isaiah 42, which says, "*¹⁰Sing unto the LORD a new song, and his praise from the end of the earth, ye that go down to the sea, and all that is therein; the isles, and the inhabitants thereof. ¹¹Let the wilderness and the cities thereof lift up their voice, the villages that Kedar doth inhabit: let the inhabitants of the rock sing, let them shout from the top of the mountains. ¹²Let them give glory unto the LORD, and declare his praise in the islands. ¹³The LORD shall go forth as a mighty man, he shall stir up jealousy like a man of war: he shall cry, yea, roar; he shall prevail against his enemies...*" The beginning of this chapter is talking about the Lord Jesus and what He is going to do in the earth. Then the Lord in verse 9 says, "*Behold, the former things are come to pass, and new things do I declare: before they spring forth I tell you of them.*" From verse 10 on, God is then speaking of the future. The former things have already taken place and now God is speaking new things to us (or things we haven't seen before because there is nothing new under the sun). So the revelation is Kedar's people are involved in the last great revival. Notice it says in verse 11, "*Let the wilderness and the cities thereof lift up their voice, the villages that Kedar doth inhabit: let the inhabitants of the rock sing, let them shout from the top of the mountains.*" These last day black people are going to be tremendous worshippers and evangelists.

The next passage I would like to look at related to black people in the last days is Zephaniah 1:1. One of the black people in the Bible that we looked at was Cush. Cush means black and was a son of Ham. Every time we find his name along with names like Mizraim, Egypt, Ham, etc., it is speaking of black people or descendents of black people. In Zephaniah 1:1, we find that Zephaniah, one of the Minor Prophets, was a black man, "*The word of the LORD which came unto Zephaniah the son of Cushi...*" Zephaniah's name means "hid of the Lord, protected by the Lord, concealed of God, treasured of Jehovah, watcher of the Lord". Cushi was a descendent of Ham and if Zephaniah was a son of Cushi, than Zephaniah was a black prophet. All of the Minor Prophets speak much of the last days. The important part is found in the name of Zephaniah. In the last days there are black people hidden of the Lord, protected by the Lord, concealed of God, watcher of the Lord, and lastly treasured of Jehovah. In the last days, God is raising up Zephaniahs.

The last passage that I would like to look at is tucked away in I Chronicles 4:38-40. This is an amazing passage the Lord led me to. In I Chronicles 4, God is giving out the genealogies of Israel and He is telling them where to go live, "*[38]These mentioned by their names were princes in their families: and the house of their fathers increased greatly. [39]And they went to the entrance of Gedor, even unto the east side of the valley, to seek pasture for their flocks. [40]And they found fat pasture and good, and the land was wide, and quiet, and peaceable; for they of Ham had dwelt there of old.*" This passage has escaped all of us, until now. The Holy Ghost led me to this passage. Ham is the father of the black race and what I Chronicles is saying is the descendents of Ham left a fat pasture and a good pasture. You see, we have been told that black people don't know anything about civilization, but come to find out Egypt was one of the greatest civilizations ever. Did you know the elevator and the refrigerator were invented by black people? Where would we be without black people? They have done tremendous things and the lies that white historians have said has brought much damage, not only to black people by creating low self-esteem in them, but also to white people because it taught them to think unrighteously towards blacks. White people in history have taken the ability to read and write from black people when black people invented the alphabet! At some point, judgment is going to come. As far as I am concerned, if God ever released me, I would literally call for a day of repentance at least for the church. If the United States government is never going to do it, we need to do it because the church purposely kept black people in bondage for hundreds of years. The church has taught black people they were beasts and that they were born to be slaves and did not teach them their glorious legacy and history that is rich. Now as archeologists are discovering more and more of the civilization where creation began, they are finding it was in Africa! We find that instead of saying all the time we have a "Judeo-Christian" heritage, we really should be saying we have a "Afro-Judeo-Christian" heritage because we can't block out the African people. The first country in the Bible mentioned is Ethiopia! Any Bible scholar knows that the first time anything is mentioned on a particular subject in the Bible it means that every time after that it is an important thing. God mentioned Ethiopia first in the Bible for a reason.

So in I Chronicles 4:40, "*[40]And they found fat pasture and good, and the land was wide, and quiet, and peaceable; for they of Ham had dwelt there of old.*" This is what black people leave behind, a peaceable, good land. Black people are not a violent race killing each other as many people think because they see it in some of the black culture. Black people were taught to do this by white people. When you take people's culture from them and rob them of education, what do you expect them to become but violent and angry? So they migrated into tribes as we see in Africa and kill each other many times, fighting for dominance just because somebody is of another tribe. This extremely contrasts the beginning of black people because we know the Egyptian civilization contained highly skilled and intelligent people. What happened?! Well, somewhere along the line, other nations took these civilizations over. This is called colonization. Look at a nation like South Africa. Their segregation lasted up until the late 1980's and early 1990's. The black people have always had two options when responding. One, fight back and kill all the white people. But there is a better one. Search the Scriptures and see what the Bible really says about the black people and the black people of Ham wherever they went left a good pasture, a wide pasture, and a quiet and peaceable pasture! Let the truth pierce our hearts and may we respond by acting on it, thereby glorifying God!

Egypt In The Last Days
Chapter 21

In this chapter I would like to look at the entire chapter of Isaiah 19 to start with as it pertains to Egypt in the last days as well as a few other passages. Once again, this will be a typical or allegorical look what God is going to do with black people in the last days. Let us begin in verse 1 of chapter 19 of Isaiah,

"¹The burden of Egypt. Behold, the LORD rideth upon a swift cloud, and shall come into Egypt: and the idols of Egypt shall be moved at his presence, and the heart of Egypt shall melt in the midst of it." Egypt undeniably speaks of black people. And God has a burden on His heart for Egypt! Egypt was used as a tool in the hand of God to torment Israel. God many times pronounced many judgments upon Egypt and most of the time we look at those passages and only consider the bad aspects of Egypt. But if you would do a word search on Egypt throughout the Bible, you will find wonderful hidden revelation about Egypt as we see in this chapter that lets you know what God's real heart is. God is *"not willing that any should perish, but that all should come to repentance"* (II Peter 3:9). So He has a burden for black people. I love the passage in Psalms 68:31 that says *"Princes shall come out of Egypt; Ethiopia shall soon stretch out her hands unto God."* Hear me, this is happening even now. Some of the greatest churches and ministers in the body of Christ all over the world are black preachers, black teachers, black worship leaders, psalmists, etc. So I believe Ethiopia right now is stretching her hands out to God. Now a lot of Isaiah 19 deals with God judging Egypt, but God's judgment is always remedial and redemptive. He is judging Egypt to ultimately bring them back to Himself.

"²And I will set the Egyptians against the Egyptians: and they shall fight every one against his brother, and every one against his neighbour; city against city, and kingdom against kingdom." We see this all the time today. All over the world many times, light skinned black people are despised by darker skinned black people. We see a lot of Spirit-filled black people, and we also see a growing number of Muslims in the black community. We see this in Africa everyday. Tribes are still wiping out other tribes. In so many nations in Africa this is happening and the world is silent.

Verse 3 begins by saying *"And the spirit of Egypt..."* I do believe every race of people have certain characteristics that they have picked up genetically or through life experiences. But God is our redeemer and He breaks the chains of the past and as we have learned, we become a new species! But there is a spirit in Egypt and it *"...shall fail in the midst thereof; and I will destroy the* counsel thereof: and they shall seek to the idols, and to the charmers, and to them that have familiar spirits, and to the wizards." How many people have asked you what your sign is? When they ask me this, I get upset. Our month we were born has nothing to do with our life. It still amazes me as a Pastor that so many people in the church read their horoscope in the newspaper everyday. This is strictly forbidden in Scripture.

"*4And the Egyptians will I give over into the hand of a cruel lord; and a fierce king shall rule over them, saith the Lord, the LORD of hosts.*" This cruel lord and fierce king is nothing other than Satan himself. This is akin to the Jews crying out for Jesus' crucifixion and saying "*His blood be on us, and on our children*" (Matthew 27:25). They brought a curse upon themselves. But the devil has been and is ruling amongst black people. There are more black men in prison in the United States than anywhere else in the world who are locked up for the rest of their lives. Somebody was motivating them to do the crimes they committed. It is the same "*spirit that now worketh in the children of disobedience*", Ephesians 2:2 says. It is a devil that whispers into many ears, "why go to school when you can sell drugs and drive a Mercedes?" This may seem hard to believe until you have lived in abject poverty. Have you even been in a situation when you didn't know where your next meal would come from? I remember the day myself standing at a bus stop in Washington D.C. with the rain pouring down and I didn't have a place to go to live. I was desperate and I understand the temptations that come in situations like that. We have to be careful with our judgments. But the fact still remains, as Ecclesiastes 10:8 says, "*He that diggeth a pit shall fall into it; and whoso breaketh an hedge, a serpent shall bite him.*" Satan is really going after to hurt God's precious black people because of the calling upon their lives.

"*5And the waters shall fail from the sea, and the river shall be wasted and dried up...*" This is talking about the river of God. It is missing. The same is seen in verse 6, "*And they shall turn the rivers far away; and the brooks of defence shall be emptied and dried up: the reeds and flags shall wither. 7The paper reeds by the brooks, by the mouth of the brooks, and every thing sown by the brooks, shall wither, be driven away, and be no more...*" Let me say something about this. A lot of black people are fed up with the black church. They consider it a "white man's" religion and they have every reason to think this because of the white oppression and dominance that has lived in this country for so long. This is why there are so many black Muslims now because when they go to the black church, they see that many of the preachers have secret and hidden sin in their lifestyles and because of the hypocrisy many times, they think what is the point? And certainly Satan is helping them think this. The church is driving black people away especially because many ministers emphasis "hyper holiness" all the while living in sin behind the scenes. They are driven away and when they think about going to a white church many times they aren't made to feel welcome there because of hidden racism.

"*[8]The fishers also shall mourn, and all they that cast angle into the brooks shall lament, and they that spread nets upon the waters shall languish...*" The fishers represent evangelists. They will try to bring in fish and it won't happen. "*[9]Moreover they that work in fine flax, and they that weave networks, shall be confounded. [10]And they shall be broken in the purposes thereof, all that make sluices and ponds for fish.*"

"*[11]Surely the princes of Zoan are fools, the counsel of the wise counsellers of Pharaoh is become brutish...*" Hear me out here. Consider people like the black nationalists which are brutish. First of all I honestly believe some of the things that these men say are true. But on the other hand, the others things they say that are so ridiculous and so offensive, you can't see the forest from the trees. In other words, it is hard to hear what they are trying to say because of who they are. Now they may have great reason to criticize. I understand that Jeremiah Wright, as bad as we heard him over our recent history cursing America, I believe in his heart he does know Jesus because I have heard him at other times where a precious anointing flowed out of him and people were coming to Jesus to get saved. Is there any one of us who are not flawed? Is there any one of us who have been deceived and believed and even taught things that weren't true and were wrong only to find out our error later on? I know many black ministers say they pray for Louis Farrakhan to get saved. Wouldn't that be something? If Louis Farrakhan stood up and said one day that he found Jesus, got saved, and now knows Jesus is the only way, the truth, and the life. But many black counselors are deceived and have become fools.

Let us jump ahead to verse 13, "*[13]The princes of Zoan are become fools, the princes of Noph are deceived; they have also seduced Egypt, even they that are the stay of the tribes thereof.*" These leaders are deceiving people. You see, the great push is to try to bring everybody together. They will try to tell you by quoting Jesus in John 10:16, "*And other sheep I have, which are not of this fold...*" to bring in this ecumenical spirit that will cause black Holy Ghost filled churches, black evangelical churches, and Muslims to get together. I will never sit on a platform and stand with people of the Muslim faith because in the heart of that religion is a horrible truth. They want to dominate the world. They want to bring their law upon everybody. So I have no desire to join forces in the spirit of ecumenicalism at all because I know Jesus Christ is the way, the truth, and the life and no man can go to the Father but by Him, period!

"*[14]The LORD hath mingled a perverse spirit in the midst thereof: and they have caused Egypt to err in every work thereof, as a drunken man staggereth in his vomit. [15]Neither shall there be any work for Egypt, which the head or tail, branch or rush, may do. ¹⁶In that day shall Egypt be like unto women: and it shall be afraid and fear because of the shaking of the hand of the LORD of hosts, which he shaketh over it...*" Let me say one thing right here. In the last days, God is shaking everything that can be shaken. He just points out here that He is also shaking the black race.

"*¹⁷And the land of Judah shall be a terror unto Egypt...*" Judah's name means "praise". So the land of Judah represents praise and worship. This passage then is saying that praise will be a torment to many of them. I wonder how black Muslims feel when they see precious Holy Ghost filled black Christians worshipping freely in Spirit and in truth. If you search the Scriptures concerning the glory of God, there is one ingredient that always seems tied to it and that is suffering. I like what one person wrote, "when a caged bird sings..." When a person has been oppressed and then set free, they will sing from a place that is so deep and unbelievable, but it will torment some when they realize the magnificence of the manifest presence of God that comes when Christian black people sing. God's glory and manifest presence is a consuming fire and for those who don't want it, it is a fearful and tormenting thing.

"*¹⁸In that day shall five cities in the land of Egypt speak the language of Canaan, and swear to the LORD of hosts; one shall be called, The city of destruction...*" God is going to bring judgment for all of the things that Egypt has done. But then verse 19 comes, "*¹⁹In that day...*" What day is this? It is the day of the Lord. "*In that day shall there be an altar to the LORD in the midst of the land of Egypt, and a pillar at the border thereof to the LORD...*" So the judgment that God sent them was simply to change them and bring them out of darkness into His marvelous light! Hallelujah! And they know longer have to sing about the darkness in their lives, but they are liberated into the glorious liberty of the children of God (Romans 8:21). But in that day, there is going to be an altar unto the Lord and a pillar at the border saying for Egypt (black people), "the Lord is our God!" This altar in the land of Egypt says true worship and intercession is going on among black people in the last days.

"*²⁰And it shall be for a sign and for a witness unto the LORD of hosts in the land of Egypt: for they shall cry unto the LORD because of the oppressors, and he shall send them a saviour, and a great one, and he shall deliver them...*" This saviour's name is Jesus Christ! He will send them a saviour! Even people who spouted words of violence and aggression, at some point, they meet the Lord Jesus and are brought to the end of themselves and instead of crying out and cursing, now all they can do is worship the Living God! "*²¹And the LORD shall be known to Egypt...*" The word "known" here is an intimate knowing, like when it said in Genesis 3, "*Adam <u>knew</u> Eve his wife*". In other words, there is going to be intimacy with God amongst black people. I've been to many black churches in my life and I will say boldly without fear that a lot of what we hear in their praise is from the soul and not the spirit. There is a reason for this because in their history, while they were being tormented and oppressed for years, they learned how to sing in the midst of their oppression, but much of it wasn't coming from the Spirit of God, but from their soul. There is a difference. I told you of the story in another chapter when I ministered at a black church years ago. They praised God for over an hour in their cultural way, but there was no glory. It was just people enjoying themselves. Then they asked me up to the front to minister with my guitar. You know, never doubt the sovereignty of God. I was prepared for that moment because of where I was born and what I went through. And I am going to be prepared for the moment when God releases me to tell black people all over the world who they really are in Jesus. Unafraid I told and showed that black church what the Bible says about true worship in the Spirit and in truth and went on to lead them into it and into the manifest presence of God. We had such a tremendous and glorious visitation. To this day, I can still see those precious black men doing a prophetic dance before the Lord and not the Pentecostal shaking. You see, neither the black culture nor the white culture is significant anymore. There is a culture that Christians have. There is a new culture for the Kingdom of God. We can't worship like black people or white people anymore. It is going to take some time to figure this out and get this done, but it will get done. The hour has come where God is raising up His true worshippers that will be able to teach His people and show them the way to worship in Spirit and in truth. The Holy Ghost is real and there is only one way to worship Him and that is in Spirit and in truth. "In Spirit" means several things. First, we allow the Holy Ghost to lead us in our worship and second it means worship always begins in our human spirit, flows out into our soul, and then ultimately into our body and that is where we dance, lift our hands, kneel, fall prostrate, etc. Worshipping "in Spirit" also includes singing in the Holy Spirit or singing in tongues. "In truth" is two-fold. First, the Greek word for truth means reality or unfeigned. This means our worship is genuine and not fake or phony. Second, "in truth" also means worshipping according to the Bible. John 17:17 says, *"thy word is truth"*. The Bible says we can shout, sing, dance, lift our hands, kneel, weep, clap, etc. The Word of God gives us all the ways we can worship Biblically. This is where we are headed. True worship is about to take place all over the earth, especially among the black people. God is going to know black people intimately as verse 20 continues, *"...and the Egyptians shall know the LORD in that day, and shall do sacrifice and oblation; yea, they shall vow a vow unto the LORD, and perform it..."* This means that black people are going to worship God in the holy of holies and obedience to the Lord will manifest itself.

"22And the LORD shall smite Egypt: he shall smite and heal it: and they shall return even to the LORD, and he shall be intreated of them, and shall heal them..." This speaks of the dealings of God. This is the same way God dealt with Israel as we see in Hosea 6:1-3, *"1Come, and let us return unto the LORD:*

for he hath torn, and he will heal us; he hath smitten, and he will bind us up. ²After two days will he revive us: in the third day he will raise us up, and we shall live in his sight ³Then shall we know, if we follow on to know the LORD: his going forth is prepared as the morning; and he shall come unto us as the rain, as the latter and former rain unto the earth." This is the principle of the dealings of God. Romans 11:22 says, "*Behold therefore the goodness and severity of God...*" Ecclesiastes 7:14 says, "*In the day of prosperity be joyful, but in the day of adversity consider: God also hath set the one over against the other, to the end that man should find nothing after him.*" Paul said in Philippians 4:12, "*I know both how to be abased, and I know how to abound: every where and in all things I am instructed both to be full and to be hungry, both to abound and to suffer need.*" Jesus in Luke 24:50 led the disciples "*as far as to Bethany, and he lifted up his hands, and blessed them.*" Bethany means two things, "house of figs or fruitfulness" and "house of affliction". You and I will never go beyond this principle of the dealings of God because without the dealings of God, we will never be perfected.

"*²³In that day shall there be a highway out of Egypt to Assyria, and the Assyrian shall come into Egypt, and the Egyptian into Assyria, and the Egyptians shall <u>serve with</u> the Assyrians...*" Egypt and Assyria hated each other. They fought all the time against each other trying to dominate each other. And "*²⁴In that day shall Israel be the third with Egypt and with Assyria...*" What does this mean? I kind of feel it means that black people (the sons of Ham), Israel (the sons of Shem), and Assyria (a type of white people) are going to come together and worship God. None ruling over each other, but all flowing together in unity brought about, not by men and their ecumenical ways, but by a Holy Word from God and people being obedient to that Word. Glory to God!

And then it says of this unity, "*...even a blessing in the midst of the land.*" Psalms 133 says beautifully, "*¹Behold, how good and how pleasant it is for brethren to dwell together in unity! ²It is like the precious ointment upon the head, that ran down upon the beard, even Aaron's beard: that went down to the skirts of his garments; ³As the dew of Hermon, and as the dew that descended upon the mountains of Zion: <u>for there</u> the <u>LORD commanded the blessing</u>, even life for evermore.*" This blessing in Isaiah 19:24-25 is the blessing of unity found in Psalms 133. Jeremiah 31:12 says, "*Therefore they shall come and sing in the height of Zion, and <u>shall flow together</u> to the goodness of the LORD, for wheat, and for wine, and for oil, and for the young of the flock and of the herd: and their soul shall be as a watered garden; and they shall not sorrow any more at all.*" Hallelujah! This is what is coming - true unity birthed by the Spirit of God, not the ideas of men (like we saw in Genesis 11). God said of the unity in Genesis 11:6, "*And the LORD said, Behold, the people is one, and they have all one language; and this they begin to do: and now nothing will be* *restrained from them, which they have imagined to do."* According to God, heathens can even come into such unity that nothing is impossible to them. What about if we have true unity because of Jesus! Imagine what will happen among the people of God!

"25Whom the LORD of hosts shall bless, saying, blessed be Egypt my people..." God is saying, "Blessed be precious black people who are my people!" Hallelujah! This is His intent and purpose for black people! I personally want to be a part of bringing this unity among God's people. How about you? When you go out to your job tomorrow and meet people on the street, or go into stores and bump into people, I pray that the Lord will touch your heart to smile at someone, especially one that is of a different color. Greet someone and hold the door for a black woman. Help or assist somebody in need. Have you ever been in the grocery store and the person in front of you doesn't have enough money? I always try to pay whatever they don't have when that happens to me. I don't need any reward in this life. My reward is letting them know that there are people who have a revelation that God so loved the world! My prayer is God changes our hearts to make us love like Him and love the world.

So much emphasis is placed on white people loving black people and rightly so. But there is going to be a journey for black people to trust white people. This is just a fact. We are going to just have to grin and bear it until we get to the other side in unity. Hundreds of years of oppression don't end over night. We are going to have to learn to be patient and merciful. Forgiveness is one thing, but restoration is another. I can forgive someone for what they did to me, but to restore the relationship takes time and effort on both parties. But every time you meet a black person (if you are white) or a white person (if you are black), I pray that no longer what comes up in your heart is something racist, but a compassion and a motivation to reach out comes forth. You and I are called to be the love of God on this earth until God brings all His people together in unity and then the glory is going to be revealed!

The next passage I would like to look at in relation to Egypt and black people in the last days is found in Psalms 68:31, *"Princes shall come out of Egypt; Ethiopia shall soon stretch out her hands unto God."* Psalms 87:4-5 speaks of who will make up Zion in the last days and black people are part of it. Zion is the place in the presence of God where men's hearts and God unite in one. Our hearts corporately as a people form a throne room for Him to come and sit upon. This is Zion and black people are included in this! But here in Psalms 68, speaking of the last days, God is going to raise up leadership out of the black church. But not only this, Ethiopia (which is obviously black people as well) will stretch out their hands to God. First, this could mean lifting holy hands to the Lord meaning praying and worshiping the Lord. But also

Ethiopia is stretching out her hands to God because she has stretched out her hands to everybody else, only to find emptiness. But when the glory falls, there is going to be such a revolution in the earth when people see the glory in the sons of God! This is why I can't understand why people don't like teaching on the sons of God. It releases the last great move of God! God perfects a people, He appears in them, and the world will see Jesus in them and they come by the millions because of it! This doesn't make them God. They will still just be "sons of God" but they will be manifesting "The Son" perfectly! So Ethiopia, a type of black people, will see that Jesus is not a white man's religion. They will see it is the only true God and will stretch out their hands to their Creator!

The next passage I would like to address is found in Isaiah 45. In verses 5-10, God is declaring His sovereignty. Verses 10-13, God starts speaking about His creation. But in verse 14, we read, *"Thus saith the LORD, The labour of Egypt, and merchandise of Ethiopia and of the Sabeans, men of stature, shall come over unto thee, and they shall be thine: they shall come after thee; in chains they shall come over, and they shall fall down unto thee, they shall make supplication unto thee, saying, Surely God is in thee; and there is none else, there is no God. [15]Verily thou art a God that hidest thyself, O God of Israel, the Saviour."* Black people are going to see the real Jesus in the last days. Moreover, verse 14 says these men are going to be men of stature. They will come to the house of God, the people of God, and they are going to have all kinds of chains and bondages. They are going to be so weary from their bondages that they are going to fall down and say "help us" (make supplication), and they are going to do that because they actually see *"Surely God is in thee; and there is none else..."* They see the hand of God in the people of God and because of that, they say there is no other God but Jesus! In the last days, there will be forerunners. When the sons of God are revealed, there will be forerunners as well. The Word will go out, like in Isaiah 60:1, *"Arise, shine; for thy light is come, and the glory of the Lord is risen upon thee..."* or like in the mount of transfiguration in Matthew 17, God's people who have loved and served Him are going to find that Jesus is going to appear in them and the world is going to see it and recognize that Jesus Christ is Lord and every knee shall bow and confess this. Many people don't like the teaching on the sons of God because the price His people will have to pay will be everything to attain to this. Not just any Christian will be a true son of God. God has to properly deal with us to begin to appear in us. God won't give His glory to another, but He will give His glory to Himself and He must be living in us to have His glory! For the sons of God, they will be able to truly say, as Paul said in Galatians 2:20, *"I am crucified with Christ: nevertheless I live; yet not I, but Christ liveth in me..."* So the presence of God or the appearing of the Lord takes place and black people who have been bound by drugs, violence, sex, poverty, etc are going to come to be free. Prison doesn't help. Islam doesn't help them, but they are going to see that Jesus is the only way! They are going to see that Jesus is not a white man's religion. On the contrary (as we have seen in this book), white people need to be grateful Jesus included them in because the presence of white people in the Bible is much less than black people. As soon as many people read much of what this book shares, racism is going to scream in their hearts and minds. They may say about me and this book, "How dare I say these things!" So I answer them right back, right now, "How dare you think like you think! Do you know history? Have you studied the Scriptures? Do you know why you believe what you believe? If you don't than you are misinformed, so don't criticize what you don't understand. A fool utters his mind before he hears a matter. So quiet your racist heart, study your Bible, search history, and then you can speak. Until then, repent!" Glory to Jesus!

Now let me say I have refrained from speaking about some people who others have spoken of as black in the Scripture because I personally could not confirm that they were. I didn't want to put anything in this book that I could not truly point to and justify as being of the Lord and in the Scripture. Now there is conjecture that Goliath was black. Also, in Judges 21:20-23 speaks of virgins who the nation of Benjamin go and marry. Let me give you some background to this situation. Previously a woman from another tribe came into Benjamin. She was raped horribly and they cut her body parts off and sent them to every other tribe. So all of Israel joined together to destroy the tribe of Benjamin and they killed all except 600 men. And so the 600 men didn't know what to do to repair and rebuild their tribe. So they told them in Judges 21:20-23 to go to these virgins that come out during a time to dance during a certain celebration. And these virgins were of the Manasseh/Ephraim tribe. Manasseh and Ephraim were the sons of Joseph. Joseph's wife, the mother of Manasseh and Ephraim was a black woman (Pharaoh's daughter). So Manasseh and Ephraim were half black tribes. So the 600 men go and take these virgins (from a half black tribe) to repopulate and rebuild the tribe of Benjamin. This is why from this point in history and forward, the tribe of Benjamin was looked down upon. They were called "little Benjamin" (Psalms 68:27). Benjamin's name means "son of my right hand". Benjamin began to be looked down upon because the marriages between the black virgins and these 600 Benjamites produced offspring that were obviously a people of color. How do we know they were a people of color? Because of the Apostle Paul who we know was a Benjamite and as he was standing in a castle before a counsel in Acts 21:37-38 wanting to speak, they said to Paul, "*Art not thou that Egyptian...*" They mistook Paul for an Egyptian. How is a man going to look like an Egyptian if he doesn't have some color and black features? But I don't know this for sure, so I didn't add Paul to the list. I think God knows I really will be persecuted by racists if I said the Apostle Paul was a black man. I will say that he did have some black blood in him though. Glory to God! But because I can't prove this,

I am not going to go there. Egypt was judged more harshly than any other nation, I believe, because of what they did to Israel.

Next, let us look at Jeremiah 43 starting in verse 8, "*Then came the word of the LORD unto Jeremiah in Tahpanhes, saying...*" Before we keep reading, let me tell you what the name Tahpanhes means. It means "beginning of the age, place of the Negro".

Continuing in verse 9, "*Take great stones in thine hand, and hide them in the clay in the brickkiln, which is at the entry of Pharaoh's house in Tahpanhes, in the sight of the men of Judah; [10]And say unto them, Thus saith the LORD of hosts, the God of Israel; Behold, I will send and take Nebuchadrezzar the king of Babylon, my servant, and will set his throne upon these stones that I have hid; and he shall spread his royal pavilion over them. [11]And when he cometh, he shall smite the land of Egypt, and deliver such as are for death to death; and such as are for captivity to captivity; and such as are for the sword to the sword. [12]And I will kindle a fire in the houses of the gods of Egypt; and he shall burn them, and carry them away captives: and he shall array himself with the land of Egypt, as a shepherd putteth on his garment; and he shall go forth from thence in peace. [13]He shall break also the images of Beth-shemesh, that is in the land of Egypt; and the houses of the gods of the Egyptians shall he burn with fire.*" First, judgment begins at the house of God. God is going to judge the black race. But in verse 12 things change. It says He will kindle a fire in the houses of the gods of Egypt and shall burn them. This akin to God burning and cleansing His people as Hebrews 10:26-27 which says *"For if we sin wilfully after that we have received the knowledge of the truth, there remaineth no more sacrifice for sins, [27]But a certain fearful looking for of <u>judgment</u> and <u>fiery indignation</u>, which shall devour <u>the adversaries</u>.*" The fire of God that comes into the child of God's life is not to destroy the child of God, but to burn the problems and adversaries in their life. So before God can fulfill His glorious purposes among black people in the last days, He must burn up the sin, idols, etc living in them. These black people have too many gods. They have too many idols God says, so He must judge and get rid of them.

But then, the beauty is, as we keep reading in Jeremiah 43:12, God "*shall array himself with the land of Egypt, as a shepherd putteth on his garment; and he shall go forth from thence in peace.*" This is the beauty of the Lord Jesus. God told Jeremiah in His calling, "*See, I have this day set thee over the nations and over the kingdoms, to root out, and to pull down, and to destroy, and to throw down, to build, and to plant*" (Jeremiah 1:10). Hosea 6:1-3 says, "*Come, and let us return unto the LORD: for he hath torn, and he will heal us; he hath smitten, and he will bind us up. [2]After two days will he revive us: in the third day he will raise us up, and we shall live in his sight...*" All of God's dealings and judgments are to bring man back to Himself. God is going to destroy the idols and the images in black people in the last days so they can serve Him with a pure heart!

Lastly, let us look in Isaiah 11:10-12. Now we know from the beginning of this chapter that this is a book speaking of the Messiah. He is speaking of the Lord all the way down until verse 6 until He starts speaking of what the Lord is going to do and how in the last days in verse 9, *"for the earth shall be full of the knowledge of the Lord, as the waters cover the sea"*. So He is speaking of the last days as we start in verse 10, *"¹⁰And in that day there shall be a root of Jesse, which shall stand for an ensign of the people; to it shall the Gentiles seek: and his rest shall be glorious..."* Let me explain this. An ensign is a sign. In the last days, God is going to have a sign to all the Gentile nations to come home to Him. What is this sign? This sign is the sons of God revealing Jesus to the earth. At some point, God is going to shake His church out of the religious sleep it is in and a people are going to arise, as Malachi 4:2 says, *"But unto you that fear my name shall the Sun of righteousness arise with healing in his wings; and ye shall go forth..."* In other words, the ensign is the sons of God coming forth for the entire world to see. It is typified in a story of Jesus when Jesus was brought out by Pilate and stood before the people and Pilate said of Jesus to the people, *"Behold the man!"* (John 19:5). Jesus spoke this revelation to me years ago. You see, we are the body of Christ. God the Father spoke to me very sweetly about this and said the day is coming when He will say to the world about the sons of God *"Behold the man!"* like Pilate did. But it will be a corporate man. Not just one man, but a many-membered company of people who will be just like Jesus and will be this ensign to the earth. Now before you get upset about this, the word "Christian" means "little Christ". This doesn't mean we are God, but we will be like Him and our calling is to reveal Jesus to the earth. I know there will be a people who will walk like Jesus, talk like Him, love like Him, live like Him, and be like Him. This doesn't mean they will be Jesus or anything foolish like that. It just means Jesus will so possess a people that the earth will see it as a sign and they are going to come to it!

"¹¹And it shall come to pass in that day, that the Lord shall set his hand again the second time to recover the remnant of his people, which shall be left, from Assyria, and from Egypt, and from Pathros, and from Cush...¹²And he shall set up an ensign for the nations, and shall assemble the outcasts of Israel, and gather together the dispersed of Judah from the four corners of the earth." All of God's people, including the sons of Cush and the sons of Egypt, are going to come home as God puts together His remnant in the last days!

What Color Is Used As A Curse In Scripture?
Chapter 22

I.   The Curse of Whiteness in Scripture

1.   Genesis 40:16-20

"*[16]When the chief baker saw that the interpretation was good, he said unto Joseph, I also was in my dream, and, behold, I had three white baskets on my head: [17]And in the uppermost basket there was of all manner of bakemeats for Pharaoh; and the birds did eat them out of the basket upon my head. [18]And Joseph answered and said, This is the interpretation thereof: The three baskets are three days: [19]Yet within three days shall Pharaoh lift up thy head from off thee, and shall hang thee on a tree; and the birds shall eat thy flesh from off thee. [20]And it came to pass the third day, which was Pharaoh's birthday, that he made a feast unto all his servants: and he lifted up the head of the chief butler and of the chief baker among his servants.:*

2.   Leviticus 13:1-5, 9-11, 18-22, 24-25, 42-43

"*[1]And the LORD spake unto Moses and Aaron, saying, [2]When a man shall have in the skin of his flesh a rising, a scab, or a bright spot, and it be in the skin of his flesh like the plague of leprosy; then he shall be brought unto Aaron the priest, or unto one of his sons the priests: [3]And the priest shall look on the plague in the skin of the flesh: and when the hair in the plague is turned white, and the plague in sight be deeper than the skin of his flesh, it is a plague of leprosy: and the priest shall look on him, and pronounce him unclean. [4]If the bright spot be white in the skin of his flesh, and in sight be not deeper than the skin, and the hair thereof be not turned white; then the priest shall shut up him that hath the plague seven days: [5]And the priest shall look on him the seventh day: and, behold, if the plague in his sight be at a stay, and the plague spread not in the skin; then the priest shall shut him up seven days more...[9]When the plague of leprosy is in a man, then he shall be brought unto the priest; [10]And the priest shall see him: and, behold, if the rising be white in the skin, and it have turned the hair white, and there be quick raw flesh in the rising; [11]It is an old leprosy in the skin of his flesh, and the priest shall pronounce him unclean, and shall not shut him up: for he is unclean...[18]The flesh also, in which, even in the skin thereof, was a boil, and is healed, [19]And in the place of the boil there be a white rising, or a bright spot, white, and somewhat reddish, and it be shewed to the priest; [20]And if, when the priest seeth it, behold, it be in sight lower than the skin, and the hair thereof be turned white; the priest shall pronounce him unclean: it is a plague of leprosy broken out of the boil. [21]But if the priest look on it, and, behold, there be no white hairs therein, and if it be not lower than the skin, but be somewhat dark; then the priest shall shut him up seven days: [22]And if it spread much abroad in the skin, then the priest shall pronounce him unclean: it is a plague...[24]Or if there be any flesh, in the skin whereof there is a hot* burning, and the quick flesh that burneth have a white bright spot, somewhat reddish, or white; [25]Then the priest shall look upon it: and, behold, if the hair in the bright spot be turned white, and it be in sight deeper than the skin; it is a leprosy broken out of the burning: wherefore the priest shall pronounce him unclean: it is the plague of leprosy...[42]And if there be in the bald head, or bald forehead, a white reddish sore; it is a leprosy sprung up in his bald head, or his bald forehead. [43]Then the priest shall look upon it: and, behold, if the rising of the sore be white reddish in his bald head, or in his bald forehead, as the leprosy appeareth in the skin of the flesh..."

3. Numbers 12:1-14

"[1]And Miriam and Aaron spake against Moses because of the Ethiopian woman whom he had married: for he had married an Ethiopian woman. [2]And they said, Hath the LORD indeed spoken only by Moses? hath he not spoken also by us? And the LORD heard it. [3](Now the man Moses was very meek, above all the men which were upon the face of the earth.) [4]And the LORD spake suddenly unto Moses, and unto Aaron, and unto Miriam, Come out ye three unto the tabernacle of the congregation. And they three came out. [5]And the LORD came down in the pillar of the cloud, and stood in the door of the tabernacle, and called Aaron and Miriam: and they both came forth. [6]And he said, Hear now my words: If there be a prophet among you, I the LORD will make myself known unto him in a vision, and will speak unto him in a dream. [7]My servant Moses is not so, who is faithful in all mine house. [8]With him will I speak mouth to mouth, even apparently, and not in dark speeches; and the similitude of the LORD shall he behold: wherefore then were ye not afraid to speak against my servant Moses? [9]And the anger of the LORD was kindled against them; and he departed. [10]And the cloud departed from off the tabernacle; and, behold, Miriam became leprous, white as snow: and Aaron looked upon Miriam, and, behold, she was leprous. [11]And Aaron said unto Moses, Alas, my lord, I beseech thee, lay not the sin upon us, wherein we have done foolishly, and wherein we have sinned. [12]Let her not be as one dead, of whom the flesh is half consumed when he cometh out of his mother's womb. [13]And Moses cried unto the LORD, saying, Heal her now, O God, I beseech thee. [14]And the LORD said unto Moses, If her father had but spit in her face, should she not be ashamed seven days? let her be shut out from the camp seven days, and after that let her be received in again."

4. II Kings 5:1-6, 8-16, 20-27

"[1]Now Naaman, captain of the host of the king of Syria, was a great man with his master, and honourable, because by him the LORD had given deliverance unto Syria: he was also a mighty man in valour, but he was a leper. [2]And the Syrians had gone out by companies, and had brought away captive out of the land of Israel a little maid; and she waited on Naaman's wife. [3]And she said unto her mistress, Would God my lord were with the prophet that is in Samaria! for he would recover him of his leprosy. [4]And one went in, and told his lord, saying, Thus and thus said

313

the maid that is of the land of Israel. [5]And the king of Syria said, Go to, go, and I will send a letter unto the king of Israel. And he departed, and took with him ten talents of silver, and six thousand pieces of gold, and ten changes of raiment. [6]And he brought the letter to the king of Israel, saying, Now when this letter is come unto thee, behold, I have therewith sent Naaman my servant to thee, that thou mayest recover him of his leprosy...[8]And it was so, when Elisha the man of God had heard that the king of Israel had rent his clothes, that he sent to the king, saying, Wherefore hast thou rent thy clothes? let him come now to me, and he shall know that there is a prophet in Israel. [9]So Naaman came with his horses and with his chariot, and stood at the door of the house of Elisha. [10]And Elisha sent a messenger unto him, saying, Go and wash in the Jordan seven times, and thy flesh shall come again to thee, and thou shalt be clean. [11]But Naaman was wroth, and went away, and said, Behold, I thought, He will surely come out to me, and stand, and call on the name of the LORD his God, and strike his hand over the place, and recover the leper. [12]Are not Abana and Pharpar, rivers of Damascus, better than all the waters of Israel? may I not wash in them, and be clean? So he turned and went away in a rage. [13]And his servants came near, and spake unto him, and said, My father, if the prophet had bid thee do some great thing, wouldest thou not have done it? how much rather then, when he saith to thee, Wash, and be clean? [14]Then went he down, and dipped himself seven times in Jordan, according to the saying of the man of God: and his flesh came again like unto the flesh of a little child, and he was clean. [15]And he returned to the man of God, he and all his company, and came, and stood before him: and he said, Behold, now I know that there is no God in all earth, but in Israel: now therefore, I pray thee, take a blessing of thy servant. [16]But he said, As the LORD liveth, before whom I stand, I will receive none. And he urged him to take it; but he refused...[20]But Gehazi, the servant of Elisha the man of God, said, Behold, my master hath spared Naaman this Syrian, in not receiving at his hands that which he brought: but, as the LORD liveth, I will run after him, and take somewhat of him. [21]So Gehazi followed after Naaman. And when Naaman saw him running after him, he lighted down from the chariot to meet him, and said, Is all well? [22]And he said, All is well. My master hath sent me, saying, Behold, even now there be come to me from mount Ephraim two young men of the sons of the prophets: give them, I pray thee, a talent of silver, and two changes of garments. [23]And Naaman said, Be content, take two talents. And he urged him, and bound two talents of silver in two bags, with two changes of garments, and laid them upon two of his servants; and they bare them before him. [24]And when he came to the tower, he took them from their hand, and bestowed them in the house: and he let the men go, and they departed. [25]But he went in, and stood before his master. And Elisha said unto him, Whence comest thou, Gehazi? And he said, Thy servant went no whither. [26]And he said unto him, Went not mine heart with thee, when the man turned again from his chariot to meet thee? Is it a time to receive money, and to receive garments, and oliveyards, and vineyards, and sheep, and oxen, and menservants, and maidservants? [27]The leprosy therefore of Naaman shall cleave unto thee, and unto thy seed for ever. And he went out from his presence a leper as white as snow."

5. Exodus 4:1-8

"*[1]And Moses answered and said, but, behold, they will not believe me, nor hearken unto my voice: for they will say, The LORD hath not appeared unto thee. [2]And the LORD said unto him, what is that in thine hand? And he said, A rod. [3]And he said, Cast it on the ground. And he cast it on the ground, and it became a serpent; and Moses fled from before it. [4]And the LORD said unto Moses, Put forth thine hand, and take it by the tail. And he put forth his hand, and caught it, and it became a rod in his hand: [5]That they may believe that the LORD God of their fathers, the God of Abraham, the God of Isaac, and the God of Jacob, hath appeared unto thee. [6]And the LORD said furthermore unto him, Put now thine hand into thy bosom. And he put his hand into his bosom: and when he took it out, behold, his hand was leprous as snow. [7]And he said, Put thine hand into thy bosom again. And he put his hand into his bosom again; and plucked it out of his bosom, and, behold, it was turned again as his other flesh. [8]And it shall come to pass, if they will not believe thee, neither hearken to the voice of the first sign, that they will believe the voice of the latter sign.*"

II. Black – A Sign of Good Health in Scripture

1. Leviticus 13:29-37

"*[29]If a man or woman have a plague upon the head or the beard; [30]Then the priest shall see the plague: and, behold, if it be in sight deeper than the skin; and there be in it a yellow thin hair; then the priest shall pronounce him unclean: it is a dry scall, even a leprosy upon the head or beard. [31]And if the priest look on the plague of the scall, and, behold, it be not in sight deeper than the skin, and that there is no black hair in it; then the priest shall shut up him that hath the plague of the scall seven days: [32]And in the seventh day the priest shall look on the plague: and, behold, if the scall spread not, and there be in it no yellow hair, and the scall be not in sight deeper than the skin; [33]He shall be shaven, but the scall shall he not shave; and the priest shall shut up him that hath the scall seven days more: [34]And in the seventh day the priest shall look on the scall: and, behold, if the scall be not spread in the skin, nor be in sight deeper than the skin; then the priest shall pronounce him clean: and he shall wash his clothes, and be clean. [35]But if the scall spread much in the skin after his cleansing; [36]Then the priest shall look on him: and, behold, if the scall be spread in the skin, the priest shall not seek for yellow hair; he is unclean. [37]But if the scall be in his sight at a stay, and that there is black hair grown up therein; the scall is healed, he is clean: and the priest shall pronounce him clean.*"

This should show us that when black is mentioned in scripture it doesn't mean something dark or wrong. Also the color white isn't always defined as pure or innocent. And that the two it seems these passages white is the one with a bad connotation.

Names Associated With Black People In Scripture
Chapter 23

I. Biblical Names and Nations Where Black People Lived

1. Ham
2. Cush
3. Cushi
4. Cushite
5. Ethiopia
6. Ethiopian(s)
7. Egypt
8. Egyptian(s)
9. Kedar
10. Phinehas (the Negro or Nubian)
11. Phut
12. Tahpanhes (Palace of the Negro – Jeremiah 43:7)
13. Canaan
14. Canaanite(s)
15. Midian
16. Elam
17. Hittite
18. Mizraim
19. Cyrene – a city in the African nation of Libya
20. Dizahab – a palace in the Sinai Wilderness
21. Gihon – a river in the Garden of Eden (believed to be the Nile)
22. Goshen – a district of Egypt
23. Hanes – a place in Egypt
24. Horeb – a mountain range in Sinai (Egypt)
25. Jeshimon – a place in the Sinai (Egypt)
26. Libya – place in North Africa
27. Memphis – city in the African nation of Egypt
28. Noph – a city in Egypt
30. On – an ancient city in northern Egypt on the Nile Delta
31. Pathros – name for upper Egypt (now known as Sudan)
32. Sinai – an area in Egypt at the north end of the Red Sea
33. Syene – an Egyptian city
34. Zoan – also an Egyptian city

Closing Prayer

I pray that I have done honor Father, to You, by telling the truth, by showing the legacy of black people in the Scriptures, by encouraging and helping them to regain that which was stolen from them, to give them an expectation and a hope for the future and for their children, and that for every race, that they would understand where they came from and how that You are not partial to any race of people, but that you love everybody. But lastly, that we all come to the conclusion that now that we have been born again, we are a new creation and a new species and we are neither black, white, brown, or red anymore. We are all now the color of amber, the color of God, with a new culture which is the culture of the Kingdom of God. We have our own language which is speaking in tongues. Help us Lord, as you said so eloquently in Psalms 45:10-11, *"forget also thine own people, and thy father's house; so shall the king greatly desire thy beauty: for he is thy Lord; and worship thou him"* and in Mark 3:33-35, *"Who is my mother, or my brethren? And he looked round about on them which sat about him, and said, behold my mother and my brethren! For whosoever shall do the will of God, the same is my brother, and my sister, and mother."* In Luke 8:21, Jesus' answer was *"My mother and my brethren are these which hear the word of God, and do it."* This will be the hardest thing for people to do and I ask you Jesus to somehow let them see that You desire man to come back to Your original intent for him, oneness, unity, peace, contentment, and be like Enoch who *"walked with God"* (Genesis 5:24). I pray that the pages of this book will open the eyes of your people's understanding and that the great scales of racism, ignorance, or apathy will fall from off their eyes and they will be replaced with clear eyes of revelation and truth. Lord, we say to You, "To You be the glory". The day is coming as You said in Zechariah 14:9, *"And the LORD shall be king over all the earth: in that day shall there be one LORD, and his name one"* and all things will be turned back to You and it will be as it was in the beginning. So be it Master. Please let the love of God be shed abroad into every heart as we vow and promise to You to treat men and women as You would have us treat them. We will not judge after the outward appearance. We will never call unclean or uncommon, what you have cleansed, for Thou *"hast redeemed us to God by thy blood out of every kindred, and tongue, and people, and nation"* (Revelation 5:9). In the mighty name of Jesus, I pray,

Amen!

Last Word

When God spoke to me to write this book, believe me I was totally and completely surprised. I had no idea what the Holy Spirit would bring out. I simply followed the Lord's instruction and began to search the Scriptures and history. I am not a great theologian. I am not an anthropologist. I'm really not even that smart to think I could write a book about the presence of black people throughout Scriptures. Trust me, I just obeyed His Word to do it. I am positive that many will find fault with much that I have written. All I ask is that you realize that it came from a pure heart. It came from a humble person who does not claim to be a scholar or any such thing. The true message of this book is that we see the great treasure black people have been to the people of God and that we give them their just due. I pray you don't approach this book in a Pharisaical way, straining to find something that I wrote was wrong. If I did write something wrong, it was done innocently and never to confuse or distort the truth on purpose. I have done my best with a difficult subject, so now it is in God's hands.

The real message of this book is that racism is evil. It has gone on far too long. We, as Christians, must not carry any prejudices or racism. Please don't hate or judge someone by the color of their skin, their culture, their social standing, or their education. Judge a righteous judgment according to the Word of God! My prayer also is that we realize we are new creations, another brand new species in the earth. As well that all our brothers and sisters in Jesus belong now to us in our new family. I hope we can learn to treat all people with respect and dignity, and that we can walk in love towards all of God's creation. Oh how I long for the day when we simply see others as God sees them. That we collectively as the body of Christ present to the world a model of love and companionship to all who call themselves believers. Maybe as the world sees us loving each other without prejudice, they will truly see Jesus in us and come to know Him because of it.

I also hope we've found true revelation about the color of God, angels, and God's people and the original man. But more than anything, we could begin to give our precious black brothers and sisters their proper due. It's way past time to do it. I pray as well that this book will encourage, strengthen, bless and help black Christians to see the great part they've played in the Kingdom of God. I have used the term black and white through this book only so that what I was saying could be understood on though I think it's best to simply call each other, brother and sister. And never let these boundaries enter our hearts and minds again.

Finally, I have no stones to throw at anyone, nor any desire to accuse or hurt anybody that is a believer. I'm just a simple man who tried to do the best he could. Lord, please bring your Body together and put an end to every kind of racism in the church. Let there be love and harmony and unity among all your people. If that happens, this book will have done its job. This book was written with a true heart to bless, and praise and thank God for all great contributions these dear precious Black Saints have made throughtout history and within God's Holy Kingdom. You truly deserve honor because you have honored Him. Thank you again.

All my heart and love,

Brother Sam

Jesus is Precious!

Bibliography

1. King James Version – Holy Bible
2. Blacks In The Bible – James H Warden Jr.
3. From Babylon To Timbuktu – Rudolph Windsor
4. The Life And Works Of Flavius Josephus – Flavius Josephus
5. Easton's Bible Dictionary – M.G. Easton
6. Hitchcock's Bible Names Dictionary – Reverend Roswell D Hitchcock
7. The Exhaustive Dictionary Of Bible Names – Dr. Judson Cornwall & Dr. Stelman Smith
8. International Standard Bible Encyclopedia, Revised Edition – James Orr (General Editor)
9. McClintock And Strong Encyclopedia – John McClintock, Strong
10. Nelsons Bible Dictionary – Herbert Lockyer (General Editor)
11. Smith's Bible Dictionary – William Smith
12. Black People In The Bible – Randolph Jackson
13. The Black Presence In The Bible – Reverend Walter Arthur McCray
14. Fausset's Bible Dictionary – Andrew Robert Fausset
15. Nave's Topical Bible – Orville J. Nave
16. Torrey's New Topical Textbook – R.A. Torrey
17. The Glory Of God – Dr. Samuel Greene
18. A Study Of Ages Past – Dr. Samuel Greene
19. Strong's Greek And Hebrew Definitions – James Strong
20. Adam Clarke's Commentary
21. Amplified Bible
22. Antiquities of the Jews – Flavius Josephus
23. Brown-Driver-Briggs Hebrew Concordance – Francis Brown, S Driver, Briggs
24. Brown-Driver-Briggs Greek Concordance – Francis Brown, S Driver, Briggs
25. Jamison, Fausset, and Brown Commentary – Jamison, Robert, Fausset
26. Keil and Delitzsh Commentary On The Old Testament – Karl Keil, Franz Delitzsh
27. The God Manual – Dr. Samuel Greene
28. Walking With God – Dr. Samuel Greene
29. Matthew Henry's Commentary – Matthew Henry
30. Unger's Bible Dictionary – Merrill F Unger, Harrison
31. Old Testament History – Afred Edersheim
32. The Bible Exposition Commentary, New Testament – Warren W. Wiersbe
33. The Bible Exposition Commentary, Old Testament – Warren W. Wiersbe
34. Theological Wordbook of the Old Testament – Gleason, Laid, Harris
35. Vines Expository Dictionary of New Testament Words – W.E. Vine, Merrill Unger
36. Young's Literal Translation – Robert Young

37. World English Bible – Michael Paul Johnson
38. Today's English Version
39. Revised Standard Version
40. New Testament In Modern Speech – Weymouth
41. New Living Translation
42. New International Version
43. New Century Version
44. New American Standard Bible
45. God's Word Translation
46. Douay-Rheims Bible
47. Darby Bible – J. Darby
48. Bible In Basic English
49. Barnes Notes – Albert Barnes, F.C. Cook
50. Evidence Of Black Africans In The Bible – Dan Rogers
51. Stories Of Black People In The Bible – Not Your Mama's Religion Articles
52. What Does The Bible Say About Racism? – Wesley Webster
53. The Origin Of Race – Cooper P. Abrams
54. People Of Color In The Bible – Rev. Robert Ash
55. One Blood – Ken Ham, Carl Wieland, Dan Batlen
56. The Black Presence In The Bible And The Table Of Nations – Rev Walter A McCray
57. The Bible And Racism – Memorare
58. Bible And Racial Issues – R McLaughin
59. Jesus' Black Ancestors – Rick Reinekens
60. Notes on – Dr. Leroy Thompson Black But Comely

Glory Publishing, Inc.
www.glorypublishinginc.com

Samuel Greene has written over 60 books and study manuals. He has spent the last 34 years of his life studying and exhaustively searching the Scriptures out of which has come material for an entire 10 year Bible College curriculum. Many men and women of God around the world use this curriculum in their schools and churches. Some of the more recent books and study manuals written by Samuel Greene include *"The God Manual"*, *"Face to Face Communion"*, *"I Am Black But Comely – The Revelation of Black People Throughout Scripture"*, *"The Sound Of God"*, *"Mystery Babylon"*, *"The Glory Of God"*, and *"The Call Of The Bride"*, plus much, much more.

For a complete listing of his books or ordering information please contact us at *(904) 721-9963* or visit our website at:
www.glorypublishinginc.com.

A Biblical Reference Dictionary Every Minister & Disciple Must Have!

THE GOD MANUAL

NOW AVAILABLE!

160 Chapters, 1160 Pages
Revealing the tapestry of God's character,
heart, & being as found in Scriptures

John 17:3 says, *"...that they might know thee the only true God, and Jesus Christ, whom thou hast sent."* The God Manual was written with hopes of seeking to reveal the correct Biblical image of who our precious Creator really is. With 160 lessons, it exhaustively teaches almost every aspect, characteristic, and attribute of God we can think of. In order to fulfill our calling to be conformed to Jesus' image, we must first know what that image is. Our prayer is that as you study these lessons your life will forever be changed, your worship increased, you realize that holiness is not an unattainable thing anymore, and most importantly you fall deeper in love with Jesus.